THE
INDONESIAN
ECONOMY

THE
INDONESIAN
ECONOMY

edited by
Gustav F. Papanek

PRAEGER

PRAEGER SPECIAL STUDIES • PRAEGER SCIENTIFIC

Library of Congress Cataloging in Publication Data
Main entry under title:

The Indonesian economy.

Includes bibliographical references and index.
1. Indonesia--Economic conditions--1945-
--Addresses, essays, lectures. I. Papanek, Gustav,
Fritz.
HC447.I558   330.9598'037   80-18752
ISBN 0-03-057429-3

Published in 1980 by Praeger Publishers
CBS Educational and Professional Publishing
A Division of CBS, Inc.
521 Fifth Avenue, New York, New York 10017 U.S.A.

© 1980 by Praeger Publishers

123456789   145   987654321

Printed in the United States of America

PREFACE

An analysis of Indonesian economic development deals with a country of considerable intrinsic importance: fifth largest in population, a significant factor in international trade in some commodities, a political and military heavyweight in Southeast Asia, and the center of a great culture. Moreover, Indonesia's economic development carries lessons for other countries, even beyond the intrinsic importance of the country. In the course of a few decades, Indonesia experimented with four quite distinct development strategies: a colonial system for which the term "dualism" was coined; political independence with continued substantial reliance on private enterprise, foreign investment, and foreign management; the later years of the Sukarno regime, with emphasis on equality, national ownership and control, and the dominance of political over economic considerations; and since 1967, a strategy that has emphasized economic rehabilitation and growth, with a major but circumscribed role for foreigners and a greater role for private enterprise than during the early 1960s. With the basic factors largely unchanged—geography, natural resources, social system, institutions, values, and attitudes—it is possible to draw important lessons on the effects of different strategies from Indonesia's experience.

Despite its importance, surprisingly little has been published on the Indonesian economy. No book has concentrated on economic developments in Indonesia since the mid-1960s. Two journals—Ekonomi dan Keuangan and the Bulletin of Indonesian Economic Studies—have provided valuable material on the economy, but space limitations have forced them to emphasize short essays. Research on the Indonesian economy suffered until the mid-1960s because economics and economists were denounced as tainted by capitalism and imperialism—hardly the best atmosphere for serious scholarly work. Thereafter many economists were heavily engaged in government policy work, with little time for in-depth analysis.

The justification for this book is the neglect of Indonesian economic development. The original impetus for the work that resulted in these essays came from the recognition by Prof. Widjojo Nitisastro, the Chairman of Indonesia's National Development Planning Board (BAPPENAS), that research could improve the factual and analytical basis for preparing the Second Five-Year Plan. He asked the Development Advisory Service of Harvard University to help organize the foreign inputs of the research program that he and his colleagues had designed. The essays therefore resulted from research carried out under the joint auspices of BAPPENAS and the Development Advisory Service. Most have been updated, revised, and extended since they were first written in the early 1970s, but a few reflect the situation at the time they were written. Moreover, some essays are completely new. However, all reflect the education we received from our Indonesian and foreign colleagues. Financial support for the work done in the early 1970s was provided by the U.S. Agency for International Development, the World Bank, and the foreign cooperation agencies of the German and Japanese governments. The Ford Foundation for many years supported an advisory group to BAPPENAS, of which the foreign researchers became an integral part. We are grateful to all of them for their assistance.

We have an even greater debt to Indonesian colleagues and friends for their intellectual and personal support. Foreign economists who spend between three months and five years in a country, as we did, always are severely handicapped in determining the reliability of data, the difference between the merely interesting and the truly important, the factors that make for change and those that just accompany it. An analysis of Indonesia's economy is particularly complex because of varied geography, complicated history, size, and rapidly changing economic policies. This complexity would have condemned most of us to embarrassing superficiality if it had not been for the generous support of Indonesian colleagues.

Their number is so large and their contribution so all-embracing that individual acknowledgments are impossible without great risk of invidious comparisons and accidental omissions. We have therefore decided to express our gratitude and acknowledge our debt by dedicating the book to our Indonesian colleagues. We hope that a permanent record of the research results proves of some value in their work.

There is another collective debt: to our foreign colleagues. Some of them participated in the research program, but their results were too time-bound, too policy-oriented, or too sensitive to warrant publication. Essays by colleagues that relied on confidential, unpublished material were left out of consideration. Other economists concentrated on immediate policy issues, as advisers or outside analysts. Discussion with them proved valuable to all of us.

I have a personal debt to Susan Fortini for coordinating the revisions of the manuscript. When one is engaged in policy-oriented, rather than more theoretical, research, one inevitably produces conclusions with which some of one's colleagues disagree. Economists are, in any case, not known for harmony of professional view.

vi

We realize that colleagues to whom we are indebted may strongly disagree with some of the views expressed in this book. Of course, they cannot possibly have any responsibility for them. Nor should it be necessary to emphasize that none of the organizations that provided financial or institutional support is in any way responsible for what follows.

CONTENTS

PART III: AGRICULTURE AND INDUSTRY

LIST OF TABLES

xix

LIST OF FIGURES

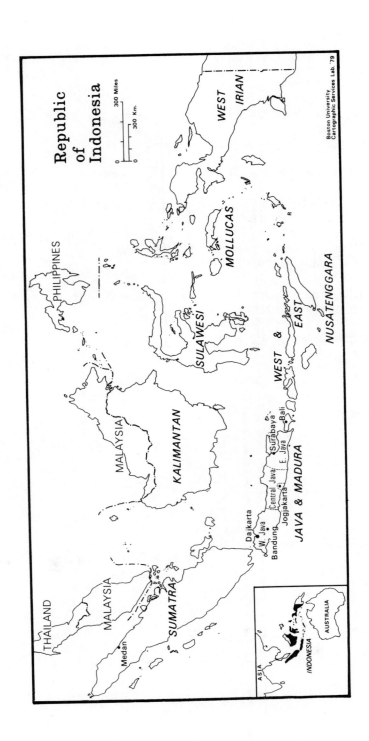

Republic
of
Indonesia

300 Miles
300 Km.

THAILAND

MALAYSIA

PHILIPPINES

MALAYSIA

KALIMANTAN

SULAWESI

MOLLUCAS

WEST
IRIAN

SUMATRA

Medan

Dajkarta
W. Java
Bandung
Central Java
Jogjakarta
E. Java
Surabaya
Bali

JAVA & MADURA

WEST &
EAST

NUSATENGGARA

ASIA

INDONESIA

AUSTRALIA

Boston University
Cartographic Services Lab. '79

PART I

GROWTH, DISTRIBUTION, AND EMPLOYMENT

1

AN OVERVIEW OF
THE INDONESIAN ECONOMY
David O. Dapice

It has been said that watching Indonesia is like watching a race between the possible and the inevitable. It is possible that the considerable natural and human resources of this vast and sprawling nation will be wisely developed for the general benefit of its people. It is inevitable that its large, and often densely packed, population will continue to increase into the foreseeable future, putting further pressure on available land, jobs, and income.

The "New Order" government under President Suharto has been setting policy since it took over from President Sukarno in 1966. To its credit, it has stopped a destructive hyperinflation, maintained a rapid rate of growth in national production, and undertaken an ambitious series of programs in education, medical care, and rural infrastructure. On the other hand, there are continuing problems with corruption at high levels and low, varying degrees of pressure on those who criticize the government, and a persistent pattern of growth being concentrated very narrowly in modern enclaves that employ few people in industries with high investment and earnings per worker. The traditional sectors, which account for seven or eight out of every ten jobs, typically have low investment and output per worker, and are growing slowly. The result is that a minority of the population enjoys a quite rapid growth in income while the large majority of the population faces slow—and in some cases zero—growth in their levels of living.

The reasons for the aggregate successes and the distributional difficulties are complex. Reasons cited by competent observers for the latter include extremely high labor intensity in traditional activities, made possible by a tradition of sharing work; wrong exchange and interest-rate policies; bureaucratic limitations and corruption;

3

pursuit of high technology for its own sake; misguided investments
and policies that created income for those already well off; inadequate tax policies; and links between the military elite and businessmen of Chinese ethnic origin. Here we cannot hope to analyze properly the full history and causality since 1965 or 1970. Rather, we
will mainly document important changes in the economy since the mid-
1960s, but always with an eye toward trying to understand why the
trends being described took place.

It is a major task in itself to describe accurately what has
been going on in Indonesia since 1970. The data base improved considerably during the 1970s, but there continue to be major problems
with much of the published data. Some of it is incorrect or inconsistent, such as the investment or import data, or the consumption survey. Other parts rely on questionable extrapolation or methodology,
and some of it may not be collected as well as it should be. These
problems, together with severe difficulties in interpreting what is
available, make it very hard to form secure judgments about many
key trends. The scholar must always test data and theories at the
same time, and often cannot be quite sure which one is correct.

In the final analysis, this data problem is not mainly technical. Attitudes toward the government among the people who must
provide the data, and among the local bureaucracy who must collect
it, are often the primary sources of error. Beyond this, there is a
tendency for higher-level bureaucrats to hide or manage data to their
own advantage. Better training will help, but changing the attitude
toward information-gathering will be a slow process. Meanwhile,
it is important to remember that margins of error are often very
large.

POPULATION

Indonesia's population exceeded 130 million in 1976, making
it the fifth most populous nation in the world. The population has
grown about 2 percent a year since 1960, and most projections have
it growing at the same rate until 2000. A major problem is the distribution of the population and its density on the "Inner Islands" of
Java and Madura. They had 82 million people in 1976 (63 percent
of the total), but only 7 percent of the land area. As a result, population densities averaged 620 per square kilometer. This is about
the highest concentration anywhere for a mainly rural population.
The "Outer Islands" had 48 million people, but spread over Sumatra,
Kalimantan, Sulawesi, West Irian, and thousands of small islands,
they average only 27 per square kilometer.

The pressure on land and resources on Java is one of the major development problems. While there have been local reports of overcrowding for more than a century, the doubling of population since 1930 and the low rate of urbanization and nonfarm activity combine to make the present situation extremely difficult. In 1976 six out of ten workers were said to be in agriculture during the slack season, when many part-time agricultural workers are not counted. A third of all farmers are landless. For those who have land, the median farm size is under half a hectare (about one acre), and few farmers operate more than one or two hectares. Labor use per hectare, crop for crop, is among the highest in the world.

There have been essentially two responses to this problem. First, there has been an aggressively pursued family planning program that is generally regarded as being quite successful. Thus far it has concentrated on Java, although efforts recently began on the Outer Islands. Acceptance of family planning has been very high on Java, and the fertility rate (the number of children a woman would have in her lifetime if she had the same childbearing experience that a cross section of the population is now experiencing) fell from 5.3 in 1967-70 to 4.9 in 1971-75.[1] However, this notable progress has not resulted in sharply lower population growth rates for two reasons. First, there were very low additions to the population in the 1940s under conditions of war, revolution, disruption, and hardship. In the 1950s birth and survival rates increased, and many more children were born and grew up. This "hollow" in the age groups kept additional numbers of women of childbearing age quite low in the 1960s, but increasingly the larger numbers from the 1950s are entering their twenties, when fertility rates are high. Thus, a substantial drop in fertility is needed simply to keep population growth down to where it had been. Second, mortality rates have been rather high and are also falling. Expected length of life increased five years from 1965-70 to 1970-75, no doubt in part reflecting better health and nutrition. Further declines in mortality rates are expected to occur in 1980-2000, offsetting about half of the expected fertility decline on Java and virtually all of the expected fertility decline on the other islands. Thus population on Java will rise nearly 50 percent between 1976 and 2001, even with a sharp further reduction in fertility. Total population of Indonesia will probably lie in the 210-220 million range by 2000.

Even though the Outer Islands have a higher natural population increase than Java, their lower densities have given rise to various schemes to move significant numbers of people off Java. It has proved very difficult to encourage large-scale migration. Different soils and social structures, poorer infrastructure, and insecurity of land tenure and income all help to explain past difficulties. Also complicating any net improvement is the flow of migrants, often educated, to Java from the Outer Islands. The result has been a steadily declining annual average net out-migration from Java, with an annual flow of about 60,000 from 1961 to 1966 and less than 15,000 from 1971 to 1976. The latter figure is only 1 percent of the annual growth in population on Java, and it does not appear that very large increases in annual flows are likely, although substantial increases are possible. Still it is not likely that transmigration will prove to be an effective safety valve anytime in the near future, although it could be an effective way to expedite and direct regional development. [2]

WORK FORCE

Compared with population, the analysis of work force changes is highly uncertain. It is no easy matter to decide whether a person is in or out of the work force when much work is done in a family or communal setting and is highly seasonal. Definitions of employment were quite strict in 1971, for example, and much looser in 1976. Simply changing the survey month from the busy harvest season to a slack season can change responses by millions of jobs. Furthermore, many people shift their occupation and even location of work during a year. They will work at agriculture, trading, construction, and services at different times and in different places, depending on the availability of employment. Placing these people neatly into occupational boxes is not easy or meaningful. Finally, there is real debate over the meaning of a job. Some self-employed people "work" long hours but perform few services and earn very little. Many economists would argue that such employment is simply too unlike a full-time job with a firm to treat it in the same way.

Typically the unemployment data in poorer countries give very little real information about the state of the labor market, save perhaps the urban, and often educated, young. Others need income so much that they find some work. They count as employed, but may have very low incomes and be on the lookout for more regular and better-paid work. In making sense of changes in occupation and labor force, it is necessary to distinguish between those who have "real" jobs and those who do not. This is not easy, but the attempt is made below.

In comparing the data from 1961, 1971, and 1976, some adjustments and consolidations are made to improve comparability and clarity. The work force is broken into four major groups:

TABLE 1.1

Population of Indonesia, 1930-76

	People (millions)				Annual Growth Rate (percent)		
	1930	1961	1971	1976	1930-61	1961-71	1971-76
Java-Madura							
Rural	N.A.	53.2	62.4	67.9	—	1.6	1.7
Urban	N.A.	9.8	13.7	15.1	—	3.4	2.0
Total	41.7	63.0	76.1	83.0	1.4	1.9	1.8
Outer Islands							
Rural	N.A.	29.5	36.0	40.2	—	2.0	2.2
Urban	N.A.	4.6	7.1	8.6	—	4.4	3.9
Total	18.9	34.0	43.1	48.8	1.9	2.4	2.5
Indonesia							
Rural	N.A.	82.7	98.4	108.1	—	1.8	1.9
Urban	N.A.	14.4	20.8	23.7	—	3.7	2.6
Total	60.6	97.0	119.2	131.8	1.5	2.1	2.0

N.A. = not available.

Sources: 1961 and 1971 are based on Population Census Reports for those years (Jakarta: Central Bureau of Statistics). 1930 comes from February 1978 Indikator Ekonomi (Jakarta: Central Bureau of Statistics), p. 138. 1976 is an estimate for October 1976 based on the March 1976 Intercensal Population Survey. It is taken from Development Policy Staff, World Bank, Employment and Income Distribution in Indonesia, no. 51 in Studies in Employment and Rural Development, Table A-5.

Group I: agriculture—this includes agriculture and mining, but agriculture accounts for 99.6 percent of the sector's jobs. The category includes estates, forestry, and fishing, as well as small-holders and agricultural workers not on estates. (Estates are cash crop plantations mostly under government management.)

Group II: manufacturing—this sector includes manufacturing, utilities, and construction. Manufacturing accounts for over 80 percent of this category, and construction for virtually all the rest.

Group III: trade—this includes trade, transport, communications, storage, finance, real estate, and business services. Trade accounts for five-sixths of employment in this group, with transport and communications taking up virtually everything else.

Group IV: services—this encompasses all community, social, and personal services, including government.

In order to improve comparability, the 1971 work force size is adjusted by setting it equal to a linear interpolation between the 1961 and October 1976 labor force sizes. This adjusts for the much stricter definition used in 1971 than in 1961 or 1976.[3] Since the 1961 and 1971 censuses were taken in September, the 1976 labor force survey taken in September through December is used rather than the March 1976 survey. Figures from the 1930 census are also shown for historical purposes.

In analyzing Table 1.2, several facts stand out. One is the continuing importance of agriculture in the total work force despite a substantial drop in its share from 1961 to 1976. In the latter year it still employed nearly three out of five workers on Java and over two out of three on the Outer Islands. If the proportion of workers engaged in agriculture were measured in March, during the peak season, rather than September or October (as in Table 1.2), in the slack season, the role of agriculture would be even larger. Another striking fact is the growing importance of trade in total employment, compared with a much more restrained rise in manufacturing. Indeed, during 1971-76 the share of manufacturing hardly changed, and by 1976 still had not reached the proportion experienced in 1930. Since output in manufacturing grew at nearly 15 percent annually from 1971 to 1976, this lack of growth in the share of the work force is particularly noteworthy.

Given the differences in population density and infrastructure, it is perhaps surprising that there is not more variation observable in the work force patterns on Java and the Outer Islands. Java has a slightly lower share in agriculture and somewhat higher shares in trade and manufacturing, and a similar share in services. Structural change in the work force is more evident in the Outer Islands despite a concentration of resources and investment on Java. The

TABLE 1.2

Distribution and Size of Work Force in Indonesia, 1930-76

(percent shares)

Sector	Indonesia				Java-Madura				Outer Islands			
	1930	1961	1971	1976	1930	1961	1971	1976	1930	1961	1971	1976
Agriculture	68.8	73.6	66.2	62.0	64.3	69.4	61.4	58.7	79.5	81.6	75.4	68.4
Manufacturing	10.6	7.8	9.9	10.1	11.6	9.1	11.4	11.3	8.3	5.2	6.9	7.9
Trade	7.7	8.9	13.5	17.3	8.5	10.2	15.9	18.9	5.7	6.6	9.0	14.1
Services	12.9	9.7	10.4	10.6	15.6	11.2	11.3	11.1	6.5	6.6	8.7	9.5
Total	100.0	100.0	100.0	100.0	100.0	100.0	100.0	100.0	100.0	100.0	100.0	100.0
Total number (millions)	20.9	34.8	44.1	51.0	14.4	22.7	28.8	33.2	6.2	12.1	15.3	17.8
Annual growth (percent)		1.7	2.4	3.0		1.4	2.4	2.9		2.2	2.4	3.1

Notes: The 1961 census includes financial employment in services, rather than in trade. This is a small error, as in 1971 financial employment was 0.2 percent of the work force. The percentage shares refer to employed people, while the absolute numbers refer to total work force.

Sources: Censuses of 1930, 1961 (adjusted to include West Irian), 1971 (adjusted to define work force consistently), and the 1976 labor force survey.

broad patterns, however, are clear. There has been a decreasing share of the work force in extractive activities, a rapidly rising share in trade and transport, and a slowly rising share in manufacturing, construction, and services.

Several questions arise: Why has manufacturing employment not grown more rapidly? Given the pressure on land, what is the nature of movement out of agriculture and the quality of nonfarm jobs available, particularly on Java? In short, is much of the work force change induced by demand factors, or is some of it basically a redistribution of existing work, reflecting intense pressures on the land and changes in work opportunities in agriculture? This broad set of issues has been addressed by various scholars, and there is disagreement about the implications of the existing data. Those who concentrate on local studies or farm- and village-level surveys are typically pessimistic about work force trends, while others point to aggregate data on consumption levels, employment patterns, and real wages in making a case for progress providing meaningful employment opportunities in recent years.*

My own approach will be to use the macro data, along with the additional evidence provided by work force status. That is, every worker is either an employer, an employee, an unpaid family worker, or an own-account worker. We know from many studies in Indonesia and elsewhere that the unpaid family and own-account workers tend to be the worst off, having no certainty of a regular income, little capital, and limited education. Inclusion of this variable is less significant in agriculture, since most of the workers there are self-employed. However, in the nonfarm sectors this status stratification is likely to be a good way of getting at the quality of job growth. A separate analysis of agricultural job gains will be made.

---

*Some of the debate has been on issues of employment, and some on the issue of poverty and income distribution. The World Bank and various government officials are most evident on the side that argues for substantial progress having been accomplished, although some work of Hendra Esmara has also been cited. On the other side, Sajogyo and others associated with the Agro-Economic Survey—such as William Collier, Benjamin White, Rudolf Sinaga, Soentoro, and Gunawan Wiradi—have argued that improvement for the poor in rural Java is more apparent than real. Other foreign scholars, such as Richard Franke, Gillian Hart, and Ann Stoler, tend to support the latter group's conclusions.

The following discussion will focus on four sectors: agriculture, manufacturing, trade, and services. As these accounted for 95 percent of all employment in both 1971 and 1976, little is lost by so narrowing the focus of work. (Over 93 percent of all job growth was in these sectors.) The nonfarm sectors increased their reported employment by a very strong 43 percent in five years, while agriculture went up 11 percent. The population over ten years of age grew only 13 percent, so the clear implication is that employment rose more rapidly than potential labor force. Combined with a rapid rate of real output growth, some observers have concluded that the period 1971-76 was a good one for employment.

When one analyzes the gains, however, a less positive picture emerges. In agriculture, for example, about 90 percent of the job gains were on Java, where land is least available, and many studies suggest that employment per unit of output was falling. Indeed, the agricultural survey data show that real wage payments per hectare fell over this period, and total hectares harvested declined over 5 percent. [4] Gustav Papanek's wage data for plantation workers on Java also indicate a decline in the real wage (see his "The Effect of Economic Growth and Inflation on Workers' Income," ch. 4 of this volume). Not only are the real wage and labor income falling, but they are absolutely very low. In the 1976 peak season, when demand for labor was high, 78 percent of all agricultural employees were paid less than the poverty-level wage of 7,000 rupiahs (Rp.) a month. A third of all job growth came in agriculture, yet most village-level observation, [5] plus aggregate data on wages and income, suggests that there are low and declining opportunities for earning adequate minimum incomes in the farm sector.

If the agricultural job gains seem questionable, many of the nonfarm improvements virtually disappear. Table 1.3 shows job growth as divided between the self-employed and unpaid family workers, on the one hand, and the employers and employees, on the other. The former group tends to have little capital and low earning power. The latter is more closely linked to the rapidly growing "modern" part of the economy.

Out of the 4.4 million new nonfarm jobs created between 1971 and 1976, fully five out of six went to those who were self-employed or unpaid family workers. Indeed, only in services was any substantial part of the job increase attributable to employers and employees. In trade and manufacturing together, there was an actual decrease in employers and employees in the five-year period, and all job gains went to the self-employed and unpaid family workers.

When the pattern of job status changes is combined with limited information available on returns to self-employed labor on Java, the overall impression is that traditional patterns of sharing work

TABLE 1.3

Worker Status and Nonfarm Job Gains: Indonesia, 1971–76

	(A) Self-Employed and Unpaid Family Workers (thousands)			(B) Employers and Employees (thousands)			Share of Growth (percent)	
	1971	1976	Change	1971	1976	Change	(A)	(B)
Trade	3,523	5,893	2,370	854	660	-194	109	-9
Manufacturing	1,093	1,979	886	1,661	1,741	80	92	8
Services	638	958	320	3,592	4,426	834	28	72
Total	5,254	8,830	3,576	6,107	6,827	720	83	17

Notes: The 1971 "employed" data were arrived at by taking "economically active" in the 1971 census and multiplying by .98—thus assuming an unemployment rate equal to that of 1976. The status and sectoral percentages were then applied to the revised total. The practical effect was to raise each category by 2.5 percent. The 1976 Intercensal Survey was used, because it alone had data on worker status. It was increased by 3.3 percent to allow for its limited geographic coverage (as compared with 1971). In both years unclassified workers were distributed on a pro rata basis over classified workers.

Sources: 1971 census, Intercensal Population Survey of March 1976.

12

may be growing. That is, additional workers are absorbed in trade, not because they are needed in any real sense to increase output, but because available work and income-earning opportunities are shared. This pattern is clearest where the data are best: in manufacturing.

> About 90 percent of this growth—i.e. manufacturing employment growth from 1970 to 1974/75, occurred in establishments of fewer than ten workers. The principal cause of this employment growth appears to have been supply side pressure of the labor market. Its principal consequence has been a decline in real value added per worker in small scale manufacturing. This decline is most pronounced on Java, where most of the small manufacturing units are located. [6]

The very small establishments are the overwhelming employers of self-employed and unpaid family workers. In 1974-75 they accounted for over eight out of every ten manufacturing workers, but less than a quarter of the value added. Putting it another way, value added per worker was about 5 percent of that in the large and medium establishments. The large and medium establishments provide most of the jobs for employees, but have increased those jobs only 1.5 percent a year, while their output has increased over 12 percent per annum. Thus, it appears that in 1971-76 the jobs with low productivity and easy entry grew the fastest and accounted for most job growth. So fast was the increase in numbers employed that average output per worker fell by about a third. The larger, high-productivity establishments accounted for most of the output growth but very few of the new jobs.

There is more uncertainty over the trend in manufacturing employment from 1961 to 1971. R. M. Sundrum argued that it is likely that there was healthy growth in manufacturing employment in that period. [7] He pointed out that while urban manufacturing employment had fallen slightly, there had been a large increase in rural manufacturing employment. He suggested that "urban spillover" meant that cities were expanding beyond their legal boundaries, and that workers were getting city jobs but not being so counted. By comparing the 1971 census with the large and medium establishment survey in 1971, and the small-scale industry survey in the next year, he concluded that comprehensively defined urban manufacturing employment grew 46 percent from 1961 to 1971, with most of that in the last four years; and rural manufacturing employment grew by a very substantial 67 percent in the same period.

I do not find this line of argument convincing insofar as it
seeks to establish that demand growth was a primary causal factor
in the changes Sundrum observed.[8] During the ten-year period private consumption grew by only 40 percent and small-scale agriculture by only 34 percent, suggesting a rate of growth for rural manufactures of only 35-40 percent. There is no way to reconcile this,
if there is constant productivity per worker, with a 67 percent increase in employment. The admittedly poor estimates of small-
scale industry show an output growth of only 28 percent in the ten-
year period—a fact noted by Sundrum but dismissed on the basis
that it was probably wrong. Yet even by 1971 displacement of hand-
pounded rice, hand looms, and other labor-intensive manufacturing
activities had been noted by observers. To the extent that employment in rural industry really did rise sharply, it was unlikely to
have been in response to a "pull" or demand causality. However,
it is possible that there was fairly rapid growth of "real" jobs in
the large and medium establishments, since they were then expanding at the expense of smaller firms using labor-intensive techniques.
As these markets have become saturated, and productivity has grown,
any increase in employees has slowed sharply.

It is impossible to draw meaningful conclusions about the increase in demand for labor by looking at the numbers said to be employed in different years. It is quite possible to have output and
measured employment growing rapidly, yet have jobs above a modest poverty-level wage growing slowly in availability, while there
are openings at very low wages or earnings for the majority of the
work force. Indeed, the pressure on income could explain some of
the extra "employment." It is difficult to determine exactly what
happened between 1961 and 1971, although most observers would
agree that conditions did improve from 1967 to 1971, as real wages
rose and the economy returned to more normal functioning. From
1971 to 1976 the data are better, and point to a slow growth in supply of good jobs and considerable evidence of overcrowding in the
poorer ones.

Many of the arguments left here will be picked up in a later
treatment of income distribution. For example, why is there no
systematic evidence of declining real wages from 1971 to 1976 if
supply-side pressure was indeed moving the system? Can one
make inferences about the causes of the apparently slow growth in
better-paying jobs? The latter point is addressed below.

OUTPUT: CHANGES IN LEVEL AND STRUCTURE

The serious problems with employment should not detract
from a significant accomplishment of the Suharto regime. From

1960 to 1967 real output in Indonesia grew about as fast as the population. Since then it has grown about 8 percent a year, and more than doubled in a decade. Real output per capita has risen over 75 percent. It is a substantial achievement to take a chaotic and stagnant economy and direct it along a path of rapid growth for a decade. Without growth, poverty can be made more bearable by sharing, but the reality of the poverty is not lessened.

It is useful to split the period under review into three parts. The first, from 1960 to 1967, includes the period of upheaval and stagnation in per capita growth. The second, from 1967 to 1971, covers the recovery of the economy and the winding down of inflation. The third, from 1971 to 1977 (which is, incidentally, the period of the revised national accounts data) includes the oil boom and its widespread effects.

There are also a number of ways to present the sectoral output data. I group agriculture (excluding forestry), trade, and services together because they account for over 85 percent of the work force and have grown more slowly than total output in recent years. I separately list forestry, mining, manufacturing, construction, public administration, and all others, which have grown rapidly in recent years. Also shown are data for consumption, investment, and trade.

The usual warnings about data quality should be repeated here. Many of the sectoral estimates are extremely rough. The investment data omit many items from coverage, and the private consumption is calculated as a residual. The 1967 estimates may be particularly low because of the disruptive effects of inflation and civil disorder, as well as unofficial barriers to trade. It would be much more correct to list the growth rates to the nearest whole number, but even then there would be a spurious impression of accuracy.

Having said all that, there is no doubt that the economy was growing very slowly in the first period and that growth picked up considerably in the second and third periods. Investment was growing as fast in three or four months in the second period as in seven years in the first. Private consumption appears to have grown more slowly than output; and if investment is understated through the lack of stock-change data, then the increase in investment and savings would be even higher than indicated. All sectors grew faster than population. Services, the slowest, is probably wrong—it is unlikely that output in this sector would lag consumption growth by so much. It was more likely growing about as fast as private consumption, perhaps 5-7 percent a year. (If services did grow at 5 percent a year in 1967-77, the subtotal in which it is included would have its annual growth rate raised by 0.20 percent.) The other striking fact in the table is the widening gap between import and export growth rates in the third period. Prior to that the two had been close. In 1971-77 imports grew by nearly 18 percent a year (in constant prices), while exports at constant prices rose only 10 percent. The reason is that oil prices did not remain constant, and that more imports could be afforded with a given volume of exports.

TABLE 1.4

Rates of Growth of National Income, 1960-77
(percent per year)

Sector	1960-67	1967-71	1971-77
Agriculture (excluding forestry)	1.7	4.2	3.6
Trade	3.5	11.3	7.5
Services	2.5	2.4	2.6
Subtotal	2.2	5.7	4.6
Forestry	-8.2	25.1	5.2
Mining	2.1	10.9	11.7
Manufacturing	2.0	14.1	13.4
Construction	-1.1	23.7	25.5
Public administration	5.0	6.5	13.6
All others	1.5	12.7	12.5
Subtotal	1.6	13.4	12.2
Total GDP, of which:	2.1	7.9	7.9
Private consumption	3.0	5.5	7.8
Public consumption	-3.1	10.1	12.3
Gross investment	0.9	26.3	13.3
Exports	1.1	7.3	10.0
Imports	2.4	6.8	17.9

Notes: The first two columns are taken from the old GNP series that ran 1960-73 and used 1960 constant prices. The third column is the new series that runs 1971-77 and uses constant 1973 prices.

Source: Statistical Pocketbook of Indonesia (various issues), Central Bureau of Statistics.

Because exports, particularly of oil, have become so important to the economy, their effect should be treated further. From 1972 to 1977 all exports rose from Rp. 754 billion to Rp. 4,119 billion, an increase of 446 percent. Import prices about doubled, and therefore real export earnings (deflated by import prices) rose 180 percent in the period. In absolute terms this is Rp. 1,350 billion in 1972 prices. Some of that increase—about Rp. 300 billion—was due to increased export volume. The balance was due to improved terms of trade. The gain due to terms of trade in 1977 compared with 1972 was about 15 percent of 1977 gross domestic product (GDP). Recent strengthening of the dollar and increases of roughly 50 percent in the official dollar price of oil exports should push the terms-of-trade effect for 1979-80 even higher. At the new exchange rate and probable level of GDP, a 20 percent effect would translate into an additional $75 per capita available due to favorable terms of trade. This surprisingly small amount serves as a reminder that, even with high-priced oil, Indonesia is scarcely a Kuwait or even a Venezuela. While the resource situation has been improved by recent events, oil earnings per capita are still modest. It also means that the increase in real GDP is equal to only two-thirds of the increase in real purchasing power from 1972 to 1977.

TABLE 1.5

Effects of Higher Export Prices on Income, 1972 and 1977
(Rp. billion)

	1972	1977
Exports (current prices)	754	4,119
Import prices	100	196
Export prices	100	388
Exports/import prices	754	2,105
Exports/export prices	754	1,062
"Terms-of-trade effect"	0	+1,043
GDP (1972 prices)	4,564	6,737

Source: Calculated from 1977 and 1978-79 Statistical Pocketbook of Indonesia (Central Bureau of Statistics).

The impact of oil shows up in another way. The shares of
different sectors in total output, valued at current prices, change
sharply. The change in constant-price shares is smaller, since
higher prices do not inflate the increase in mining's share. This
difference is shown in Table 1.6.

The preceding tables clearly indicate an astonishing rate of
structural change compressed into a decade. An economy that in
the 1960s had over 50 percent of its output in agriculture, and another 20-25 percent of output in trade and services, has shifted to
one in which other sectors now account for fully 50 percent of total
output. The rising shares of savings and investment, particularly
in current prices, is no less striking. In 1967 investment net of
depreciation was little greater than zero, and gross savings was
zero. By 1977 both savings and investment had grown to a respectable 20 percent of total output. And many government "consumption" programs, as in education, in fact have an investment component in them, though they are not so counted. The structural
change, combined with the doubling of output, means incredible
scaling up of spending: real investment multiplied fourfold in a
decade; construction, manufacturing, and mining tripled or better.
Managing this pace of change is difficult under favorable conditions.
Given the initial labor intensities and the modest bureaucratic ca-
pabilities extant in 1967, it is perhaps not surprising that the growth
has been uneven and often undesirable.

Another striking fact is that in spite of the oil boom and the
higher rates of investment that it has helped to finance, there has
been no discernible tendency for output growth rates to increase.
It might be said that 1967-71 represents recovery, and that in the
absence of new injections of investment, a slowdown would have
been experienced. There is an element of truth in this, but the
spurt in growth had seemingly run out by 1970, when output was at
an all-time high, fully 27 percent above 1967 (a growth of 8.5 percent per year) and 46 percent above 1960. Yet growth from 1971 to
1974, when investment averaged 17 percent of output, was 9.5 percent per year, while growth from 1974 to 1977, when investment
was 20 percent of output, was only 6.5 percent per year. (The oil
boom revenues were spent on a large scale only since 1975, so the
division is a proper one.) It appears that a higher rate of investment produced a lower rate of growth, even when catch-up factors
are largely allowed for.

It is likely that this is a real paradox, not merely a result of
poor data. If anything, statistical coverage of certain Pertamina
investments was becoming worse in the mid-1970s, and correction
of biases would probably accentuate rather than diminish the findings. It seems likely that the government's shift to highly capital-

TABLE 1.6

Changes in Sectoral Output Shares, 1960–77
(percent)

Sector					

Current Prices

Sector	1960	1967	1971	1977	
Agriculture	53.9	54.0	44.8	31.3	
Mining	3.7	2.7	8.0	19.4	
Manufacturing	8.4	7.3	8.4	9.5	
Construction	2.0	1.7	3.5	4.8	
Trade	14.3	17.6	16.1	16.1	
Public administration	4.5	4.8	5.9	7.3	
Services	6.2	7.0	4.9	3.2	
All other	7.0	4.9	8.4	8.4	
Total	100.0	100.0	100.0	100.0	

Constant Prices

Sector	1960	1967	1971	1971*	1977*
Agriculture	53.9	51.8	46.1	44.0	34.7
Mining	3.7	3.7	5.6	9.9	12.2
Manufacturing	8.4	8.4	9.3	8.8	11.9
Construction	2.0	1.6	2.8	3.0	4.6
Trade	14.3	15.8	17.8	16.7	16.2
Public administration	4.5	5.5	5.2	5.9	8.0
Services	6.2	6.4	5.2	4.5	3.3
All other	7.0	6.8	8.0	7.2	9.1
Total	100.0	100.0	100.0	100.0	100.0

Current Prices

	1960	1967	1971	1977	
Private consumption	79.7	92.7	77.1	67.4	
Public consumption	11.5	7.3	9.3	10.9	
Gross investment	7.9	8.0	15.8	18.9	
Exports	13.3	8.7	14.4	21.6	
Imports	12.6	16.9	16.6	18.8	
"Savings"	8.7	0.0	13.6	21.7	

Constant Prices

	1960	1967	1971	1971*	1977*
Private consumption	79.7	85.3	77.6	72.1	71.6
Public consumption	11.5	8.0	8.7	9.4	11.9
Gross investment	7.9	7.4	13.7	15.6	21.4
Exports	13.3	12.5	15.1	16.1	18.0
Imports	12.6	12.9	15.1	13.2	22.4
"Savings"	8.7	6.9	13.7	18.5	16.6

Notes: An asterisk means that constant prices of 1973 are used; unstarred items use constant prices of 1960. "Savings" is equal to gross investment plus exports minus imports. It is in quotation marks both because of its unreliable value due to its residual method of calculation, and because grants that finance imports are, arguably, not validly deducted from investment.

Source: Central Bureau of Statistics.

intensive, long-payoff projects, along with poor purchasing and
negotiation for many of those projects, led to a distinct increase in
the capital-output ratio. Essentially, even when correcting for the
gestation of investments, it took a lot more postboom investment to
"buy" the same increment in growth as preboom investment did.
How much more is uncertain, but the range is certainly between 50
percent and 80 percent more investment needed per unit of output
growth. Thus, the government chose a path that provided less
growth and did little to improve employment.

GOVERNMENT SPENDING

There were violent fluctuations in the real value of government
spending in Indonesia during the 1960s and 1970s. During most of
the 1960s, the rapid inflation and slow tax collections caused a decline in real spending that was only partly made up by deficit spending. In 1967 deficits essentially stopped. Revenues and expenditures
rose thereafter, but it was not until the 1970-71 fiscal year that real
spending finally equaled that of 1961, the previous peak. Since 1970-
71 real spending by 1978-79 has quadrupled, with routine spending
more than tripling and development spending quadrupling. The share
of the development budget in total spending rose from 30 percent in
1968 to over 50 percent in 1978-79. Table 1.7 provides a capsule
summary of changes in routine and development spending.

The meaning of government spending in this context should be
made clear. It covers all central government spending, including
contributions to lower levels of government and equity contributions
to quasi-public corporations. However, it does not comprehend all
spending by lower-level units, nor all capital spending by quasi-
government corporations. In particular, the spending of Pertamina—
the State Oil Company—is not included unless part of its resources
come from an equity contribution of government. Since many loans
for state-owned corporations require government backing, the development budget is not a complete picture of where government-
controlled resources are being allocated. Beyond this, the distinction between routine and development spending is less clear than
might be wished. It does not exactly correspond to current and
capital budgets; and although some entries could be switched to
either budget, on balance the current budget, if available, would be
larger than the routine spending.

The depressed levels of spending in the mid-1960s had a devas-
tating effect on the bureaucracy. As real salaries fell below the
subsistence level, practices such as multiple job holding, charging
fees for services, and outright corruption increased rapidly.

TABLE 1.7

Routine and Development Spending, 1961–79

Year	Billion Current Rupiahs			Index of Real Spending (1969–70 = 100)		
	Routine	Development	Total	Routine	Development	Total
1961	N.A.	N.A.	.088	—	—	113
1966	26	4	30	88	23	65
1968	150	58	208	84	49	75
1969–70	217	118	335	100	100	100
1970–71	288	170	458	121	131	124
1972–73	438	298	736	148	192	163
1974–75	1,016	962	1,978	193	338	244
1976–77	1,630	2,154	3,784	231	531	336
1978–79	2,744	2,556	5,299	320	548	400
1980–81	5,500	5,000	10,500	443	741	548

N.A. = not available.

Note: Deflation by the Jakarta Consumer Price Index. For all years except 1978–79, figures are actuals; for 1978–79 they are budget estimates.

Sources: Realized expenditures of 1961 from 1968–1969 Statistical Pocketbook; realized spending of 1966 through 1978–79 from April 1979 Indikator Ekonomi, p. 83; 1980–81 budget from December 1979–January 1980 Indonesia Development News, Vol. 3, Nos. 4–5, p. 1; inflation rates are calculated from the Jakarta cost of living index, except for 1980–81, which is estimated at 15 percent.

Repair of roads and irrigation facilities was neglected. This led to an accumulation of problems in both physical infrastructure and bureaucratic practices. The physical problems presented obvious targets for rehabilitation, and eased the burden of planning in 1967–71. The decline in bureaucratic morale and capability was perhaps more serious, and certainly was longer-lasting in its effects. Even with adequate salaries at the lower government levels and nearly adequate salaries (counting legitimate fringe benefits) at higher levels, there are persistent difficulties with corruption and poor performance. [9] While these would have been problems in any case, given the thin ranks of experienced and educated high- and middle-level civil servants and the rapid increases in real spending, the legacy of the 1960s doubtless intensified the difficulties.

The structure of spending in the routine budget has changed rather little, though in years when large subsidies for food are needed, the shares going to ordinary spending for personnel and materials fall. Typically, a little over 40 percent of the routine budget goes for personnel expenses, about 20 percent for materials, 20 percent for regional subsidies, 10-15 percent for debt service, and the balance for such items as food or petroleum subsidies and general election expenses.

The development budget has had rather more significant changes. Unfortunately, it is only since 1974–75 that a sectoral breakdown including project aid has been available. Prior to that the local rupiah budget was broken down, but project aid was not. However, in the earlier period local revenues and program aid were 75-80 percent of the total development budget, so the impression they give is not likely to be very misleading. In Table 1.8 sectoral shares in development are given for 1969–70 to 1973–74, which covers Pelita I, the First Five-Year Plan, and for 1974–75 through 1978–79, the Second Five-Year-Plan period. A budget estimate for 1979–80, the first year of Pelita III, is also shown.

The trends in Table 1.8 need explanation. For example, "agriculture and irrigation" spending includes a variable but substantial payment to subsidize fertilizer imports. It has averaged about 30 percent of government expenditure for that sector over the last five years, but rose as high as 83 percent in 1974–75, when the share of the sector reached an unusually high 31 percent of total development spending. "Industry and mining" does not include Pertamina investments. "Transportation, communications, and tourism" includes the very expensive, recently completed satellite system that raised the share of that sector while it was being installed. The most notable declining share was for regional development, which basically consists of grants to lower levels of government for specified categories of expenditures, such as road repair

TABLE 1.8

Sectoral Shares of Development Spending, 1969–70 through 1980–81

(percent)

Sector	Pelita I	1974–75	1975–76	1976–77	1977–78	1978–79	1980–81
Agriculture and irrigation	31.4	30.9	18.9	17.8	17.6	16.9	14.7
Industry and mining	2.4	7.2	8.4	9.8	6.4	9.0	15.1
Electric power	6.0	8.1	8.6	10.9	10.3	10.8	15.1
Transport, communications, and tourism	18.1	12.9	22.9	20.0	16.5	15.8	14.1
Transmigration and manpower	0.3	0.3	0.7	1.3	2.8	5.0	5.9
Regional development	21.1	14.3	9.5	9.3	11.6	11.0	9.6
Education	7.7	5.2	8.0	6.6	9.8	11.0	11.4
Family planning, health, and welfare	3.3	2.3	2.6	2.2	3.3	3.6	3.9
Housing and water supply	1.7	0.7	1.0	1.3	4.2	2.4	2.8
Defense	2.8	2.3	2.5	2.9	2.6	4.7	7.7
Government capital contributions	3.4	10.8	9.3	11.4	8.8	3.3	3.6
Other	11.8	5.0	7.6	6.5	6.1	6.5	11.2

Note: Pelita I covers 1969–70 through 1973–74.

Source: Nota Keuangan (various years); Ministry of Finance.

and drainage. However, the meaning of a declining share in this period is simply moderate growth in absolute terms. For example, even though the share for regional development fell almost by half from Pelita I to 1978-79, its rate of growth in terms of real spending grew over 11 percent a year from 1973-74 to 1978-79, a cumulative increase of over 70 percent. Those sectors, such as industry and transmigration, that had a large increase in their share, obviously had their resources multiplied many times over. The share of defense spending, which had been held at a remarkably low 2-3 percent for most of the period, jumped sharply in 1978-79, reflecting concern by the armed forces, after severe difficulties in Timor, that better equipment was necessary.

It is a pity that there is not a data base to put together a consolidated investment budget for the public sector. For the development budget is not unreasonable taken by itself: a third of the budget to agriculture, regional development, and transmigration; a sixth to education, health, and housing; a third to industry, electricity, transport, and communications; and the rest widely spread over the other categories. It is when the quasi-public corporations are included that the picture begins to tilt decidedly toward large, capital-intensive projects. Some of this pattern of allocation is the legacy of Pertamina's past management. By 1976 it had negotiated a number of large and corruptly costly projects, with the financing coming from huge, unauthorized borrowings. When the loans were added up, it was found that Pertamina's debts exceeded those of the rest of the government, including even those incurred during the Sukarno period. Yet the past is no longer an adequate explanation for the new projects being discussed and sometimes approved, many of which seem to be of low priority and poor payoff in terms of employment, foreign-exchange earnings, or a properly calculated rate of return. It may be that bureaucratic and political pressures bias budgetary decisions toward this type of project.

Future directions of budgetary allocation will be influenced by the new round of increased oil revenues, again providing large amounts of "outside" rupiah at a time of inflationary pressures generated by the November 1978 devaluation. (The sections on government revenue and inflation define and discuss the issue of "outside" rupiah.) There is also the continuing problem of expanding administrative absorptive capacity. In this situation capital-intensive projects with high returns make sense. They will productively utilize revenues, with minimal inflationary effects. Waste can be easier to control administratively in large projects than in highly decentralized ones. If the political process allows efficient selection and implementation of these large projects, they could move the oil revenue forward to the time when they begin generating profits—perhaps to a future when administrative capacity has grown to use more funds efficiently in implementation of labor-intensive projects. A simple alternative strategy would be to borrow less and pay back more, thus improving future borrowing capacity while maintaining an equal resource availability. Choosing the proper mix of borrowing, well-selected large projects, and an appropriate rate of expansion for employment-intensive spending will be a major problem confronting policy makers.

A related issue is that of the subsidy to domestic petroleum products. Raising these prices to anywhere near world levels would be politically difficult and somewhat inflationary, but also would provide large amounts of domestic rupiah that could be used to finance internal spending with only modest inflationary impact. Up to 1978-79 the budgetary practice was to ignore the forgone revenue, with a negative revenue item debited if Pertamina lost any money on domestic sales. Now the subsidy is treated as an expenditure, but it still does not equal the economic subsidy effectively paid—the difference between what customers pay and what the fuels cost or could fetch in world markets. The true economic subsidy in 1978-79 exceeded Rp. 150 billion, and by late 1980 the annual rate of subsidy will exceed Rp. 1,500 billion. (This is after taking account of the 40 percent increase in domestic prices announced in 1979.) Balancing the political, economic, and equity variables involved in this problem will be another major task in the years ahead.

GOVERNMENT REVENUE

Government revenues are collected for a number of different reasons. They provide the resources by means of which spending can be undertaken without generating inflation. They can be used to redistribute income. And the tax system can direct investment toward socially efficient uses by correcting market signals that do not reflect relative availability of a good. As Table 1.9 indicates, virtually all of the rapid revenue growth in recent years (relative to GDP) has come from oil and aid. If the tariffs collected from the imports financed by those exports and aid are added, then nearly 80 percent of absolute revenue growth has been from these sources, and less than 20 percent from income or property taxes. This fact, combined with other policies, has meant that the revenue policy has not succeeded in any of the three major purposes outlined above, even though real revenues have grown very rapidly.

There are many facets to this de facto policy of relying on oil and aid for a large and increasing fraction of total revenues. One problem is simply that it is risky. If oil prices were to soften,

TABLE 1.9

Indonesia Revenues from Oil, Aid, and Other Sources, 1960 to 1980-81

Year	Revenues in Billion Current Rupiah				Index of Real Revenue		Revenue/GDP	
	Total	Oil	Aid	Other	Total	Other	Total	Other
1960	.054	(.004)		.05	82	144	.13	.12
1966	13	(1.5)		11.5	29	51	.04	.04
1968	208	33	58	117	75	80	.10	.06
1969–70	335	66	91	178	100	100	.12	.07
1970–71	465	99	121	245	125	124	.13	.08
1972–73	748	231	158	359	176	159	.15	.07
1974–75	1,986	957	232	797	254	192	.18	.07
1976–77	3,690	1,635	784	1,271	337	218	.23	.08
1978–79	5,302	2,309	1,036	1,957	398	276	.23	.08
1980–81	10,557	6,430	1,502	2,625	551	258	.28	.07

Notes: All years are actual figures. The GDP for 1978–79 and 1980–81 are estimated. Deflation is by the Jakarta consumer price index, except for 1980–81, when it was estimated at 15 percent. Total revenues = oil revenues + aid revenues + other revenues.

Sources: All actuals are from Central Bureau of Statistics sources, except for oil and aid revenues for 1960 and 1966, which are taken from Dietrich Lerche, "The Indonesian Tax System" (unpublished paper). 1980–81 budget estimates are from Phyllis Rosendale, "Survey of Recent Developments," B.I.E.S., no. 1 (March 1980): 12.

physical oil exports to fall, or aid to decline, there would be little capability in place to switch to other tax sources for additional revenue. Arguably, the economy is more open to instability because of this.

Reliance on oil and aid revenues tends to be inflationary. When oil is pumped from the ground at little domestic resource cost, and then exported, the result is that foreign exchange is delivered to the government and the revenue "appears" from "outside." Net borrowing and grants similarly "create" foreign exchange. If this foreign exchange is used for imports, the results are not inflationary. But if the dollars are turned into rupiah and spent on local resources, the immediate inflationary effect is similar to that of printing rupiah. To the extent that the government wishes to spend oil or aid revenues ("outside" rupiah) on domestic goods and services without aggravating inflation, it will have to raise "inside" rupiah from income, sales, or property taxes. About three-quarters of all revenues are from "outside" sources, but only one-third to one-half of government spending goes directly for imports. The overall impact has been that demand for inelastically supplied goods, which are not effectively traded, has been so strong that their prices, and the overall price index, have increased much faster in Indonesia than in most other countries.*

The effect of taxes on resource allocation will be discussed in more detail later. The basic point is that many tariffs, quotas, and export taxes have encouraged inefficient investment. Modest positive steps have been taken to encourage labor-intensive cigarette and soda-bottling plants by placing higher sales taxes on more capital-intensive methods. But the overwhelming thrust of the tax system, in conjunction with investment review, licensing, and lending procedures, has been to distort rather than to improve the allocation of investment.

The argument concerning redistribution is clear and direct. Income and property taxes don't amount to much. Income taxes in 1977-78 accounted for less than 1 percent of private consumption (not income), and probably less than 1.5 percent of the income of

---

*This discussion is elaborated analytically in the next section, "Inflation." It should simply be noted here that restraint on money supply growth is not practically feasible as a means of controlling this inflation because of the size of the government sector and the effects that extreme credit restriction would have on remaining sectors. An explicit decision about the size, type, and financing of government spending is needed.

the upper 20 percent of income recipients (approximately the percentage supposed to be liable). The tax on urban property is similarly modest, with recent estimates of its average cost being about one rupiah per 1,000 rupiah of market valuation. Both taxes are collected haphazardly, with many legally liable taxpayers simply refusing to pay. Penalties are seldom applied, and least often to the influential. More common is a process of tax negotiation, particularly for income tax, payments being made to the tax collector in order to avoid higher assessed liability. In short, in terms of average yield or incidence on the highest income classes, the taxes on income and property are not significant.

The defacto policy of restricting taxation of incomes and property can be defended on some grounds. Income taxes are very difficult to collect in both technical and political terms. Revenues for much of the period were growing rapidly, and the main problem was the effective use of the seemingly ample sums available. Increasing collections of these taxes would have meant diverting scarce administrative talent to relatively low-priority or low-payoff activities. Other observers maintain that it has mainly been reluctance to take on powerful interests that has slowed this kind of tax effort, although other considerations may also have been present to a lesser degree.

This is not to suggest that no progress was made in tax administration during the 1970s. This is not the case. Tax rates were cut, yet tax revenues, even after adjusting for the growth of the tax base, rose. There is some indication that the ratio of actual to legally due collections increased. Yet there are still severe problems, much tax negotiation, and an inability of the tax collectors to determine what is actually due. This leads to widely varying payments for those in similar financial positions and a general cynicism about the process of tax collection.*

INFLATION

Inflation has been one of the few constant factors in the Indonesian economy, as Table 1.10 indicates. The government has consistently increased the money supply much faster than real output, and the result has been double-digit inflation in most years. From 1962 to 1968 prices more than doubled each year and rose

---

*A program designed to ease this problem for corporate income tax was announced in early 1979. It is expected that predictability of corporate tax liabilities will be improved as a result.

TABLE 1.10

Inflation and Money Supply Growth in Indonesia, 1940–51 to 1979
(annual rates, percent)

Period	Inflation	Money Supply
1940–51	32	28
1951–56	12	22
1956–61	28	39
1961–66	330	279
1966–68	148	127
1968–71	11	42
1971–78	19	32
1967	171	132
1969	17	61
1971	4	28
1973	39	41
1975	19	33
1977	11	25
1978	8	24
10/78–6/79 (annual rate)	32	N.A.

N.A. = not available.

Notes: The Jakarta cost of living index is used from 1959; prior to that an earlier low–income Jakarta index is used. The 1973 inflation rate has been raised to allow for understatement due to changing rice varieties. Money supply refers to currency and demand deposits. The money growth rates reflect December-to-December changes; inflation is year to year.

Sources: Statistical Pocketbook of Indonesia, Bank of Indonesia Weekly Bulletin, International Monetary Fund publications. See also G. Papanek and D. Dowsett, "The Cost of Living Index, 1938–73," Ekonomi dan Keuangan 23 (June 1975): 181–206.

about 800 times in the period. Since 1968 prices have roughly sextupled, or risen at an annual rate of about 17 percent, as measured by the Jakarta cost of living index, a widely used index based on a 1957-58 survey of spending patterns of industrial workers in Jakarta. Recent work by the Central Bureau of Statistics has produced a new urban consumer price index with 150 goods rather than the 62 items included in the earlier index, a more up-to-date and representative market basket, and a wider geographic base. It seems likely that the new index, with a base of 1977-78, will show somewhat higher rates of inflation than the present one. It was published beginning in April 1979.

Because of differences between urban-rural and Java-Outer Island consumption patterns and prices, there is an entire family of price indexes that attempt to capture inflation for at least some important basic goods for various geographic groups. Most of the inflation rates in the 1970s, as measured by these indexes, have been fairly close to the Jakarta index shown below. A puzzling exception is the price index for the nine basic commodities for the rural Outer Islands. It has grown at only 16 percent a year, while all urban areas and rural Java registered inflation of 19 percent since 1971. The cumulative gap of about 20 percent is hard to explain.

The relationship of money growth and inflation has not been entirely stable. In the 1940s and most of the 1960s, the turnover of money increased as prices rose faster than money supply. In the 1950s and since 1968 the opposite has held true, with money growth outstripping inflation. From 1968 to 1971 this difference was very large, as the economy became remonetized following recovery from the hyperinflation that had encouraged people to reduce their real holdings of money. Since output has risen to 8 percent a year and the cash-using sectors (as opposed to subsistence) have grown even faster, it is probably fair to say that during the 1970s any increase in money supply in excess of output growth in the monetized sector of the economy was inflationary. This is essentially a long-run observation, and does not account for the inflationary spurt felt after the November 1978 devaluation.

The pattern of inflation has been uneven, with food prices rising more than others. The September 1978 food index in the Jakarta cost of living index was nearly four times the September 1971 level, while housing, clothing, and other goods and services rose to only 2.4 to 2.8 times their earlier level. Because food has a weight of 63 percent, the overall index rose 3.5 times. During this same period the rupiah cost of imports rose to only about 2.4 times its September 1971 level. In other words, food prices behaved as if food were largely untraded, while housing and services (and clothing) rose only slightly more than import costs.

It is a bit of a puzzle why money supply growth should be so directly inflationary in an open economy. When goods trade freely, one would expect rapid increases in money or credit to result in higher levels of imports rather than in higher prices of traded goods. Some nontraded goods, facing bottlenecks in production, might increase rapidly in price if their supply were inelastic; other nontraded goods, with substantial excess capacity, would be elastically supplied, and higher relative prices would not be needed to increase output for that group. Many things happened between 1971 and 1978 (during which time the rate of the rupiah to the dollar was fixed)— such as the slide of the dollar against other currencies, an increase in trade restrictions, and more aggressive enforcement of existing regulations—and all of them should be reflected in the import price index.

If domestic food prices really did quadruple while world (dollar) prices of food roughly doubled, then the clear implication is either that food prices were controlled (the government has a monopoly on rice imports) or that food was not a traded good. With some minor exceptions, and two major ones of rice and wheat, very little food is imported. The reasons for this are unclear, but may involve difficult import procedures and high costs. It is otherwise difficult to explain a wholesale price of $183 per metric ton for corn in the Jakarta wholesale market, but only $100 per metric ton in the United States. Transport costs should not exceed 10-15 percent, and there are no tariffs on the importation of corn. This is not a problem of short-run lags, since there has been a large discrepancy since 1975. (In 1974 the Jakarta price was 10 percent over the U.S. price.) In any event, it is evidently true that the economy is less open than it appears to be and that imports are not keeping prices down, as would normally be expected.*

It is also true that some nontraded goods, such as land and skilled manpower, are in fixed supply (or are growing slowly relative to demand) and have gone up quite sharply in price. However, since housing costs even in Jakarta rose no faster than imports since 1971, we must assume that the direct effect of higher land costs on consumer prices (aside from food) has been modest. In general, one would expect most nontraded goods to be supplied fairly elastically.

---

*Jakarta wholesale rice prices were 82 percent of Thai prices for rice in 1971, but 113 percent of them in 1977. Thus, domestic rice prices tripled in that period while Thai rice prices (in dollars) only doubled. In the case of rice, government policy caused faster domestic than world inflation.

Another possible explanation lies in the general role of government and the charges it imposes on business activity. As Clive Gray noted, it is a common practice for civil servants to demand and receive quite substantial side payments for various reasons.[10] It is not known if these payments have increased sharply over time as a fraction of output, but they certainly add to the cost of doing business. They also may prevent potential price-reducing competition. In that sense the direct and indirect costs of government intervention may have generally contributed to a situation in which inflation was worse than it otherwise would have been.

The policy dilemma with respect to inflation may usefully be viewed as part of the larger macroeconomic situation. Generally accepted long-term goals include increasing employment and indigenous (as opposed to Chinese or other foreign) entrepreneurial activity, in order to put growth on a politically sustainable and economically solid basis. Yet the ability of the government to spend money efficiently for these long-term goals is limited. Furthermore, in the short run, inflation, income taxes, and higher fuel prices are very unpopular. Yet spending large amounts of "outside" rupiah on domestic goods and services is inflationary unless "inside" rupiah are also collected (in the form of income taxes or higher prices for domestic petroleum products). If the outside rupiah are spent largely on imports, little employment is generated and the entire thrust of government spending may aggravate dualistic tendencies. If the government skews procurement prices and credit in favor of labor intensity, the Chinese will tend to be primary beneficiaries. Thus, the tradeoffs between inflation dualism, taxes, employment generation, and Chinese vs. indigenous entrepreneurs are linked. It is quite difficult to put together a consistent policy that balances the various goals and pressures in the short and long runs.

One reason the policy problem is so intractable is that the banking system is dominated by a few state-owned banks with major problems. Several of the banks have difficulty functioning as lending institutions. Bad loans are a recurring problem, and solvency is not assured even with very high margins between borrowing and lending rates. Reports of illegal payments to bank officers are common, and traders are reported to pay over 10 percent per month for "informal" credit. Official lending rates are 1.5 to 2.5 percent per month, and the spread between official bank and free-market rates is presumably some indication of the real cost and difficulty of obtaining bank loans. Further, virtually all banks have problems as development institutions. Their ability to loan intelligently to small farmers, traders, or manufacturers is limited; their capacity to assist this class of borrowers in improving operations is even more deficient. Too much pressure on the banking bureaucracy to move funds earmarked for small businesses results in bad loans; too little pressure, and the rate of disbursements slows drastically. There often seems to be little room between these two states, and it is difficult to get labor-intensive activities to "take off" if rates of return have to exceed 200 percent per year—which is equivalent to the 10 percent per month that now has to be paid for nonbank loans.

There are a number of possible solutions to the present predicament. The general outline will be to improve administrative capability in the government and banking bureaucracy so that more domestic and labor-intensive-oriented spending and lending can be efficiently pursued. Slow progress in collecting "inside" rupiah and adroit use of Chinese entrepreneurial talent will also be required to combine reasonable price stability and intelligent relative prices with a pattern of development that is broadly enough based to command popular support. It is uncertain, however, if this type of policy response would be supported fully by the coalition now largely influencing decision making.

FOREIGN TRADE

Exports

Exports can play a major role in shaping the rate and kind of growth a nation experiences. A rapid rate of aggregate export growth can assure a plentiful supply of foreign exchange and adequate imports. It is also possible to direct the economy's product mix toward those goods that use plentiful domestic resources, such as labor or natural resources. Doing this can create jobs or, if the natural resources are low-cost, generate government revenue.

Indonesia's export record is very good in the aggregate but mixed with regard to its structure of output. Most of the growth in value has come from oil, timber, and minerals. These goods can create significant revenues, and deserve to be pursued for that reason. However, they are not major sources of employment. The record with other exports is spotty. The value of this group was able to surpass the 1960 level only after 1972, and since then there has been very rapid growth in export value. This is due in large part to favorable price trends. A major weakness has been the very sluggish volume growth in rubber and coconuts, two of the major cash crops in terms of employment and income. Coconut exports have virtually ceased because of slow output growth and growing internal demand. Rubber exports have fluctuated, but the 1977 volume was within 2 percent of that in 1970, as was production. There have been successes with other export crops. Solid-to-spectacular output gains have been achieved in coffee, palm oil, tobacco, tea, and pepper. However, unless coffee prices are very high, this group does not approach the other in value, and never comes close in terms of total employment.

Besides the sluggish growth of important traditional crops, there has been slow growth of labor-intensive manufactures. Some nontraditional exports have appeared, but the important ones have not been labor-intensive. Cement, fertilizer, and steel exports have come from government-subsidized or -supported capital-intensive plants. Fish and seafood exports now surpass $100 million, but are gathered and processed mainly by foreign ships. In these cases few jobs are created. Because of various subsidies or protection or a lack of normal taxation, the fact of export activity does not necessarily mean that world-level costs have been reached. Some of these exports may become profitable without subsidies and with normal taxes, but that is not yet the case for this group.

There has been some job creation through differential taxation of logs and processed wood. Logs pay a 20 percent export tax, while any kind of processed wood, even rough-cut sawn wood, pays no tax.* There is room for further growth in these activities. But up to 1978 little had happened in textiles, clothing, electronics, or other exports that could create tens of thousands of jobs. One reason for this was certainly the exchange rate, which, at least against the dollar, was unchanged from 1971 to 1978 while domestic costs rose rapidly. This problem was addressed with a 50 percent rupiah devaluation against the dollar in November 1978. There remains, however, a network of regulations that hinder exports. For example, shortly after the devaluation the Ministry of Trade began to ban exports or limit them in order to fight inflation. Beyond this, the costs of getting permission to export are often great, and port handling and processing costs can be prohibitive. The decision to devalue was a bold one, clearly aimed at improving the structure of output and job opportunities rather than directed primarily at saving or generating foreign exchange, at least in the short to medium run. But much better followup and implementation will be needed if the intended purpose of the devaluation is to be achieved. Development of labor-intensive exports may well be critical to foreign-exchange

---

*An important and little-noted problem with this kind of large differential export tax is that there is a very high effective protection on the export activity of sawing wood. Quite inefficient operators can receive high profits under this tax regime.

earnings in the longer run, since estimates of oil reserves are modest (if uncertain) and domestic petroleum consumption is growing much faster than production.

In summary, as Table 1.11 indicates, there has been an explosive growth in the value of Indonesian exports—nearly a tenfold jump in seven years. This is a welcome change from the decline or stagnation of much of the 1960s. Five-sixths of recent gains have come from the oil, minerals, and timber group, which is better at generating revenues than employment. The record for traditional cash crops has been mixed, with rubber and coconut the biggest disappointments; most other crops have done well in volume and value. Other, nontraditional exports have appeared, but they generally are not labor-intensive. These have been held back by high domestic costs and cumbersome regulations. The problem in exports, as in the economy generally, is to harness the dynamism of the modern dualistic sector and somehow direct it into products that will generate a better distribution of jobs and incomes.

Imports

The import data of Indonesia are a relatively weak statistical series. The coverage of the data during the mid-1960s was particularly weak, since national policies virtually insured widespread smuggling and underinvoicing. These problems were slowly brought under control, or at least reduced, in the mid-1970s. Since then poor coverage of at least some Pertamina imports and increasing protection may have caused further problems. Certainly the charges published in the 1979 anti-smuggling drive suggest that these problems are still significant.

There are three series that can be used to indicate imports, and they seldom agree closely in level or trend. The letter-of-credit data are recently the lowest; the customs, next; and the balance of payments (BOP) the highest. Since the customs figures allow a breakdown by type of import (the BOP do not), they are useful; but even they fell $2.5 billion short of the BOP estimate of imports for 1977-78. That is, the BOP figure was about 40 percent higher than the customs figure. Under these circumstances it is difficult to make secure judgments about many import trends or their composition. Table 1.12 illustrates the data problem.

With these caveats it is nevertheless clear that in 1961 imports peaked in dollar and volume terms for that decade, with the decline of the mid-1960s made up by the early 1970s. From 1971 to 1978 the dollar value of imports rose six to seven times, a near tripling in terms of constant prices. Since 1973 there has been no

TABLE 1.11

Exports of Indonesia, 1960-77
(million dollars)

Product	1960	1965	1970	1972	1974	1977	Share of Growth (percent) 1965-70	Share of Growth (percent) 1970-77
Oil and gas	221	272	434	965	5,133	7,194	40	71
Other minerals	57	42	78	90	303	366	9	3
Timber	2	2	101	231	726	961	25	9
Other nonoil	561	392	496	534	1,144	2,118	26	17
Rubber	317	222	261	196	487	595	9.7	3.5
Coffee	N.A.	32	66	72	101	634	8.5	6.0
Palm Oil	N.A.	27	37	42	166	193	2.5	1.6
All other	244	111	132	224	390	696	5.3	5.9
Total exports	841	708	1,109	1,820	7,306	10,639	100.0	100.0
Exports of goods and services as percent of GDP	13.3	5.3	12.8	16.5	16.8	18.9		
Other nonoil exports as percent of GDP	6.4	N.A.	5.6	4.8	4.4	4.6		

N.A. = not available.

Notes: Exports of goods and services as percent of GDP is taken from national income accounts data. Other nonoil exports as percent of GDP is taken by multiplying the dollar value by the relevant exchange rate and dividing by GDP in rupiah.

Sources: Bank Indonesia and Central Bureau of Statistics.

TABLE 1.12

Imports of Indonesia, 1970-71 to 1978-79
(million dollars)

	1970-71	1972-73	1974-75	1976-77	1977-78	1978-79 (est.)
Balance of payments	1,242	1,870	5,616	7,920	8,658	9,366
Customs	1,111	1,651	4,349	6,013	6,204	6,900
Letter of credit	1,205	1,617	4,218	4,245	4,958	4,988
			Distribution of Imports (percent)			
Customs basis						
(calendar year) consumer goods	25.1	16.1	18.4	16.1	17.7	18.2
Intermediate goods	37.6	38.3	41.2	35.7	39.4	39.3
Capital goods	37.2	45.6	40.4	48.2	42.9	42.5

Sources: Indikator Ekonomi, various issues, Central Bureau of Statistics; B.I.E.S., vol. 14, no. 1; B.I.E.S., vol. 15, no. 2; Monthly Bulletin, various issues, Bank Indonesia.

clear shift in the share of imports devoted to consumer goods, capital goods, or intermediate goods—although there have been fluctuations reflecting large capital or rice purchases in particular years. The aggregate trends are fairly certain, and consistent with other data; the data on import patterns are less reliable.

The growth of imports by nearly 200 percent in real terms, while real income grew only 70 percent, is notable. It implies an import increase of 25-30 percent for a 10 percent increase in income. Since import prices rose less than domestic prices in this period, the measured increase in import demand reflects both a price effect (relatively cheaper imports) and an income effect. Given the poor data base, no convincing effort has been made to disentangle these effects. However, the government itself is, directly and indirectly, a major importer. It accounts for most capital imports and much rice, kerosene, and many intermediate goods imports. The extent to which the government itself will respond to price incentives is uncertain. But it is likely that one major reason for the devaluation of November 1978 was the feeling that higher prices for capital equipment would encourage more labor-intensive techniques. It remains to be seen if the 50 percent rise in rupiah prices of many imports will act to do this or to slow down import growth relative to income. While no foreign-exchange problems are likely in the near future, some progress on this front is likely to be increasingly important if the volume of oil exports falls, as many expect it to.

Balance of Payments

The BOP of Indonesia improved drastically in the 1970s. In spite of rapid increases in imports and service payments, the growth of exports and capital inflows allowed a healthy reserve position to be built up. The Pertamina crisis did result in sharp falls of reserves in the first three quarters of 1975, as unexpectedly large debts came to light and had to be paid. The billion-dollar decline in reserves was reversed in late 1975, and by the end of 1976, reserves had returned to the $1.5 billion level of year-end 1974. Since then reserves have increased, and were near $2.5 billion at the end of 1978. This amounts to about four months of nonoil imports,* well within normal rules of thumb for a prudent level of reserves. (In 1967 reserves were $6 million, or four days of imports.)

---

*Imports by foreign oil companies and by Pertamina for producing, refining, transporting, and marketing oil are often treated separately as "oil imports." They are largely financed from oil production, and do not need reserves to back them.

Perhaps a more important consideration is the debt-service ratio. In the 1979-80 budget, debt servicing alone is $1 billion, and amortization puts the total over $1.5 billion. However, with net oil exports rising, total exports in 1979-80 should be well over $11 billion and the debt-service ratio should fall from the 16 percent level of 1978-79 to 13-14 percent in 1979-80, and lower levels thereafter. This assumes further borrowing at both concessional and market rates of real amounts roughly similar to those of past years. Lower levels of borrowing are now quite possible and would further reduce future payments.

This past success and optimistic short-to-medium-term outlook does not mean that no problems exist. As Table 1.13 shows, some trends are unfavorable and the twin pillars of past gains—buoyant oil exports and large concessional borrowing—may not be growing much in real terms throughout the 1980s.* Controlling imports and service payments would then be quite important.

If real import capacity were to grow by less than 6 percent a year from a 1979-80 base—and this is quite possible—then a significantly lower income elasticity of imports will be needed to make 6-7 percent real GDP growth compatible with similar growth rates in imports. The devaluation was, in part, aimed at beginning a shift away from import-intensive growth patterns and encouraging a type of growth more compatible with the eventual slowdown in the growth of foreign-exchange resources that is expected.

AGRICULTURE

Agriculture is a key sector for a number of reasons. First, it is the primary source of food. Since Indonesia is already the largest rice importer in the world, and because the amount of traded rice is small relative to world production, a bad crop year in Indonesia and in major rice-producing areas can—and periodically has—produced severe shortages and very high prices.

Agriculture is also important as a source of foreign exchange, and as a major element of the economy of most of the Outer Islands. While petroleum exports displaced traditional exports in the 1970s, future growth in foreign exchange will depend in part on progress in traditional cash crops. The income levels of many small farmers also depend on this.

---

*There seems to be significant disagreement about the longer-run potential for oil production. Some observers believe exports can rise even with increasing domestic consumption. Others foresee declining production and exports.

TABLE 1.13

Balance of Payments, 1971-72 to 1978-79

(million dollars)

	1971-72	1973-74	1975-76	1977-78	1978-79
Exports, f.o.b. (+)	1,374	3,613	7,146	10,732	11,502
Oil	510	1,708	5,273	7,225	7,561
Nonoil	784	1,905	1,873	3,507	3,941
Imports, c.i.f. (-)	1,394	3,399	6,020	8,658	9,310
Oil	145	461	930	1,417	1,675
Nonoil	1,249	2,938	5,090	7,241	7,635
Services, net (-)	478	970	1,980	2,764	3,205
Oil	241	606	1,205	1,363	1,679
Nonoil	187	364	775	1,401	1,526
Current account	-448	-756	-854	-690	-1,013
Oil	+204	+641	+3,138	+4,445	+4,207
Nonoil	-652	-1,397	-3,992	-5,135	-5,220
Capital inflow, net	626	1,116	490	1,394	1,597
(official)[a]	400	643	1,995	2,106	2,210
Other[b]	226	473	-1,505	-765	-613
Change in reserves	+100	+360	-364	+651	+584

[a]"Official" flows are intergovernmental or other aid flows. It excludes borrowing by governmental entities on commercial terms.

[b]Nonaid portfolio borrowing, direct investment, debt service, special drawing rights, errors, and omissions.

Sources: B.I.E.S., vol. 13, no. 2; vol. 14, no. 3; vol. 15, no. 2.

1969 - 1979

TABLE 1.14

Food Crop Production in Indonesia, 1968-77
(1,000 tons and rice-equivalents)

	1968	1970	1972	1974	1976	1978	Annual Average Growth 1968-78	Annual Average Growth 1974-78
Rice	11,670	13,140	13,183	15,844	15,844	17,600	4.2	2.7
Corn	3,166	2,825	2,254	3,011	2,572	3,855	2.0	6.4
Cassava	11,356	10,478	10,385	13,031	12,191	12,961	1.3	-0.1
Sweet potatoes	2,364	2,175	2,006	2,469	2,381	2,235	-0.6	-2.5
Soybeans	420	498	518	589	522	571	3.1	-0.8
Peanuts	287	781	282	307	341	439	4.3	9.4
Rice-equivalents[a]	19,454	20,287	19,701	23,529	23,414	26,798	3.3	3.3
Index of GDP food crop output[b]	100	104	112	126	132	137	3.6	2.8

[a]Conversion to the calorie equivalent of rice. Coefficients are 1.0, .989, .303, .269, .335, and 1.517, respectively.

[b]Constant price index of farm food crop output. Includes crops above plus fruits and vegetables. It excludes copra, tea, coffee, sugar, fish, and livestock.

Source: Central Bureau of Statistics.

41

A final issue concerns the trends in employment opportunities and in earnings in agriculture, particularly in Java. This is an area in which there has been much research and a nearly equal degree of disagreement.

As Table 1.14 shows, the trends in food production have been somewhat irregular, but rice has been a strong performer, reflecting the heavy emphasis on irrigation, research, extension, and credit in the BIMAS and INMAS packages.* The 1976-77 slowdown in rice production was overcome in 1978 and 1979, when crops averaged about 17.5 million tons, apparently in response to improved fertilizer distribution efforts and the partial overcoming of a particular type of pest. Corn, cassava, sweet potato, and soybean production has been irregular and often sluggish, with per capita, and in some cases physical, declines. Peanuts have seen quite rapid increases in output. Overall, the caloric output has risen 1 percent faster than population while the value of crop output has risen about 3.5 percent a year over the decade. This is much better than the declining per capita food output over the 1960-67 period.

The sources of output growth are curious. Irrigated rice yields and unirrigated rice yields each went up by about 2.5 percent a year from 1968 to 1976. However, the area planted to irrigated rice has gone up nearly 2 percent a year, while the area devoted to upland (dry) rice has fallen over 3 percent annually, so the output of all rice has risen by 3.7 percent a year. While their area has declined quite unexpectedly, yields of corn, cassava, and sweet potatoes experienced greater increases of 3.3 percent, 2.8 percent, and 4.2 percent a year. This is greater than the 2.5 percent annual yield increase for rice. One can only assume that some of the fertilizer and insecticides pushed in the rice production program have also been used for these crops. That they have responded to these inputs better than specially selected rice strains have is surprising. One possible explanation is that nonrice yields are low relative to those of nearby countries, while rice yields are rather high. Thus, there may be an element of "catching up" in the nonrice yields while higher irrigated rice yields proceed from an already high level.

Even with these factors the superior yield performance of the nonrice foods is remarkable, and has led to a new emphasis in agricultural policy. There seems to be widespread agreement that getting rice output to grow more than 3-4 percent a year will be difficult,

---

*These acronyms stand for slightly different packages aimed at improving yields of irrigated rice by choosing proper seeds and by using adequate fertilizer and pesticides.

while nonrice food crops have relatively more potential for "easy" output gains. Thus, the Third Five-Year Plan projects a 3.5 percent annual gain in rice output, but a 5.6 percent gain in total caloric output, with especially sharp gains projected in corn and cassava. The output targets are ambitious ones that will be difficult to attain. Gains in future output will depend on the adequacy of efforts in plant breeding, extension work with much more complex packages, administrative implementation of tertiary irrigation and new lands programs, and marketing. While improvement in these diverse areas can be expected, it is uncertain that the pace of progress will be sufficiently rapid to fulfill the plan's targets.

Cash Crops

As Table 1.15 indicates, certain cash crops have done quite well, while others—particularly the portion grown by smallholders—have languished. Estate output has generally been quite strong.

It is useful to remember that population growth on the Outer Islands has been about 2.5 percent per year, and that cash crop production is concentrated there, so that any output gain less than 22 percent has failed to raise income in per capita terms for areas outside Java.

Why have estates done so well since 1969 while smallholders have suffered declining per capita output? An obvious factor is government investment, which has focused on rehabilitating estates but has done relatively little to upgrade smallholder productivity. This was partially a response to the 1960-69 period, during which estates suffered from inadequate care and their output stagnated, while smallholders raised output by 26 percent. It is also true that both the exchange rate and interference with marketing by local (and sometimes national) authorities have tended to discourage investment by smallholders. The upshot of this is that smallholder productivity per unit area or per tree is quite low relative to other countries in spite of very favorable natural conditions.[11]

If output is to be increased, particularly for smallholders, a number of steps need to be taken. First, the prices of many of these crops must improve. Copra, for example, is virtually banned from export, and even interisland transport is closely managed in order to protect high-cost oil extraction plants on Java.[12] Devaluation will have little impact if regulations forbid trade. Second, many of the illegal or irregular fees and excessive marketing margins must shrink. The ratio of farm-gate to export price must rise. Third, both technical assistance and long-term credit extension will be needed to encourage replanting of trees that will not yield for

TABLE 1.15

Cash Crop Production in Indonesia, 1969–77
(1,000 tons)

	1969	1971	1973	1975	1977	Percent Change 1969–77
Rubber						
Estate	223	239	247	244	249	12
Smallholders	558	572	599	536	570	2
Copra (smallholders)	1,220	1,147	1,233	1,370	1,440	18
Coffee						
Estates	14	19	10	15	17	19
Smallholders	161	178	140	155	166	26
Tea						
Estates	40	47	53	55	63	58
Smallholders	31	24	14	14	16	-48
Sugar						
Estates	723	834	811	1,004	1,105	53
Smallholders	220	221	199	223	260	30
Cloves (smallholders)	11	14	27	19	26	136
Pepper (smallholders)	17	24	29	23	39	129
Palm oil (estates)	189	249	290	411	497	163
Tobacco						
Estates	7	8	8	7	9	33
Smallholders	75	69	69	74	91	21
Smallholder cash crop GDP index	100	100	110	106	115	15
Estate cash crop GDP index	100	107	106	127	147	47
Total cash crop GDP index	100	104	108	113	125	25

Sources: B.I.E.S., vol. 14, no. 2; vol. 15, no. 1; Statistical Pocketbook of Indonesia, 1972–73; and Central Bureau of Statistics, 1977–78.

several years. Although some steps are being taken, the ability of the government to create a coherent and effective policy remains to be demonstrated. Without well-coordinated effort, the problem of creating adequate income and employment growth in many parts of the Outer Islands will be extremely difficult.

Income Distribution in Agriculture,
and Policy Options

In the section on the work force, it was stated that there was some disagreement about past trends in income-earning opportunities in agriculture, especially on Java. There is a basic agreement on some points, however:

1. Poverty is a serious problem in rural Java, with at least 50 percent of families in 1976 living under the poverty level of Rp. 3,000 per month per capita. [13]

2. Landlessness has increased as the number of farms has grown more slowly than rural families. From 1963 to 1973 farms on Java grew by 4 percent while the farm labor force grew by 10 percent from 1961 to 1971. [14]

3. Tenants and sharecroppers account for a declining fraction of farmland, from 45 percent in 1963 to 30 percent in 1973. [15]

4. While real wage payments per hectare have declined over 20 percent since 1971, real per hectare returns have risen 50-100 percent. [16]

5. The area of farmland on Java declined by 3 percent from 1963 to 1973; an even sharper decline in area harvested was observed between 1971 and 1976. [17]

6. Many specific technical changes, such as tractors, rice hullers, and sickles, have reduced labor demand per unit of output. [18]

7. Levels of labor utilization are extremely high on Java compared with other countries, and it seems likely that minimal reorganization of effort and technical changes could result in increased output with less labor. [19]

Thus, there seems to be widespread agreement that poverty and growing landlessness constitute a serious problem; that commercialization and technical progress can, and do, displace labor and concentrate agricultural incomes; and that a potential exists for considerable displacement of labor. There is disagreement over the extent to which labor has been displaced, the direction of real wage rates and incomes of the poor, and the extent to which rural incomes have become more concentrated.

The policy challenge within agriculture is to find a way to maintain or even increase income-earning opportunities while maintaining some forward momentum with regard to better yields. As farmers shift to using more fertilizer and purchased inputs, there will be a natural reluctance to share the harvest with literally hundreds of people (as was done before). Social pressure may keep this practice alive for a while longer, but the combination of increasing population densities on the land and economic incentives to exclude large numbers who would collectively get a large (and hard to control) share of the harvest will be difficult to resist. Without productivity growth there will be no way out of poverty: with it there will be severe pressure—perhaps sooner than later—on the landless and near-landless who make up about half of the population.

There is no fixed set of policies, because this situation is unique in degree, if not in kind. Restricting certain types of technology that do less to increase output than to displace labor—such as tractors—is one possibility. Putting more emphasis on increasing irrigation use and intensifying crop rotation, particularly for smaller farms, is another. Using government funds for reforestation, public works, and transmigration has also been suggested. Land reform or cooperative arrangements of various types are less likely solutions, because of both political difficulties and administrative inefficiencies. There is little doubt that the performance of agriculture in providing a basic livelihood for millions of landless is a very serious problem, perhaps the hardest one facing policy makers. Widespread displacement of landless workers could cause immense suffering, trigger rapid and disastrous urbanization, and probably create problems of maintaining order.

INDUSTRY

There was an extremely rapid rate of industrial growth in the 1970s, with a tripling of real output since 1968. This compares with virtual stagnation in 1961-67. The composition of this output in terms of both product mix and type of establishment producing the output has changed dramatically. While aggregate manufacturing output grew 13.5 percent a year from 1971 to 1977, the output of small-scale establishments with one to nine workers grew between 1.5 and 5 percent a year,[20] which suggests that establishments with ten or more workers grew about 17 percent per year. Thus, the share of the larger establishments increased from two-thirds to four-fifths of total manufacturing output in that period. It is perhaps more surprising that employment in the small-scale industries is estimated to have risen about 12 percent a year from 1971 to 1974-75 and 1976, while employment in large-scale industry grew slowly if at all—certainly less than 2 percent a year. Again, the very striking pattern of low employment and high output gains in the "modern" sector is combined with high employment and low output gains in the traditional sector. Output per worker in the modern (large and medium establishments) sector is growing at 15 percent per person per year, while output per worker in the traditional (small-scale) sector is falling by perhaps 8-10 percent a year.

Some of the rapid productivity increases in the modern sector are due to changes in the composition of output. Cement, fertilizer, steel, and petrochemicals are beginning to account for a significant fraction of total output, and inclusion of these capital-intensive industries in the total will raise output per worker. Also important is the displacement of labor-intensive technologies by capital-intensive ones in the textile, soft drink, tire, rice milling, other food processing, and wood processing industries. Table 1.16 illustrates the progress in production over 1969-70 to 1977-78.

These increases—most very large, except for some light consumer goods—reflect a low initial base, considerable import substitution, and a growing internal market. For the output in food and beverages, tobacco, and textiles and apparel—which accounts for about two-thirds of total employment and about 45 percent of value added in large and medium firms—the future growth in demand is not likely to come from further displacement of imports. Those sectors will either grow about as quickly as domestic demand or find export markets. There is virtually no significant export of these manufactures at present, unless processed raw materials such as sawn wood, palm oil, crumb rubber, and tea are counted. However, there have been growing exports of fertilizer, cement, and steel, reflecting excess capacity in these government-backed industries.

The record in industry, as elsewhere, is one of very large gains in particular areas, usually the capital-intensive ones. The capacity of the Indonesian industrial sector to supply major parts of its own domestic demand has grown tremendously and, with an effort, some of its industry should prove competitive enough for large export trade. But much of the past investment has been in industries or techniques with high costs and doubtful comparative advantage. The automobile assembly industry is perhaps the most commonly and justifiably cited example, but some food processing, chemicals, pharmaceuticals, and heavy industries could equally well be mentioned.

The reasons for this rapid growth of high-cost industries are threefold. First, the tariff system has been set so that it often creates high rates of protection. If Louis Wells is correct, this

TABLE 1.16

Production of Selected Goods in Indonesia, 1969-70 and 1977-78

Item	Unit	1969-70	1977-78	Coefficient of Multiplication
Urea	1,000 tons	85	990	4.6
Caustic soda	1,000 tons	1	7	7.0
Sulfuric acid	1,000 tons	—	20	—
Reinforcing iron	1,000 tons	5	240	48.0
Steel pipes	1,000 tons	2	120	60.0
Steel cables	1,000 tons	—	98	—
Zinc plate	1,000 tons	9	185	20.5
Paper	1,000 tons	17	84	4.9
Automobiles (assembly)	1,000 units	5	84	16.8
Motorcycles (assembly)	1,000 units	21	272	13.0
Car tires	1,000 units	366	2,339	6.4
Cycle tires	1,000 units	2,205	7,382	3.3
Batteries, car	1,000 units	32	575	18.0
Cigarettes	billion pieces	30	64	2.1
Fabrics	million meters	450	1,333	2.9
Textile yarn	1,000 bales	182	678	3.7
Vegetable oil	1,000 tons	290	308	1.1
Soap	1,000 tons	133	195	1.5
Glass bottles	1,000 tons	12	54	4.5
TV sets	1,000 units	5	482	96.4
Radios	1,000 units	364	1,000	2.7

Sources: Presidential Address, August 17, 1971; and March 1978 Pidato Pertanggungjawban, Department of Information, Jakarta.

48

creates a quasi-monopoly situation in which a "taste for technology" can be indulged that does not maximize profits but does make management easier.[21] Second, the exchange rate against the dollar remained constant from 1971 to 1978 while domestic costs rose much more than foreign (import) costs. This made imports of capital goods and consumer goods increasingly attractive, and encouraged capital-intensive investment. Third, the government offered inducements to investment in the form of capital subsidies: lower interest rates, rebates on tariffs on capital goods, and accelerated depreciation. All these steps lowered the cost of capital. Finally, the government itself was committed to an ambitious investment program in capital-intensive industries, which was perhaps the only way to spend large amounts of money rapidly without a major inflationary impact.

The structure of growth could possibly swing back toward one in which the large and medium firms in labor-intensive industries increase their employment. The devaluation should help; and if follow-up steps to simplify tax and trade procedures, and to rationalize the tariff system, are undertaken and can begin to succeed, the market and administrative signals should be better than in the recent past. The government seems to recognize the importance of fostering small-scale and labor-intensive industry, and may be prepared to be more selective in its choice of capital-intensive projects. Time will tell if these inclinations can be realized through translation into effective policies.

SUMMARY AND CONCLUSIONS

The 1970s saw a distinctly different set of external conditions, policies, and political-economic processes at work than previously. Many of the changes were positive—lower birth rates; less inflation; more savings, investment, exports, and growth; better education and health care; and somewhat higher average food production and consumption. Some of these successes have created new problems. When input costs go up and yields increase, agriculture becomes more commercialized and income-earning opportunities are reduced for poorer peasants. When there is new industrial investment, traditional activities are displaced and few new jobs are created as an offset. Other problems have simply reflected government inattention, inaction, or inefficiency: the slow growth of nonrice food crops compared with Thailand; of tree crops compared with Malaysia; of manufactured exports compared with Korea or the Philippines; or of transmigration.

To be sure, there has been forward motion on a number of policies. Issues such as family planning, overvaluation of the rupiah, and the need for better selection of large projects have been largely or partly dealt with. Others are not very far along, such as coordinating government ministries so they will work together, or getting basic reforms in the civil service and in the banking, income tax, and tariff systems. Because the country is large and diverse, and many of the problems are difficult and complicated, the improvement needed in planning and coordination is especially critical. A more decentralized and "from the bottom up" approach is needed if local opportunities are to be seized, but some central supervision and coordination need to be exercised.

The next few years will be ones in which government revenues and foreign exchange should be adequate, assuming that oil prices continue near their present real level. Many long-postponed or poorly executed initiatives can be begun or restarted. Programs can be formulated and tested, and management skills developed. It is likely that the real contribution of oil and aid will fall, perhaps sharply. At that time quite substantial increases in other exports, import substitution, and other taxes will be needed to keep income growth on track and provide for adequate job creation. If initiatives in the areas mentioned are further delayed or fall victim to inertia and corruption, the outlook for equity in the short-to-medium run and for income growth in the longer run is poor.

With all the pros and cons, there seems little doubt that there exists the human and physical capacity to accomplish many difficult things, if the society and government can manage a concerted effort to focus their own energies. This issue of the government's ability to mobilize and involve more of the population will be considered below.

Much of what happened in the 1970s can be understood as an attempt to compromise between conflicting goals with inadequate managerial and technical resources. There has been a tremendous explosion of resources available, as oil revenues, foreign aid, and private foreign investment and capital inflow have grown from little or nothing to 15-20 percent of GDP. A government that began with very widespread poverty, few skilled people, and major difficulties in integrating regions and political groups into a unified framework, has had to make a number of difficult economic, social, and political decisions. The solutions it has selected build on a wholly interventionist view of the state.

It has been taken for granted since the formation of the Indonesian Republic that the state must play a significant role in the economy. The banks, utilities, oil production and distribution, shipping, railroads, fertilizer, and iron and steel industries are state-owned or –dominated. In addition, the state controls or close-ly licenses trading in cash crops, and has a monopoly on rice im-ports. It owns most of the estates, and has substantial investments in textiles, electronics, salt, and drugs. It controls major foreign and domestic investments through granting special inducements to investors that meet certain specified conditions.

This pattern of government involvement and control was es-tablished under the Dutch (in spite of various episodes of "liberal-ism" in the nineteenth century); and though the direction and modali-ties of government involvement have changed since Sukarno, the magnitude has increased rather than diminished. There are various power centers in the government that try to direct or influence its economic involvement. It is not really enough to say "the military" is important. The various military divisions, services, and par-ticular high-ranking individuals often espouse different policies and administrative practices.

Negotiation and conflict between various groups in the mili-tary, ministries or subministry units, Bank Indonesia, the state-owned banks, the technocrats, BULOG (the Food Logistics Board), and assorted Chinese (or Chinese-Indonesian) and foreign investors show up in a number of ways. Announced policy measures reflect only the first stage of decision making—in terms of exchange rate, tariff policy, interest rates, taxes, and investment priorities. At least as important is the implementation of the announced policies. Exactly where government spending or credit goes, who controls it, how well or poorly taxes or tariffs are collected, and to what extent programs are funded represent another major level of decision and conflict that is too often ignored.

It is clear that the poor and the indigenous village capitalists associated with the Islamic parties have not been well represented in most past debates on policy or influential in the allocation of re-sources. The government bureaucracy, the upper levels (at least) of the military and their Chinese business associates, many foreign investors, the service and technical personnel employed by these groups, and large landowners have been favored. There has been a growing theoretical acknowledgment of the need to spread the bene-fits of growth to previously excluded groups. Pessimists and critics would say a corrupt (or at least self-serving and entrenched) bureau-cracy and military are not about to dismantle the system that has served so well to enrich them. Even supporters must acknowledge that the technical and administrative problems of transmigration, increasing upland or Outer Island crop production, or encouraging small-scale industry are formidable, as are the difficulties of re-ducing corruption or usury to the point that it no longer prevents de-centralized domestic activity from growing under its own power.

However, the resiliency of the society should not be dismissed.
There are increasing numbers of competent and concerned individuals, and the political situation has more fluidity under the surface
than the predetermined parliamentary structure at first suggests.*
It is true that the important decisions are not made at the ballot box,
but that observation does not say very much about how decisions are
made.

As Bruce Glassburner has pointed out, much of the critical
foreign analysis of Indonesia has been leftist in a bad sense[22]—un-
balanced, determined to be wholly negative, suspicious of the present regime because of its use of foreign aid and investment, foreign
advisers, and greater use of market-oriented economics than the
previous regime. He might have added that the birth of the regime
in 1965-66 was marked by the killing of hundreds of thousands by
both the army and rightist groups, and that large (if diminishing)
numbers of political prisoners are still detained. But it is the rise
of conspicuous consumption and clear deterioration in income distribution, combined with reliance on foreign capital and investment,
that has convinced most radical analysts that reform is hopeless.
This has also led them to ignore or deprecate the real accomplishments of the 1970s.

My own observations lead me to believe that hope for reform
is not merely wishful thinking. Many groups in the military come
from rural Java, and wish to improve conditions there. There is a
growing concern about the threat of external military aid being linked
up with disaffected internal groups and a desire to reduce this potential difficulty by improving conditions. Others realize that a more
sustainable type of growth will need to rely less on foreign borrowing
and oil and more on domestic resources; and this type of growth
would be, and needs to be, more equitably distributed. It is very
difficult to know how this national uneasiness with past excesses of
consumption, corruption, and income distribution will express itself.
There is a rise in Islamic organization that may become a focal point
of change. Perhaps the main point is that there is now a considerable
ability to use available resources to reorient priorities, and at least
some inclination to do so. Foreign pressures are relatively weak,
and in any case Indonesia has a considerable degree of policy independence.+

----

*Because a large number of the parliament seats are given over
to appointed delegates of the ruling party, defeat is virtually impossible.

+The notion that foreign advisers control or even heavily influence policy is overblown. As one who has observed the process of

It is difficult to know what kind of coalition might support equitable policies, or if there will be adequate capacity to effectively implement any positive policy decisions. Perhaps the present lack of effective formal political feedback will be a decisive roadblock to improving bureaucratic responsiveness, although a patchwork of certain types of critical journalism, government-sponsored university research, and extraordinary anti-corruption activities may be a workable expedient.

In a sense the question facing the Indonesian economy is what growth-oriented policies are politically acceptable—that is, will they create adequate opportunities for indigenous capitalists and laborers? Growth will almost certainly create tendencies toward inequality. But an improved macro framework, better credit and investment policies, and improved administration may create enough progress in the slower-growing sectors to satisfy their demands. Such efforts will almost surely require a greater degree of political and economic participation. The system's capacity to redirect growth and increase political participation is highly uncertain, but there are groups that see their self-interest as lying in this direction. The race between the possible and the inevitable is still on, and the outcome is not a foregone conclusion.

NOTES

1. The figures are taken from an annex of an unpublished paper by C. Chandrasekaran, "Population Trends and Prospects in Indonesia." A modified version appears in C. Chandrasekaran and Sam Soeharto, "Indonesia's Population in the Year 2000," Bulletin of Indonesian Economic Studies (B.I.E.S.) 14 (November 1978): 86-93.

2. There has been considerable debate about the possible scale, cost, and appropriate methods for future transmigration,

---

interaction between advisers and policy makers, I believe it is fair to say that foreign advisers are sometimes listened to; their analysis is sometimes used; but many other factors enter into a position, and many purely domestic and bureaucratic groups further contribute before any policy is decided. Foreign advisers seldom participate closely in the implementation, which is at least equally important. The strategic decisions seem to be domestic; the tactical policy decision will more often involve foreign advice; the implementation of the policies usually is purely domestic. Foreign advisers seem to influence the pace, more than the direction, of change.

with some experts holding high expectations of future potential.
For a good survey see Suratman and Patrick Guinness, "The Changing Focus of Transmigration," B.I.E.S. 13 (July 1977): 78-101.

3. This technique was used in Development Policy Staff,
World Bank, Employment and Income Distribution in Indonesia,
Table A-12.

4. Anne Booth, "The Agricultural Surveys 1970-75,"
B.I.E.S. 15 (March 1979): 59.

5. A good summary and commentary on these studies and
their differences from some of the macro data is available in
Benjamin White, "Political Aspects of Poverty, Income Distribution, and Their Measurement: Some Examples from Rural Java,"
paper presented at an Asia Society seminar, Singapore, November
21-25, 1977.

6. Taken from summary sheet of Donald Snodgrass, "Patterns and Trends in Small-Scale Manufacturing, 1970-1976,"
mimeographed (Cambridge, Mass.: Harvard Institute of International Development, 1978).

7. R. M. Sundrum, "Manufacturing Employment, 1969-1971,"
B.I.E.S. 15 (March 1979): 59-65. See Peter McCawley and Maree
Tait, "New Data on Employment in Manufacturing," B.I.E.S. 15
(March 1979): 125-36, for a view contradicting Snodgrass; and a
comment by Donald Snodgrass and David Dapice, "Employment in
Manufacturing, 1970-77: A Comment," B.I.E.S. 15 (November
1979): 127-31.

8. An excellent summary of the difficulties faced in compar-
ing 1961 and 1971 employment data can be found in Gavin Jones,
"Sectoral Employment-Output Coefficients in Indonesia Since 1961,"
B.I.E.S. 15 (March 1979): 80-92.

9. See Clive Gray, "Civil Service Compensation in Indonesia,"
B.I.E.S. 15 (March 1979): 85-113; H. W. Arndt and R. M. Sundrum,
"Civil Service Compensation: A Comment," B.I.E.S. 15 (March
1979): 114-24.

10. Gray, "Civil Service Compensation in Indonesia."

11. Alan Strout, "Aspects of Agricultural Productivity on
Java and the Outer Islands," paper presented at a conference sponsored by the Carnegie Institution and the State Department (Washington, D.C., November 1978), indicates the extent of the productivity gap.

12. Howard Dick, "Survey of Recent Developments," B.I.E.S.
15 (March 1979): 30-31.

13. National Socio-Economic Survey (SUSENAS), Fifth round,
1976, Central Bureau of Statistics.

14. Anne Booth and R. M. Sundrum, "The 1973 Agricultural
Census," B.I.E.S., vol. 12, no. 2, pp. 90-105.

15. Ibid.

16. Booth, "The Agricultural Surveys," pp. 45-68.

17. Booth and Sundrum, "The 1973 Agricultural Census," p. 93; Statistical Pocketbook of Indonesia, 1972-73 and 1977; Central Bureau of Statistics.

18. White, "Political Aspects of Poverty . . . Rural Java."

19. Strout, "Aspects of Agricultural Productivity . . . Outer Islands."

20. Calculated from data in Snodgrass, "Patterns and Trends in Small-Scale Manufacturing," for 1970-71 to 1974-75.

21. Louis Wells, "Men and Machines in Indonesia's Light Manufacturing Industries," B.I.E.S. 9 (November 1973): 62-72.

22. Bruce Glassburner, "The Political Economy of the Soeharto Regime," B.I.E.S. 14 (November 1978): 24-51. One of the better radical analytical pieces is Richard Robison, "Toward a Class Analysis of the Indonesian Military Bureaucratic State," mimeographed summary of his Ph.D. dissertation from Sydney University in 1978. Glassburner gives qualified praise to Franklin Weinstein, Indonesian Foreign Policy and the Dilemma of Dependence (Ithaca, N.Y.: Cornell University Press, 1976).

2
INCOME DISTRIBUTION AND
THE POLITICS OF POVERTY
Gustav F. Papanek

Data on income distribution universally have a high margin of error. This is particularly true for Indonesia. Therefore it is necessary to rely on fragmentary and indirect evidence to analyze what has happened. This essay and the one that follows are based on sketchy data, and everything that follows should be preceded by caveats. Instead, all warnings are expressed in these introductory sentences. Conclusions also can be affected by the time period analyzed and the questions emphasized. While this essay and the following one by David Dapice may give the impression of drawing contradictory conclusions, they are, in fact and on the whole, consistent.

Neither relies much on the usual macroeconomic indicators of income distribution, for reasons that Dapice expounds at some length. The Dapice analysis is concerned with income changes between 1971 and 1976. He concludes that there is no evidence that the poor benefited significantly from rapid growth in these years. Since average per capita income increased about 6 percent per year during the same period, it is clear that the income of the wealthier groups must have increased rapidly and that income distribution became substantially less equal.

This essay, on the other hand, compares Indonesian income distribution with that of other countries, and concludes that it is relatively egalitarian. It also provides some evidence that the real income of important groups of the poor increased over the period 1965-67 to 1977-79, a much longer time span than that analyzed by Dapice.

There is spotty, indirect evidence supporting a distinction between improvement for the poor between 1966 and 1970 and little change between 1970-71 and 1978-79. Dapice compares increases in income and changes in staple calories and rice consumption in the 1970s as an indicator of the real income of the poor. One can extend the analysis for rice to the period 1956-67 to 1974-75. The average income elasticity of rice was 0.5; that is, for every 10 percent increase in income, rice consumption increased 5 percent. Upper income groups have an elasticity of 0.36; and the lower the income, the higher the elasticity. To obtain the elasticity of 0.5 that prevailed from 1965-67 to 1974-75, therefore, the income of the poor must have increased substantially.

The most useful evidence is from wage data. Real wages on plantations and in industry declined from the early 1950s to the mid-1960s, and rose very substantially thereafter until 1970. The next two years showed little change, with another decline beginning during the inflationary period in late 1972 and continuing to 1974. Wages rose again thereafter, but on Java's plantations and in the textile industry reached only the 1970-71 level by 1977-78. A separate series for construction workers shows no clear trend between 1976 and 1979. Spotty data for six Javanese villages indicate only a 28 percent per annum increase in real wages of agricultural workers in the 1970s. Thus there is support for Dapice's conclusion that the real incomes of the poorer groups changed by less than did the average income in the country during the 1970s.

The main conclusion of this essay is that most of the major, politically important groups gained from the rapid growth since 1966, but that many landless laborers, smallholders, and urban workers selling mainly labor may well have been excluded from the benefits of growth since 1970. It is, of course, this group that forms the bulk of the poor majority that Dapice concludes probably has not benefited from development since 1970. Within the limits of available data, the two analyses are complementary, not conflicting, in this respect. Both also suggest some deterioration in income distribution in the 1970s. In short, even if Indonesia remains egalitarian compared with other countries, and even if the poor are better off compared with the 1960s, it is the likelihood of recent deterioration in income distribution that may be most significant for attitudes toward the income distribution issue in Indonesia.

The mid-1960s were a disastrous period for Indonesia's economy. When an economy is in shambles, most groups suffer; and, not surprisingly, it was the poor majority who suffered most. The return to a more normal economy, fostered by the stabilization program and the concern with economic efficiency of the new regime, provided economic benefits to many groups, certainly including some, and perhaps most, of the poor. The 1970s probably was a period of renewed deterioration in income distribution, which only conscious government policies could reverse.

BASIC TRENDS

Whatever the shortcomings of data, one thing is reasonably clear: Indonesia has been an egalitarian society in comparison with other countries. Unlike other countries it did not have a large group of really wealthy landowners, businessmen/industrialists, or aristocrats. Overall indexes confirm this: calculations of Gini coefficients for Indonesia tend to be around 0.3, while those for similar less-developed countries are 0.5 or higher (Brazil, 0.6; Iran, Philippines, Thailand, 0.5). While the Indonesian data leave out considerable income received by the rich, this is true of all countries—the wealthy everywhere fear the tax collector—so the difference is probably a real one.

For whatever these indexes are worth, they show no significant change in the basically egalitarian nature of Indonesian society in the 1960s. The deterioration in equality of the overall indexes that is seen by some analysts is not a constant trend, is probably smaller than the margin of error in the estimates, and still leaves Indonesia in the class of egalitarian countries. More important is the fact that all these indexes deal with a partial picture only—the rural areas, or the urban areas, or Jakarta—and it is quite possible to have an improvement in overall income distribution while there is deterioration in the distribution in both rural and urban areas. If a large number of the rural poor move to the city, and in the process increase their income substantially, income distribution in the country as a whole will have improved. Yet since rural incomes are below urban incomes, this movement can show up as deterioration in both the rural and urban statistics.

The overall data on what has happened to the absolute income of the poor equally lack clarity. We know that the supply of food grains per capita declined from about 185 kilos in the late 1950s to 170 kilos in the late 1960s, then increased to about 190 kilos in 1973 and 1974 and to 195 kilos by 1977-78. There is more food available, but it is not clear who is eating this additional food. Normally one would expect that an increase in the supply of food grains benefits particularly the poor, who spend more of their income on food grains than the rich do. On the other hand, if increased income has gone wholly to the rich, an increase in the food supply will not help the poor. The Consumer Surveys (SUSENAS), in calculations by Dwight King and Peter Weldon, show wild fluctuations in rice consumption of the poor, indicating the unreliability of the data, especially in any single year.[1] For whatever they are worth, they show roughly the same rice consumption for the bottom 40 percent in 1969-70 as in 1963-64.

In short, all one can conclude from the macro data is that Indonesia was an egalitarian society, compared with other countries, and that changes in relative income distribution cannot be documented from the usual macroeconomic indicators.

GROUPS WITH HIGHER INCOMES SINCE 1965

When one examines fragmentary data on specific groups, one finds that most politically important groups have had a substantial increase in real income since 1965.

1. Plantation, industrial, and other workers. The most useful data are for workers, largely unskilled, on plantations, in industry, and on public works projects. As is obvious from a subsequent essay, the real wages of these workers declined very sharply to the mid-1960s and then rose even more sharply to the early 1970s. Real income changed somewhat less, because multiple job holding was easier until 1965 and more difficult thereafter, but the basic trend is unmistakable: workers' income has risen very substantially since 1965.

2. Migrants to the city. One estimate is that low-income migrants to Jakarta increased their income by roughly 85 percent.[2] Again the estimate can be way off and the increase will still be substantial. With an increase in city jobs and migration, a larger group of rural poor has benefited from the substantial improvement that a movement to the city brings.

3. Professional, intellectual, technical groups; military. Both jobs and pay have increased for engineers, civil servants, technicians, economists, and so on, as the government's development program has expanded and foreign firms, Pertamina, and others have bid for their services. Those who have access to housing also have benefited from renting out their houses, especially in Jakarta. The military has increased its role in government at all levels, as well as in government and semi-government enterprises. Its income in most cases seems to have increased even more than that of the professional-intellectual-technical groups.

4. Farmers. Here one is on less certain ground. As irrigation systems have been rehabilitated, some cultivators have benefited from higher output. Others have been able to buy inputs at lower cost and to sell products at higher prices as transportation improved. Food-grain production increased 25 percent from 1968 to 1974, while its prices rose more than the prices of industrial products (especially textiles), so the income of cultivators selling food grains should have improved substantially. In fact, an analysis by Irlan Soejono of farmers' income in eight Central Java villages showed an increase between 1968-69 and 1973-74 (in constant prices)

in the net return from paddy of 128 percent and in returns from all sources of 113 percent.[3] Moreover, the share of the poorest 60 percent increased from 22.6 percent to 24.6 percent over the same period, and the share of the poorest 20 percent from 2.7 percent to 4.3 percent. As a result, the Gini coefficient declined from 0.533 to 0.495. These admittedly limited results support the notion that cultivators, even those on small holdings, had a massive increase in absolute income.

There are undoubtedly cultivators whose output has not increased, who have no surplus to sell, and who have not benefited from increased food-grain production and prices. But the Soejono data suggest that they are few in number and that there remains the question of whether they are of political importance.

5. Businessmen/industrialists. This too is a mixed group. A majority has probably profited from greater imports, more investment, and higher production, often in partnership with foreign investors. Another group lost out in competition with new enterprises (see below).

In short, most of the groups that are politically active and important seem to be substantially better off now than in 1965—the middle class, the military, industrial and agricultural workers, and the majority of cultivators and businessmen. The increase in absolute income has been substantial, even if we do not know what has happened to relative incomes of broad groups.

GROUPS WITH LOWER INCOMES SINCE 1965

The major groups that have lost in economic terms since 1965 are more difficult to identify. Of course the political leadership of the Sukarno era and those identified with the Communist party and other opposition groups have lost, but so have more specific economic groups. What has happened to others is less clear.

1. Businessmen/industrialists. Government patronage remains important for success in business and industry, although its significance declined with the abolition of import licensing and other regulations. Still, access to credit at preferential rates and to various licenses remains crucial to most firms. At the same time, access to foreign technology, capital, and sometimes markets has become more important. Enterprises that have neither public nor foreign patrons appear to have lost out in the competition. A significant proportion of the losers comes from the practicing Muslim (Santri) group.

2. Landless rural workers and some smallholders. The great unknown is the impact on the income of the rural poor, the landless and near landless in the rice areas of Java and Bali, and the smallholder rubber producers. On the one hand, the reports of the Agro-Economic Survey show a decline in harvesters' income with a shift from crop shares to cash payment and from the harvest knife or blade (ani-ani) to the sickle.[4] There has been a rapid decline in women's income from the hand pounding of rice (C. P. Timmer and others), and studies show declining labor compensation in rice production.[5] (R. Montgomery estimates a 20 percent decline in man-days worked in shifting to high-yielding varieties of rice; Soejono, a 14 percent decrease in wage payments for preharvest labor from 1968-69 to 1973-74, although the number of man-days used increased, suggesting a substantial decline in wage rates.[6])

On the other hand, the expansion of multiple cropping increases labor use (Montgomery estimates an increase of over 10 percent between 1961 and 1971), and greater output requires more labor in handling and in other nonfarm activities.

There is, therefore, conflicting evidence on what has happened in the past. But a continuing shift to commercial agriculture will eventually squeeze hundreds of thousands from agriculture.

So far there appear to have been no obvious political consequences as the income of some landless and smallholders has declined while that of others has increased, with the proportions unknown. Those who have lost in most cases remain in their villages and, like peasants elsewhere, unless they are very hard pressed, have not expressed their discontent. The ones who have moved to the cities have still experienced an increase in income. However, the likelihood is great that in the future there will be hundreds of thousands of families whose income in the rural areas will drop as the opportunity for harvest and other agricultural work does not rise with population. When they are forced into the cities in large numbers, they may become a significant political force, if the nature of development is such that they can no longer find an improved income there.

POLITICS OF POVERTY AND INCOME DISTRIBUTION

The argument so far has stressed that practically all politically important groups benefited from development since 1965. If that is the case, then why were there riots in 1973-74 that had economic grievances as one of their main causes?

To the extent that economics played a role, there probably were several relevant factors, some of which may well recur in the future:

1. Sharp temporary setbacks to the poor. Indonesia, like other countries with an economy highly vulnerable to the vagaries of the weather, of the world market, and of accidents, inevitably experiences serious setbacks from time to time. Unless government policies are carefully designed to avoid this, the impact of these setbacks will be felt particularly by the lower income groups. This is precisely what happened in Indonesia in 1972-73. As a result of a temporary shortage of food grains, especially rice, food prices rose sharply. With nominal wages lagging, real wages declined.

2. Conspicuous consumption by the rich. The setbacks to the poor are likely to be more obvious and resented if conspicuous consumption by the rich continues unabated. Moreover, in general, income disparities are widely known only if they take the form of differences in consumption, since very few people know the income of the rich but many can see the cars they drive, the houses they live in, and the parties they give. The income differences in Indonesia may have been less great than in India and Pakistan, but the rich in those countries had learned to keep their wealth more discreetly hidden. Also, during some periods much of the income of the rich in South Asia was used for investment, not for conspicuous consumption. In contrast, in Indonesia the period after 1968 saw an obvious rise in conspicuous consumption (and conspicuous investment; for instance, in government office buildings), especially in Jakarta. High living by the rich continued unabated during 1973-74, a period of real suffering for many urban poor. One index of conspicuous consumption is the ownership of passenger cars and motorcycles.

TABLE 2.1

Motor Vehicles in Indonesia, 1963-77
(percent change)

	Passenger Cars	Buses	Trucks	Motorcycles
1963-66	+25	-13	+21	+44
1966-70	+34	+20	+10	+56
1970-74	+41	+29	+63	+115
1974-77	+41	+52	+67	+80

Source: Statistical Pocketbook (various issues).

It is also obvious that the number of buses, used by the poor, increased far less rapidly than passenger cars, used by the rich, and motorcycles, owned by the middle class and the sons of the rich. The contrast with the Sukarno period is again instructive. As in the case of real wages, the poor did not benefit from that regime's populist stance. As the economy deteriorated, the number of buses declined. Development after 1967 clearly benefited the poor—the number of buses increased substantially—but it increased conspicuous consumption even more rapidly.

3. Perception of government held by the poor majority. Almost regardless of the rate of growth and of normal (nonrevolutionary) changes in income distribution, the economic well-being of the poor majority in a country like Indonesia improves only slowly. They remain poor in absolute terms. The poor in Jakarta may have very nearly doubled their premigration income, but in 1972 their daily income averaged less than Rp. 300, at best $20 a month.[7] They, like other poor, therefore live partly on hope. It can then be highly important whether government is seen as concerned with the poor and as attempting to improve their lot, or as indifferent and concerned only with the wealthy.

Conspicuous consumption by the rich is one indication to the poor that the government is doing little to take from those who have, to give to those who need. The way in which setbacks to the economy are handled can be another important signal. When inflation speeded up in 1973 and other economic difficulties emerged, there was no announcement that belt-tightening would be required and would primarily affect the rich. Nor were there announcements to impose new taxes and restrictions on conspicuous consumption. Some of these steps were taken after the riots of 1974. But in 1973 the tendency was to deny that there was a crisis, and to suggest that prices had risen very little, when every shopper knew what rice really cost.

Specific government policies can be a more obvious signal to the poor majority. In fact, the Jakarta city administration, by banning sidewalk vendors and bicycle rickshaws (betjaks) from the lucrative center-city areas, immediately reduced the income of two important and reasonably well-organized low-income groups. While the poor in other occupations reported increased incomes from 1971 to 1972, these two groups said theirs dropped by 20 and 40 percent, respectively. These actions could also be seen as the clearest possible signal and symbol: hurting the income of the poor, so the rich can drive their cars and patronize their shops more easily.

4. Resentment of the excluded elites. Indonesia did not have a major ethnic group that was excluded from the benefits of development and that used political means to get a share (like the Bengalis

in Pakistan and the South Indians at an earlier stage). The major
ethnic minority, the Chinese, was, on the contrary, powerful in
business, though not otherwise. But Indonesia did have one significant group that lost: the businessmen and industrialists who lacked
government or foreign ties, and their families. A substantial proportion were practicing Moslems (Santri) who had other reasons
for negative feelings toward the government. Their political vehicles had been undermined or destroyed, their values were outraged
by nightclubs and massage parlors, and they disliked the prominent
role of foreigners and ethnic Chinese in the economy. To these
concerns was added their economic loss, inflicted by competition
from enterprises run by what they could well regard as an unholy
coalition of military with a non-Islamic cultural background
(abangan), Chinese managers, and foreign capital. Particularly
galling was the feeling that their loss in the competition was not due
so much to the greater efficiency of the coalition as to its access to
cheap credit, to government concessions on taxes, tariffs, and
permits, and to other forms of government patronage.

It is not surprising, if one accepts this analysis, that the riots
in Bandung and Jakarta had as their targets the rich, the coalition
of foreigners (Japanese), corrupt officials, and Chinese, and the
market into which the government tried to push the sidewalk vendors,
nor that betjak drivers were reported to be prominent in both dis-
turbances.

GOVERNMENT POLICIES

The short-term policies adopted by the government in 1974
were well-designed to deal with several of the major problems discussed. Indonesia, unlike countries in South Asia, has the economic
resources to provide economic benefits to most politically important groups, and the government effectively used increased oil revenues to stabilize the price of rice and of food grains in general.
Real wages rose again in 1975 and 1976 as food-grain prices stabilized. In addition the government announced curbs on conspicuous
consumption and on the role of foreign investors, and plans that
pay more attention to income distribution and poverty. That is, it
took steps to reassure indigenous businessmen, to prevent deterioration in real wages, and to change the poor majority's perception of
the government's economic strategy.
In the short term, Indonesia has the resources to enable the
government to improve the economic position of politically important groups. Whether it can deal with the longer-term problems of

income distribution and poverty depends on the economic strategy it follows. Even $10 billion income, mostly from oil, is not enough to provide jobs, and therefore income, to the additions to the labor force and to those squeezed out of agriculture, if a substantial proportion of the resources are used for conspicuous consumption and conspicuous investment. Moreover, there is no guarantee that oil revenues of that magnitude will continue to flow and that net borrowing, based on assumed oil revenues, will continue to make a major contribution to Indonesia's resources.

CONCLUSIONS

There is no persuasive evidence that Indonesia's relatively egalitarian income distribution has significantly changed since 1965. In terms of absolute income, a number of politically important low-income groups experienced a considerable decline in their income until the mid-1960s, and have benefited from a substantial improvement since then. Therefore, as economists usually analyze income distribution and poverty, there appear to be no serious problems in Indonesia: distribution seems to have remained egalitarian and the income of many poor has improved.

But these macro indexes are not all that matters. When Indonesia experienced the inevitable economic setback in 1972-74, it was some of the poor who appeared to bear the brunt. At the same time conspicuous consumption continued, government was perceived as little concerned with the hopes and needs of the poor majority, and as favoring foreigners, resident Chinese, and abangan military over indigenous businessmen. The government acted quickly to restore the income of wage earners and other poor who purchase most of their food, and announced steps to curb the consumption of the rich and the role of outsiders. Unlike Pakistan after 1965, it acted to deal with both image and reality with respect to poverty in the short term. The further rise in relative oil prices in 1979 substantially eased the resource problems.

But it appears that income distribution deteriorated throughout the 1970s, and the crucial question for the future remains: Will Indonesia use the limited but significant resources available to provide jobs at a rate sufficient to keep the urban proletariat from swelling to unmanageable proportions? It does not have the resources of an Iran (much less those of a Saudi Arabia), and therefore has to manage them carefully. If it uses a substantial proportion for consumption by the rich, another large fraction for low-productivity investments, and much of the rest to prevent the dissatisfaction of the poor majority from being expressed (by subsidizing their consumption), it may find itself in the trap that other countries have fallen into: resources inadequate to simultaneously complete costly ongoing investment projects and to meet the demands of the wealthier groups for access to accustomed consumer goods, and the demands of the poor for continued subsidization of their consumption. Whether that point is reached sooner, later, or not at all, depends not only on the wisdom with which resources are managed but also on whether there is a substantial decline in resources available. If the Pertamina debt problems had coincided with a drop in oil prices, the crisis would already have faced Indonesia. If oil prices remain high in real terms and social pressures maintain the system of labor and income sharing (involution), serious problems can be postponed for a long time. It would obviously be risky to plan on the assumption that real oil income will continue to rise during the 1980s and that migration to the cities will remain relatively slow.

NOTES

1. Dwight King and Peter Weldon, "Income Distribution in Java," Economic Development and Cultural Change 25 (July 1977): 699-712.

2. G. F. Papanek and Dorodjatun Kuntjoro Jakti, "The Poor of Jakarta," Economic Development and Cultural Change 24, no. 1 (October 1975): 1-27.

3. Irlan Soejono, "Growth and Distributional Changes of Incomes in Paddy Farms in Central Java 1968-74," Bulletin of Indonesian Economic Studies (B.I.E.S.) 12, no. 2 (July 1976): 80-89.

4. W. Collier et al., "Agricultural Technology and Institutional Change," Food Research Institute Studies 12, no. 2 (1974).

5. C. Peter Timmer, "Choice of Technique in Rice Milling in Java," B.I.E.S. 9, no. 2 (July 1973): 57-67; W. Collier et al., "Choice of Technique in Rice Milling in Java: A Reply," B.I.E.S. 10, no. 1 (March 1974): 121-26.

6. R. Montgomery, "The Link Between Trade and Labor Absorption in Rural Java" (Ph.D. diss., Cornell University, 1974); Irlan Soejono, "Growth and Distributional Changes . . . 1968-74," pp. 80-89.

7. G. F. Papanek and Dorodjatun Kuntjoro Jakti, "The Poor of Jakarta."

3
TRENDS IN INCOME DISTRIBUTION AND LEVELS OF LIVING, 1970-75
David O. Dapice

In the previous essay there was some discussion of the disagreement among observers about the trends in income distribution and absolute levels of living in Indonesia and rural Java. This essay examines the data from the period 1970-75 in detail, and attempts to reach a conclusion about what happened. The major primary sources on which to base any judgment are the 1969-70 and 1976 consumption surveys, the food balance sheets, the GDP accounts, and the two employment censuses. Other observers have analyzed income distribution in this period, but most of them have used only the consumption surveys, [1] or perhaps one other source. Gustav Papanek has completed a study of wage rates, included in this book, which is also helpful in analyzing this period.

The most direct way of finding out what has happened with respect to income distribution and absolute levels of living is to use the two consumption surveys. They recorded information from thousands of families on both money and physical expenditure. If the collected data are broadly accurate, they should answer the questions posed. Because of the controversy surrounding this topic, it should be clear that many observers doubt that the consumption surveys are correct.

THE SUSENAS CONSUMPTION SURVEYS*

Before reviewing the surveys, some general caveats are in order. First, virtually everyone agrees that the survey estimates

---

*SUSENAS is the National Social-Economic Survey, which recorded consumption data. Round four was in 1969-70 and round five was in 1976.

of spending are better than those of income. Most income groups, including the top ones, report net borrowing (spending more than income), and this is impossible if the sample is representative of the population. (It is exceedingly unlikely that there is no gross household savings in any income group, or in the aggregate.) Second, since saving is done mainly by the rich, income typically is less equally distributed than spending. (But if saving behavior is stable, the trends in expenditure shares should still be good indicators of changes in income shares.) Third, there are major questions concerning seasonality and deflation procedures in the consumption surveys. Most studies have compared the January-April periods in 1970 and 1976 rather than use the full 1969-70 or 1976 information. Results are highly sensitive to the periods compared and to the deflation method chosen.

A typical comparison exercise has been cited by R. M. Sundrum in his summary of the Perrera-Budianti work. In Tables 3.1 and 3.2 changes in real spending by geographic regions and income groups are shown. The big spending gains and increases in inequality were in urban Java. Rural Java had no reported change in income distribution and a moderate rise in spending. The Outer Islands grew quite slowly and, on balance, saw an increase in equality, as measured by spending. The gains by the poor in Table 3.2 are most striking in rural Java, where their real spending increased faster than that of any group but the rich in urban Java. Similarly, the rural poor on the Outer Islands had faster growth than any other group on the Outer Islands, and overall the spending of the rich grew more slowly than that of the poor or of the middle-income group.

These surprising conclusions may well be wrong. In using only January-April for 1970 and 1976, a significant bias was introduced. Further, the deflators used do not correspond to the price indexes implicitly generated by the SUSENAS survey data. Finally, the SUSENAS coverage itself appears defective. These points are complicated but crucial, so further elaboration is needed.

The 1969-70 survey collected data in October through December of 1969 and January to April of 1970. The earlier round omitted Kalimantan (one of the Outer Islands) and a few other small provinces covered in the later round. The 1976 survey covered the entire year in three four-month rounds. The October-December 1969 spending was considerably higher than the January-April 1970 spending, while the reverse was true in 1976. The last round (September-December) was considerably lower than the first. (Since the fasting month and subsequent feasting period were included in both years, they cannot account for the observed pattern.) Thus, considerable differences, even on Java, can be generated simply by

TABLE 3.1

Increases in Real per Capita Spending and Changes in Inequality in Indonesia, 1970 and 1976

Region	Real Spending		Percent Increase	Gini Coefficient		1976 Price Index (1970 = 100)
	1970	1976		1970	1976	
Java–Madura						
Rural	1,029	1,228	19	.30	.30	284
Urban	1,714	2,461	44	.33	.40	297
Total	1,144	1,456	27	.32	.36	288
Outer Islands						
Rural	1,712	1,842	8	.33	.30	244
Urban	7,070	2,248	9	.30	.31	299
Total	1,759	1,914	9	.33	.30	255
Indonesia						
Rural	1,272	1,449	14	.34	.30	266
Urban	1,819	2,385	31	.33	.37	298
Total	1,351	1,619	20	.35	.35	274
Memo:* GDP estimate real private consumption, all Indonesia	1,920	2,678	40			

*Refers to National Income Account estimates of real private consumption per capita.

Notes: Real spending is in 1970 rupiah per capita per month. The Gini coefficient is a measure of overall inequality; a higher value means that inequality has increased.

Source: L. N. Perrera and Sri Budianti, "Economic Growth and the Distribution of Income in Indonesia," a monograph cited in R. M. Sundrum's "Income Distribution, 1970–76," B.I.E.S. 15, no. 1 (March 1979): 138–40.

using different rounds. For example, spending in rural Java was 3.37 times as high in January-April 1976 as in that period of 1970, but only 2.89 times as high in September-December 1976 as in October-December 1969. For all Indonesia a similar but less pronounced pattern exists. These differences are large, and reduce confidence in a comparison based on any single round.

TABLE 3.2

Average Real Spending Increase, by
Expenditure Group, 1970-76
(percent)

	Poorest 40 Percent	Next 30 Percent	Richest 30 Percent	Total
Java				
Urban	21	25	50	40
Rural	28	13	17	19
Total	24	19	28	27
Outer Islands				
Urban	10	8	7	9
Rural	22	6	4	8
Total	20	7	7	10
Indonesia				
Urban	19	17	34	29
Rural	26	16	6	12
Total	24	18	16	19

Note: Original data presented for decile groups.

Source: L. N. Perrera and Sri Budianti, "Economic Growth and the Distribution of Income in Indonesia," a monograph cited in R. M. Sundrum's "Income Distribution, 1970-76," B.I.E.S. 15, no. 1 (March 1979): 138-40.

Furthermore, the inflation rates calculated from various price indexes are generally lower than those indicated by the prices people say they paid in 1969-70 and 1976. One scholar did this calculation of implicit inflation just for January-April 1970 and 1976. His findings are summarized in Table 3.3 and compared with the Perrera-Budianti rates.

TABLE 3.3

Estimates of Inflation in Indonesia, 1970–76:
Price Index for January–April 1976
(January–April 1970 = 100)

	Perrera–Budianti	Implicit SUSENAS	Poorest 40 Percent	Middle 40 Percent	Richest 20 Percent
Rural Java	284	329	346	322	307
Urban Java	297	298	299	294	302
Rural Outer Islands	244	259	282	251	218
Urban Outer Islands	299	276	270	243	267
All Indonesia	274	294	N.A.	N.A.	N.A.

N.A. = not available.

Source: SUSENAS calculations by Om Nijhawan, "Indonesia: Poverty and Inequality" (1978) (World Bank internal memorandum).

In the rural areas the implicit inflation rates are considerably higher than those reported by the price indexes used by L. N. Perrera and Sri Budianti. In the Outer Islands urban areas the implicit inflation is lower, and on urban Java it is the same. Overall, the inflation rate reported by the survey was 7 percent more than that generated by price indexes. More significantly, the rural poor had a higher inflation rate than the middle or top groups. Thus, the bottom groups would need a higher nominal spending increase (with their consumption patterns) than the better-off simply to match their progress.

If we put these observations about seasonality together with the higher implicit inflation rates, we get a spread of results.

TABLE 3.4

High and Low Estimates of Real Spending Changes
Using Implicit Inflation Rates
(percent)

	High Estimate	Low Estimate	Average of High and Low	Estimates of Perrera-Budianti
Rural Java	2	-12	-5	19
Urban Java	37	25	31	44
Rural Outer Islands	7	8	6	8
Urban Outer Islands	15	9	12	9
All Indonesia	12	4	8	20

Note: Implicit inflation rates from January-April 1970 and 1976 are used to deflate both periods. Comparisons are of like periods in 1969 and 1970 with 1976.

Sources: Calculated from SUSENAS IV and SUSENAS V, Central Bureau of Statistics, Jakarta. The implicit inflation rates are from Om Nijhawan, "Indonesia: Poverty and Inequality" (1978) (World Bank internal memorandum).

I do not wish to advance the low figures in Table 3.4 as the "correct" ones any more than the high or average estimates. It is apparent, however, that the range of estimates generated is generally lower than that using official price indexes or only the January-April periods. Furthermore, the rural lower-income groups have their real spending gains cut or become negative. In the January-April periods alone the gains are reduced from the Perrera-Budianti 28 percent to 2 percent for the bottom 40 percent in rural Java and from 22 percent to 6 percent for the bottom 40 percent in the rural Outer Islands. In other periods there are even declines in real spending for the poor.

Given this spread of results, there is obviously room for disagreement. It would seem generally reasonable to use as much information as possible (the excluded provinces in 1969 seem not to affect the results very much) and rely on price as well as expenditure data from the survey. This would result in the use of the "average" column in Table 3.4. But is that number likely to be correct? Again—and unfortunately—probably not.

The SUSENAS surveys seem to say that real per capita spending rose 4-12 percent in a six-year period. The national income account estimates put the figure at 40 percent. While the gross domestic product (GDP) estimate of private consumption is calculated as a residual and is open to challenge, the major source of error is likely to be underestimated investment. Even if the additional error in investment in 1976 were 10 percent more than 1970 (a reasonable upper limit), the growth in per capita private consumption would still be 36 percent. While somewhat better coverage of output over time may also bias the GDP estimate upward, it seems likely that any plausible set of corrections would still give a GDP per capita consumption growth several times that suggested by the SUSENAS surveys, as shown in Table 3.4.

One major source of the understatement appears when one attempts to find evidence in the surveys of the rapid increase in purchases of luxury durable goods.* The entire category of "other

---

*Some data are given to illustrate the growth in consumption:

	1970	1976	Percent Change
Registered cars (1,000)	239	421	+76
Registered motorcycles (1,000)	440	1,419	+222
Air departures to foreign countries, excluding tourists (1,000)	69	303	+339

Sources: Statistical Pocketbook of Indonesia 1972-73 and 1977-78, Central Bureau of Statistics.

durable goods," which excludes furniture, household utensils, and similar items, amounted to only $2 per capita in 1976, or little over $250 million. Yet in 1976, 75,000 new cars and 267,000 new motorcycles were assembled and sold. Many others purchased used cars and motorcycles as the old ones were traded in. On these two goods alone, the excluded consumption may amount to $1 billion, or 5-6 percent of total reported consumption. Lesser but still substantial shortfalls appear to exist for foreign travel, gasoline, and some of the more expensive household durable goods, such as air conditioners and refrigerators. My own guess is that excluded upper-income consumption equals at least 10 percent of total reported consumption. Adding it to reported consumption would eliminate much of the differential if a 35 percent increase in real per capita consumption is assumed.

Further evidence in support of the likelihood of an adverse trend in income distribution comes from the data on food consumption. We will concentrate on the consumption of calories from the four basic staples of rice, corn, cassava, and sweet potatoes. The demand for these calories was calculated by Peter Timmer on the basis of 1976 survey data. His findings with regard to the expenditure elasticity, by expenditure group, are shown in Table 3.5.

TABLE 3.5

Expenditure Elasticity for Staple Calories in 1976

Monthly per Capita Expenditure Group	Percent of Population		Percent of Spending		Expenditure Elasticity	
0- 1,999	15.4		5.8		.80	
2,000- 2,999	23.7		13.7		.47	
3,000- 4,999	32.4		29.6		.39	
5,000-10,000	22.6	28.5	32.8	51.0	.16	.08
10,000 +	5.9		18.2		-.24	

Sources: Peter Timmer, "Food Policy Analysis and Protein Calorie Malnutrition" (1978), p. 10 (unpublished paper prepared for the World Bank, Washington, D.C.). The spending data are based on the SUSENAS surveys.

This shows that the poor will, unsurprisingly, increase their percentage of staple calorie consumption by nearly as much as their real spending, while the better-off buy proportionately fewer staple calories as their spending increases, and the very rich actually buy fewer calories.* If expenditure actually increased by equal percentages for all groups, we would expect a 35 percent increase in real spending to be consistent with an 8 percent increase in staple calorie consumption. In other words, the weighted expenditure elasticity is about .23 for all of Indonesia, and about .30 for rural Java.

In fact, the SUSENAS surveys show a small decline in staple calorie consumption. The food balance sheets, using production and trade data, show a 2 percent per capita increase. In either case the ratio of change in calorie consumption to increase in real spending is very low, and possibly negative. The data for rural Java are more decisive, with a 5 percent decline in staple calories registered by the SUSENAS surveys. The only other major influence evident would be that food prices rose more than prices in general. However, because food is 75-80 percent of total spending for most people, the weight of food in price indexes is so high that the extent to which food prices grow faster than general price indexes is very limited. In rural Java it appears that food prices increased perhaps 10 percent more than a general price index over the period. This relative shift in prices cannot begin to account for the decline observed in staple calorie intakes. By far the main explanation is likely to be that real incomes of the poor did not increase much if at all.

AN ALTERNATIVE CALCULATION

Because the preceding analysis differs significantly from the conclusions drawn by others from the recent SUSENAS data, additional support may be useful in establishing this pattern of income concentration. There are, unfortunately, few alternatives. The one chosen here is crude, and essentially splits the economy into just two groups. Changes in income distribution within the two groups would obviously affect the distribution of income by decile group. This exercise does not attempt to estimate a full-blown income distribution, only to indicate general directions of change.

---

*In 1979 very similar patterns occurred for rice consumption alone. In 1969-70, lower-income groups had rice-expenditure elasticities well in excess of unity.

The procedure is simple. All sectors in the national income accounts are allocated to either a "modern" or a "traditional" group. Where data are adequate, output within a sector is divided and allocated partly to each group. A similar allocation is done for employment, so that output per worker and its changes from 1971 to 1976 (the years of the two employment censuses) can be broadly discerned. Because of data limitations, only the food-crop portion of agriculture, manufacturing, and trade are divided. All other sectors are placed directly into a single group. The allocation is shown below.

"Modern" Group	"Traditional" Group
Part of food crops	Part of food crops
Estates	Smallholders' cash crops
Forestry	Animal husbandry
Mining	Fishing
Large- and medium-scale manufacturing	Small and cottage manufacturing
Construction	Informal trade
Utilities	Services
Formal trade	
Transport	
Finance	
Government	

Much could be criticized in this allocation, but on balance it is likely to be a minimum estimate of trends in concentration, since in many sectors the distribution of income is likely to have become more concentrated.

A brief review of the sectoral allocation in agriculture, manufacturing, and trade will be useful to document procedures before summarizing the trends in output and employment in the "traditional" and "modern" groups.

In agriculture there has to be a division between "traditional" and "modern" groups in the food-crop sector. I put all landless and near-landless in the first group; all others, in the second. We assume that the "traditional" group gets all labor payments plus all nonlabor output from the land they own. Labor payments are available for wet rice cultivation for 1971-75 (they fall in real terms), but only 1975 data are available for dry rice and nonrice cultivation. It is assumed that 1975 labor income was constant from 1971 to 1976 for this latter group. For wet rice, 1975 labor income is used for 1976. The landowners in Java who own less than .50 hectare (the bottom 60 percent) and the landowners on the Outer Islands who own less than about .75 hectare (the bottom 40 percent) were put in the "traditional" group.* The calculations of income allocation in the food-crop sector (in billion 1973 Rp.) is shown below.

	1971	1976
Labor income	196	167
Small farm output share (16 percent)	198	254
"Traditional" share	394	421
Total GDP food-crop output	1,436	1,755
"Modern" share	1,042	1,334

Source: Agriculture surveys (1970-75); 1973 Agricultural Census; official GDP accounts.

All of the biases in this are in the direction of understating the trend toward inequality. To the extent that technical progress favored larger farmers, that access to low-cost credit grew more quickly for larger farmers, or that control of output through various arrangements to buy crops at low prices increased for smaller farms, the assumption of their share of total farm area being equal to nonlabor output share will be wrong.

The employment in each group is estimated as follows. The 1963 and 1973 Agricultural Censuses allow interpolation and extrapolation of trends to find the number of farms in 1971 and 1976— 13.4 million in 1971 and 14.3 million in 1976. Of these, 7.0 and 7.4 million were placed in the "small" ("traditional") category, leaving 6.4 million and 6.9 million "large" (and therefore "modern") farms. We will assume two workers per large farm, plus an estimated .7 million estate and forestry workers in 1971 and .9 million in 1976.† Thus, the rough food-crop sector employment estimates (in millions of workers) are:

	1971	1976
"Traditional"	19.8	20.6
"Modern"	13.5	14.7

---

*It is important to note that this is the area of farmland, not sawah (wet rice fields). Only about half of the farmland is sawah. According to the 1973 Agricultural Census, average farm size is .28 hectare for Java and .41 hectare in the Outer Islands.

†These figures are derived from the employment census and surveys in 1971 and 1976, plus other information on estate and forestry employment.

It should again be emphasized that the definition of "traditional" farmers has been restricted to landless and near-landless peasants. If we could observe which parts of the "modern" group had materially benefited in the 1970s, we might redraw the line and make the "modern" group much smaller.

The manufacturing sector is easier to divide because of surveys of large-, medium-, and small cottage-scale industries. We find that employment in large and medium industries remained about 1 million, while workers in small and cottage industries increased from 2.0 to 2.9 million. "Modern" output rose from Rp. 328 billion to Rp. 744 billion, while the other group's output rose from Rp. 162 billion to Rp. 186 billion.

In trade we will assume that all self-employed and unpaid family members are "traditional," while all employers and employees are "modern." We will further assume that trade activity of the modern and traditional groups can be estimated by taking 32 percent (1971) and 35 percent (1976) of the commodity output (agriculture and manufacturing) generated by each group. This is a crude procedure, but probably is not seriously wrong. The results are shown below.

	"Traditional" Sector		"Modern" Sector	
	Output (billion 1973 Rp.)	Employment (million)	Output (billion 1973 Rp.)	Employment (million)
1971	335	3.8	588	.90
1976	410	6.4	940	.70

We can now summarize the results in billion 1973 Rp. and millions of workers.

	Agriculture	Manufacturing	Trade	Other	Total
"Modern" output					
1971	1,454	328	588	1,347	3,717
1976	1,832	744	940	2,439	5,955
"Traditional" output					
1971	987	162	325	250	1,724
1976	1,112	186	410	284	1,992
"Modern" employment					
1971	13.5	1.0	.9	3.3	18.7
1976	14.7	1.1	.7	4.0	20.5
"Traditional" employment					
1971	19.8	2.0	3.8	3.3	28.9
1976	20.6	2.9	6.4	3.7	33.6

The trends in average output per worker and work force shares are striking.

	Output per Worker (1,000 constant 1973 Rp.)		Percent of Work Force	
	1971	1976	1971	1976
"Traditional"	60	59	61	62
"Modern"	199	290	39	38

The rather generously defined "modern" group has a nearly 50 percent gain in income per worker, but a slightly declining share of the work force. The "traditional" group has essentially level output per worker and a slightly increasing share of the work force. Given the extreme roughness of these calculations, the only secure finding is that a large group of workers—say between half and three-quarters—is little, if any, better off. A smaller fraction of the work force—most likely smaller than the 38 percent shown above— is considerably better off. This broad finding is consistent with the employment trends noted in the previous essay and with the food consumption data from the SUSENAS surveys. Income distribution has become worse in this period (1971-76).

ABSOLUTE LEVELS OF LIVING

The emphasis in this essay has been on trends in the share of income and spending. However, it is also important to try to trace what changes have occurred in the absolute level of living.[2] There are a number of dimensions to this concept, such as nutrition, health, and education. The evidence reviewed here will be partial, but helpful in giving some indication of trends since 1970.

Food consumption, as calculated from the national food balance sheets, shows a 5 percent rise in total calories available per capita from 1969-70 to 1976. Similar calculations of total calories with the SUSENAS data are difficult, but staple calories showed essentially no change in the period. Foods such as wheat and oils were increasing rapidly in use, and probably caused average urban calorie intake in Java to remain level or increase slightly. In rural areas of Java, it is likely that average calorie intake fell a few percentage points. The Outer Islands probably saw modest gains in total calorie consumption. Protein intake per capita, which is also short of requirements, did not change. Overall, the picture is one of small changes in intake, with the Outer Islands, and perhaps urban Java, gaining, and rural Java losing. The SUSENAS data do not reveal any clear differences in changes in intake by most expenditure groups from 1969-70 to 1976.

Mortality rates are another commonly used indicator of levels of living. From census data in 1971 and 1976, we observe a small decline in mortality rates from 21 to 20 per 1,000 population. This continues a long-standing downtrend from 1946-51, when the mortality rate was 34 per 1,000, to 1956-61, when the rate was 27.6 per 1,000. The pace of decrease has slowed, with 1966-71 having a rate of 22.4 and 1971-76 one of 19.8 per 1,000.[3] Thus, death rates have been declining even when consumption levels were not increasing, as in the mid-1950s. The slower rate of gain might be attributed either to its being harder to achieve reductions, or to modest advances in health and nutrition. Since other Southeast Asia countries have much lower death rates, it would appear that the latter explanation is a better one.[4]

The enrollment ratios in primary and secondary schools rose rapidly in the 1970s. The primary school enrollment ratio rose from 71 percent to 85 percent, and the secondary school rate from 12 percent to 18 percent. This probably reflects both increased government spending and efforts to widen educational opportunities, and the increased ability and demand of upper income groups for continued schooling for their children.

Overall, then, the 1970s was a period of progress in many indicators used for levels of living, but with a wide dispersion and—possibly—some declines for selected parts of the population. It is likely that average nutrition, health, and education improved. It is less clear whether the poor in rural Java benefited much, if at all, particularly in terms of food intake.

SUMMARY

The findings presented here are not particularly surprising. The 1970s was a period of rapid, even violent, structural change in the Indonesian economy. Progress was highly uneven, leaving behind many who were not well-equipped to take advantage of new jobs, technologies, and opportunities. There is little doubt about the considerable growth in average consumption, or the concentration of that growth in the upper fifth (or so) of the population. The major uncertainties are what degree of income inequality is acceptable to society, and what policies hold out realistic hope of continuing growth and also of doing more for the groups who have been excluded thus far. It is resolving those uncertainties, rather than refining the estimates of income distribution, that deserves high priority at this time.

NOTES

1. Major (mimeographed) studies include "Employment and Income Distribution in Indonesia," issued in 1978 by the Development Policy Staff of the World Bank, Washington, D.C.; Hendra Esmera, "Pertumbuhan Ekonomi, Pembagian Pendapatan dan Tingkat Kemiskinan di Java-Madura, 1967-76," issued in 1978 by LIPI, the National Academy of Sciences of Indonesia; L. N. Perrera and Sri Budianti, "Economic Growth and the Distribution of Income in Indonesia," a monography cited in R. M. Sundrum's "Income Distribution, 1970-76," B.I.E.S. 15, no. 1 (March 1979): 137-44; Ingrid Palmer, "Rural Poverty in Indonesia with Special Reference to Java," issued in July 1976 by the International Labor Organization, Geneva; and Sayogyo, "The Poverty Line and Minimum Food Needs," issued by the Bogor Agricultural Institute, Bogor, Indonesia. Also see David Dapice, "Income Distribution: A Comment," and R. M. Sundrum, "A Reply," B.I.E.S. 16, no. 1, pp. 86-93.

2. Dwight King and Peter Weldon, "Income Distribution and Levels of Living in Java 1963-70," Economic Development and Cultural Change 25, no. 4 (July 1977): 699-711, discusses the reasons for investigating levels of living, must use rice consumption as the major indicator.

3. Development Policy Staff, World Bank, "Employment and Income Distribution in Indonesia," Annex 1, pp. 8-10.

4. In 1970, Thailand had a rate of 10 per 1,000; the Philippines, 12 per 1,000; Sri Lanka, 8 per 1,000; and Malaysia, 7 per 1,000. See World Tables, 1976 (Baltimore: Johns Hopkins University Press, 1976), pp. 506-08.

4
THE EFFECT OF ECONOMIC GROWTH AND INFLATION ON WORKERS' INCOME
Gustav F. Papanek

Rapid economic growth in Indonesia since 1967 has benefited only the rich, it is argued by some. Data on changes in real wages are the best evidence available on this issue.

Since little reliable information exists on Indonesian income distribution or the absolute income of the poor, it is particularly useful to develop an index of changes in the income of a major section of the lower income group: the wage earners. Unfortunately only scattered data are available on the largest group of wage earners, those who work on rice and other smallholdings, and those data are of questionable reliability. Consistent series exist only for plantation and industrial workers, with scattered information on others. However, evidence for other countries, similar to Indonesia in important economic characteristics, is that wages in different sectors and occupations move broadly together, including rural/ agricultural wages and those in the informal urban sector. [1]

In Indonesia unskilled workers' wages also move broadly together over time, both in the country as a whole and in different regions. This provides indirect evidence that labor markets are sufficiently integrated so that the wages of any large group of unskilled workers can be taken to reflect the wages of most unskilled workers in the same area and at the same time. Therefore the wage series for workers on estates (plantations), which is quite complete and comprehensive, can be used as an indicator of wage

The help of the Biro Pusat Statistik (the Central Statistical Bureau) is gratefully acknowledged.

changes for unskilled workers in general during years when other
data are not available or are not sufficiently detailed. While it is
therefore plausible that the trends in rural wages were quite similar to those for the plantation (and manufacturing) wages examined
here, this cannot be demonstrated.

The margin of error in Indonesian wage and price data, as in
the other statistics, is high, increased by intermittent upheavals,
including Japanese occupation, the revolution that brought independence, and the runaway inflation of the mid-1960s. Therefore, at
best, only major changes are of significance. On the other hand,
major changes have taken place in the economy, so it is possible to
trace the effect of such changes on real wages with a good deal of
reliability.

THE EFFECT OF STAGNATION AND GROWTH

There have been two major trends in the real wages of unskilled
Indonesian workers: a drastic decline as the economy suffered setbacks and stagnation up to the mid-1960s, and then an equally dramatic rise accompanying rapid economic growth. It is interesting
that the decline occurred despite a pro-labor government policy,
rising political power for workers, and effectiveness of trade union
organization, while rising wages accompanied a steady decline in
the political and economic power of organized labor.

The highest real wage on Java's plantations, the only category
for which there are data, seems to have occurred during the colonial
period. Of course, the margin of error is very great when one
makes comparisons over long periods, especially when different
currencies are involved, massive price changes have taken place,
and two different data sources have to be used. However, comparing only the purchasing power for rice, the principal staple, in order to avoid price index problems, confirms the real wage data. It
appears that on Java's plantations real wages in 1938 were Rp.
5,194 a month in 1969 prices, almost 80 percent higher than in
1972, the post-Sukarno high point for permanent workers, and 15
percent higher than in the highest post-World War II year (1953).
The wages in the colonial period were higher despite the workers'
relatively weak political and trade union position, and little concern
with income distribution on the part of the colonial government.
Using the same price indexes, municipal workers' wages in 1938
Jakarta can be estimated at Rp. 7,774 a month and industrial workers' wages at Rp. 5,160, both in 1969 prices.[2] Both are substantially above the real wage for industrial work during 1955-70 (see
Table 4.5). In short, these sources suggest that with less population

pressure than subsequently, a well-functioning economy, and low food prices, workers' wages seem to have been relatively high prior to World War II.

During the 1940s the economy deteriorated very sharply as a result of war, Japanese occupation, and revolutionary struggle. As a consequence, by 1951 the real wage appears to have dropped by roughly one-third compared with the colonial period. Rehabilitation of the economy again raised the real wage, and a postwar high point seems to have been reached in 1952-53.

From the 1950s on, the wage data are somewhat more reliable, since a single source is available and can be checked against other information. For the next decade the economy stagnated, and per capita income probably declined slightly. At the same time workers' political and trade union power increased substantially. Despite this, by the mid-1960s both plantation wages (on Java and Sumatra) and industrial workers' wages generally were half or less than half of what they had been eight-ten years earlier (Table 4.1). The real wages for textiles paralleled those for all of industry. Industrial wage movements, therefore, were not due to structural changes in industry during this period of decline.

The actual decline in real wages was probably somewhat less than the data indicate, because the value of wages in kind may be reflected in the data only incompletely and with a lag. Wages in kind were to be reported at market value. However, it is certainly possible that firms did not bother to adjust the reported value when prices rose during the year, but made adjustments only once a year. Reporting constant wages in kind during a year of rapid inflation would overstate the decline in real wages. There may also have been other deficiencies in reporting. However, analysis of a few individual firms that bought the goods used to make payments in kind confirmed that there was a sharp decline in real wages, even after taking account of payments in kind.

Real income did not decline by as much as real wages. First, plantations and some industrial firms were required to take on additional workers, some of whom had to appear only to collect their pay. They could do other work and earn another income. By the mid-1960s the number of workers on plantations had increased by about 17 percent (Table 4.2). There is no comparable trend for industry. It is known that the labor force of some firms did increase, while others remained unchanged or may even have declined. Second, income was also maintained because it became increasingly possible for workers to divert to their own use some of the inputs and outputs of many enterprises, or otherwise to supplement their income at the expense of the firms they worked for. The decline in workers' income was, therefore, not as sharp as the wage data indicate.

However, since the number of workers on plantations increased by less than 20 percent, while the wage rate dropped by 60 percent or more, the decline in the income of workers as a group undoubtedly was massive; it is difficult to believe that appropriation of inputs and outputs was adequate to compensate for the more than 50 percent decline in the total wage bill.

TABLE 4.1

Longer-Term Movements in Real Wages, Mid-1950s-Early 1970s
(percent)

	Mid-1950s to Mid-1960s	Mid-1960s to Early 1970s
Plantations		
Java	−67	+114
Sumatra	−37	+54
Indonesia	−63	+91
Industry		
Large scale	−50	+58
Medium scale	−34	+98
Medium scale	−69	+210
Household servants	−66	

Sources: See Tables 4.3-4.6.

TABLE 4.2

Estimated Employment on Plantations: 1955–76

	1955		1963		1966		1972		1976	
	Worker per Hectare	Workers (1,000)	Worker per Hectare	Workers (1,000)	Worker per Hectare	Workers (1,000)	Worker per Hectare	Workers (1,000)	Worker per Hectare	Workers (1,000)
Rubber	0.45	205	0.56	226	0.56	207	0.43	152	0.55	225
Tea	1.25	83	1.43	92	1.54	92	1.25	72	1.46	87
Coffee	0.83	36	0.83	31	1.00	36	0.87	28	0.77	29
Sugar	0.42	21	0.77	55	0.53	37	0.67	48	0.70	81
Palm oil	0.24	22	0.31	27	0.33	31	0.26	26	0.22	40
Average/total	0.47	367	0.61	431	0.59	403	0.53	326	0.56	462

Note: Total workers = hectares producing crops times workers per hectare.

Sources: Hectares of producing crops from Biro Pusat Statistik (BPS), Statistical Pocketbook (various years); worker per hectare calculated from reporting estates—see BPS, Statistik Upah Karyawan Perkebunan (Wages Paid on Estates) (various years).

The deterioration in the economy was so severe that real wages could not be maintained, despite workers' power and government policies designed to favor them. The income was simply not there. Even if workers, management, and officials (civil and military) obtained the entire value of output, with no income going to the owners (mostly the government after nationalization), the workers' share was not adequate to prevent a severe deterioration in their real wages and income. Other, more powerful participants in the income could protect their interests more effectively than could the workers.

Since, in general, the average wages for three to four years are compared with the average for another three to four years, annual fluctuations are not involved. Statistical artifacts or accidents are, if not ruled out, greatly reduced. The data reflect powerful economic forces that reduced the real wages of all workers on plantations and in industry to a severe, really brutal, degree.

The plantation wage series were compiled separately for all Indonesia (including several islands with a small plantation sector), for Java and Sumatra, for several crops (rubber, tea, sugar, and coffee), and in all cases for permanent, temporary, and permanent plus temporary workers. All these series showed exactly the same trends.

By contrast, since the mid-1960s workers' real wages show a strong upward trend. By the early 1970s plantation wages were up over 90 percent compared with the mid-1960s, and industrial workers' wages increased 58 to 98 percent or more (Table 4.1). It is clear that with general prosperity and rapid economic growth, workers' real wages improved dramatically as well. This happened despite a radical decline in workers' political power and ability to organize. Real income lagged behind real wages, as it had during the period of wage decline, since multiple jobholding and illegal income supplementation became more difficult for workers. Plantation employment declined some 25 percent (Table 4.2); but since real wages rose by much more, the wage bill was up by more than a third. In industry employment seems to have roughly doubled, so workers benefited from a near doubling of both real wages and employment.

Further evidence that real wages fell, then rose, and that both were substantial changes, comes from a variety of sources. Industrial real-wage series were separately calculated for this essay and by Mark Pitt (see Table 4.5), and showed roughly the same movements. Since both calculations used the same basic sources, however, this is not really independent evidence. Careful compilation of data from a single foreign industrial firm shows wages declining 30-40 percent from their high point in 1952 until

TABLE 4.3

Plantation Real Wages and Prices, 1951–78
(monthly wages, 1969 prices)

	All Indonesia			Java		Sumatra	
	Price Change (percent)	Real Wages Temporary and Permanent Workers	Permanent Workers	Price Change (percent)	Real Wages Temporary and Permanent Workers	Price Change (percent)	Real Wages Temporary and Permanent Workers
1951	65.0		3,416				
1952	5.0		4,333				
1953	2.5	4,647	4,507	0	4,167	6.3	5,118
1954	4.9	4,669	3,564	8.3	4,074	5.9	5,259
1955	37.2	2,896	3,035	35.9	1,633	37.0	3,622
1956	11.9	3,110	3,176	13.2	2,698	6.8	3,705
1957	4.5	3,130	3,258	5.0	2,694	1.3	3,850
1958	47.8	2,528	2,844	41.3	2,308	66.3	2,768
1959	26.5	2,079	2,555	27.0	1,659	26.3	2,948
1960	26.4	1,869	2,596	27.4	1,426	22.0	2,793

Year	(1)	(1 comb.)	(2)	(2 comb.)	(3)	(3 comb.)	(4)	(4 comb.)	(5)	(5 comb.)	(6)	(6 comb.)
1961	33.1		1,796		2,299		34.0		1,263		32.2		2,874
1962	167.0	524	—		—		164.0	550	—		200.0	511	—
1963	134.0		1,392		1,671		147.0		1,056		103.0		2,023
1964	93.0	7,280	—		—		110.0	7,868	—		49.1	5,942	—
1965	284.0		—		—		295.0		—		270.0		—
1966	898.0		1,636		2,216		889.0		1,261		994.0		3,237
1967	193.0		1,123		2,274		183.0		749		227.0		2,835
1968	161.0		1,490		1,968		153.0		1,082		159.0		2,607
1969	8.1		2,390		2,407		9.2		1,820		8.1		3,508
1970	11.4		2,805 } 2,762		2,878		12.3		2,201 } 2,166		7.0		4,221 } 4,163
1971	6.6		2,718		2,878		9.2		2,130		2.7		4,105
1972	9.9		2,724		2,919		10.5		2,224		5.2		4,173
1973	52.7		2,342		2,663		49.8		1,849		71.5		3,332
1974	30.9		2,306		2,456		30.0		1,952		21.2		3,111
1975	12.2		2,533		2,696		16.3		2,078		3.3		3,852
1976	17.0		2,689		2,716		17.7		2,041		13.5		4,576
1977	16.1		2,716 } 2,715		2,751 } 2,777		16.7		2,208 } 2,132		17.5		4,256 } 4,277
1978	10.8		2,713		2,803		7.6		2,055		26.8		4,298

Sources: Nominal wage data from BPS, Statistik Upah Karyawan Perkebunan (yearly). Deflated by urban food prices from G. F. Papanek and D. Dowsett, "The Cost of Living, 1938–1973," Ekonomi dan Keuangan (July 1975), for years through 1973; 1974–78 constructed on the same basis from BPS, Indikator Ekonomi (various issues).

TABLE 4.4

Semiannual Wage Changes for Plantation Workers, 1972-78
(temporary and permanent workers—
monthly wages, 1969 prices)

		All Indonesia		Java		Sumatra	
		Prices (percent)	Wages	Prices (percent)	Wages	Prices (percent)	Wages
1972	I	2.6	2,671	2.8	2,077	-1.0	4,311
	II	14.1	2,756	15.0	2,329	12.6	4,193
1973	I	29.0	2,264	27.9	1,701	36.0	3,665
	II	22.2	2,392	19.4	1,965	37.9	3,071
1974	I	29.5	2,101	17.8	1,710	13.8	3,032
	II	1.8	2,489	3.4	2,156	-5.9	3,362
1975	I	7.5	2,440	8.6	2,031	4.9	3,545
	II	9.4	2,662	10.3	2,117	6.3	4,241
1976	I	8.6	2,706	9.0	1,946	5.2	4,961
	II	6.0	2,671	6.0	2,136	9.0	4,190
1977	I	5.8	2,695	4.9	2,177	9.9	4,169
	II	6.9	2,752	8.0	2,227	4.9	4,265
1978	I	6.1	2,675	2.7	2,022	21.3	4,281
	II	2.1	3,001	1.8	2,337	4.2	4,504

Notes: I = January-June, II = July-December. Some differences from Table 4.3 because not all of the same cities were available for 1974-75.

Sources: Nominal wage data from BPS, Statistik Upah Karyawan Perkebunan (yearly). Prices for 1972-73 from G. F. Papanek and D. Dowsett, "The Cost of Living, 1938-1973," Ekonomi dan Keuangan (July 1975); 1974-78 constructed on the same basis from BPS, Indikator Ekonomi (various issues).

1965, and then increasing by 55 percent until 1972. The number of workers in this firm actually declined from 1956 on, and was down about 20 percent by 1972. Since labor is a small fraction of the total costs for this enterprise, the impact on labor income of economic deterioration or recovery was less than in labor-intensive plantations and firms, but it was substantial nevertheless. At its low point the firm was operating at only 10 percent of capacity, and labor income had to decline together with the deterioration of the firm.

An index of real wages for household servants, also compiled by Mark Pitt, covers the period 1950-64 (Table 4.6) and shows an even more drastic decline. From their high point in 1953-54 they fell by 70 percent to their low period exactly a decade later.

A similar pattern of initial decline, then substantial rise, prevailed in the state electricity enterprise. Real wages, including all benefits, declined from 1961 to 1965, until they were slightly over half of what they had been, then rose by almost 4.5 times to 1969 (Table 4.7). These data again overstate the early decline and later rise, since payments in kind would show up on the books at the controlled prices, while the price index used to deflate the nominal wage presumably uses market prices. Even taking this into account, it is clear that government officials also experienced a substantial deterioration in income until 1965, and an improvement thereafter.

There was an exception: wages for public works employees in Sumatra Province did not rise from 1967 on. It may be that political power had been more effective in keeping wages up until 1966-67 for this group of government workers than for others. Deteriorating earnings need not constrain a government department, as they do plantation management, from raising wages in response to workers' pressure. That these casual, unskilled workers in a less prosperous area earned more in 1966 and 1967 than plantation employees in more prosperous regions of Sumatra, suggests the possible aftereffects of earlier political pressure. With a change in government policies, the pressure of migrants from Java on the wage level may then have forced real wages down in 1968.

In short, the absolute income of workers, mostly unskilled, declined during periods when the economy as a whole degenerated or stagnated, and rose when it grew rapidly. Political and trade union power, and government professions of concern with income distribution, seemed to make little difference, or at least were not enough to overcome the effects of economic change.

TABLE 4.5

Real Wages in Industry, 1951-77

	Monthly Wages (1969 prices)							Yearly Wages (1973 prices)	
	Large-Scale				Large and Medium	Foreign Firm Unskilled	Large Unskilled (new series)	Large	Medium
	Daily/Weekly		Monthly						
	Manuf.	Text.	All	Medium					
1951						3,163			
1952						4,335			
1953									
1954								110,300	
1955	3,490	3,457	12,910	2,216	3,961	3,710		102,600	
1956								100,400	
1957						4,389		97,600	
1958						4,397		80,500	27,500
1959	2,704	2,688	9,295	1,720	3,300	6,646		78,400	35,000
1960	3,068	3,151	9,816	2,076	3,788	6,810		71,600	33,300
1961						6,186		69,500	35,000
1962	1,753	1,803	3,903	1,025	1,919	4,131		46,000	20,700
1963	1,604	1,464	3,234	686	1,613	3,382		50,400	20,800
1964						3,210		46,800	
1965						2,632		51,400	23,500
1966						3,960		55,200	18,700
1967						3,585		67,800	
1968						2,609			
1969						3,124			

Year								
1970	4,011*				3,475			
1971		3,515	2,142	3,110	3,718		74,100	37,600
1972 I					(3,725)	(6,021)		
1972 II					(4,890)	(5,847)		
1972 I, II				5,144	4,311	5,938	83,700	43,200
1973 I					(5,889)	(5,136)		
1973 II					(5,904)	(4,664)		
1973 I, II					5,897	4,904	84,400	44,000
—								
1975	3,856*			4,916				
1976	3,907*			5,098				
1977	4,014*			5,231				

*For these years figures were not separately available for production (daily/weekly) and office (monthly) workers. Only a weighted average of both was available and is shown. Therefore 1970 to 1977 data are comparable, but are not fully comparable with 1955 to 1963 data.

Notes:
Daily/weekly-paid workers are production workers.
Monthly-paid workers are office workers.
"All" workers = weighted average of daily/weekly and monthly workers.
"Manuf." = all manufacturing.
"Text." = textiles.
"Large and Medium" = weighted average; total wage bill divided by total workers.
"New series" = only data for 69 firms that consistently reported were compiled.
Nominal wages were deflated by an urban food price index for Java, Sumatra, all Indonesia.

Sources: "Large and medium" from BPS, "Industrial Census," Statistical Pocketbook (various years), for 1955–72; 1975–77 from Industrial Statistics, vol. I, Survey of Manufacturing Industries (for these years); yearly wages from Mark M. Pitt, "Alternative Trade Strategies and Employment: Indonesian Country Study," unpublished draft prepared for the National Bureau of Economic Research project "Alternative Trade Strategies and Employment in Less Developed Countries"; urban food price index from G. F. Papanek and D. Dowsett, "The Cost of Living, 1938–1973," Ekonomi dan Keuangan 23 (June 1975): 181–206.

TABLE 4.6

Real Wages for Public Works, Office, and Household Workers, 1950-73

Year	Monthly Wages, 1969 Prices			Household Servants Index (1954 = 100)
	Public Works	INPRES (daily)	Office Workers	
1950				85
1951				67
1952				81
1953				98
1954				100
1955				90
1956				85
1957				80
1958				72
1959				70
1960				62
1961				56
1962				34
1963				35
1964				28
1965				—
1966	4,507			—
1967	4,864			—
1968	1,988		24,328	—
1969	2,492		23,969	—
1970	2,913	116	26,234	—
1971	3,417	119	27,905	—
1972 I	(3,517)			
1972 II	(2,482)			
1972 I, II	3,004	126	30,498	
1973 I	(2,061)			
1973 II	(1,731)			
1973 I, II	1,887	114	35,184	

Notes: Public works labor data for Sumatra only. INPRES is a locally administered public works program. Data are for Java; these are planning figures, not actuals. Workers were paid daily.

Sources: Public works data from Public Works Dept.; INPRES figures reported by each kabupaten (county), wage statistics are simple averages of kabupaten figures; office workers data from one foreign firm; household workers from Mark M. Pitt, "Alternative Trade Strategies and Employment: Indonesian Country Study," unpublished draft prepared for the National Bureau of Economic Research project "Alternative Trade Strategies and Employment in Less Developed Countries," using data from Almanac Indonesia 1968.

TABLE 4.7

Long-Term Movements in Real Wages,
State Electricity Enterprise, 1961-69
(index of total labor costs per employee,
deflated by food index)

Year	Index		Year	Index
1961	82		1966	100
1962	69		1967	134
1963	51		1968	133
1964	80		1969	220
1965	49			

Sources: Labor costs from C. Manning (Ph.D. diss., at
Australian National University); food prices from G. F. Papanek
and D. Dowsett, "The Cost of Living, 1938-1973," Ekonomi dan
Keuangan (June 1975).

WHY DID GROWTH AFFECT WAGES?

One can speculate on why real wages in Indonesia did not behave as they should, according to the labor-surplus theories—why
did they decline, presumably below "subsistence" or the traditional
wage, in periods of economic stagnation and rise above these norms
when rapid growth took place? Presumably "subsistence" is not a
physiological concept for the regularly employed, especially not in
Indonesia, but is in part culturally defined; and views of an "acceptable" wage are subject to change. When the economy declines,
workers are forced to accept less; there is an increase in misery,
but not outright starvation (for instance, people shift from rice to
cassava, and postpone even minimal clothing purchases). There
may also be pressure to look more actively for bits of income from
supplementary labor and trade, especially by children and women.

One plausible hypothesis that fits into the labor-surplus theories is that the reservation price of wage labor is largely determined by the income in the only alternative open to everyone: self-
employment, either as an individual or on the family land. Instead
of working for wages, the worker can always help out on the family
land, if any; pull a bicycle rickshaw; pick up cigarette butts, and so
on. The social marginal product in these occupations may be zero,

but compensation is usually equal to the average product. On the family land the worker shares equally in income, eating the common meal and staying in the family house, even if his or her departure would cause no loss in output. Even the compensation of much non-family labor in agriculture appears to be related to the average, not the marginal, product. As long as harvest labor, for instance, receives a share in the harvest, not a fixed cash wage, its income will change with the average product, even if there are more harvesters than needed, so that the marginal product is zero. Similarly, in informal urban occupations one more rickshaw puller may not add to the convenience of passengers if there are already too many; but if no one lowers the price as a result, the newcomer will receive the new, lower average product as his share.

The mechanism that prevents a reduction in price until it equals the marginal product is now under examination, and a study has been completed on the relationship of the average product in agriculture to the real wage in three other countries and Indonesia.[3] It confirms, in general, a significant relationship between agricultural output per capita—the presumed reservation price below which workers will not take wage jobs—and the real wage. However, for Indonesia a rigorous test is difficult because neither national accounts nor agricultural output indexes are available for part of the period under review. But rice production per capita for the rural population was stagnant from 1953 to 1958. From 1958 on, national income data are available, and show continued stagnation until 1965 in value added per capita for the rural population in both farm food crops and all agriculture. At best, average product per capita seems to have stagnated between 1953 and 1965. From 1965 on, the per capita value added increased some 2.8 percent per year for food crops and 2.2 percent for all agriculture until 1970, then continued to increase, though at a slower rate.

The postulated relationship of changes in agricultural output and in other self-employment activities with real wages may be the principal reason for falling wages to the mid-1960s and rising wages thereafter. Another factor was ability to pay in the wage sector, combined with delays and difficulties in returning to self-employment, particularly in agriculture. Clearly, wages dropped far more than the reservation price—that is, the average product in agriculture. If the system is symmetrical, wage earners should return to self-employment. But that is not as easy as the opposite move. When family members move from self-employment on a small plot in Java to plantation work, everyone in the family can have higher income, since there is one less person to feed. Support for such a move should therefore be strong. A family member coming back from plantation labor makes everyone worse off economically. Therefore the pressure should work against it. Moreover, the plantation or industrial worker may have acquired a vested interest in a house, a garden, a school for his or her children, access to better health facilities, and even secondary income-producing occupations.

For all of these reasons there may be a ratchet effect. When plantation or industrial wages rise, workers may respond quite quickly by moving out of self-employment and into wage labor, but wages may have to fall a great deal before enough workers move back to self-employment to raise the wage rate. [4]

If such a ratchet effect works, and if the ability to pay of many enterprises is driven down by the general state of the economy, as it was in Indonesia in the late 1950s and early 1960s, then it is not surprising that plantation and industry wages dropped very sharply, far more than the average product in agriculture, the bellwether of self-employment. Somebody had to pay for the losses incurred by the enterprises as a result of shortages of inputs, inadequate spare and replacement parts, and an exchange rate that often made legal export of plantation crops unprofitable, regardless of efficiency. It is not surprising that it was the workers who paid, if they had few realistic alternatives to plantation or industry employment.

Other factors besides the effect of the average self-employment product and the inability to pay when profitability declined sharply affected real wages. One was the rate of inflation and the tendency of nominal wages to lag behind rapidly rising and/or accelerating prices. Moreover, when the economy is flourishing, it can make sense for the profit-maximizing manager to increase wages, to improve workers' physical ability to work, and to reduce absenteeism, turnover, theft, damage to equipment, and the likelihood of conflict with labor. Even if other workers are available at a lower (constant) wage, the task of hiring new employees and the risk that they cannot be fired if the profitability turns out to be temporary, may make higher (including overtime) wages for existing workers a preferred alternative. Finally, in prosperous times employers may be willing, for noneconomic reasons, to give workers a share of the increased income, and workers may demand higher wages for the same reasons. Even though new workers may be available at lower wages, employers may respond to their own noneconomic objectives and to workers' pressures in profitable periods, both for noneconomic reasons and to avoid turnover costs.

THE EFFECT OF INFLATION

In addition to the effect of the state of the economy, price changes also affected real wages. That wages often tend to lag

behind price changes is well-known, and is generally confirmed by
the Indonesian experience. Changes in real wages were generally
and primarily the result of changes in prices, not in nominal wages.
Over the short term, when prices dropped, or the rate of price
increase declined, real wages tended to rise; when price rises accelerated, real wages tended to decline. But the correlation between real wages and prices is far from perfect, since wages are
obviously influenced by other factors.

Nominal wages will lag behind prices either if adjustments
to compensate for price rises are made only at the end of a year,
or if wages are adjusted in anticipation of price rises but the antici-
pations are not correct. Both the rate of inflation and the rate of
change in inflation can matter. For instance, if prices in year 1
rise 10 percent, and wages are adjusted at the end of the year to
compensate for this increase, then wages will have gradually declined from 0 to 10 percent over the year, until the adjustment re-
stores the original real wage at the end of the year. The higher the
rate of inflation, the greater the average loss over the year. However, if wages are adjusted in anticipation of future inflation, in an
attempt to keep real wages constant, and anticipated inflation is
assumed to equal past rates, then a change in the rate of change
will affect real wages. For instance, if inflation is regularly 10
percent and wages are adjusted at the beginning of the year by 15
percent to compensate for this anticipated rate of inflation, then a
rise in the inflation rate to 20 percent will reduce real wages.

Nominal wages are significantly correlated with price changes,
which they tend to lag by about two years. In 1953-67 inflation was
both high and accelerating. The rate of inflation was another factor
contributing to the decline of real wages during 1953-67. Subsequently, declining and lower inflation contributed to rising wages.
The secular deterioration in the economy from the mid-1950s to the
mid-1960s both raised prices and lowered per capita output; and
both, in turn, resulted in declining real wages. For the early 1950s
to the mid-1960s, income in self-employment dropped and inflation
rose. With declining per capita production and rising unrequited
exports (smuggled out to finance capital flight), accompanied by a
rapid expansion of the money supply, both declining reservation
wages and rapid inflation contributed to falling wages. Conversely,
stabilization thereafter meant both more stable prices and higher
per capita output, which produced rising wages.

On a year-to-year basis the correlation between changes in
prices and in real wages is not always strong. The highest rates
of inflation were in 1965 and 1966, yet real wages on plantations
and in industry increased between 1964 and 1966 (see Tables 4.3
and 4.5). The third highest annual rate of inflation was recorded

in 1967, but real wages in industry rose (Table 4.5) although plantation wages in general declined. On the other hand, real wages dropped in 1973, when inflation was far less than in 1967. It is reasonable to hypothesize that two factors disturbed the general relationship between rapid inflation and real wages when annual changes are examined: the secular trend in the economy, already discussed, and expectations.

Expectations will influence real wages if nominal wages are adjusted to meet expected price changes, in order to keep expected real wages reasonably steady. If expected prices are based on past price changes, then any acceleration or deceleration in the rate of change will mean that nominal wage changes undershoot or overshoot price changes. Then, when inflation accelerates, real wages tend to drop, because the acceleration is unexpected; when inflation slows, real wages tend to rise, because the deceleration is usually unexpected. The evidence bears out this hypothesis. There were seven years of significant acceleration in price rises (1955, 1958, 1961, 1962, 1965, 1966, and 1973). In addition, during 1968 price rises slowed, but not by as much as had been expected after the unusual success in slowing inflation in 1967. In all eight years it can be assumed that the magnitude of future price increases was underestimated. For five of these years there are plantation wage data and in all five of these years wages dropped significantly (see Table 4.3). For workers in industry, the picture is less clear-cut and, especially in large-scale industry, undoubtedly was influenced by political and economic pressures and the changing composition of reporting firms. Nevertheless, in a small majority of cases, wages did decline in these years. On the other hand, there were six years of significantly decelerating prices (1956, 1957, 1964, 1967, 1969, and 1975 were all years when the price increase was less than half of what it had been in the previous year). In five of these six years, real wages remained essentially stable, or rose. The year 1967 is a clear exception, and political factors may have played an overriding role.

Nominal wages sometimes lagged behind price changes for a considerable period of time. The regression analysis (see Table 4.8) generally shows that nominal wages change by 60-80 percent as much as prices in the same year, and sometimes, but by no means always, catch up in the following year. More clear-cut evidence on timing comes from the most recent period. Prices started to rise dramatically in September 1972, but nominal wages generally continued to rise at only the same rate as in the past. As a result real wages of most workers dropped sharply over an 18-month period. By the second half of 1974, inflation had been greatly reduced and real wages started to rise again. It required another

18 months before real wages again approximated the level of the second half of 1972 (Table 4.4). Thus the inflation-caused drop in real wages lasted three years in total.

TABLE 4.8

Regression Analysis of the Effect of Prices on Wages
(plantation workers)

Nominal Wages	Constant	Price-Current	Price-Lagged	R^2
Indonesia	-0.02	0.71	0.30	0.99
	(-0.6)	(25.7)	(9.7)	
Java	0.05	0.79	-0.09	0.91
	(0.4)	(10.5)	(-3.9)	
Sumatra	0.08	0.61	-0.01	0.96
	(1.0)	(16.5)	(-1.0)	

Notes: For both permanent and temporary workers, n = 20.
Figures in parentheses = t-statistics.
Source: See Table 4.3.

On the other hand, two foreign firms (one manufacturing, Table 4.5; one with office workers, Table 4.6) managed not only to protect their workers, but also to give them an increase in real wages despite inflation. In both cases the costs of labor, especially unskilled labor, were not a significant consideration. Clearly the impact of inflation was most serious for the lowest-paid, most vulnerable workers.

The serious impact of the inflation of 1972-73 on the real wages of low-income workers came after a period of rapid improvement. Since 1968 plantation workers on Java, for instance, had doubled their real wage. The sharp drop over the next 18 months, 27 percent in their case, probably was especially noticeable (and resented) as a result. Public works employees had seen a 75 percent improvement and an even more severe deterioration (51 percent in 18 months). By late 1973 the dissatisfaction of wage earners likely was acute.

TABLE 4.9

Effect of Price Stability, Growth, and Inflation
on Real Wages, 1963-76
(percent)

	Mid-1960s to 1972	1972-74	1974-76
Plantations			
Indonesia	+145	-23	+28
Java	+268	-27	+19
Sumatra	+48	-28	+51
Industry	+218	-23	
Public works	-22 to +77	-51	
Foreign firms			
Industry	+65	+37	
Office	+25	+15	

Notes: Unlike Table 4.12, which compares multi-year averages in order to reduce accidental fluctuation, Table 4.9 uses single
years or half-years to compare low points and high points in real
wages.

Periods covered are as follows: Plantations—1967 to 1972-II,
1972-II to 1974-I, 1974-I to 1976. Industry—Large and medium,
1963-72; new series, 1972-I to 1973-II; these figures almost certainly understate the decline, since the sample included mostly
capital-intensive firms, many of them foreign, for whom labor is a
small share of total cost. The other series (large/medium monthly
and yearly) overstate the increase for 1963-72 and understate the
subsequent decline. There was a substantial change in composition
of the industrial sector, with an increasing proportion of capital-
intensive and foreign firms having a much higher proportion of
skilled workers. The "new series" is somewhat more reliable because it uses reports from exactly the same panel of firms.

Public works—The decline is for 1966 to 1972-I, the increase
for 1968 to 1972-I, hence a range in the first column. The decline
from 1972-76 in the second column is for 1972-I to 1973-II. Foreign
firms—1968-72, 1972-73.

Sources: Tables 4.3-4.6, 4.8-4.9.

REAL WAGES SINCE 1970

There is little question that real wages increased substantially from their low point in the mid-1960s to the early 1970s as a badly shattered economy was rebuilt. What has happened since then is less clear. Rapid economic growth has continued, even accelerated, since 1972; but it has been capital-intensive growth, requiring relatively few workers. The labor force has continued to increase as well, and with it, the demand for jobs. What has happened to the demand for labor in agriculture is in dispute. If, as has been argued, work and income sharing is declining in the rural areas, a large number of workers would no longer receive a share that is closer to the average product than to their marginal product. Their reservation price, equal to their earning ability in agriculture, would decline.

On balance, it is not clear a priori whether real wages should have continued to increase after 1970. Even if the reservation price of landowners was raised by increased average income from self-employment in agriculture, a stagnant or declining income for the landless in rural areas and those in the informal urban sector would mean a stagnant or declining reservation price for those most likely to take wage employment. In fact, it is clear that the income of a substantial group in the informal urban sector—the bicycle rickshaw pullers and the peddlers—has declined since they were excluded from large parts of Jakarta and other cities.[5] The rural wage, on the other hand, may have gone up slightly since 1970—at about 2 percent a year—(Table 4.10), although the data are spotty in the extreme. It is at least plausible that the reservation price of labor has not risen, and that there is therefore no a priori reason, from either the demand or the supply side, for wages to have risen since 1970.

In fact, the real wage for plantation workers in 1977-78 was about the same as it had been in 1970-71. The rise since 1974 simply compensated for the fall between 1972 and 1974 that resulted from accelerating inflation. The period was clearly affected by the inflationary spurt after 1972, and therefore may not be a very good test of what is happening to wages over the longer term. However, further confirmation for the thesis that plantation wages have been stagnant since 1970 comes from three other facts: (i) there was no significant change in real wages between 1970 and 1972, before the inflationary spurt; (ii) by 1978, four years after the sharp inflation of 1973-74, the real wage was still slightly below 1970-71; and (iii) the small decline for all of Indonesia is the result of a 6 percent increase in Sumatra, not a labor surplus area, and a 2 percent decline in Java, where the underemployment problem is acute (Table 4.3).

TABLE 4.10

Real Wages for Agricultural Workers
Preparing Rice Fields, 1966-77

Period	
1966-70	1.4
1970-74	1.7
1974-77	1.85
1977-79	1.95

Notes: Data collected from six villages on Java. Preliminary
unpublished data in real terms. Averages for several years used to
reduce random fluctuations. Rice prices used to deflate money
wages. Probably kilos of rice per day. Data for 1979 are generally
for the first half-year only, which tend to be higher than for the
second half-year. Probably an overestimate, therefore.
   Source: Rural Dynamics Study, Agro-Economic Survey,
Institute of Agriculture, Bogor.

A new series for construction workers is consistent with the
conclusion that stagnation in real wages continued to 1979 in the
labor-surplus area. For all of Indonesia (except for Sumatra, where
the series is incomplete), real wages of unskilled workers rose
only 3 percent in 1976-79, or 1 percent a year, on the average.
However, that increase was due to a rise in Jakarta and in the Other
Islands. For Java except Jakarta, there was actually a 10 percent
decline. (Including Jakarta there was still a 2 percent decrease;
see Table 4.11.) It is, of course, on Java that one would find concentrated any problems of increasing landlessness or of forced migration to the cities, because job opportunities were declining in the
villages. That real wages were rising in Jakarta suggests at least
some success for the policy of restricting migration to that city.
   These series also confirm the impact of inflation on real
wages. As inflation was slowed somewhat in 1977, and even more
in 1978, wages of all workers, including the unskilled, rose. Even
on Java outside Jakarta, real wages of unskilled workers rose by
8 percent in these two years. But as the rate of inflation doubled
and tripled in 1979, wages of that group dropped by 17 percent.
Other groups of construction workers experienced a similar decline
in 1979 that brought their wages back to where they had been in 1976.

TABLE 4.11

Real Wages for Construction Workers, 1976-79
(in April 1977-March 1978 prices)

	1976	1977	1978	1979
Jakarta				
Price increases (percent)		10.8	8.6	25.1
Daily paid workers				
Skilled	920	882	952	822
Semiskilled	611	603	629	600
Unskilled	466	517	566	555
Employees (monthly)				
Management	53,381	53,221	54,253	55,699
Executive	33,657	34,467	34,846	31,844
Others	29,029	30,306	29,609	29,035
Java, excluding Jakarta				
Price increases (percent)		10.4	5.3	27.2
Daily paid workers				
Skilled	714	728	773	697
Semiskilled	518	533	589	557
Unskilled	404	423	435	362
Employees (monthly)				
Management	54,579	59,766	63,568	57,710
Executive	33,669	38,283	40,997	38,683
Others	20,421	24,907	23,324	20,504
Java, including Jakarta				
Price increases (percent)		10.5	6.1	26.2
Daily paid workers				
Skilled	766	767	818	743
Semiskilled	541	551	599	568
Unskilled	420	447	468	410
Employees (monthly)				
Management	54,279	58,130	61,239	56,457
Executive	33,666	37,329	39,460	36,974
Other	22,573	26,257	24,895	22,637

	1976	1977	1978	1979
Indonesia, except Sumatra				
Price increases (percent)		10.0	5.7	24.1
Daily paid workers				
Skilled	743	766	829	738
Semiskilled	543	548	606	584
Unskilled	385	403	440	396
Employees (monthly)				
Management	51,194	53,614	56,579	53,012
Executive	32,546	34,541	36,691	34,482
Other	21,374	23,897	24,418	22,754
Sumatra				
Price increases (percent)		13.8	6.6	27.9
Daily paid workers				
Skilled		878	862	734
Unskilled		496	482	432
Employees (monthly)				
Management		52,243	59,021	56,549

Notes: The Indonesian-language descriptions of the various positions were not translated literally, but used to describe the position that seemed to be involved. (For instance, a literal translation of "other craftsmen" was changed to "semiskilled workers.") "Java, excluding Jakarta" is a simple, unweighted average of the real wages for West, Central, and East Java. "Indonesia" adds real wages for Jakarta, Bali, and South Sulawesi to the three Java provinces. A simple, unweighted average of the six real-wage figures was used. Data for Sumatra were not available for 1976, and were therefore excluded from the total, since the series would otherwise not have been comparable. For 1979 last quarter wages were generally not available; average of first three quarters used. The price increases for 1979 were calculated on a November 1978 to November 1979 basis. Nominal wages deflated by urban cost of living index for Jakarta, Bandung (West Java), Jogjakarta and Semarang (Central Java), Surabaja (East Java), Denpasar (Bali), Unjung Pandang (South Sulawesi), Medan, Padang, Palembang, Tandjungkarang (Sumatra). Where the index for more than one city was used, a simple, unweighted average was constructed.

Source: BPS, "Rata-Rata Upah Pekerja, Perusahaan Bangunan" ("Construction Workers' Wages"), various (undated typescript) issues 1976-79 for nominal wages.

Slight further evidence comes from a tiny sample of agricultural workers in six villages, collected by the Agro-Economic Survey. Using four-year averages to reduce random fluctuations, the real wages of unskilled workers on rice (hoeing) increased by 21 percent between the late 1960s and the early 1970s, but only by 14 percent in the 1970s (compare 1977-79 with 1970-74). The latter increase, a low 2 percent a year from a small sample, is probably not much greater than the margin of error (Table 4.10).

Industrial workers' wages also provide confirmation, although they appear to show quite a different pattern. Between 1970 or 1971 and 1972 there was a substantial increase in large- and medium-scale industrial wages, as shown in three different series in Table 4.5. For 1972 to 1973 or 1975 all series show essentially stagnation. The only series that continues beyond 1975 shows a further increase of 6 percent to 1977. While industrial wages show considerable increase between 1970-71 and 1975-77, these increases can largely be explained by changes in the structure of industry, to more skill-intensive activities, and to larger, more capital-intensive firms paying higher wages. If one examines wages in a single industry, textiles, one finds a 4 percent decline between 1970 and 1975 and a comparable rise in 1975 to 1977. The result is a 1977 wage practically identical with that in 1970, although even within that industry there probably was a shift to more capital- and skill-intensive types of firms.

Apparently there was a decline in the proportion of workers in medium-scale, labor-intensive, relatively low-wage firms and industries, and a rise in the proportion of higher-paid workers in larger firms, in more skill- and capital-intensive industries. That is, the increase of 68 percent in the real industrial wage between 1970 and 1977 seems to reflect more an increase in the dualistic structure of industry than an increase in the income of the broad mass of unskilled wage earners.

All of these wage calculations may need to be adjusted to an unknown degree for an implicit temporary rice subsidy during the inflation of the mid-1970s. When market prices of rice rose rapidly, the Food Logistics Board (BULOG) reportedly provided rice to public or state enterprises at a lower price. Since the price index used to deflate nominal wages is based on market prices, ignoring such an implicit subsidy, the resulting decline in real wages from 1972 to 1974 would be overstated. Real wages for state enterprises—nearly all plantations and many large-scale industrial firms—would be higher, by an unknown amount. However, if this implicit subsidy came to an end when prices stabilized in 1974 or 1975, as was reported, then the real wages calculated here are underestimated for only one to three years in the mid-1970s. The comparison between 1970-71 and 1976-77 remains accurate.

In sum, as far as one can tell from the limited data available, real wages for unskilled workers rose dramatically as the economy was restored to functioning between 1967 and 1970, but stopped rising thereafter. The number of skilled industrial workers continued to expand and their real wages probably rose as well, so average industrial wages continued to rise after 1970 as the skill mix of industry changed; but the far larger group of unskilled workers probably saw little further increase in wages after 1970. There may have been a small increase (less than 10 percent) in some series or a small decline (2 percent) in others, but the best guess is that there was little change in real wages from 1970 to 1979, in the labor surplus areas of Java.

INCOME DISTRIBUTION AND WAGES

Data on real wages provide only limited information on income distribution. However, it is clear that the average per capita income in Indonesia did not decline anything like the roughly 50 percent fall in real income estimated for wage earners between the mid-1950s and the mid-1960s. Economic stagnation during this period therefore worsened not only the absolute, but also the relative, position of workers on plantations and in industry. Their incomes are likely to have reflected the incomes of other wage earners in construction, trade, and services, and, in line with the model sketched earlier, of self-employed, unskilled workers in the rural and urban informal sectors. Workers in general, therefore, most probably experienced a deterioration in relative, as well as absolute, income to the mid-1960s.

Conversely, from the mid-1960s to 1970, real wages and income of workers increased much more than the average per capita income. Therefore, it is highly probable that wage earners and many self-employed benefited substantially, both relatively and absolutely, from the rapid recovery of the economy between 1967 and 1970. In this respect income distribution probably became more equitable during the recovery period. Certainly the rich were not the only ones to benefit from rapid growth in the late 1960s.

The situation after 1970 is more equivocal and disquieting. Since the real wages of unskilled workers seem to have stagnated between 1970 and 1977, at least on Java, while per capita income increased 5-6 percent a year, there probably was a deterioration in income distribution, at least in the wage-paying sectors.

Those in the plantation and industrial sectors obviously are not among the really poor. Their annual wage is between 100 and 200 percent of the average per capita income. If there are two incomes, but five consumers, in an average family, plantation and industrial workers would have a per capita income somewhat below the average, say in the third or fourth percentile of the income distribution. Except for the one survey of four villages mentioned and other scattered evidence, little is known about the absolute or relative income of the bulk of the really poor: the landless laborers, those with tiny holdings of land, the casual workers in the city. Industrial and plantation workers are part of the modern, organized, high-income sectors. Although they are among the poor members of these sectors, their incomes, like those of others in the modern part of the economy, is higher than incomes in the traditional, partly subsistence, small-scale sector. Income distribution in general, therefore, could have deteriorated during periods in which modern-sector wages were rising. However, it has been suggested earlier, and is discussed in more detail elsewhere, that incomes of unskilled workers move together whether they are on plantations, in industry, in the informal sector, or self-employed. In Indonesia there has been relatively little government intervention since 1966 that would raise the incomes of a labor elite. If it is therefore reasonable to believe that labor incomes generally rise and fall together, then stagnation or decline in available wage series to 1966 and since 1970 indicates deterioration in income distribution. Conversely, the rapid rise in wages means greater equality.

Within the wage-earning group different trends can be observed. In the 1970s the level of real wages for Javanese plantation workers never reached the levels of 1956 and 1957. It was only 60 percent of the admittedly more dubious figure for 1953. On the other hand, the higher-income Sumatran plantation workers substantially exceeded their 1956-57 wages in the 1970s. As a result the gap between Java and Sumatra widened from 20 percent in the mid-1950s to 50 percent in the 1970s (Table 4.3), primarily because, when the economy deteriorated from the mid-1950s to the mid-1960s, the real wages of plantation workers on Java dropped by about twice as much as those on Sumatra (Table 4.13). The regional disparities were further increased in the 1970s. By 1976-77 Sumatran wages were 6 percent above those for 1970-71, while Java's were 2 percent below the earlier average (Table 4.3).

Data on real wages in construction allow one to extend the comparison to 1979. The 1979 real wage of unskilled workers was above that for 1976 in Bali (+7 percent), Sulawesi (+29 percent), and Jakarta (+19 percent), while in the rest of Java it had decreased (-10 percent), suggesting that regional differences widened further. Similarly, wages of unskilled public works laborers in one north Sumatra province in 1971-72 did not reach the level of 1966-67 (Table 4.6). That province is, in economic terms, more an extension of Java than it is part of Sumatra. In short, regional income disparities increased as the pressure of population on Java kept wages down.

In industry there were differential changes as well. During the period of decline in real wages (mid-1950s to mid-1960s), employees of foreign firms apparently suffered the least. Presumably those firms had the greatest surplus to be tapped. Unskilled workers in industry in larger industrial firms suffered less than those in smaller firms or white-collar workers. Their real wage dropped by half (see "Daily/Weekly" workers, Table 4.5). Their political and economic bargaining power enabled them to gain a larger share than other groups of the income accruing to the industrial sector. Workers in medium-scale industry, with less bargaining power and, in many cases, less of a surplus to tap, saw their wage reduced to less than one-third of what it had been. If data were available on small-scale firms, their workers, with the least bargaining power, would almost certainly have proved to suffer even more. The upper income groups in industry (clerical, technical, management), paid on a monthly basis, had the least political weight and lost the most, with their real wage dropping to one-quarter of what it had been.

What happened, as a result, to income distribution within industry during 1955-65 is difficult to estimate with any precision. The highest income groups (monthly paid workers) and the lowest (employed by medium-scale firms) suffered the most, while those in the middle (production workers and all workers employed by foreign firms) lost much less. However, since there are many more workers employed by medium- (and small-) scale firms than there are in the highest income group, income distribution within industry most probably deteriorated during the period of economic decline.

Detailed data do not seem to be available on the effects of growth, since 1968, on the distribution of income within industry. However, workers in medium-scale industry gained substantially more than those in large-scale firms if one compares 1963 and 1970. The lower-income workers therefore seem to have gained more from growth, just as they lost more from deterioration, than their somewhat better-paid counterparts.

Within the construction industry, wage disparities became more pronounced in the labor-surplus regions. For Java, excluding Jakarta, unskilled workers' real wages declined between 1976 and 1979 while the wages of semiskilled workers, and of all white-collar employees, rose. In the other regions there is no clear-cut pattern, with unskilled workers sometimes doing as well as or better than other groups. Of course all of these data are for only four years, so not too much should be read into them.

In sum, since wage earners as a whole lost during the period of deterioration, and among wage earners the position of the lower-income groups deteriorated the most (plantation workers in Java versus those in Sumatra, employees of medium-scale versus large-scale industry), there seems little doubt that with respect to wage earners, income distribution became less egalitarian as the economy stagnated. Conversely, during the period of rehabilitation (mid-1960s to early 1970s), wage earners as a group gained substantially and within that group the poorest gained the most, so income distribution improved in that respect. However, between 1970 and 1976-78 wage earners may have gained little or nothing, and this stagnation may reflect that of other lower-income groups. Since rapid growth in national income continued, income distribution is likely to have deteriorated. This conclusion is clearly consistent with that reached in the preceding essay, although it is based on different sources of information.

THE EFFECT OF COMMODITY PRICES

In a well-functioning labor market, one that is efficient in economic terms, wages for unskilled workers would be similar in different occupations and regions. But real wages in Indonesia differed greatly by regions. Workers on rubber or tea plantations in Sumatra were in the 1960s generally able to buy 50-70 percent more rice with their wage than those in Java. Regional disparities are obviously substantial and have been increasing.

Such regional differences are well-known in most countries, a result of relative labor scarcities and imperfect labor markets. In Indonesia substantial differences existed in real wages for workers producing different commodities in the same region. Moreover, relative real wages on plantations in Java moved in different directions from year to year for workers producing different crops. To a substantial extent—45 out of 75 cases—when the price of the commodity produced increased relative to other crops, the real wage also increased and vice versa. This correlation between prices of commodity produced and wages runs counter to economic theory.

A plausible explanation is similar to part of the explanation advanced for the correlation between the general economic situation and wages. If prices for a commodity rise and plantation income is higher, management may be both more willing and more able to raise wages, for both economic (profit-maximizing) and noneconomic (trouble-avoiding) reasons: to keep workers' goodwill, avoid disruptions, improve workers' well-being, and encourage greater effort to raise output.

TABLE 4.12

Regression Analysis: Real Wages and Commodity Prices, 1953–72

Real Wages =	Constant	Commodity Prices	Price Level	State of Economy	R-Square	F	D.W.
	-0.08 (-2.5)	0.26 (2.0)	0.03 (3.0)	0.16 (3.5)	0.24	8.7	2.4
	0.07 (-2.2)	0.26 (2.0)		0.16 (3.1)	0.16	7.9	2.6
	-0.8 (-0.3)	0.31 (2.3)	0.03 (2.6)		0.13	6.1	2.3

Notes: All plantation (estate) crops for which appropriate commodity prices could be found were included in the analysis. Most such crops are produced primarily for export, and the world market price is more relevant than the domestic price. For sugar, consumed domestically, the domestic price was used. The analysis covered rubber, coffee, tobacco, sugar, and tea, and the periods 1953–63 and 1966–72. (The year 1962 was arithmetically interpolated.)

For the price level the second derivative was used to represent changes in the rate of price increase or decrease.

A dummy variable distinguished the period before 1965 from the period after 1966.

For real wages, the dependent variable, the change from the previous year was used.

Ordinary least-squares regressions were calculated for the 85 observations available.

Figures in parentheses are t-statistics.

Sources: See Table 4.3.

In addition to management's increased ability and willingness to raise wages when enterprises are more profitable, workers' expectations are likely to rise with profitability. As a result there may be greater costs to a given, unchanged wage, with greater disruption and lower productivity if the workers' (higher) expectations are not met.

An attempt was made to provide more rigorous support for this hypothesis by postulating that the share of wages in value added is a reasonable proxy for profitability, and that whenever that share deviates too much from the "normal" (that is, the average), real wages will be adjusted to bring them back near the average. This test did not give consistent and significant results, but this may be due less to an incorrect hypothesis than to faulty specification (for example, the deviation of the wage share from the average may not reflect profitability) and inadequate data (changes in value added can be estimated only by finding some price for the commodities and multiplying by reported output—and both are likely to be inaccurate, especially during periods when the official exchange rate is a multiple of the effective rate). Using relative commodity prices as a proxy for profitability, by comparing changes in the price of a particular crop with the changes in prices of all plantation crops, does show a correlation between movements in relative prices and real wages in roughly two-thirds of the cases. Of course that test suffers from various defects, most notably the failure to take account of other causal variables. In a multiple-correlation analysis for permanent workers only, relative commodity prices proved to be highly significant, but the general explanatory power of the equation was low.

CONCLUSIONS: FACTORS INFLUENCING CHANGES IN REAL WAGES

Trends in Indonesian wages contradict the argument that rapid economic growth does not benefit the lower-income groups, that it benefits only the rich. Indonesian data also consistently contradict an assumption of the labor-surplus theories: that real wages remain constant in labor-surplus economies until all the disguised unemployed are absorbed, that there is a perfectly elastic supply of labor at the prevailing wage, determined by custom or subsistence needs. Rather, it appears that real wages were influenced by the rate of growth of the economy and whether the pattern of growth was labor-intensive, the rate of inflation, and factors other than the rate of growth that affected profitability.

TABLE 4.13

Percentage Changes in Wages and Prices over Time, 1957–75

	Plantation Labor			Manufacturing		Household Servants
	All Indonesia	Java	Sumatra	Large	Medium	
Long-term trends						
Mid-1960s/mid-1950s	-63	-67	-37	-50	-34	-66
	(1953-57 to 1963, 1966, 1967)			(1954-57 to 1963-66)	(1958-60 to 1963, 1965, 1966)	(1953-55 to 1962-64)
Early 1970s/mid-1960s	91	114	54	58	98	—
	(1963, 1966, 1967 to 1970-73)			(1963-66 to 1971-73)		
Sharp price changes						
Early 1970s						
Prices, previous	417	408	460			
current	8.7	10.2	5.9			
Wages	86	98	36			
Time period	1966-68 to 1969-71					
				New Series		_Public Works_
1972-74						
Prices	104.1	80.0	113.4	52.7		71.5
Wages	-23.8	-26.6	-27.7	-22.5		-50.8
Time period	(1972 II to 1974 I)			(1972 I to 1973 II)		(1972 I to 1973 II)
1974-75						
Prices	19.7	23.9	4.9			
Wages	26.7	23.8	39.9			
Time period	(1974 I to 1975 II)					

Notes: Since Indonesian real wages show a steady trend and not much annual fluctuation, an average of the beginning years/half-years has been compared with an average of the final years/half-years to show the trend in its clearest form. Prices are annual averages for the later period. However, for 1972-74 the price increase for 1973 has been shown. "Previous" prices show rapid inflation in late 1960s; "current" prices show relative stability in 1969-71.

Sources: Tables 4.3-4.6.

113

The last point, with relative prices of the commodity produced by a group of workers used as a proxy for profitability, was tested in the regressions of Table 4.12. The other two factors are tested in the regressions of Table 4.14 (with the effect of the rate of inflation also shown in Table 4.13), which are quite typical of a much larger number of regression analyses carried out with the same variables. In general, at least the current-price variable and the rate of (labor-intensive) growth (dummy) variable proved quite significant.

The state of the economy influenced wages through several causal linkages.

First, the reservation price of labor. If, as a result of rapid growth, income in self-employment increased, workers would logically demand a higher wage before they accepted wage employment. Conversely, when the economy stagnated or deteriorated, workers in agriculture receiving a share of the average product, because they share in the income from the family land or are sharecroppers or because they receive a fixed share in the harvest, would see their income stagnate or decline, and would be willing to work for the same or a lower wage than previously. The situation would be similar for self-employment outside of agriculture. When the economy deteriorates, those who share in the income of an activity, from shoe shiners to ditch diggers to construction workers, find their income declining and, as a result, lower their reservation wage.

More specifically, the income of many self-employed persons approximates the average, not the marginal, product in the activity, because there is work sharing and income sharing. Most wage earners are hired only if their marginal product equals or exceeds their wage. But there is a group that shares in the agricultural income and in some informal-sector activities, but whose income and reservation wage can be reduced by the decisions of employers or government. One important part of this group is the agricultural workers, who have shared in the harvest under traditional social arrangements. That is, harvesters as a group receive a share of the harvest regardless of the number of people who participate, even though a much smaller number could bring in the harvest at less cost to the landlord. Once the landlord decides to reduce the number of harvesters in order to increase his income, the income of some workers may drop so low that they are forced into commercial wage employment (if available) or, more likely, into self-employment areas where there are few barriers to entry, such as petty trade. Similarly, when the government reduces the earning opportunities of bicycle rickshaw pullers or street peddlers, it may force them into other forms of self-employment. In either case

TABLE 4.14

Plantation Wages Regressed on Prices and the State of the Economy, 1953-75

	Constant	Current Prices	Lagged Prices	State of Economy	R^2
Permanent Indonesia	0.16 (0.16)	0.53 (0.94)	-0.07 (-0.43)	1.23 (1.02)	0.15
Permanent Java	-0.03 (-0.7)	0.71 (36.4)	0.13 (2.48)	0.09 (1.7)	0.99
Permanent Sumatra	0.02 (0.38)	0.65 (22.45)	0.07 (1.75)	0.08 (1.03)	0.98
Temporary Indonesia	-0.001 (-0.003)	0.70 (8.55)	-0.12 (-8.7)	0.01 (0.02)	0.94
Permanent and temporary Indonesia	0.03 (0.66)	0.72 (27.15)	0.28 (9.08)	0.11 (1.68)	0.99
Permanent rubber	-0.002 (-0.04)	0.74 (26.10)	0.02 (3.14)	0.07 (1.16)	0.99
Permanent coffee	-0.02 (-0.4)	0.61 (25.01)	0.02 (3.08)	0.13 (2.52)	0.99
Permanent and temporary rubber	-0.04 (-0.58)	0.75 (20.39)		0.18 (2.03)	0.97
Permanent and temporary coffee	-0.02 (-0.41)	0.62 (20.86)		0.16 (2.37)	0.97

Notes: Figures in parentheses = t statistics. Table generally covers 20 years. Dependent variable is the nominal wage. The "State of Economy" variable is a dummy, distinguishing the period 1953-63 from 1966-75.
Source: Table 4.3.

115

the average product in these unprotected, "open" self-employment activities drops as more people enter, and with it their reservation wage.

A stagnant average product in agriculture from 1953 to 1965 is, then, consistent with a declining reservation price for labor, and consequently declining wages, if the larger landlords, civil servants, military, and others appropriated a slightly larger share of stagnant output. They would leave the landless and smallholders with a smaller average income and lower reservation wage. This phenomenon would be aggravated if a decline in the income of the middle class, industrial workers, and others also decreased the demand for, and therefore the average income of, the self-employed in the cities. During rapid recovery from 1967 to 1970, average self-employment income probably grew quite rapidly, and with it the reservation price of labor. Since 1970 the more slowly rising average product in agriculture, combined with a reduction in social and political pressures for work sharing and income sharing in the rural areas and declining opportunities for some self-employment in the cities, could have kept the reservation price from rising.

If large numbers have had to abandon relatively well compensated work and income-sharing activities, it would explain why plantation wages have not risen since 1970, although the average product in agriculture has continued to increase. The increased average income may no longer be shared among all in the rural sector, and the reservation price of agricultural labor therefore may not have been rising with the average product.

Second, the willingness and ability to pay more for economic reasons. With rapid growth, more enterprises are likely to be profitable and to experience increased demand, than in a stagnant or declining economy. They would then have good economic reasons to raise wages for existing employees rather than hire new ones at the prevailing wage if there are turnover costs, there is the risk that the additional employees cannot be fired if the demand increase proves temporary, higher wages reduce absenteeism, theft, disruption, and other problems that now become more costly. That is, the returns from increased labor productivity exceed the increased wage cost, and hiring additional labor is a more costly option for raising output.

Third, employees' expectations. Employers may find it particularly worthwhile to raise wages if the profitability of many enterprises has raised employees' expectations and failure to raise wages causes more output-reducing activities than occurred during the period when the enterprise was not profitable. In other words, a given wage that is acceptable and provides sufficient incentives to employees when the enterprise is losing money may result in output-reducing actions when the enterprise is profitable.

Fourth, employers' noneconomic objectives. Managers of enterprises usually do not have maximum profit as their sole objective. They can be willing to raise wages when they can afford to do so, even if there is no economic need for higher wages, simply because they prefer a more contented labor force. It is not unreasonable, after all, to prefer having cheerful people around, rather than those who scowl and mutter.

All four reasons probably contributed to the substantial fall in wages when the economy deteriorated to the mid-1960s and the substantial rise thereafter, when the economy improved.

The second factor influencing real wages, the rate of inflation and changes in that rate, is more conventional. Nominal wages will lag behind prices: (i) if wages are adjusted for price changes with a lag and (ii) if the current rate of inflation is expected to continue, nominal wages are adjusted beforehand in line with that expectation, in order to stabilize real wages, and inflation then accelerates. If both phenomena occur simultaneously, nominal wages will lag considerably behind rapidly changing prices. Real wages will fall when inflation is high and accelerating, while wages will rise when it is low and decelerating.

Both mechanisms for adjusting nominal wages for changes in prices can coexist, either because some enterprises adjust wages retroactively and others prospectively, or because most enterprises do some of both. There is good evidence that this was the case in Indonesia, and that high and accelerating inflation in the mid-1960s contributed to lower real wages; that low and decelerating inflation in the late 1960s contributed to rising wages; and that renewed acceleration of inflation from 1972 to 1974 sharply lowered wages, while bringing inflation under control thereafter raised wages again from 1974 to 1976. Even lower inflation in 1978 produced a sharp increase in real wages in construction, while a doubling of the inflation rate sharply reduced real wages in 1979.

Finally, profitability is, of course, influenced not only by the state of the economy as a whole but also by international price movements and the efficiency of management. These other factors in profitability can influence wages, in the same way as changes in profitability due to the role of growth.

CONCLUSIONS: WAGE TRENDS AND THE
EFFECT OF POLICIES

In Indonesia, as a result of the impact of growth, of commodity prices, and of changes in the prices of wage goods (the rate of inflation), workers' real wages changed substantially between 1953 and 1979.

Wage earners in industry, on plantations, and elsewhere suffered from the stagnant economy until 1967 and benefited from rapid recovery thereafter. In any country, when income declines, the struggle for a share is bound to be fierce; and it is more likely that wage earners will be among the losers than that the ruling elite will be. In Indonesia even policies to benefit workers specifically, including those that forced an increase in the number of workers employed, were not effective for workers as a whole, since they contributed to stagnation in the economy at the same time. Workers would, of course, have benefited the most from a government that both increased growth and adopted specific measures to redistribute income in their favor.

The losses of wage earners as a result of economic stagnation were not only absolute but also relative. Within the wage-earning group it was the lowest income receivers who lost the most. When income rose with rehabilitation, it was the poorer groups who benefited the most. Since 1970, however, it appears to be the skilled workers in capital-intensive industries, as well as workers in Sumatra, who have gained, while unskilled workers in labor-intensive industries and plantation workers on Java have not. Increasing the demand for labor by emphasizing labor-intensive activities would, by increasing the number of jobs in the relatively well-paying modern sectors, reduce the number of workers in self-employed work and income-sharing activities while increasing the demand for their output. As a result the reservation wage, and with it wages in the economy as a whole, would rise. The capital-intensive pattern of investment in the 1970s, in contrast, contributed to stagnation in real wages.

Gains or losses in income were partly due to changes in the reservation price of labor. This in turn depends on the average product in self-employment activities, especially in agriculture, and how that is shared among landlords, tenants, and workers. Government policies that increase output in agriculture can therefore raise wage income throughout the economy. Equally important is the avoidance of policies that reduce self-employment income in the cities or that reduce the share of the lower income groups in agriculture (for instance, by "tractorization" of agriculture). Labor-intensive works programs can also increase the reservation price of labor, and thus affect not only the income of those employed but of others as well.

Regional income distribution for wage earners worsened. With rising population pressure on Java, the poorer wage earners fell behind those in regions with a better population-resource ratio. It would obviously be desirable to accelerate population movements out of, and job movements into, Java.

Government price-stabilization programs and policies were crucial in some years, in preventing a drop in workers' real income and a deterioration in income distribution. In more general terms, government policy on the prices of wage goods can be a powerful tool for influencing real wages.

Since real wages were also affected by the prices (earnings) of the commodities produced, policy on the prices of output (such as export taxes) could be used as another tool to affect the income of workers. However, real wages did not adjust quickly or fully to changes in relative output prices. Therefore, changes in commodity prices had a disproportionate effect on profits, and commodity tax changes were required to avoid excess profits on rising prices and substantial deficits on falling ones.

Nominal wages did not adjust quickly to changes in the price level, even when price increases were concentrated in wage goods. Presumably wages therefore will adjust even more slowly to price changes concentrated on goods consumed by the middle- and upper-income groups. Therefore, in the exchange rate government has a potential tool for influencing the real foreign-exchange cost of labor. A higher exchange rate might result in substantially more employment at only a somewhat lower real wage.

If short-term, but potentially brutal, declines in real wages are to be avoided, with all their consequences in terms of social and political tension, prices of wage goods need to be stabilized.

In short, the wage-determination mechanism or model described here implies that the principal longer-term determinant of the price of labor, and therefore a major determinant of income distribution and the absolute income of the poor, is the reservation price of labor in traditional, work- and income-sharing sectors. Since the reservation price depends on the number of workers in those sectors and the value of their output, the crucial policy variable determining the income of the poor majority is the number of jobs created in the commercial sector in relation to the number of persons seeking such jobs, either as additions to the labor force or because they are driven out of the traditional sectors. Over the longer term, then, the real wage depends on the rate of increase in population; the decline in income-earning opportunities in some traditional, work- and income-sharing activities as a result of technological, social, or institutional change (such as elimination of hand-pounding of rice, commercialization of rice harvesting); the number of new jobs in the commercial sector, determined by that sector's growth rate and its labor intensity; the growth in output in the traditional sector, determined by demand for its services and its costs.

Government policies that increase the demand for unskilled labor will raise wages, even in the labor-surplus economy of Java, and thereby improve the absolute income of the poor. Since Indonesia already has a high rate of economic growth, a crucial question for poverty alleviation is the pattern, that is, the labor intensity, of that growth. In the short term the stabilization of prices of wage goods is crucial to real wages; in the longer term job creation is crucial.

Neglect of either or both can result not only in hardship but also in political problems. The relatively widespread support for agitation against the Sukarno government in 1964 was probably affected by the sharp decline in real wages that had taken place throughout the economy for a decade. In the same way the support for the agitation started by students in 1973-74, and the lack of such support for similar agitation in 1977-78, may have been influenced by declining wages in the earlier period and by rising wages in the later period. Not unexpectedly, both short- and long-term economic changes had important political consequences. The near stagnation in wages during the 1970s, while average income was rising rapidly, implies serious problems for the future if not corrected soon.

NOTES

1. The countries are India, Pakistan, and Bangladesh in G. F. Papanek, "Real Wages, Growth, Inflation, Income Distribution and Politics in Pakistan, India, Bangladesh and Indonesia," Discussion Papers 29 and 30 (Boston: Department of Economics and Center for Asian Development Studies, Boston University, 1978). (Mimeographed.)

2. Plantation and municipal workers' wages calculated from A. van Merle, man. ed., Selected Studies on Indonesia by Dutch Scholars; industrial workers' wages, from H. J. van Ooorschot, Industrial Development in Indonesia.

3. Papanek, "Real Wages . . . Indonesia."

4. The proposed mechanism is more clearly specified in ibid.

5. See G. F. Papanek and Dorodjatun Kuntjoro Jakti, "The Poor of Jakarta," Economic Development and Cultural Change 24, no. 1 (October 1975): 1-27.

5

MIGRATION, EMPLOYMENT, AND EARNINGS
Bisrat Aklilu and John R. Harris

Received theory and empirical research have long postulated and verified that the initial phases of economic development involve a transfer of human, physical, and financial resources from the relatively sluggish regions and sectors (rural areas and agriculture) to the more dynamic and expanding regions and sectors (urban areas and secondary and tertiary activities). While structural change through such a transfer of resources has its associated benefits and costs, there is a consensus that, on balance, the process leads to a net positive effect on factor productivities and, hence, on total production as well as regional and sectoral distribution. (For a recent challenge to this generalization, see Lipton 1976.)

Such an optimistic macro evaluation of the process of economic development, however true it may be, is of limited value to national planners. Policy makers in developing countries have lately realized that development, in the short run, has certain negative features that are often disproportionately borne by certain groups. The issues of unemployment, poverty, and more skewed income distribution are examples of important problems with such immediate impact that solutions cannot be left solely to long-run adjustments.

Indonesia is an example of a developing country that has long experienced a rate of urbanization that outstrips the rate of employment creation in the expanding industrial, manufacturing, and service sectors. Policy makers therefore have attempted to stop or slow down the rapid urbanization of major cities. The most dramatic example was the declaration of Jakarta as a "closed city" to new migrants in 1971. This was bound to fail, since the policy had to be framed without an adequate understanding of the fundamental causes of population movements.

To obtain a better understanding of the causes and effects of population movements, a survey of migration was conducted in 1973 by the Indonesian National Institute of Economic and Social Research (LEKNAS). The survey was sponsored by the National Development Planning Board (BAPPENAS), since an understanding of the nature, structure, and determinants of labor earnings was crucial for employment-oriented development strategy for the Second Five-Year Plan.

One of the major objectives of the migration survey was a careful examination of the nature of the various labor submarkets, through identifying the skill and education requirements, the means of entry, the wage determination mechanism—in short, the income-earning opportunities of migrants in both "formal" and "informal" urban sectors. This essay reports some of the findings with respect to migrants in Java.

SAMPLING METHOD OF THE SURVEY

An explanation of the sampling method will be helpful in understanding the results. The survey was undertaken in 24 cities of various size in all of Java, North, West, and South Sumatra, and South Sulawesi. Since these cities are of different sizes and are spatially distributed, they have different economic structures that provide a range of opportunities, thus enabling us to capture information on migrants with different socioeconomic backgrounds.

The rukun tetangga (RT), the smallest administrative unit in Indonesia, was the basic enumeration unit used for both the 1973 migration survey and the 1971 census. The RT is composed of about 40 to 50 households. Within each of the 24 cities, the survey included two different types of population samples. The major (household) sample was drawn by randomly selecting a list of RT from the official city lists. The total number of RT selected in each city was based on the target number of interviews set for that city and the number of migrants expected in each RT. All migrants residing in each chosen RT were interviewed. A migrant was defined by the survey as any person 15 years of age or over who had moved from outside of the city of the interview in the previous five years (since January 1, 1968).

In the course of the household survey, this sample was found to exclude the more recent and lowest-income migrants. The sampling bias was mainly a result of the administrative system of Indonesian cities, which at times fails to "officially recognize" the dwellings of the very poor—those living as squatters, in cardboard shelters, under bridges, and so on. In some cities, such as Jakarta, in order to be officially acknowledged as belonging to an RT, the system required households to obtain identity cards whose costs were prohibitive to recent and poor migrants. (Gordon Temple has estimated the cost as equivalent to 15 days' urban labor. See Temple 1975, p. 57.)

In an attempt to correct the upward bias of the household sample, a purposive cluster sample was taken of those occupations and areas likely to be frequented by migrants, including squatters, petty traders, bicycle rickshaw or trishaw (betjak) drivers, and prostitutes. A target number of interviews of migrants belonging to the above four groups was undertaken, although the sampling frame is unknown.

This essay deals with all migrants, the household as well as the four cluster samples, in the 14 cities of Java. Table 5.1 gives the sample sizes in the different categories for those cities.

The specific questions that the present study will deal with are the following:

1. How the labor force participation rates and unemployment rates vary among migrants.
2. The major occupations migrants are engaged in, compared with their occupations before migration as well as their first occupations after migration—that is, the occupational mobility of migrants.
3. The structure and pattern of employment in the formal and and informal sectors.
4. The determinants of earnings of migrants who are employed.

SOME CHARACTERISTICS OF THE MIGRANTS

The age, sex, and educational characteristics of migrants are shown in Table 5.2. The age profile shows that the migration is dominated by the young. About 70 percent of both male and female migrants are under 25 years of age, with the largest group in the 15–18 age bracket. Less than 11 percent of the migrants of both sexes are over 36 years of age.

The educational distribution of the migrants indicates a rather strong relationship between migration and education. Over one-third of the migrants have at least a junior high school diploma, while about a fifth have graduated from a senior high school. Compared with the adult population of either urban or rural areas in Indonesia, the migrants have better education (Table 5.3). The difference is largely due to somewhat higher educational attainment by female migrants than other female urban dwellers, and more education at

TABLE 5.1

Populations of Survey Cities in Java, 1973

City or Area	1971 Population (1,000)	Household Sample	Squatters	Petty Traders	Trishaw Drivers	Prostitutes	Total Sample
Jakarta	4,576.0	3,080	213	322	238	356	4,209
Central Java							
Surakarta (Solo)	414.3	845	45	194	147	50	1,281
Purwokerto	658.9	373	48	102	48	25	596
Semarang	646.6	910	94	168	193	99	1,464
Tegal	106.0	342	74	50	73	72	611
West Java							
Bandung	1,200.4	1,124	97	194	166	100	1,681
Sukabumi	96.2	421	30	91	128	36	706
Tjirebon	178.5	411	—	105	95	—	611
East Java							
Surabaja	1,556.3	2,003	185	408	198	195	2,989
Malang	422.4	721	49	46	97	49	962
Jember	122.7	405	24	49	75	25	578
Kediri	178.9	288	24	25	24	25	386
Madiun	136.2	392	23	49	76	22	562
Jogjakarta	342.3	947	47	195	144	50	1,383
Total	10,635.7	12,262	953	1,998	1,702	1,104	18,019

Sources: Total in column one from BPS, Population of Indonesia, 1971 Census; totals in all other columns from 1973 Survey of Migration.

TABLE 5.2

Age, Sex, and Educational Characteristics of Migrants: Java, 1973

(percent)

Educational Level	Male						Female					
	Age					All Male	Age					All Female
	15-18	19-21	22-25	26-35	36+		15-18	19-21	22-25	26-35	36+	
No education	3.3	3.7	5.9	15.3	25.9	9.0	11.4	16.4	18.4	30.2	49.0	21.0
Primary education, no diploma	21.0	19.3	28.81	30.3	32.3	25.1	28.7	25.7	29.8	27.0	21.8	27.3
Primary diploma	29.4	22.0	28.7	25.5	20.3	25.7	25.4	18.2	19.8	19.7	15.7	21.2
Junior high diploma	32.1	10.6	12.0	10.6	10.6	17.0	26.2	13.7	14.2	10.9	8.8	16.8
Senior high diploma	7.6	22.1	14.3	11.5	7.1	12.7	5.2	13.6	12.4	8.4	3.6	8.4
Academy or university	6.5	22.2	10.9	6.8	3.8	10.5	3.1	12.5	5.4	3.7	1.1	5.4
Number of migrants	3,226	2,518	1,817	2,310	1,382	11,253	2,573	1,421	945	1,006	637	6,582

Note: Total responses differ in number between tables because of non-response to certain questions.
Source: 1973 Survey of Migration.

125

TABLE 5.3

Percentage Distribution of the Indonesian Population
15 Years and over, by Educational Attainment, 1971

Educational Attainment	Urban		Rural	
	Male	Female	Male	Female
No school or less than elementary diploma	34.0	55.6	68.0	83.0
Elementary school	33.7	25.6	25.6	14.6
Junior high school	17.6	11.9	4.5	1.9
Senior high school	11.8	6.1	1.7	0.5
Academy or university	2.9	0.9	0.2	0.0
Total	100.0	100.0	100.0	100.0
Number of people	5,833,230	6,011,226	26,013,605	28,454,419

Source: BPS, Population of Indonesia, 1971 Census, ser. D, as reported in Suharso et al. (1976), p. 51.

126

the academy and university levels for male migrants (10 percent) than other urban males (3 percent).

The percentage of women migrants who have earned diplomas is consistently lower than that of men migrants at all levels of education. This is also true for the adult Indonesian population of both urban and rural areas.

The fact that migration to the cities of Java is dominated by the young and those with some education is consistent with the now generally accepted economic explanations of migration decisions. In view of the fact that migration alters the lifetime income of the participants, it is evident that the expected rate of return from migration is higher for the young and educated, thereby inducing them to move. This finding about the effect of human capital on migration decisions has been found to be true in Africa (Barnum and Sabot 1976) and Latin America (Schultz 1971; Yap 1976).

With respect to marital status, approximately equal proportions (42 percent) of the migrants of both sexes are married (Table 5.4). However, virtually all of the remaining males report themselves as single (never married), while some 20 percent of the females are widowed or divorced. It is a general pattern in Indonesia for females to marry much earlier than males, and divorce is quite common. However, given the regional and ethnic variations in the status of women, custom, inheritance law, and so on, it is hard to know fully the meaning, causes, and implication of the apparent association of family breakup and migration for Indonesian women.

TABLE 5.4

Percentage Distribution of Migrants' Marital Status: Java, 1973

Marital Status	Male	Female	Total
Single	52.8	36.5	46.8
Married	42.5	41.1	42.0
Widower/widow	2.7	9.8	5.3
Divorced	2.0	12.0	5.9
Total	100.0	100.0	100.0
Number of people	11,392	6,627	18,019

Source: 1973 Survey of Migration.

Half of the male migrants and 36 percent of female migrants revealed that they had visited their city of present location at least once before making the migration decision. Such prior visits provide migrants firsthand information about the nature of the labor market, the status of previous migrants, and the amenities as well as adverse conditions that await them. In short, visits to the prospective city of migration, before the decision to migrate is taken, will reduce some of the element of risk inherent in moving to a new situation.

More than 75 occupations were listed by the migrants and were grouped under 15 general categories. (A list of the 75 occupations and the categories to which they are assigned is given in the appendix.)

Tables 5.5 and 5.6 show the distribution of migrants by previous job (job before migration) and present job (the job the migrant had at the time of the interview). The most striking observation for both the male and female migrants is the high rate of declared unemployment before migration. The rate is 16 and 17 percent for males and females, respectively, before migration, and falls dramatically to 3 and 3.6 percent after migration. The differences in the unemployment rates of migrants of different ages and educational backgrounds, and the policy implications of these figures, are discussed in detail in a later section of this essay.

Agriculture constituted the single most important occupation before migration, accounting for 24 and 14 percent of the total male and female migrants, respectively. The other important occupations were services and trade, and 8.5 percent of the female migrants indicated that they were previously domestic servants. The other urban-oriented occupations, although not important as sources of previous employment, had quite a few migrants distributed among them. This would suggest that the rural areas, although important, are by no means the sole source of migration.

THE URBAN LABOR MARKET

Early extensions of the Harris-Todaro expected-income model of migration (Harris and Todaro 1970) assumed that the urban informal sector easily absorbs recent migrants who are unable to get "prized" modern-sector jobs. Since then, those concerned with employment and unemployment in less-developed countries have attempted to clarify the nature and structure of the informal sector, and its relationship to the formal sector, through the goods it produces and services it performs (Webb 1975; Mazumdar 1975; Sethuraman 1974). The ILO study of Kenya argued that the informal

TABLE 5.5

Occupations of Male Migrants Before and After Migration: Java, 1973

Occupation	Occupation Prior to Migration		Percent Who Report Present Occupation Same as Premigration Occupation	Present Occupation		Percent Whose First Occupation in City Was Same as Present Occupation
	Number	Percent of Total		Number	Percent of Total	
Student	3,163	29.5	69.4	2,252	20.4	97.3
Housewife	—		—	—	—	—
Agriculture	2,641	24.6	1.5	45	0.4	73.3
Traditional transport	175	1.6	80.6	1,907	17.3	96.2
Motor transport	75	0.7	80.0	134	1.2	92.3
Domestic service	250	2.3	12.0	134	1.2	71.1
Peddling service, and trade	413	3.9	50.6	1,399	12.7	90.3
Settled service, and trade	876	8.2	63.0	1,941	17.6	92.6
Daily worker	289	2.7	25.3	480	4.3	71.6
Production/manual	349	3.3	28.9	602	5.4	81.1
Lower clerical	367	3.4	77.9	714	6.5	95.7
Manager-administrator	263	2.5	66.5	386	3.5	95.2
Scavenger	69	0.6	94.2	436	3.9	90.3
Unemployed	1,763	16.4	7.3	336	3.0	93.2
Other	26	0.2	67.9	266	2.6	—
Total	10,719	99.4		11,032	100.0	

Note: Totals do not necessarily add to 100 percent because of rounding.
Source: 1973 Survey of Migration.

TABLE 5.6

Occupations of Female Migrants Before and After Migration: Java, 1973

Occupation	Previous Occupation		Percent Who Report Present Occupation Same as Premigration Occupation	Present Occupation		Percent Whose First Occupation in City Was Same as Present Occupation
	Number	Percent of Total		Number	Percent of Total	
Student	1,490	22.7	66.9	1,036	15.8	97.6
Housewife	1,712	26.1	73.8	1,943	29.6	96.4
Agriculture	921	14.0	0.2	3	—	—
Traditional transport	3	—	—	18	0.3	—
Motor transport	2	—	—	4	—	—
Domestic service	558	8.5	39.2	657	10.0	84.1
Peddling service, and trade	89	1.4	31.5	175	2.7	85.6
Settled service, and trade	276	4.2	46.7	440	6.7	89.6
Daily worker	19	0.3	—	20	0.3	80.0
Production/manual	92	1.4	41.3	373	5.7	93.8
Lower clerical	40	0.6	47.5	119	1.8	93.6
Manager-administrator	96	1.5	55.2	140	2.1	94.6
Scavenger	27	0.4	88.9	232	3.5	99.0
Prostitute	66	1.0	93.9	1,124	17.1	99.0
Unemployed	1,130	17.2	11.3	234	3.6	83.3
Other	42	0.6	—	46	0.7	—
Total	6,563	99.9		6,564	99.9	

Note: Totals do not necessarily add to 100 percent because of rounding.
Source: 1973 Survey of Migration.

sector, far from being transient, is a permanent source of employment for a sizable portion of the urban labor force (ILO 1972). In
recognition of its efficiency, in that factor use in this sector is much
closer to a reflection of opportunity costs, the study advocated that
governments should abandon the negative attitude that has often led
them to adopt policy measures that discriminate explicitly or implicitly against the sector and in favor of the formal sector.

There is little disagreement that urban labor markets are differentiated with respect to one or more of the following conditions:
terms of employment; scale of operation, particularly in the use of
capital; hours of work per day; conditions of entry and extent of
labor turnover; nature of wage determination. Nevertheless, there
is a growing consensus that the distinction between the two sectors
is not as sharp as earlier studies have suggested. Distinctions between the formal and informal sectors are even fuzzier in Indonesia
than in some countries in Africa or Latin America. Unlike Kenya
or Brazil, Indonesia does not have minimum-wage legislation or
strong labor unions that differentiate and protect the interests of the
labor force in the modern sector.

However, in order to test some of the standard hypotheses
about the informal sector and to permit comparison with other work,
we have categorized the different occupations into formal and informal sectors, using two criteria.

The first criterion used information about the employer as the
determining factor. Those who are self-employed or are employed
by family, friends, or strangers were classified as belonging to the
informal sector, while those who worked for government or large
private firms were classified in the formal sector. Under this definition 78 percent of the male and 80 percent of the female migrants
were found to be in the informal sector.

The second criterion distinguished the two sectors on the basis
of information about the nature of the occupations (see Tables 5.5
and 5.6). Migrants in the categories of lower clerical, manager-
administrator, and manual production workers were placed in the
formal sector, while all other occupations were classified as belonging to the informal sector. Eighty percent of the male and 81
percent of the female migrants were in the informal sector under
this definition. Whether one uses the first or the second criterion,
roughly the same percentage of migrants is in the informal sector;
therefore we have used the second criterion for purpose of analysis.

Tables 5.7 and 5.8 show the labor force participation rates of
the migrants by education and by age. Eighty percent of the male
and 55 percent of the female migrants are in the labor force. The
participation rate is, however, much higher for migrants without
elementary school diplomas, with an average rate of 97 percent for

TABLE 5.7

Labor Force Participation of Migrants, by Sex and Education: Java, 1973

	Male Education						All Male	Female Education						All Female
	1	2	3	4	5	6		1	2	3	4	5	6	
Number of observations	1,014	2,783	2,778	1,868	1,379	1,170	10,992	1,314	1,790	1,389	1,162	546	351	6,552
Percent in formal sector	5.6	6.9	9.4	15.6	42.3	22.9	15.1	4.6	9.0	10.8	7.3	20.9	8.3	9.5
Percent in informal sector	91.6	91.6	83.0	33.9	21.3	5.5	61.5	72.9	61.6	34.0	11.3	12.1	5.1	41.6
Percent unemployed	2.5	1.6	3.1	3.2	7.2	1.6	3.0	4.3	3.2	4.1	3.5	2.9	2.0	3.6
Percent active participants in labor force	99.7	99.7	95.5	52.7	70.8	30.0	79.6	71.8	73.8	48.9	22.1	35.9	15.4	54.7
Percent students	0.3	0.3	4.5	47.3	29.2	70.0	20.4	0.5	0.6	9.9	44.8	23.8	63.5	15.7
Percent housewives	—	—	—	—	—	—	—	17.7	25.6	41.2	33.1	40.3	21.1	29.6
Percent not in labor force	0.3	0.3	4.5	47.3	29.2	70.0	20.4	18.2	26.2	51.1	77.9	64.1	84.6	45.3
Unemployment as percent of labor force	2.5	1.6	3.2	6.1	10.1	5.4	3.8	5.2	4.3	8.4	16.0	8.2	13.0	6.5

1 = no education.
2 = less than elementary diploma.
3 = elementary diploma.
4 = junior high diploma.
5 = senior high diploma.
6 = academy or university.

Source: 1973 Survey of Migration.

TABLE 5.8

Labor Force Participation of Migrants, by Sex and Age: Java, 1973

	Male					All Male	Female					All Female
	Age						Age					
	15-18	19-21	22-25	26-35	35+		15-18	19-21	22-25	26-35	35+	
Number of observations	3,168	2,477	1,825	2,250	1,346	11,066	2,573	1,422	944	1,005	634	6,578
Percent in formal sector	8.8	13.1	20.1	21.1	19.2	15.4	12.1	9.2	6.9	8.3	6.8	9.6
Percent in informal sector	48.9	49.5	70.2	76.0	75.0	61.3	37.7	44.4	64.0	43.5	43.3	41.8
Percent unemployed	3.3	3.9	2.2	2.0	3.6	3.0	4.4	1.8	2.1	1.6	9.1	3.6
Percent active participants in labor force	61.0	66.5	92.5	99.1	97.8	79.7	54.2	55.4	73.0	53.4	59.2	55.0
Percent students	39.0	33.5	7.5	0.9	2.2	20.3	29.1	16.9	2.1	1.2	1.9	15.7
Percent housewives	—	—	—	—	—	—	16.7	27.7	44.9	45.4	38.9	29.6
Percent not in labor force	39.0	33.5	7.5	0.9	2.2	20.3	45.8	44.6	27.0	46.6	40.8	45.3
Unemployment as percent of labor force	5.4	5.9	2.4	2.2	3.7	3.8	8.2	3.2	4.0	3.0	15.5	6.5

Source: 1973 Survey of Migration.

males and 65 percent for females. The participation rate is also higher for migrants above the age of 22. This is to be expected, since the younger migrants, those between 15 and 21, have a higher proportion continuing education (see also Table 5.8; the percentage of migrants who are students falls sharply with age). For females the relationship between age and labor force participation is not as strong as for males, since the percentage of housewives increases markedly in higher age groups. These data on participation should be used with caution, since it is quite likely that housewives participate in the labor force to supplement the family income, usually in service or trade activities. However, in the absence of solid information about secondary occupations, we have treated housewives and students as not participating in the labor force.

As anticipated, the percentage of migrants in the formal sector increases with educational level. It should be noted, however, that the formal sector is a relatively minor source of employment for migrants. Only 15 percent of the male and 10 percent of the female migrants are in it.

In fact, it is doubtful whether the conventional distinction between formal and informal sectors serves any purpose in the Indonesian context. Systematic institutional differentiation between the sectors as a result of legislation, organized union activity, and labor practices of government and parastate organizations has not been far-reaching, as is the case in many countries, particularly in Africa. Rather, Indonesian labor markets exhibit most of the characteristics of competitive markets, with only small differentials attributable to institutional factors.

UNEMPLOYMENT, EDUCATION, AGE, AND THE SEARCH PROCESS

The Harris-Todaro model postulates that urban unemployment is a result of a high wage differential between rural and urban areas. In such a situation migrants may decide to move to areas with higher expected wages even in the face of substantial urban unemployment. The recent generalization of this model by J. Harris and R. Sabot regards unemployment as a partial outcome of a "search for better-paying jobs in the face of wage dispersion and imperfect information" (Harris and Sabot 1980, p. 48). Thus unemployment is regarded in part as an alternative "productive" activity whose output is accurate information about the different jobs that are available, and their associated pay and working conditions.

Since unemployment in the Harris-Sabot version entails a financial cost for those engaged in it, and the benefits of engaging in extended search are uncertain, it is likely that individuals with higher levels of education will remain unemployed while searching for jobs for longer periods than those with less education. This is true for two reasons: first, the more educated face a wider dispersion of potential wage offers, so the gains accruing to further search will be longer; and second, the empirical relation between family income and economic status and education makes it more likely that the educated will be able to finance their subsistence requirements during an extended period of search. This proposition is supported by the Indonesian evidence. The last row of Table 5.7 shows unemployment as a percentage of the labor force of migrants with different levels of education. For both males and females, the rate of unemployment increases with education. The highest unemployment for males is that of the migrants with senior high school diploma. The rate is 10.1 percent, compared with the average of 3.8 percent for all males in the sample. The highest rate of unemployment for females is the junior high school diploma holders with 16 percent unemployment, followed by the academy or university graduates (13 percent). The average unemployment rate for all females is 6.5 percent.

The proportion unemployed also drops with age for both sexes. This reflects the fact that the percentage of migrants with higher education decreases with age. Furthermore, almost all of the unemployed are seeking their first job in the particular urban labor market. Therefore, younger migrants are also disproportionately recent arrivals and recent graduates or school leavers.

Finally, we should note that the average unemployment rate for both sexes after migration is much lower than either the rate before migration or the urban or rural rate for all Java. The unemployment rate as a percent of the labor force is 3.8 and 6.5 after migration for males and females, respectively, compared with the premigration rates of 23 and 33 percent (Tables 5.5 and 5.6). The corresponding figures for all age groups in urban and rural Java are 12.2 percent and 7.6 percent (Sethuraman 1974, pp. 6-49).*

---

*At first glance these data seem surprisingly high, but they reflect the census findings of 1971, which refer only to open unemployment. The usually published unemployment figures are much lower, but are the percentage of the **population** unemployed. Since labor force participation rates also appear suspiciously low for the age groups in the early twenties, it is not surprising that unemployment is a much larger proportion of the labor force. Furthermore, it should be noted that the census was taken in September, a "slack"

All of this suggests, contrary to recent speculation by many observers, that absorption of the urban lumpenproletariat is not the

---

time in agriculture in Java. Comparison with the Intercensal Population Survey taken in March 1976 (a peak period) suggests that almost 7 million persons more are found working in agriculture in Java in March than in September; this is largely confirmed by comparison of unpublished labor force surveys taken in March and September 1976. Furthermore, there is marked seasonal variation in migration corresponding to reduced hours of work for those who are employed in September relative to March. These suggestive and preliminary findings are at least consistent with the observation that the 1971 census data represent unemployment at its highest point in the year. Sethuraman's calculation of the relevant unemployment rates are shown below.

Unemployment as a Percent of Labor Force
by Region, 1971

	Urban		Rural	
Region	All Age Groups	10–29 Age Group	All Age Groups	10–29 Age Group
West Java	19.5	26.6	14.0	17.9
Central Java	8.0	12.8	4.2	5.9
Jogjakarta	6.1	10.5	2.8	4.5
East Java	10.5	16.5	6.6	8.6
Jakarta	12.8	16.7	—	—
All Java	12.2	17.6	7.6	10.1

Source: Data drawn from BPS, Population Census 1971 (Jakarta: BPS, March 1974).

Sethuraman also gives cropping intensity indexes from the 1963 Agricultural Census of 1.05, 1.57, and 1.53 for West, Central, and East Java, respectively, which further confirms the allegation that there is likely high seasonal variation in unemployment in rural areas. Our survey data are inadequate to demonstrate the extent to which migration to urban areas substitutes seasonally varying employment in rural areas with steady employment in urban areas as the basis on which "expected incomes" are calculated. It is also possible that a fluid pattern of seasonal and circular migration enables people to combine peak periods of agricultural employment

essential aspect of the labor absorption problem in Java—rather, the difficult and central problem is the productive absorption of an unemployed and underemployed rural labor force. The essential puzzle is why so few of the rural unemployed are rushing to urban labor markets, where it seems safe to conclude that rural-urban migrants manage to find some kind of employment rather quickly. This is particularly true of less-educated migrants—it is only the better-educated who can afford the luxury of remaining unemployed until they find a good job. The poor have to take anything that is available in order to survive, and this they find relatively quickly.

OCCUPATIONAL MOBILITY AFTER MIGRATION

Do migrants remain in the same occupation after migration, or do they move into occupations that provide higher income and/or more security? Some answers, though tentative, may be derived from Tables 5.5 and 5.6. The third column of each table gives the percentage of migrants who retained their previous occupation after migration.

As expected, the striking change is for those who were engaged in agriculture. Only 1.5 percent of the male and 0.2 percent of the female migrants who were previously in agriculture remained in that occupation after migration. Of course this change reflects the structure of employment opportunities in rural and urban areas, with agriculture being dominant in the former and insignificant in the latter. (There is some truck gardening and fishing employment among residents of urban areas, and these are included in agriculture.)

The majority of the male migrants remained in the occupation they were in prior to migrating, the only major exceptions being male domestic servants, daily workers, and production workers: 12 percent, 25 percent, and 29 percent, respectively, remained in their premigration occupation. The majority of the female migrants in occupations other than prostitution and scavenging changed their occupation after migration. This may be due to the fact that women often have to give up their previous occupation when they migrate with a spouse or family. They are thus forced to look for jobs different from the ones they had held.

---

with urban employment in the slack seasons. Graeme Hugo (1977) suggests that at least in West Java such circular migration is of considerable magnitude and probably rising over time.

Tables 5.5 and 5.6 also show the structure of unemployment at the time of interview as well as the percentage of migrants whose current job is the same as the first job they obtained after migration. For both males and females there appears to be very little occupational mobility subsequent to migration. However, we include data only on migrants who had moved within the previous five years, and there may be mobility within these broad occupational categories. In short, the time span of five years may be too short to detect the true pattern of occupational mobility, although this is doubtful, given the fact that most of the observed mobility occurs within the first two years and Gustav Papanek and Dorodjatun Kuntjaro Jakti (1975) reach similar conclusions using a ten-year reference period.

DETERMINANTS OF EARNINGS

We need to understand the relative importance of personal factors (human capital) and institutional features of labor markets in determining earnings of individuals when they become employed. Therefore, earning functions were estimated for the sample of employed migrants. The logarithm of monthly earnings was regressed on sets of dummy variables representing education, age, year of migration, employment sector, pay period, occupation, and city of migration. The general model used is of the following form:

$$LnI_j = A_0 + \sum_i b_i E_{ij} + \sum_i c_i A_{ij} + \sum_i d_i Y_{ij} + \sum_i e_i M_{ij} + \sum_i f_i P_{ij}$$

$$+ \sum_i g_i O_{ij} + \sum_i h_i C_{ij}$$

where

I_j = monthly income of migrant j

E_{ij} = education level i of migrant j [j=1, no formal education; 2, less than elementary diploma; 3, elementary diploma; 4, junior high school diploma; 5, senior high school diploma; 6, academy or university diploma (omitted)]

A_{ij} = age group i of migrant j[+i=1, 15–18; 2, 19–21; 3, 22–25; 4, 26–35; 5, 36–65 and over (omitted)]

Y_{ij} = arrival year i of migrant j [i=1, 1968; 2, 1969; 3, 1970; 4, 1971; 5, 1972, 6, 1973 (omitted)]

M_{ij} = employer/occupation i of migrant j [i=1, self-employed peddler; 2, self-employed in trade or service; 3, self-employed in other occupation; 4, wage-employed by stranger; 5, employed by large private firm or government; 6, working for family (omitted)]

P_{ij} = pay period i of migrant j [i=1, daily; 2, monthly; 3, weekly or biweekly (omitted)]

O_{ij} = occupation i of migrant j [i=1, domestic servant; 2, scavenger; 3, prostitute; 4, other (omitted)]

C_{ij} = city i of migrant j [i=1, Jakarta; 2, Surabaja; 3, Malang; 4, Jember; 5, Kediri; 6, Madium; 7, Jogjakarta, 8, Solo; 9, Semarang; 10, Tegal; 11, Bandung; 12, Sukabumi; 13, Tjirebon; 14, Purwakarta (omitted)].

The reported monthly income, which is our dependent variable, merits some comment. The survey of migrants asked each person his/her pay period and the amount of cash and/or the cash value of income received in kind from the primary occupation, per pay period. Depending on the pay period, the migrants were further asked to state the average number of days worked in a week and the average number of hours worked in a day. The cash and kind payments were added, and daily and weekly pay was converted to a monthly equivalent using the number of days or weeks worked per month. Major difficulties were encountered when these data were first analyzed, since some of the reported wage figures were unrealistic for the reported pay period. An almost case-by-case study of reported wages that were extreme outliers was undertaken, and in most cases the mistakes were identified and subsequently corrected.* The distri-

---

*The exact changes that were performed are documented in the author's working titles and are available on request. In brief, a relatively few (less than 3 percent of the cases) outliers made the mean wage estimates unusable and the standard errors enormous. However, analysis of the median wages in different categories suggested that these estimates were extremely reasonable. (Professor Alden Speare of Brown University has reported analysis of this sample, using median wages.) The kind of problem encountered would be a distribution of daily wages with 97 percent of the observations between Rp. 75 and 300 per day, with a median of 150. But the rest would be in a range of 2,000 to 8,000, with two or three cases of 70,000 and 80,000. The mean of such a distribution would be 900 (six times the median), with a standard error of 1,500.

Clearly, something was strange. On further analysis, it became clear that the observations in the 2,000-8,000 range corresponded closely to the distribution of monthly-equivalent earnings of

bution of the final wages was quite reasonable when compared with wages paid to workers in the national public works development program (INPRES) and other published wage figures. In summary, our measure of income is the monthly income, cash and in kind, from the migrant's primary occupation.

The education variables are used to capture one major element of human capital, it being hypothesized that higher education will lead to higher income. It was decided to characterize education by a series of discrete dummy variables rather than as a continuous variable, such as number of years of schooling. Some earlier analyses of the data, and observations of the ways in which educational requirements for jobs are set, suggested that receipt of a specific certificate of completion or diploma is the most appropriate measure of educational attainment, since it combines attendance and achievement levels.

Age is included to capture a number of effects—maturity, commitment to the labor force, experience—that are probably nonlinear. The year of migration can be taken as a proxy for experience in the

---

the rest of the sample with similar educational and occupational characteristics. Therefore, these earnings were taken as monthly rather than daily. It is evident that errors like these were compounded when these daily rates were multiplied by the 22–28 days reported being worked per month. Similarly, there were a few monthly wages reported that were obviously daily wages, although we were unable to determine whether the errors were in response, coding, or punching. In all cases we attempted to preserve the median values when these transformations were being made.

Our confidence in the edited income data was further increased by noting that the variance of the income in cash plus income in kind is relatively smaller than the variance of either of the components. Since we know that income in cash and in kind are substitutes in the Indonesian context, the data suggest that the enumerators were collecting "real" data on the components of income. However, we are less certain that the conversion of daily wages to monthly income is completely reliable. Attempts were made to obtain average daily income and number of days worked per month. However, a number of biases could arise in reporting, particularly by the large number of self-employed whose daily incomes fluctuate considerably day by day. While the resulting estimates appear "reasonable," we have continued to include pay period as a dummy variable in all of the statistical analyses, in order to reflect any consistent bias that arises from this conversion procedure.

particular labor market, allowing the migrant to learn about and find better opportunities.

The employer-occupation categories represent the effect of institutional and structural factors in determining income. Self-employment includes returns to both labor and capital. Therefore, it is divided into those with more substantial capital (settled stalls or shops) and self-employment in working for family. In the latter category, income in kind and in cash are very difficult to disentangle, but the numbers are relatively small. Finally, there are two main divisions in wage-earning employment: employment by a "stranger" (in the Indonesian context this corresponds roughly to informal-sector employment), which is distinguished by respondents from employment by a large private firm or government. Thus, these categories represent the major institutional segmentation of the labor market between employment by large-scale organizations, usually characterized as the "formal sector," and the range of informal-sector employment relationships. Various types of self-employment and participation in family-run businesses are fairly straightforward and, as suggested previously, combine both returns to labor and returns to capital. But the final informal-sector category, being employed by a "stranger," is less clear-cut. The dividing line between this category and employment by a large private firm is fuzzy at best, and the classification used is that offered by respondents. In general, this category represents an employment relationship in which the worker knows and identifies the employer personally, suggesting that the employer is a small-scale entrepreneur employing a relatively small number of workers. The exact nature of the personal relationship between such employers and their workers, in the absence of direct family connections, can vary widely. It is our impression that most often such entrepreneurs hire workers who are known to them through networks of friends having the same geographic or ethnic origin, and that such an employment relationship is determined by both social and contractual arrangements.

Pay period was included as a separate set of variables for two reasons. First, as mentioned earlier, there may be a consistent statistical bias in converting daily wages to monthly incomes—most likely this bias is upward, as a result of overestimating the number of days worked per month and the average income per day. Second, daily wages include self-employed and casual workers, while monthly wage contracts characterize the "formal sector," and include substantial measures of both job security and income. Furthermore, monthly contracts more often include a substantial amount of income in kind, such as rice allowances.

Three further occupational categories represent special institutional arrangements that should be controlled for in any analysis of earnings. Domestic servants are frequently hired on the basis of family relationship, and frequently receive nonreported income in kind because they live and eat as part of the household unit. For both reasons their reported income is likely to be considerably lower than their real income. Scavengers represent the most excluded group within the economy. They are individuals who do not participate in any of the regular or informal labor markets, but manage to eke out an existence through collecting scrap materials that can be sold. They generally live in temporary cardboard or bamboo hovels, occupy abandoned railroad cars, or camp under bridges. Most of their reported income is income in kind, which was converted to an income equivalent by the interviewers. Virtually all of these scavengers are self-employed. Finally, prostitutes constitute a separate occupational category. Mostly self-employed, they occupy a position to which some social stigma is attached. Furthermore, their effective earning years are very limited. For these reasons one would expect their reported earnings to be higher than what they could earn in other occupations.

The final set of variables represents the different urban labor markets. Differences in earnings among cities will vary, ceteris paribus, by differences in the economic structure of the particular labor market, the supply of labor to that area via migration, variations in cost of living, and differences in amenities. In a world with good information, mobile populations, and efficient and cheap transportation, migration should serve to make small, if not entirely eliminate, disparities in real earning opportunities among labor markets. Hence, in a perfectly integrated spatial economy, coefficients of specific cities would not be expected to be significantly different from each other. However, in addition to reflecting real earnings differentials among cities, the fact that surveying was done by different teams in different cities may cause coefficients to reflect a systematic interviewer bias in recording incomes.

Since all of the independent variables have been entered in the form of dummy variables, one category from each set has to be eliminated in order to prevent singularity in the matrix to be inverted. The regression coefficient for each dummy variable represents the partial effect of that variable on income. As such, it is differences between coefficients in the same set that are significant, more than whether each or all are significantly different from zero, which is the basis of the reported "t" statistic.

Finally, it can be questioned whether these variables can, and should be, entered as completely independent variables, since there are likely to be significant interactions between variables such as age, education, occupation, and pay period. In fact, we did experiments with several dimensions of interaction through an analysis of variance, and concluded that little was to be gained by including specific interaction terms in the regression. The estimated coefficients have been relatively robust with respect to specification changes; and furthermore, by estimating the regression in logarithmic form, the variables enter multiplicatively. The one form of interaction that was consistently important was between sex and all other variables. Therefore, we have estimated separate equations for males and females, which is equivalent to full interaction between sex and all other variables.

The estimated regression equations are presented in Table 5.9.

The selected independent variables that are used in the regression model explain 26 percent and 43 percent of the variation in the log of monthly earnings of males and females, respectively. The analysis shows that both human capital (education) and structure of the labor market (employer-occupation interaction, pay period) are important determinants of migrants' earnings. But the importance of these variables varies for males and females.

EDUCATION

Noting that the regression coefficients on the dummy variable represent the partial effect on income of being in a particular category relative to the omitted category, the result of the education coefficients clearly represents the return to higher levels of education. Since the omitted category is the highest educational level, academy or university degree, our result shows that the lower a migrant's educational attainment, the lower the earnings.

Table 5.10 shows the estimated earnings of one particular class of male and female migrants. The table clearly shows that income increases substantially with education. Other things being equal, a male with a primary school diploma will earn 11.3 percent more than one who attended school but did not obtain the diploma, and 28 percent more than one who never attended school at all. Statistically, we can identify these marginal returns to education. However, the total returns to education are undoubtedly higher, since education also helps to determine employment status and occupation. For instance, the probability of being a monthly paid employee of a large firm is much greater for a secondary school graduate than for one with no schooling. Yet the correlation between education and those variables is not so high as to invalidate the measures we have estimated in log-linear forms. Of course, education and professional and managerial status are closely related. In this case we preferred

TABLE 5.9

Earnings Functions for Migrants in 14 Cities of Java, 1973

Independent Variable	Male		Female	
	b^a	t^b	b^a	t^b
Education				
E_1 (no education)	-0.328*	18.04	-0.287*	6.82
E_2 (less than primary)	-0.269*	16.32	-0.221*	5.07
E_3 (primary)	-0.220*	13.53	-0.176*	3.99
E_4 (junior)	-0.185*	11.12	-0.086	1.87
E_5 (senior)	-0.107*	6.57	-0.014	0.29
Year of migration				
Y_1 (1968)	0.099*	7.49	0.041	1.58
Y_2 (1969)	0.079*	6.03	0.025	1.04
Y_3 (1970)	0.094*	7.32	0.026	1.15
Y_4 (1971)	0.094*	7.03	0.020	0.92
Y_5 (1972)	0.062*	5.01	0.007	0.37
Age				
A_1 (15-18)	-0.025	0.568	-0.088	0.99
A_2 (19-21)	-0.014	0.325	-0.068	0.75
A_3 (22-25)	-0.014	0.311	-0.077	0.86
A_4 (26-35)	0.032	0.072	-0.041	0.45
A_5 (36-65)	0.077	1.746	-0.026	0.29
Employer/occupation				
M_1 (self-employed, peddling)	-0.049*	3.789	-0.043	1.27
M_2 (self-employed, settled)	0.028*	2.302	0.146*	5.43
M_3 (self-employed, other)	-0.052*	3.229	-0.024	0.30
M_4 (stranger)	-0.041*	3.815	0.051*	3.04
M_5 (government/large private)	-0.008	0.694	-0.005	0.20
Pay period				
P_1 (daily)	0.050*	4.74	-0.116*	6.07
P_2 (monthly)	0.064*	5.10	0.147*	6.42

144

	b^a	t^b	b^a	t^b
Occupation				
O_1 (domestic service)	-0.316*	11,263	-0.287*	10.59
O_2 (scavenging)	-0.400*	24,064	-0.098*	3.42
O_3 (prostitution)	—	—	0.416*	18.43
City				
C_1 (Jakarta)	-0.051	0.00	0.181*	5.36
C_2 (Surabaja)	0.016*	2.725	0.042	1.22
C_3 (Malang)	-0.014	0.722	0.112*	2.84
C_4 (Jember)	-0.123	0.611	0.191*	3.75
C_5 (Kediri)	-0.162*	4.844	0.120*	2.91
C_6 (Madium)	-0.162*	6.76	0.037	0.88
C_7 (Jogjakarta)	-0.098*	4.71	0.057	1.32
C_8 (Solo)	-0.053*	2.54	0.124*	3.35
C_9 (Semarang)	-0.097*	4.87	0.074*	2.03
C_{10} (Tegal)	-0.032	1.41	0.057	1.38
C_{11} (Bandung)	-0.011	0.53	0.203*	5.06
C_{12} (Sukabumi)	-0.050*	2.27	0.155*	3.33
C_{13} (Tjirebon)	-0.102*	4.59	0.247*	4.16
Constant^c				
$(E_6, Y_6, A_6, M_6, P_3, O_4, C)$	3.9326		3.575	
$\bar{R}^2$	0.26		0.43	
S.E.E.^{d}	0.25		0.29	
N	8,303		3,040	

*Statistically significant at the 5 percent level.

$^a b$ is the standard linear regression slope coefficient.

$^b t$ is the value of student's t. Values greater than 2.0 indicate significance at the 5 percent level—two-tailed test.

^{c}Constant is the estimated value of the regression for the omitted categories of the dummy variables.

^{d}S.E.E. is the standard error of estimate of the regression.

Source: Estimated from data gathered in the 1973 Survey of Migration.

145

TABLE 5.10

Estimated Monthly Earnings of Migrants Aged 26–35 Who Migrated
to Java in 1973: Employed by a Stranger and Paid
Monthly, by Educational Attainment

Educational Level	Male			Female		
	Rp.	Index $(E_i = 100)$	Percent Change from Lower Level	Rp.	Index $(E_i = 100)$	Percent Change from Lower Level
No formal education (E_1)	3,959	1.00		3,556	1.00	
Less than primary diploma (E_2)	4,535	1.15	15.0	4,140	1.16	16.0
Primary school diploma (E_3)	5,077	1.28	11.3	4,592	1.29	11.2
Junior high diploma (E_4)	5,503	1.39	8.6	5,649	1.59	23.2
Senior high diploma (E_5)	6,585	1.66	19.4	6,668	1.88	18.2
Academy or university diploma (E_6)	8,426	2.13	28.3	6,886	1.93	2.7

Source: Estimated on data from 1973 Survey of Migration.

to attribute the earnings to education, and did not include such occupational categories among the independent variables.

It is interesting to note the interaction between education and sex. On the average, women earn less than men, but part of this is due to their lower average educational attainment. Table 5.10 suggests that women receive lower wages than men at both low and high levels of education. With no formal education, being employed by a stranger, and receiving a monthly wage, a 26-35-year-old woman who migrated to Jakarta in 1973 would earn 12 percent less than a man in the same situation. Beginning at this lower base, the proportional increments to income occurring from some primary schooling and completion of primary school are the same for women as for men—their earnings remain approximately 12 percent lower than for men at each level. However, the apparent returns to junior high school completion are greater for women than for men, with earnings being equal (actually slightly, but not significantly, higher) to those of males at that level. However, women seem to experience virtually no further gain in going beyond senior high school, and receive lower incomes than do men at this level. We do not have a good explanation of this—it may merely be that we had very few observations for women with university diplomas.

How do our predicted monthly earnings of migrants with different educational attainments compare with the observed wage rates in Jakarta? According to BAPPENAS internal records, INPRES, which is a public works program in the rural and urban areas of Indonesia, paid average daily wages in Jakarta in 1971-72 of Rp. 200, Rp. 350, and Rp. 400 for unskilled, semiskilled, and skilled workers, respectively. This implies a monthly wage of Rp. 5,000, Rp. 8,750, and Rp. 10,000, respectively, for 25 workdays per month. Compared with these figures, our predicted earnings are a bit on the low side. However, when account is taken of the lower coefficient for daily wage payment, our estimates seem reasonable and are approximately in line with the estimates reported by Papanek and Kuntjaro Jakti (1975) for comparable occupation groups.

YEAR OF ARRIVAL AND AGE

The year of arrival, which is a measure of the number of years the migrants have been in their new environment, should affect earnings because of gains in experience, better information, and adaptation to and acquisition of skills needed in urban areas. Consequently, we had expected a positive, but not necessarily a linear, relationship between length of residence and income. While this was found to be true, particularly for males, the income gain due to additional years of urban residence is very small, and differences after one year of residence are negligible. Similarly, the age coefficients, which also reflect experience and maturity, while of the expected pattern, are not statistically different from each other. These findings are wholly consistent with our earlier evidence of the low degree of post-migration occupational mobility.

EMPLOYER-OCCUPATION

Our regression model allows us to study the net effect of institutional and structural factors on the earnings of migrants after allowing for the effect of the standard human capital variables, such as education and age. The structural variable used in our study classifies the migrants by their relationship with their employer: self-employed, employed by family or friend, employed by a stranger, and employed by a large private firm or government. It should be recalled that the formal-informal sector classification was also based on relation to employer, with those employed by a large private firm or government being in the formal sector while all the rest were categorized as informal sector.

Given the fact that the informal sector is highly differentiated into numerous types of activities, which results in a wide range of earnings, it was found useful to further disaggregate the self-employed migrants. Consequently, they were classified into self-employed who are engaged in peddling services and trade, self-employed in settled services and trade, and self-employed in other occupations.

The result shows that even after allowing for the human-capital variables, the type of employer has an effect on the migrants' earnings. Being self-employed in settled service or trade was found to bring the highest income for both males and females. Part of this high income is return to capital. The next highest income is registered in the formal sector—jobs with large private firms or the government—for males, but in the informal sector—employed by a stranger—for females. Self-employment in peddling service or trade, which is presumably the easiest job to enter, is found to have low earnings, thus reflecting the high degree of competition in that sector.

Perhaps the most noticeable and significant are the relatively small differences in income arising from segmentation of the labor market. For males, earnings in small-scale self-employment (peddling and other) and wage employment by strangers are not significantly different. These are approximately 10 percent lower than earnings for those employed by large-scale organizations or by family enterprises. Earnings in larger-scale self-employment are 6 percent higher than in large-scale organizations, which reflects returns to capital for the former. The results for females are only slightly different: small-scale self-employment and employment in large-scale enterprises pay similarly. Employment by strangers yields significantly greater earnings: 40 percent higher than the formal sector. Clearly, the formal sector does not provide better opportunities for females than do easy-entry alternatives. It is not clear why earnings are higher in employment by "strangers," although some degree of personal relationship with employers may explain this difference. Finally, females who achieve entrepreneurial success do much better in relation to other alternatives open to them.

As expected, domestic service pays only half as much as other occupations, but this is largely accounted for by unreported income in kind. Scavengers are grossly disadvantaged—males earn about 40 percent of the level in wage employment, and females about 70 percent of the wage alternative. But prostitutes earn more than 2.5 times what they could earn otherwise. These differences are what one would expect. Daily paid workers, both male and female, apparently earn only slightly less than monthly paid workers. Although these differences are not statistically significant, it must be noted that the margin of potential error is large in converting daily wages to monthly equivalents. Moreover, a daily paid worker is in a much less secure situation than his or her monthly paid counterpart.

SPECIFIC URBAN AREAS

Adding a set of dummy variables for specific cities improves the statistical fit of the regressions. However, no obvious systematic relationships between city characteristics and the coefficients emerge, although we intend to analyze these results further. It is interesting to note that Jakarta and Surabaja, the two largest and fastest-growing cities, have coefficients that are not greatly different from smaller cities in their regions. With some exceptions, earnings are highest in West Java and lowest in Central Java, which is consistent with regional differences in income and reported wages in other surveys. The omitted city is Purwokerto, a middle-sized city in Central Java.

CONCLUSIONS

This essay has investigated the employment and earnings of Indonesians who migrated to the 14 major cities of Java between 1968 and 1973. We were particularly interested to understand the migrants' labor force participation, the structure and pattern of their employment in both the formal and the informal sectors, the extent of their occupational mobility, determinants of earnings of those receiving wages, and the rate of employment and characteristics of the unemployed.

Consistent with almost all other empirical evidence, the migration stream was dominated by the young (70 percent of both sexes were under 25) and the relatively more educated (only 9 percent and 21 percent of the males and females, respectively, had no education). Though migration may alter the lifetime income of all participants, it tends to be more attractive to the young and educated, for whom the expected gains from moving are highest.

One of the most striking results is that the average unemployment rate after migration is much lower than either the rate before migration or the urban or rural unemployment rate for all of Java. The unemployment rate as a percentage of the labor force is 3.8 and 6.5 after migration for males and females, respectively, compared with the premigration rates of 23 and 33 percent. Though this high rate of premigration unemployment may be overstated and difficult to interpret, given the nature of unemployment figures in countries like Indonesia, it is a clear indicator that the problem facing migrants in urban areas is not the lack of jobs per se, but the meagerness of the income they receive for their work. Since migrants constitute the "working poor," efforts to improve their condition require policy measures that increase their productivity more than the design of policies that attempt to expand employment opportunities in general. This is particularly important because over 75 percent of the migrants are self-employed in the informal sector.

The result of this study strongly supports the argument by Harris and Sabot (1976) that unemployment results from a search for better-paying jobs in situations where there is imperfect labor-market information coupled with significant dispersion of wages. Unemployment, as a search process, entails a financial cost and offers uncertain benefits. Hence, we would expect unemployment to be concentrated among those most likely to benefit from a longer search for high-paying jobs and who have the means to support themselves while engaging in this "productive" but currently nonincome-earning activity. Our data show that for both male and female migrants, the rate of unemployment is directly correlated with education. The less educated, who are also the poorest migrants, have the lowest unemployment rate because they cannot afford to remain unemployed and are not motivated to engage in an extended search, given the limited range of potential job offers open to them.

Finally, our earning-function estimates for the sample of employed migrants indicated that both human-capital factors and institutional and structural factors determine earnings. However, the effect of the institutional factors appears to be relatively small, while education and ownership of capital contribute significantly to income. Differences in income arising from segmentation of the labor market are small for males and nonexistent for females. The "formal sector" does not provide better opportunities than the "informal sector." This finding is reinforced by the observation that Indonesia has adopted few of the institutional features, such as minimum wages and organized collective bargaining, that define segmentation between labor markets within most developing economies. Therefore, distinctions between "formal" and "informal" sectors of the Indonesian economy do not have any economic meaning.

Although this essay does not present evidence on rural-urban earnings differentials, it is clear from other findings of our survey work that such differentials are positive but relatively small. The vast majority of migrants interviewed indicated that they believed their life situation had been improved by migration, and this is consistent with the evidence on income.

The Harris-Todaro model of migration has drawn attention to excessive migration and high levels of urban unemployment being caused by institutionally maintained rural-urban earnings differentials. In a sense Indonesia becomes the test of what happens in the absence of such differentials. The evidence is clear that in these circumstances unemployment is quite low, earnings differentials are positive in order to compensate for transport and other costs of moving, and migration flows respond to urban demands for more labor. It is also evident that urban migrants in these circumstances earn low incomes that correspond to the low incomes of nonmigrants. But this purposely shifts emphasis away from migration and urbanization per se, and forces the policy maker to concentrate on alleviating poverty in both urban and rural sectors.

In conclusion, it should be stressed that migration is one of the few relatively more accessible means of improvement at the disposal of a significant majority of the rural people. This and previous studies continue to support the idea that at least the private, if not social, benefit of migration is positive, and that migration is a rational and informed decision triggered by the differentials in expected income and opportunities. If some migrants continue to survive in conditions of extreme poverty even after they move to the cities, it is a further indicator of the marginal and difficult alternatives they had faced, and left, in the countryside. Consequently, no policy package aimed solely at the prevailing urban "problem" could ameliorate the condition of migrants or the urban working poor.

Elimination of factor-price distortions, adoption of a rational trade policy, and encouragement of small-scale, labor-intensive production activities, while contributing to the improvement of the condition of the urban poor, are likely to intensify the flows of migration from rural to urban areas unless effective action is taken simultaneously to raise rural incomes. Thus the welfare of migrants, like the welfare of the urban and rural poor, rests in the adoption of the above policies within an employment-oriented strategy of overall development, whose main components are integrated rural development and labor-intensive urban industrialization.

REFERENCES

Barnum, H., and R. Sabot. 1976. Migration, Education and Urban Surplus Labor. Paris: OECD.

Harris, J., and R. Sabot. 1980. "Urban Unemployment in LCD's: Towards a More General Search Model." In Essays on Migration and the Labor Market in Developing Countries, edited by R. Sabot. New York: Westwood, forthcoming.

Harris, J., and M. Todaro. 1970. "Migration, Unemployment and Development: A Two-Sector Analysis." American Economic Review 60, pp. 126-42.

Hugo, Graeme. 1977. "Circular Migration." Bulletin of Indonesian Studies (October 1977): 57-66.

International Labor Office. 1972. Employment Incomes and Equality. Geneva: ILO.

Lipton, Michael. 1976. "Migration from Rural Areas of Poor Countries: The Impact on Rural Productivity and Income Distribution." Paper presented at IBRD research workshop on Rural-Urban Labor Market Interactions. Washington, D.C.: World Bank. Mimeographed.

Mazumdar, D. 1975. "The Urban Informal Sector." World Bank Staff Working Paper no. 211. Washington, D.C.: World Bank. Mimeographed.

Papanek, G. F., and D. Kuntjaro Jakti. 1975. "The Poor of Jakarta." Economic Development and Cultural Change 24, no. 2, pp. 1-27.

Schultz, T. P. 1971. "Rural-Urban Migration in Colombia." Review of Economics and Statistics 53, pp. 157-63.

Sethuraman, S. V. 1974. "Urbanization and Employment in Jakarta." World Employment Programme Research Working Paper. Geneva: ILO. Mimeographed.

Suharso et al. 1976. Rural-Urban Migration in Indonesia. Jakarta: LEKNAS.

Temple, G. 1975. "Migration to Jakarta: An Empirical Search for a Theory." Ph.D. dissertation, University of Wisconsin.

Webb, R. 1975. "The Urban Traditional Sector in Peru." Washington, D.C.: The World Bank. Mimeographed.

Yap, L. Y. L. 1976. "Rural-Urban Migration and Urban Underemployment in Brazil." Journal of Development Economics 3, pp. 227-43.

APPENDIX: CLASSIFICATION OF OCCUPATIONS USED FOR ANALYSIS

Student
Housewife
Agriculture
  Landowner
  Sharecropper
  Seasonal laborer
  Plantation worker
  Fisherman
  Shepherd
Traditional transport
  Trishaw (betjak) driver
  Cart/carriage driver (drawn
  by horse or bullock)
Motor transport
  Driver of taxi, bus, truck,
  locomotive, ship, airplane
  Bemo, helicak driver
Domestic servant
  House helper
  Children helper (governess)

Peddling services/trade
  Junk seller
  Nonfood seller
    Water
    Fuel
    Household items
    Cloth
  Food seller
    Cooked
    Uncooked
  Barber
  Laundryman, car washer
  Bootblack
  Photographer
  Knife sharpener
Settled services/trade
  Salesperson
  Waiter/waitress
  Junk seller

Nonfood seller
  Water
  Fuel
  Household items
  Books
  Cloth
Food seller
  Cooked
  Uncooked
  Restaurant
Barber/beautician
Repairman
Dressmaker/shoemaker
Maintenance worker in work-
  shop
Compounder or seller of tra-
  ditional medicines
Go-between for selling goods
Handicraft worker
Photographer
Butcher
Daily worker
  Construction, road projects
  Stevedore at harbor or railway
  Business companies
Production/manual
  Janitor, office guard, etc.,
    in private or government
    office
  Production worker
  Postal and telecommunications
    clerk
  Transportation company
    worker
  Graveyard gatekeeper
  Plumber
Lower clerical (private and
  government)
  Trainee
  Administrative worker
    (manager not included)
  Cashier, bookkeeper, etc.

Clerk in bank, insurance com-
  pany, business
Manager/administrator
  Extension worker in agricul-
    ture, family planning, etc.
  Physician
  Pharmacist
  Teacher, religious or public
    school
  Translator
  Managerial staff of private or
    government office
  Researcher
  Contractor
  Foreman/supervisor
  Editor/reporter
  Consultant
  Teacher of private courses
    (language, cooking, etc.)
  Salesman/detail man
  Irrigation/waterpump super-
    visor
  Designer/architect
  Lawyer/judge
Prostitute
  Call girl
  Brothel
  Streetwalker
Scavenger
  Paper collector
  Cigarette butt collector
  Collector of metal, glass, etc.
  Beggar
Other
  Actor
  Military
  Retired civil servant
  Athlete
  Betjak (trishaw) owner
  Cook
  Brothel keeper
Unemployed

6

AN EXPERIMENT IN RURAL EMPLOYMENT CREATION: THE EARLY HISTORY OF INDONESIA'S KABUPATEN DEVELOPMENT PROGRAM

Richard Patten, Belinda Dapice, and Walter Falcon

Few countries have initiated major public works programs consciously designed to create rural capital by using labor-intensive techniques. The People's Republic of China has used such an approach in a major way, and there have also been modest attempts in India, Tunisia, and Ethiopia. One of the largest (certainly the best-documented) efforts to create employment through a public works program has been in Bangladesh (then East Pakistan).[1] But the number of national efforts is small, and the total amount of employment thus created remains extremely small relative to the labor forces of many poor countries.

Given this limited experience, Indonesia's attempts to initiate a rural employment program have aroused understandable interest. Java has one of the highest population-to-resource ratios of any major region in the world. It is also one of the poorest regions, having been plagued by rampant inflation, economic stagnation, and growing unemployment during much of the late 1950s and early 1960s. Given these preconditions, the potential for a publicly financed employment program appeared substantial, and a country-wide program was initiated in 1970. The scheme, the Kabupaten Development Program (KDP), continues on an expanding basis, and its evaluation is still in progress. Hence only a preliminary report on the program as it existed in 1973-74 is possible in this essay.

─────────────

This essay covers the period 1969-70 through 1972-73 only, and corresponds to the years when the senior author was involved with the program.

INDONESIA'S EMPLOYMENT PROBLEM
IN PERSPECTIVE

Indonesia has the dubious distinction of being one of the most densely populated less-developed countries. In some agricultural areas of Central Java, population density exceeds 2,000 per square kilometer. For all of Java, the density is approximately 500 per square kilometer; and even when the Outer Islands are included, the figure is still greater than 50. Nearly half of Indonesia's farms are less than one acre, and 70 percent are less than one hectare. Even with a labor-intensive rice agriculture, there is a large amount of underemployment in the countryside. The lack of productive job alternatives is especially acute in seasonal terms, because rainfall patterns limit the number of crops that can be grown. Even in irrigated areas, which tend to be the most heavily populated, there is strong seasonality in terms of the labor used within agriculture.

This picture of population pressure in rural areas is made even more stark by an examination of recent trends in labor-force estimates. Population has been growing by more than 2 percent annually. Widjojo estimated that the male labor force would increase by 50 percent between 1961 and 1976, [2] and that between 1966 and 1971 the working-age population would increase by 1.8 million annually, of which 1.3 million would be in the 15-19-year-old group. Hence, for both political and economic reasons, a strong government concern with employment was understandable.

In spite of difficult preconditions, the policy framework was generally favorable for the creation of productive employment for this large and rapidly growing labor force. Since 1966 a major effort has been made to allow factor prices to approximate social opportunity costs: the basic interest rates for secured loans have been between 12 and 24 percent annually; the foreign-exchange market has been relatively free and flexible; wage rates have been very low and largely unaffected by union pressures; and land continues to be held under a fairly egalitarian system.

C. P. Timmer has argued persuasively that, in fact, factor pricing has not been "correct," as appears on the surface, because of tariff preferences on capital goods, credit rationing at preferential interest rates to particular groups, and certain organizational biases that result in overly capital-intensive projects. [3] Nevertheless, of all the major capitalist countries of the developing world, it is difficult to think of many examples in which the economist's main recommendation on employment—get factor prices in line— has been implemented so well. In spite of a relatively favorable institutional and policy milieu, however, rural unemployment remained a very serious problem. It was not surprising, therefore, that policy makers turned to a specific job-creation program.

ORIGINS OF THE KABUPATEN PROGRAM

The formal history of the works program can be traced to the middle of 1969. By that time the Indonesian government had implemented a set of monetary, fiscal, and trade policies that had curtailed much of the earlier economic chaos. The initial economic discussion surrounding the First Five-Year Plan (1969-70 through 1973-74) had focused on price stability and rehabilitation, with particular emphasis on restoring rural infrastructure. A concern with jobs was certainly not the central focus, although brief consideration was given to increasing employment in cottage industries and expanding job opportunities through an industrialization program. Indeed, most discussion of employment centered on gotong royong, or voluntary labor contributions.

One manifestation of this outlook was the Desa Program. Beginning in 1969, each desa (village) was given Rp. 100,000 (about $2,500) annually by the central government for the purchase of materials from outside the village area. Together with voluntary labor from within the town, these inputs were meant to form the beginning of a decentralized improvement program.

A second program, closer to the KDP in conception, was the Padat Karya (Labor-Intensive Works) Program, which had begun on an experimental basis in 1963-64. Under this program American food aid was used as in-kind compensation for workers on infrastructure projects in poor areas. These projects typically included attempts at road construction, river dredging, irrigation, and reforestation. [4]

Beginning in 1969, the Padat Karya Program was expanded considerably. At the same time discussions on employment began to have a slightly different emphasis. Labor-intensive investment was still considered important, but primary concern shifted to the income problems of the poorest groups in the countryside. These groups often supplied the "voluntary" labor, but received little in the way of direct wages or other benefits.

As the dimensions of the employment and income problems became clearer, President Suharto and key members of his government decided to implement the KDP throughout the 281 kabupatens (counties) of Indonesia.

The KDP was established formally with Instruction of the President, no. 1, 1970, and is therefore known popularly as the INPRES Program. This instruction assigned program responsibility to the ministers of Interior, Finance, and Planning, who, in turn, issued further decrees. These directives laid down allocations, detailed the character of eligible projects, outlined local responsibilities, and described the accounting and reporting systems.

Projects eligible for the program, as described in the joint decree of the three ministers, were required to meet the following criteria:

To be labor-intensive in construction and to be designed to expand permanent employment opportunities

To use local manpower and materials, and to avoid as much as possible the use of imported goods

To increase production of goods and services in the shortest possible time

To increase the participation of the people in development

To be sound technically

To be carried out with labor paid the normal wage prevailing in the area, not with voluntary or partially voluntary labor

To be planned and supervised with the staff already available in the kabupaten

To be complete and economically useful in and of themselves, without depending on any other project financed through another program

To be completed within the financial year.

A further instruction of the Minister of the Interior specifically prohibited the construction of offices, purchase of vehicles and equipment other than hand tools, and the loan of funds for commercial enterprises.

A close reading of these objectives raises questions about their internal consistency and about which goals were to dominate in particular projects. But the directives set an important tone for the program. It was clearly recognized from the beginning that the projects would be relatively small and would be located close to the homes of the people who would work on them. These factors in turn dictated that the decision-making authority be decentralized. The kabupaten level of government was chosen as the level that might best provide the right projects and requisite administrative and technical skills. In practice, therefore, KDP built or rehabilitated market roads, irrigation systems, flood-control embankments, small bridges, drainage systems, fish-landing harbors, produce markets, bus stations, and fresh- and saltwater fish ponds.

FUNDING OF THE PROGRAM

The program, from its inception, involved per capita contributions to the kabupatens from the central government.* An impor-

---

*The exception has been sparsely populated kabupatens, where a minimum allocation was set. This level was Rp. 5 million in

tant part of the success of the INPRES Program was due to this simple and equitable procedure. It avoided much of the political infighting over allocations, and it did not necessitate an overly centralized control structure.

During the first year the allocation was Rp. 50 ($.12) per capita, and involved total funds of Rp. 5.7 billion ($14 million). Though small by many standards, it nearly doubled resources controlled by local governments. In succeeding years the per capita contribution grew rapidly. Although a portion of the increase was only nominal because of inflation, the real contribution nonetheless increased substantially between 1970 and 1973 (see Table 6.1).

TABLE 6.1

Allocations Under the Kabupaten Development Program,
1970-71 to 1973-74

Year	Per Capita Amount (Rp.)	Total Amount* (billion Rp.)
1970-71	50	5.7
1971-72	75	8.8
1972-73	100	12.8
1973-74	150	19.2

*Until mid-1971 the exchange rate was Rp. 378 = U.S. $1.00; for the rest of the period, the rate was Rp. 415 = U.S. $1.00.

Sources: Atar Sibero, "Program Bantuan Pembangunan Kabupaten/Kotamadya," Ekonomi dan Keuangan Indonesia 21, no. 2 (June 1973); and Departemen Dalam Negeri, Lampiran Pidato Kenegaraan Republik Indonesia (August 1973), ch. 1.

In addition to the "standard" allocation, an incentive scheme was instituted beginning in 1972-73. Kabupatens that had reached their targets on the collection of land taxes became eligible for an additional allocation, which totaled about Rp. 338 million in 1972-73.

1970-71, but has increased each year, so that in 1973-74 the level was Rp. 12 million per kabupaten.

This amount was raised to Rp. 742 million in 1973-74; and with the encouragement of the incentive, the kabupatens showed substantial increases in the revenue they collected on their own.

DESIGN OF THE PROGRAM

The implementing procedures of the program were designed from the outset to protect central, provincial, and kabupaten interests. The planning process starts at the local level, typically beginning in October for the following fiscal year (April through March). At that time the kabupaten engineering staff estimates the amount and price for each item of material and labor, and the length of time required to complete each project. Following compilation of all the projects, the local program is sent to the provincial government over the signatures of the bupati (chief official of the kabupaten) and the heads of the kabupaten sections for public works, agriculture, planning, and manpower. At the provincial level the planning staff checks first to see that the prescribed procedures have been followed. For example, the manpower officer checks the estimates of labor requirements and the wages proposed to see that they are in line with those prevailing in the area. (An indication of regional and vocational variations in wages is shown in Table 6.2.)

Based on the technical judgment of his staff, the governor issues a detailed letter of approval for each project, including the names of the people who will supervise each project and the name of the treasurer for each. This approval is conveyed to the bupati, the local and provincial branches of the Bank Rakyat Indonesia, and the central government.

As soon as full agreement has been reached with the central government and the release has been issued, kabupaten governments proceed with invitations to tender bids. All projects are completed by contractors chosen through competitive bidding, except in remote areas where there are no contractors. In such cases the kabupaten staff hires the laborers and secures the materials directly on the kabupaten's own account.

On each project site a sign is erected that gives relevant details of the project, including its cost, starting and completion dates, name of the contractor, and kabupaten officials responsible for supervision. This identification helps to insure that the public knows at least some details of what is happening, and is one part of the "open management" instituted in the program. During the construction, teams from the provincial and central governments make on-the-spot inspections. The provincial government makes a final inspection of each project to see that it has been constructed to specification.

The foregoing plan of organization and operation, presented deliberately with detail, helps to underscore why the KDP has generally been so successful. First, the policy makers who conceived it understood the seasonal nature of the employment problems and the benefits to be derived from labor-intensive rural investments. Second, these officials understood the need for decentralized decision making on specific projects, and they also recognized the necessity of having an open management and control system to insure that the employment and development objectives would not be compromised. Indeed, one of the most impressive features of the program has been the care with which the planning has been done and the manner in which central and local interests have been balanced.

IMPACT OF THE PROGRAM

For program planning and evaluation at all levels of government, it was important to record conditions prevailing initially. Consequently an inventory of real infrastructure (roads, bridges, and irrigation systems) was completed for each kabupaten. Sample results, illustrated in Tables 6.3 and 6.4, show the enormity of this task. Obviously, completing the inventories was in itself a significant accomplishment that added substantially to the information base for local and regional planning. These surveys established the magnitude of required rehabilitation and provided information essential for designing new infrastructure. Although the age of most of Indonesia's irrigation systems had long been known, it was necessary to document the serious disrepair of roads and irrigation structures in order to realize the full extent of the deterioration that had taken place in the 1950s and early 1960s.

Physical Accomplishments

As is shown in Table 6.5, the KDP projects (in expenditure terms) have concentrated heavily on roads and, to a lesser extent, on bridges and irrigation facilities. Of the estimated total of about 50,000 kilometers of kabupaten roads, about 11,500 kilometers (23 percent) were rehabilitated under the program by the end of 1972–73.

Data on the physical results of rehabilitation and new construction under the program are shown in Table 6.6. Although most of the work undertaken through 1971–73 represented rehabilitation, there was some shift toward new projects in the 1973–74 funding proposals. Projects tended to be concentrated on Java, as indicated

TABLE 6.2

Daily Wage Rates for Different Types of Work: 1972–73

(Rp.)

Province	Unskilled Laborer	Semiskilled Laborer	Skilled Laborer	Foreman	Supervisor	Mechanic	Night Watchman
Aceh	N.A.	N.A.	N.A.	N.A.	N.A.	N.A.	N.A.
North Sumatra	225	325	375	275	325	350	225
West Sumatra	175	275	325	225	300	325	175
Riau	250	350	400	375	475	500	300
Jambi	225	300	375	350	400	400	250
South Sumatra	225	350	400	300	350	350	275
Lampung	225	300	350	250	275	300	200
Bengkulu	250	350	400	300	350	375	275
D. K. I. Jakarta	200	300	400	400	—	350	250
West Java	175	275	300	250	300	250	175
Central Java	125	200	250	200	275	250	125
D. I. Jogjakarta	95	140	185	175	175	190	120

Region							
East Java	125	225	275	250	325	275	150
West Kalimantan	350	450	475	425	475	500	300
Central Kalimantan	350	425	500	450	450	500	350
South Kalimantan	225	325	375	325	375	300	250
East Kalimantan	400	600	750	650	900	600	400
North Kalimantan	250	350	425	300	350	350	260
Central Sulawesi	200	325	450	300	450	300	175
South Sulawesi	N.A.	N.A.	N.A.	N.A.	N.A.	N.A.	N.A.
Southeast Sulawesi	175	350	500	225	375	450	175
Bali	120	175	200	150	200	175	140
West Nusatenggara	150	250	275	225	250	225	150
East Nusatenggara	N.A.	N.A.	N.A.	N.A.	N.A.	N.A.	N.A.
Maluku	175	250	300	250	290	275	250
Irian Jaya	225	350	450	450	525	425	420

N.A. = not available.

Source: T. A. Salim and Ishandora, "Daftar Upah Harian beberapa jenis pekerja tiap Kodya/Kabupaten Tahun 1972/73" (Jakarta: BAPPENAS, August 1972) (mimeographed).

TABLE 6.3

Irrigation Structures to Be Rehabilitated or Built: Bantul Kabupaten, Indonesia

Irrigation Structure	Year Built	Irrigated Area (ha.) At Present/Before Rehabilitated — Initial	Irrigated Area (ha.) At Present/Before Rehabilitated — Before Rehabilitated	Irrigated Area (ha.) After Rehabilitation	Canals (km.) Total Length	Canals (km.) To Be Rehabilitated	Construction (cu. m.) Grand Total	Construction (cu. m.) To Be Rehabilitated	Other Structures (no.) Grand Total	Other Structures (no.) To Be Rehabilitated
Klep Trihudadi at Afvoer Trihudadi	1942	47	47	47	—	—	4,435	4,435	—	—
Sl. Madejan, Kali Krusuk	1940	342	270	342	6,000	650	11,828	4,328	1,160	145
B. Karangtengah at Kali Tjeleng	—	—	—	55	2,200	300	18,792	9,042	350	95
B. Gumungkumtji at Kali Winongo Lama	—	75	60	100	—	400	—	5,557	—	—
Sl. Vanderwijk at Kali Progo	1940	264	264	417	4,000	360	11,912	1,912	750	250
Sl. Pasangan Klodran at Kali Bedog	1942	206	190	206	6,000	750	20,250	2,475	750	30
B. Kasaran II at Kali Winongo Ketjil	1944	121	121	121	—	—	3,500	3,500	—	—
B. Butuh at Afvoer Sulang	1947	43	30	43	300	100	3,180	3,180	—	—

Description	Year									
Penutupan Kali Winongo Ketjil sepandjang kota Bantul	—	—	—	—	—	—	4,700	4,700	—	—
Pasangan Penahan Tanah B. Panggang at Kali Winongo Kecil	—	—	—	—	400	400	1,525	1,525	—	—
Tl. Pelaman at Slokan Hadeyan, K. Krusuk, and Onderdam	1940	137	75	137	6,000	—	11,828	1,000	—	—
Onderdam B. Mojo at Kali Winongo	1959	—	—	—	—	—	3,250	2,250	300	200
B. Sirihan at Kali Sirihan	1950	60	20	60	—	—	5,750	5,750	—	—
Ps. Penahan Tanah Tuk	—	80	60	80	—	—	1,800	1,800	—	—
Siphon Metuk at Kali Wingo	1959	200	200	200	1,500	—	2,250	1,100	—	—
Total		1,575	1,337	1,808	26,400	2,960	105,000	52,554	3,310	720

Source: Bantul Kabupaten Planning Staff.

165

TABLE 6.4

Roads and Bridges to Be Rehabilitated or Constructed: Bantul Kabupaten, Indonesia

Road Direction (from — to —)	Part of Road to Be Rehabilitated from Km. — to —	Length (km.)	Number of Very Poor Roads	Bridges Total	Bridges To Be Rehabilitated or Constructed
Bantul–Srandakan	Km. 17–23	6	6	2	—
Batas kota Jogja–Imogiri	4–12	8	8	4	2
Batas kota–Parangtritis	13–28	15	15	1	1
Batas Jogya–Ambarwinangun	3–5	2	2	2	1
Kotagede–Karangsemut	6–13	7	7	2	2
Palbapang–Samas	22–25	3	3	1	1
Palbapang–Barongan	—	—	—	2	1
Barongan–Klegen	19–28	9	9	3	3
Barongan–Imogiri	14–16	2	2	1	1
Grojokan–Plered	7–11	4	4	1	1
Dongkalan–Gamping	4–10	6	6	2	1
Jodoglegi–Gesikan	15–17	2	2	2	2
Gesikan–Sedayu	17–30	13	13	5	5
Sapuangin–Sambong	20–28	8	8	6	6
Srandakan–Trihudadi	23–29	6	6	—	—
Wiyoro–Ngipik	7–9	2	2	1	1
Kotagede–Plered	—	—	—	1	1
Barongan–Siluk	14–18	4	4	1	1
Siluk–Bibal	18–24	6	6	1	1
Dogongan–Kretek	18–30	12	12	16	4
Pades–Nulis	15–16	1	1	—	—
Klangon–Gunungmojo	19–21	2	2	1	1
Piyungan–Munggur	14–16	2	2	—	—
Klodran–Bejen	16–17	1	1	—	—
Imogiri–Karangtulen	16–17	1	1	—	—
Total		122	122	55	36

Source: Bantul Kabupaten Planning Staff.

TABLE 6.5

Percent of Funds Allocated for Various Types
of Projects, 1971-72 and 1972-73

Project	1971-72	1972-73
Roads	55.2	56.1
Bridges	16.2	16.3
Irrigation	14.7	14.4
Markets	8.0	6.1
Other	8.8	7.1

Source: Dirjen Pemerintahan Umum dan Otonomi Daeran, Departemen Dalam Negeri, Laporan Pelaksanaan Bantuan Untuk Pembangunan Kabupaten dan Kotamadya Tahun 1971/72 dan Rencana Untuk Tahun 1972/73.

TABLE 6.6

Physical Results of the Kabupaten Development Program
in Indonesia, 1970-71 to 1972-73

Project	1970-71	1971-72	1972-73
Roads (km.)	2,711	3,585	4,962
Bridges and culverts (m.)	5,919	16,533	22,428
Irrigation (1,000 ha.)	99	120	160
Dams (no.)		168	220
Canals (km.)		710	464
Control structures (no.)		452	355
Markets (no.)		144	112
Reforestation (ha.)		2,718	6,938
Number of projects		2,393	2,828

Source: Atar Sibero, "Program Bantuan Pembangunan Kabupaten/Kotamadya," Ekonomi dan Keuangan Indonesia 21, no. 2 (June 1973).

TABLE 6.7

Number of Kabupaten Projects, by Province and Type, 1972–73

	Total	Roads	Bridges	Irrigation	Markets	Drains	Culverts	Other
D. I. Aceh	216	45	66	28	14	13	44	6
North Sumatra	157	84	34	18	4	7	—	10
West Sumatra	116	82	16	5	1	3	1	8
Riau	35	17	11	4	—	2	—	1
Jambi	62	9	38	9	1	1	1	3
South Sumatra	125	24	50	1	12	1	34	3
Bengkulu	39	3	6	9	1	—	—	20
Lampung	41	8	8	17	—	—	8	—
D. C. I. Jakarta	6	1	1	3	1	—	—	—
West Java	527	147	161	70	16	10	114	9
Central Java	443	165	133	115	1	3	17	9
D. I. Jogjakarta	22	7	3	10	1	—	—	1
East Java	443	177	109	100	32	2	2	21
West Kalimantan	27	9	8	8	1	—	—	1
Central Kalimantan	12	4	2	3	2	—	—	1
South Kalimantan	46	16	15	—	4	—	5	6
East Kalimantan	12	5	3	—	2	—	1	1
North Sulawesi	39	10	19	6	—	2	2	—
Central Sulawesi	21	7	8	2	4	—	—	—
South Sulawesi	161	44	87	22	1	2	5	—
Southeast Sulawesi	19	7	7	2	—	—	3	—
Bali	37	20	4	10	—	—	3	—
West Nusatenggara	82	21	16	24	9	—	3	9
East Nusatenggara	111	13	10	24	2	—	62	—
Maluku	10	2	2	1	2	—	1	2
Irian Jaya	19	10	2	—	1	4	2	—
Total	2,828	937	819	491	112	50	308	111
	(100%)	(33%)	(29%)	(17%)	(4%)	(2%)	(11%)	(4%)

Source: Dirjen Pemerintahan Umum dan Otonomi Daeran, Departemen Dalam Negeri, Laporan Pelaksanaan Bantuan Untuk Pembangunan Kabupaten dan Kotamadya Tahun 1971/72 dan Rencana Untuk Tahun 1972/73.

168

in Table 6.7, but there was some activity in every province. Overall, it is clear that the program was widespread throughout the country from its inception.

For obvious reasons it is almost impossible to evaluate the aggregate impact of 3,000 small projects. In order to learn important details of some of these projects, numerous case studies are planned, and a few have already been completed.[5] From these studies and from the available aggregate data, it is possible to reach a few preliminary conclusions about the impact of the program on the economy.

Employment Creation

The breakdown of planned expenditures under the program for 1972-73 is shown in Table 6.8. Wages and local materials account for nearly 70 percent of the expenditures. Assuming that about 80 percent of the primary cost of local materials is local wages, approximately 60 percent of all program funds have gone for the hiring of labor.* Assuming an average length of employment of 100 days (which appears reasonable, given the types of projects undertaken and their average length) and using average local wage rates, annual employment rose from 200,000 to over 400,000 persons during the first three years of the program (see Table 6.9).

Since a principal objective of the program has been to create employment for the poor and the landless, it is important to determine exactly who is benefiting from these jobs. In most of the cases studied, it appears likely that the majority of unskilled workers employed were casual workers from the immediate project area, rather than workers regularly employed by a contractor and brought into the area. However, aggregate figures for the shares of these two groups are difficult to estimate. One survey team found that on a dam project, which had been under way for almost a month at the time of the visit, a total of 3,427 man-days of labor had been expended, of which casual labor represented nearly 90 percent.[6] However, this percentage is perhaps atypically high. The same team's study of two completed road projects found that 45 percent and 54 percent of total man-days (for direct labor) represented casual labor.[7]

---

*Many of the local materials are rocks, hand-pounded aggregate, and the like. Most of the value of these items is the labor required to transport and prepare them for use in construction.

TABLE 6.8

Expenditures Planned for Kabupaten Projects, 1972-73

	Million Rupiah	Percent
Wages	3,285.2	27.9
Local materials	4,815.1	40.7
Other materials	2,114.1	17.7
Equipment	338.4	2.0
Compensation	154.4	1.3
Other	1,243.4	10.4
Total	11,950.6	100.0

Source: Dirjen Pemerintahan Umum dan Otonomi Daerah, Departemen Dalam Negeri, Laporan Pelaksanaan Bantuan Untuk Pembangunan Kabupaten dan Kotamadya Tahun 1971/72 dan Rencana Untuk Tahan 1972/73.

TABLE 6.9

Number of Men Employed an Average of 100 Days: Kabupaten Program, Indonesia, 1970-71 to 1972-73

Period	Number
1970/71	200,000
1971/72	302,000
1972/73	435,000

Source: Y. B. de Wit, "The Kabupaten Program," Bulletin of Indonesian Economic Studies 9 (March 1973): 65 ff.

On the other hand, field visits by the authors to several projects in process showed that the majority of laborers were permanent employees of itinerant contractors. On one dam project, for example, local persons were employed only for grading of the river embankments leading to the dam site. It was clear in this instance that use of casual, unskilled, local labor was limited, and that many of the unskilled jobs were being performed by permanent employees of the contractor. Obviously, projects range from those that employ local, casual workers almost exclusively to those that use outside labor already employed by the contractor almost exclusively.

The record on the use of local materials versus goods imported from outside the project area is equally difficult to evaluate on an overall basis.* Case studies indicate considerable variation among projects, and suggest that expenditure on local materials may not be as high as had been hoped. On road projects, for example, a large part of the budget sometimes went for the purchase of asphalt, which Indonesia both produces and imports.[8] Some dam projects manifest similar characteristics.[9] In one case study a large proportion of the dam construction materials came from outside the project area, though only cement and reinforcing rod used foreign exchange. Bamboo, palm trunks, crushed rock, and some lumber were the main items coming from within the project area. An estimate of the large amounts of labor embodied in these materials is shown in Table 6.10.

Of those employed directly on KDP projects, most workers were from the poorer groups in terms of income and ownership of land, homes, and livestock. In a 25 percent sample of workers in one study, average ownership of wet-rice land was only 0.15 hectare. Only about 37 percent owned any land at all, and 23 percent did not own a dwelling of any kind. Average household income of these workers was about Rp. 54,000 ($130) per year, implying an average annual per capita income of about Rp. 10,800 ($26), far below the estimated annual per capita income of Rp. 17,500 for West Java, where the project was located.[10] Another study of one project showed that 84 percent of the workers had incomes of Rp. 500 (about $1.25) or less per month, again substantially below average.[11] At these income levels the additional income from the jobs generated by INPRES projects will, for the most part, be spent on

---

*Part of the difficulty of evaluation hinges on the definition of "imported." In some studies "imports" refer to foreign purchases, while in other analyses it refers to purchases from neighboring kabupatens.

TABLE 6.10

Labor Involved in Preparing and Transporting Local Materials:
One Dam in West Java

Materials	Amount	Man–Days for Preparation	Man–Days for Transport	Total Man–Days	Means of Transportation
Bamboo (pcs.)	3,000	—	49	49	truck
Kawung wood (pcs.)	88	—	11	11	person
Lumber (planks)	50	18	1	19	person
Rock (cu. m.)	1,025	3,075	1,743	4,818	person
Sand (cu. m.)	245	271	330	601	truck
Limestone (cu. m.)	90	76	115	191	truck
Terracing materials (cu. m.)	135	149	196	345	truck
Cement (sacks)	450	—	13	13	truck
Iron rods (tons)	7	—	—	—	truck
Water gates (pcs.)	3	—	2	2	truck
Total		3,589	2,460	6,049	

Source: Bureau for Economic and Social Research, Faculty of Economics, "Pengaruh Impres Tahun 1970/71 dan 1971/72 Terhadap Kegiatan Ekonomi dan Kesempatan Kerja."

increased consumption of food, clothing, housing, and health services, thus generating additional employment.

Completion of a project has a further impact on the economy of the immediate area. Rehabilitation of a badly damaged irrigation system, for example, generally means a change in cropping patterns. This point is illustrated by the Parakan Raden dam project of West Java, which affects an area of 502 hectares, 52 of which had been irrigated before rehabilitation. The remaining 450 hectares represented new wet-rice area and had previously been planted to cassava and tubers. As a result of rehabilitation under INPRES, two rice crops can now be planted. The Padjadjaran University survey team's calculations show an increase in income of almost Rp. 84,000 per hectare. [12] The increased output will also lead to increased fertilizer demand and greater utilization of processing units and marketing systems. A major impact will be on additional employment within the farming sector. Cultivation of one hectare of wet rice typically involves about 250 man–days (really man–days and woman-days) of labor per crop, so that 450 hectares planted to rice twice a year would represent approximately 225,000 days of labor. The net addition to employment depends on the crop replaced. In the case of cassava, which involves about 133 days of labor (and in this case was planted only once a year), the net addition would be on the order of 165,000 days. Moreover, this labor would be needed on a continuing annual basis.

This example may be extreme, but without detailed knowledge of the circumstances of each project, it is impossible to calculate the aggregate impact of all irrigation projects on employment. Potentially the effect is substantial but, as shown in Table 6.11, employment generation depends on the previous condition of the irrigation facilities and on the changes in cropping patterns that occur after rehabilitation. Considering both the direct and some of the more obvious indirect effects of irrigation and other projects, it appears that the overall contribution of the works program is significant. In 1972-73, for example, the direct increase in labor on project construction was approximately 43.5 million man–days. The additional irrigated area of 160,000 hectares added (conservatively) 16 million man–days. (This change also represented an increment in long-run employment.) When other indirect effects of nonirrigation projects are included, the program can probably be credited with a direct and indirect effect of around 70 million man–days, or about 0.3 to 0.4 million man-years of relatively "full-time" employment. Compared with the large (but quantitatively unknown) pool of underemployed labor, or the addition to the potential labor force of 1.8 million persons per year, it is clear that the KDP, while significant, is not a panacea. Perhaps the greatest shortcoming of the KDP is its small size.

TABLE 6.11

Labor Use on Selected Crops, East Java and South Sulawesi

	Man-Days per Hectare per Crop		Approximate Length of Crop Cycle (months)
Crop	East Java	South Sulawesi	
Wet rice	325	170	6
Corn[a]	160	135	5
Peanuts[a]	165	130	5
Soybeans[a]	80	—	5
Sugar[a]	690	—	15
Tobacco[a]	390	—	6
Dry rice	250	—	7
Corn[b]	140	105	5
Peanuts[b]	155	100	6
Soybeans[b]	55	—	4
Tobacco[b]	260	210	6

[a]Wet land.
[b]Dry land.
Source: B. Dapice, Sri Widayati, and W. P. Falcon, "A Report on Cropping Systems and Seasonal Employment in East Java and South Sulawesi" draft paper (Agro-Economic Survey and BAPPENAS/Harvard Research Project, Jakarta, June 1973, mimeographed).

Other Effects

In addition to the direct and indirect employment effects, other changes result from the completion of a project. A new road or bridge, for example, might affect the general level of economic activity by lowering the cost of transport.

A case study of three road projects carried out in Blora kabupaten in Central Java under INPRES I, II, and III indicates that the real price of agricultural commodities in the rural markets affected by rehabilitation of roads rose about 15-17 percent between 1969 and 1972, relative to prices in comparable villages without road repair. It appears that completion of the roads also resulted in a smaller increase in prices of imported goods in the affected market than in the market unaffected by road upgrading. The combination of price changes for both local agricultural commodities and goods brought in from outside resulted in a substantial rise in real income for the population in the project area. [13]

The impact of a new road or bridge on general economic activity in the area can also be significant. The road projects studied above facilitated production and transportation of timber by allowing more trips with larger trucks. In addition, economic activity in general increased, as evidenced by new shops, new traders in the market, and even a new market in one of the villages along the road.

Even with perfect data, calculating the economic impact of a road or market presses the limits of benefit/cost theory. Consequently, it is not possible to come to a precise conclusion backed by careful quantitative analyses. Nevertheless, it is possible to provide a broad qualitative evaluation of the overall program and its impact.

ADMINISTRATION AND ITS LIMITS

An evaluation of the effectiveness of the INPRES program to date and a projection of the possibilities for expansion require an understanding of the need for employment and infrastructure, and also of the administrative strengths and problems involved in trying to meet these needs.

Decentralization and Participation

Widespread employment in the construction of infrastructure can be achieved only through working on hundreds of small projects simultaneously. Each project may be small and simple, but the total of people employed, kilometers of roads, or number of irrigation systems constructed or rehabilitated can be large. The simultaneous implementation of hundreds of small projects requires a high degree of decentralization in the making of decisions about priorities, detailed engineering, and project timing.

More than 1,000 people are involved in choosing project priorities in the 28 kabupatens. Five hundred additional staff are concerned with engineering detail, and at least 200 more with scrutinizing the projects before the governor gives approval. Supervision of the projects in construction takes over 1,000 people, and at least 500 members of the staff of the Bank Rakyat Indonesia (BRI) are involved in the financial system.

The administrative problem has been to divide the entire job into component parts, with each level of government and each official given appropriate responsibility. The level of competence is obviously not uniform among all bupatis, engineers, or planning personnel. Therefore, a successful program must start with relatively simple planning and progress to more sophisticated projects.

Administrative Limits

Once the basic routines of project preparation, scrutiny, and implementation have been established, the strategy should be to increase capacity to plan and implement successful projects. How quickly this capacity should be enlarged is a question of timing and constant surveillance. If the breakdowns are so general that the central and provincial teams visiting the province and kabupaten cannot give sufficient help to repair the administrative breakdowns within the year, the program has been pushed too fast and must have a period of consolidation.

Thus the evaluator is faced with the problem of looking at the program while it is in process, and must ask the right questions—not whether there are any problems in the program, but whether there are so many problems that they cannot be solved without unacceptable losses.

The greatest of the continuing problems of the program is undoubtedly the problem of communication. Communication with many kabupatens is physically difficult, with a minimum of two weeks needed for some kabupatens even to be reached by telegram. Moreover, a serious lack of communication exists between individuals at the same level. The dictum that "Anything that can be misunderstood will be misunderstood" applies with extra force when instructions must be conveyed indirectly to a large number of people of widely varying administrative skills and capacities. The communications problem is exacerbated by the inability of the central government to announce the level of expenditures for the program before the budget speech in January.

By 1972-73 the basic framework of the program—the planning methods and the information requirements—seems to have been reasonably well understood. The kabupaten staffs seemed generally able to follow the routine required to prepare a one-year program. Expansion in the size of a one-year program is more work, but not a different routine, and therefore presented no great administrative or technical problems at the kabupaten level.

The technical inspection of plans is within the capacities of the provincial engineering staff, provided they are given sufficient time to do the work. The central government's inability to disclose budget figures before January reduces the time available for the provincial staff to do its work to less than two months. This problem could be eased if projects were planned by the kabupatens and scrutinized by the provincial staff in advance of the year in which they are to be carried out.

There have been some weaknesses in the planning staffs of three or four provincial governments, caused mainly by a misunderstanding, in the early stages of the program, of its importance relative to other programs. Lower-level staff were unable to deal with the local officials and the central government. This problem is being corrected, though some difficulties remain.

The flow of funds through the bank is reasonably smooth. The method of authorizing funds based on a monthly expenditure schedule per kabupaten, with the BRI branch debiting the central account, now seems simple and obvious; however, it took three years to develop. It is still subject to disruption if the governors or their staffs feel that the problems of monitoring the progress of a project, making on-the-spot inspections, or insisting on proper reporting from the bupatis are too difficult. In these instances the governors have a tendency to attempt an additional pre-audit system for all expenditures, thereby slowing down the projects and destroying the possibility of smooth, timely implementation. At the same time, these pre-audit systems tend to turn the provincial officers into clerks who sign contractors' bills, precluding the carrying out of their normal functions as monitors. Pre-audit rules are in violation of the system set down in the central government's instructions, however, and generally the violations are eliminated after a few weeks or months.

The reporting system formerly entailed a simple monthly report from the kabupaten that was used and summarized by the provincial government. This system was revised at the beginning of 1972-73, but it took nearly a year for the revised system to be understood. More generally, when procedures are changed in a major way, it appears to take at least this long for them to become fully implemented.

To summarize, at the end of three years of the kabupaten program, the basic methods of planning, technical scrutiny, implementation, and reporting for a one-year set of projects appeared to be in place and working. There did not seem to be insurmountable administrative constraints preventing an increase in the size of the program, provided that the growth of the program did not involve major shifts in basic methods.

Project Selection, Costs, and Standards

On the whole, project selection seems to have been generally good, although specific questions have been raised in a number of cases. For example, the upgrading of certain roads in Central Java, which were already in moderately good condition, probably had only a small economic impact on the community. There also have been complaints that certain village leaders selected road and irrigation projects that would benefit themselves or particular groups. It would be naive to believe that politics in this form did not enter the decision process, as it does everywhere else. On the whole, however, the prevailing judgment seems to be that funds were used well, if not perfectly.

Much conjecture and few facts surround the questions of corruption under the KDP. The general impression of knowledgeable observers is that the record of the KDP is probably better than most other development programs in Indonesia, although there is variation by project and province. One of the important factors in controlling corruption has been the publication and posting of allocations, unit costs, and expenditures.

Research is now under way that will provide a more detailed assessment of the costs and engineering standards of the kabupaten program. Several provincial and kabupaten engineers reported that the work is on a par with that of other development projects. On the other hand, there have been reports of inadequate shoulders on some roads and insufficient attention to the drainage aspects of a number of road projects. Clearly, the question of standards and required maintenance is largely unexplored at the present time.

In terms of unit costs, the KDP data are quite impressive. The planning data shown for 1971-72 in Table 6.12 require confirmation on a case-study basis, but on the whole are lower than for similar development projects constructed under different programs.

THE FUTURE

It has been asked whether there are enough projects at the kabupaten level to continue the KDP program for a reasonable length of time. Clearly, it would be a serious mistake to build up a system of administration to provide a large share of the supplementary employment required in the rural areas, only to find, suddenly, that there was no more work to be done. In a country that had an inadequate infrastructure in 1945 and maintained it inadequately for 25 years, the question might be rephrased (albeit pejoratively): "How long can the government spend money at the rate of 35 cents per capita per year on rural public works before it completes all of the infrastructure work that needs to be done?" Since the question is asked seriously, a serious answer will be attempted.

TABLE 6.12

Kabupaten Projects, Volume and Costs, 1972–73

Type of Project	Physical Volume	Cost (Rp.)	Unit Cost (Rp.)
Roads	5.0 million km	6.8 bill.	1.4 mill. per km.
Bridges	19.4 million m.	2.0 bill.	101,456 per m.
Dams and reservoirs	389.8 million cu. m.	845 mill.	2,168 per cu. m.
Irrigation channels	463,715 km.	490.3 mill.	1.1 mill. per km.
Other irrigation	355 items	201 mill.	56,611 per item
Marketplaces	266,286 cu. m.	745 mill.	2,797 per cu. m.
Drains	90,803 km.	233 mill.	2.6 mill. per km.
Culverts	3,054 cu. m.	25.3 mill.	8,290 per cu. m.

Source: Dirjen Pemerintahan Umum dan Otonomi Daerah, Departemen Dalam Negeri, Laporan Pelaksanaan Bantuan Untuk Pembangunan Kabupaten dan Kotamadya Tahun 1971/72 dan Rencana Untuk Tahun 1972/73 (Jakarta, 1973).

A preliminary evaluation indicates that in Java the rehabilitation of present infrastructure should be completed before 1990 at the present rate of expenditure. A few kabupatens in Java have exceptional circumstances: one kabupaten located next to Surabaja, which is already over 70 percent irrigated, will have its roads and irrigation fully rehabilitated by 1980. In the Outer Islands, where the requirement per capita for transport infrastructure is much greater, the length of time needed to complete rehabilitation at present spending levels will be longer.

There is, of course, no reason to stop work after rehabilitating the infrastructure, much of which existed before World War II. After rehabilitation is complete, the kabupatens could well start on the development of new infrastructure required by modern agriculture and by the growth of urban trading centers.

The idea that there will not be a sufficient number of economically viable infrastructure projects at the kabupaten level to use the resources that could be made available appears to be based on a misconception. The misconception is that at least Java and Bali were well-supplied with roads in the past, and that rehabilitation of the previous system will be adequate to meet present needs. In fact, even these two islands could be considered well-supplied with roads only if it is agreed that most rural communities are to be semi-isolated, and to be based only on subsistence agriculture with minimal purchased inputs and marketed surpluses. Since most of the rural areas of these two islands have not achieved an acceptable level of economic development, the road network will have to be more dense than in the past, and a much higher percentage of the water available will have to be utilized in organized irrigation systems.

In 1973-74 the kabupatens began the preparation of a long-term plan indicating the present known requirements for new infrastructure. This plan would not be the final word on what can be done, but the formalization of current ideas. It must be adjusted as agriculture develops and as population densities change.

The full documentation of such plans for each kabupaten will involve the work of several thousand people at the kabupaten level who know the local conditions and who can fit their knowledge into a conceptual framework provided by the central government. The opportunity for making such long-term plans at the local level is one of the most important long-run effects of the INPRES program.

NOTES

1. For a survey of the East Pakistan program, see J. W. Thomas, "Rural Public Works and East Pakistan's Development,"

in <u>Development Policy II: The Pakistan Experience</u>, ed. W. P. Falcon and G. F. Papanek (Cambridge, Mass.: Harvard University Press, 1971). For a general review of rural works programs, see also International Bank for Reconstruction and Development, "Public Works Programs in Developing Countries: A Comparative Analysis," Staff Working Paper no. 224 (Washington, D.C.: IBRD, February 1976).

2. Widjojo Nitisastro, <u>Population Trends in Indonesia</u> (Ithaca, N.Y.: Cornell University Press, 1970).

3. C. P. Timmer, "Choice of Technique in Indonesia," in <u>The Choice of Technique in Developing Countries</u>, ed. C. P. Timmer et al. (Cambridge, Mass.: Harvard Studies in International Affairs, 1975).

4. For a description of the program, see Department of Manpower, "Padat Karya Labor Intensive Works Program" (Jakarta: the Department, April 1, 1970). Evaluations of several projects have also been completed. See, for example, Labor-Intensive Research Team, "Labor Intensive Research in Java and Madura" (Jakarta: the Team, 1972). The Padat Karya and Kabupaten development programs have grown to be complementary rather than competitive in character. In 1970-71 the Padat Karya Program provided employment to an estimated 40,000 persons in 43 <u>kabupatens</u>.

5. See, for example, Bureau for Economic and Social Research, Faculty of Economics, "Pengaruh Inpres Tahun 1970/71 dan 1971/72 Terhadap Kegiatan Ekonomi dan Kesempatan Kerja" (Bandung: Padjadjaran University); Manpower Research Project, Department of Manpower, "Penelitian Project Inpres I-II-III, Kabupaten Blora/Jawa Tengah Djalan Kabupaten" (Jakarta); Management Center, Faculty of Economics, "Konsekwensi Sosial Ekonomis Projek 2 Inpres" (Jogjakarta: Gadjah Mada University).

6. Bureau for Economic and Social Research, Faculty of Economics, "Pengaruh Inpres Tahun 1970/71 dan 1971/72 Terhadap Kegiatan Ekonomi dan Kesempatan Kerja."

7. Ibid., pp. 97-107.

8. Manpower Research Project, Department of Manpower, "Penelitian . . . Kabupaten."

9. Bureau for Economic and Social Research, Faculty of Economics, "Pengaruh . . . Kerja."

10. Ibid., pp. 45 ff. Based on an average of five persons per family.

11. Manpower Research Project, Department of Manpower, "Penelitian . . . Kabupaten," ch. C.2.

12. Bureau for Economic and Social Research, Faculty of Economics, "Pengaruh . . . Kerja," p. 44. The cost calculations

here included only costs of seed and fertilizer, and land tax. They did not take account of labor costs.

13. Manpower Research Project, Department of Manpower, "Penelitian . . . Kabupaten," ch. B. 2.

PART II

PRICES, PUBLIC FINANCE, FOREIGN TRADE, AND INVESTMENTS

7

A SHORT MACROECONOMIC
MODEL OF THE INDONESIAN ECONOMY
Daniel M. Schydlowsky

Indonesia's development objectives, like those of most other countries, are medium- to long-term ones. Income is to be raised, the distribution of income is to be improved, the structure of the economy is to be modified, and so on. The attainment of these goals is expected to take time, and in order to move purposefully toward them, a long-term development strategy has been evolved. To some extent a formal economic model underlies that strategy.

On the other hand, day-to-day policy is dominated by short-run considerations and needs, particularly of the balance of payments. It could not be otherwise in an economy as open as the Indonesian one, in which trade is of fundamental importance and that operates with a completely free foreign-exchange market, where capital flows in and out without barriers.

With day-to-day and month-to-month policy focusing on the short run, and monetary and fiscal policy managed to protect the country's balance of payments and price stability, the short run obviously has an impact on the long-term development. The succession of short runs becomes the long run, and inevitably the succession of short-run policies has long-run consequences. Therefore, if short-run policies are not properly integrated into the long-run development strategy, the long-term goals are unlikely to be achieved. The predominance of short-run exigencies over long-term goals is not uncommon, and it is to right the balance that medium-term planning is desirable. Yet if medium-term planning is divorced from short-run needs, it risks becoming a dead letter. Hence the great importance of short-term as well as medium-term planning.

The model presented here was developed in 1971-72 and completed in 1973 as an aid in formulating short-run policy. At that time Indonesia had achieved virtual price stability relative to the international price level, and behaved like a veritable textbook open economy—that is, its price changes were overwhelmingly imported. Thus the model is fundamentally concerned with quantity changes, prices being given to the economy from outside. It is specifically designed to be useful for the following purposes: to aid in understanding and appraising the observed developments of the economy, in particular the growth of income and changes in balance of payments, international reserves, bank credit, and monetary stock; to provide guidelines for formulating a reasonable short-run policy for stabilizing the level of income and, in particular, the level of international reserves; to aid in developing consistency between short-run policy and long-term or economic development policy.

Evidently conditions have changed somewhat since the formulation of this model, principally in regard to price formation. The economy has not become more closed, but the explosion of Indonesia's international purchasing power as a result of the increase in the price of its oil exports has caused import demand to grow at a pace far exceeding the supply possibilities of the importing infrastructure. As a result, the short-run supply function of imports is no longer infinitely elastic, and excess demand has produced price rises as well as increases in imports. One economic agent's prices being another's cost, a modest price-cost spiral naturally ensued. This price-determination mechanism is not incorporated into the model. As a result the model is applicable only to 1973-76 if all variables are viewed as defined in nominal terms and separate price equations are added. However, the model's validity once again increased as the enormous expansionary pressure of the oil price increase spent itself. The renewed spurt in oil prices in 1979 may again reduce the direct applicability of the model, although one would expect the economy now to be much better able to handle rapid expansions in import demand, precisely because the 1973-76 experience forced the importing infrastructure to grow considerably. In the absence of rapid and large increases in the demand for imports that overwhelm the importing infrastructure, the structure of the model remains appropriate, even if its parameters may have to be reestimated. It is the conviction that 1973-76 were unusual years and that the earlier structure is again relevant that justifies the presentation of the model, updating of which is not feasible at present. In addition, the model has general applicability to open economies that have considerable unemployment and do not use import quotas as a general policy. In this wider context the approach adopted here, focusing on the structure of typical markets and relating the monetary and real sides of the economy through explicit behavioral relationships, offers valuable insights into the macroeconomic behavior of newly industrializing less-developed countries.

The first two sections present a description of the functioning of the major commodities and service markets of Indonesia, and develop a core model of the macroeconomic functioning of the Indonesian economy. This core model includes the main behavioral characteristics of the Indonesian economy, distilling from them the country's macroeconomic adjustment mechanism and its consequences, particularly for the balance of payments. "The Quasi Dynamics of the Model" develops a version of the model sufficiently dynamic to be applicable to annual Indonesian data. "Calibrating the Model" provides estimates of the parameters of the model and tests the quality of its calibration for the period 1970-72. "Policy Analysis with the Model" illustrates the economic analyses that can be undertaken with the model's help, and "Forecasting with the Model" presents a formal forecast developed with the model. The comparative statics of the model, as well as the data sources, are presented in appendixes.

THE MARKETS FOR GOODS AND SERVICES

Before proceeding to specify a macro model for Indonesia, it is useful to discuss how the major markets for goods and services work in this economy. For it is the structure and adjustment mechanisms in these markets that will determine the structure of the macro model and make it a useful representation of the country's economy. For analytical purposes it is useful to distinguish four different kinds of goods and services in the Indonesian economy: export goods, import-competing goods, services, and nontraded goods.

Export Goods

Output and price equilibrium in export commodities is the result of the interactions of domestic supply conditions with world price, as modified by the relevant export duty. Since Indonesia is a relatively small supplier in world markets of all its exports, except for oil and timber, the demand curve facing it in the world market is infinitely elastic over the relevant range; that is, Indonesia can sell any amount within its range of supply at the going world price. Furthermore, with the exception of coconut oil and rubber, no significant domestic demand for these export products exists. Figure 7.1 illustrates the resulting equilibrium: DwDw represents the world demand curve, drawn flat to indicate the smallness of the Indonesian supplies to the world market; below it is drawn a parallel line D'wD'w, showing net revenue to the

Indonesian exporter when he sells in the world market. The difference between the two represents export taxes (CESS and others) and port charges. DD is the domestic demand for the export commodity concerned. SS represents the domestic supply schedule and reflects existing technology, domestic cost conditions, managerial capacity, and so on. Equilibrium takes place with an output PX, determined by the intersection of the supply curve and the curve representing world demand less export taxes. Domestic offtake is given by the intersection of the domestic demand curve DD and the D'wD'w curve reflecting international demand less export taxes. The domestically consumed quantity is therefore X^d and the quantity exported is the difference between PX and X^d.

FIGURE 7.1

The Domestic Market for Export Goods

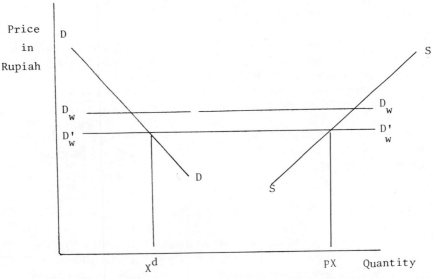

The situation regarding oil is surprisingly similar. Indonesia is a significant supplier of oil on the world market, but it has tied its price to that emerging from negotiations on Middle Eastern oil, so for practical purposes it is a price taker in this market as well. This circumstance, combined with the existence of considerable domestic consumption, allows us to include oil in the common analysis of export products.

The case of timber appears to be somewhat different, on the surface. The timber export sector is rather clearly distinct from the sector producing timber for domestic use, regarding both type and quality of wood and organization of the economic activity. Export timber is shipped almost wholly by foreign enterprises to their downstream affiliates. The export price obtained is therefore not an arm's-length price but, rather, a device for splitting the profits of the Indonesian logging operations between the domestic operation and the foreign parent. Since all the factors of production except labor are largely foreign-owned, it is useful to think of Indonesia as exporting labor and taxes, rather than timber. Such a view is justified because foreigners repatriate or otherwise retain control of all export proceeds other than the funds needed to pay Indonesian labor and taxes. Naturally such a "net timber export" concept reveals a much lower value of exports than does a "gross" concept. Furthermore, in terms of market structure, we can then interpret Figure 7.1 as referring to prices and quantities of wages and taxes in export timber production.

Taking all the export goods together, the following fundamental conclusions emerge from this analysis:

The level of output of export goods is independent of domestic demand for them; its determinants are domestic supply conditions and world price (f.o.b. Indonesia), less applicable export taxes and port costs.

The level of exports is the difference between total output of export goods and domestic demand for these goods.

The domestic wholesale price for export goods is the world price, less existing export taxes and port charges.

The domestic retail price is equal to the world price, less export taxes and port charges (= domestic wholesale price), plus domestic retailing and transportation costs.

Summarizing these propositions, we can write:

(a) supply of exportables: $PX = PX[P_{fob}^{e} (1-t_x^{e}) - PTChg^{e}]$

where PX = value of production of export goods at world prices (f.o.b.)

P_{fob} = export price

t_x^{e} = export taxes

$PTChg^{e}$ = port charges on exports

(b) supply of exports: $X = PX - xY$

where $X =$ value of exports at world prices (f.o.b.)

$x =$ marginal (= average) propensity of the domestic market to absorb export goods*

$Y =$ gross domestic income

(c) domestic price of exports: $P_d^e = P_{fob}^e (1-t_x^e) - PTChg^e$

$+ RTChg^e$

where $P_d^e =$ domestic retail price

$RTChg =$ domestic retailing and transportation costs

Import-Competing Goods

Into this category fall most of the agricultural and industrial goods produced in Indonesia. Characteristically, for these products domestic demand at the existing price exceeds domestic supply, and the difference is made up by imports. Figure 7.2 shows the formation of equilibrium in these markets: DD is again the domestic demand curve, SS is the domestic supply curve, and WW is the world supply curve, drawn flat to reflect the fact that Indonesia is a small buyer in world markets.[†] W + T, W + T shows the same world supply curve, as modified by import duties imposed by

---

*In order to keep the equation in f.o.b. prices, this coefficient represents absorption of goods in f.o.b. prices in relation to gross domestic product measured at domestic (retail) prices. Equality of marginal and average propensities is used for simplicity's sake. See "Calibrating the Model" for the manner in which the coefficients are empirically estimated.

[†]The occasional exception is rice; in some years Indonesia has been a sufficiently large buyer to affect the price. However, in such cases the government has endeavored to keep the domestic price constant while adjusting the trade taxation (in this case the Food Logistics Board's [BULOG] loss) to absorb the higher import cost.

Indonesia and port charges and costs of importing.* Equilibrium takes place at point D_0, where the domestic demand curve intersects the adjusted supply curve of imports. (The total supply curve then becomes the line SS_0D_0.) Domestic supply is shown by point S_0, given by the intersection of the domestic supply curve and the adjusted supply curve of imports. The horizontal difference between D_0 and S_0 represents imports of the respective goods. (Since 1974, Indonesia has made increasing use of import prohibitions. These measures transfer the affected commodities from the category of import-competing to the category of nontraded goods.)

FIGURE 7.2

The Domestic Market for Import-Competing Goods

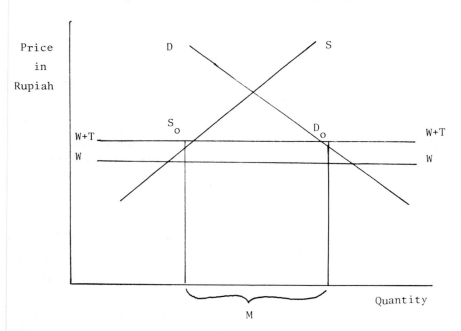

---

*Note that the actual tariff incidence will affect price formation. Hence nominal tariffs must be reduced by the relevant exemptions, undervaluations, evasions, and so on. Note also that if the importing capacity (such as ports) is strained, W + T, W + T will slope upward.

It will be noted that in this case conclusions very similar to those pertaining to export goods result:

The level of output of import-competing goods is independent of the domestic demand for them; its determinants are domestic supply conditions and world price (c.i.f. Indonesia), plus applicable import taxes, port charges, and importing costs.

The level of imports is the difference between total domestic demand and domestic supply of these goods.

The domestic wholesale price for import-competing goods is determined by world price, as modified by existing import duties, port charges, and other importing costs.

The domestic retail price is equal to the world price plus import duties, port charges, and other importing costs (= domestic wholesale price), plus domestic retailing and transportation costs.

Summarizing these propositions algebraically, we can write:

(a) Supply of import competing output:

    (i) Agricultural output:

$$A^* = A^*[P_{CIF}(1 + tm_a + ptm)]$$

    where A^* = quantity of agricultural goods domestically supplied, measured at domestic wholesale prices

        P_{CIF} = import price

        tm_a = average import duty on agricultural goods

        ptm = average rate of port charges and other importing costs

    (ii) Industrial output:

$$I^* = I^*[P_{CIF}(1 + tm_I + ptm)]$$

    where I^* = quantity of industrial goods domestically supplied, measured at domestic wholesale prices

        tm_I = average import duty on industrial goods

(b) Demand for imports:

$$M^{dom} = (A^d - A^*) + (I^d - I^*) + m_a^* A^* + m_I^* I^*$$

where M^{dom} = quantity of imports demanded, at domestic wholesale prices

A^d = quantity of agricultural goods demanded, at domestic wholesale prices

I^d = quantity of industrial goods demanded, at domestic wholesale prices

m_a^* = import requirement for intermediate goods per unit of agricultural output, at domestic wholesale prices

m_I^* = import requirement for intermediate goods per unit of industrial output, at domestic wholesale prices

Note that the first term on the right-hand side measures the shortfall of domestic supply of agricultural goods from domestic demand; the second term measures the same item for industrial goods. The last two terms reflect intermediate input needs. The nature of the equation can be seen even more clearly if we reorder terms to group similar elements together. Then

$$M^{dom} = \underbrace{A^d + I^d}_{\substack{\text{demand for} \\ \text{finished goods}}} - \underbrace{(A^* + I^*)}_{\substack{\text{domestic supply} \\ \text{of finished goods}}} + \underbrace{(m_a^* A^* + m_I^* I^*)}_{\substack{\text{demand for} \\ \text{imported} \\ \text{intermediate} \\ \text{inputs}}}$$

However, imports need to be defined in c.i.f. prices, and the above expressions were specified in domestic wholesale prices. Thus deflators must be defined to translate one set of prices into another. This can be readily done if we recall that domestic wholesale prices equal c.i.f. plus tariffs plus port and other importing costs. Then

$$M = \frac{A^d}{1 + tm_a + ptm} + \frac{I^d}{1 + tm_I + ptm} - \frac{A^*}{1 + tm_a + ptm}$$

$$- \frac{I^*}{1 + tm_I + ptm} + \frac{m_a^* A^*}{1 + t'm_a + ptm} + \frac{m_I^* I^*}{1 + t'm_I + ptm}$$

where M = quantity of imports demanded, at c.i.f. prices
$t'm_a$, $t'm_I$ = average tariffs on agricultural and industrial inputs, respectively

It is now useful to simplify notation. Let us define:

$$A = \frac{A^*}{1 + tm_a + ptm} \qquad\qquad I = \frac{I^*}{1 + tm_a + ptm}$$

$$m_a = m_a^* \frac{1 + tm_a + ptm}{1 + t'm_a + ptm} \qquad\qquad m_I = m_I^* \frac{1 + tm_I + ptm}{1 + t'm_I + ptm}$$

Let us also recognize that demand for agricultural and industrial goods depends on income. Then we can define marginal (= average) propensities to spend on agricultural (a) and industrial (i) goods:

$$\frac{A^d}{1 + tm_a + ptm} = aY \qquad\qquad \frac{I^d}{1 + tm_i + ptm} = iY$$

Using our simplified notation and the propensities to spend, we can restate the import equation as follows:

M =	(a+i)Y	−	(A + I)	+	$(m_a A + m_I I)$
	demand for finished goods		domestic supply of finished goods		demand for imported inputs

or, alternatively:

M =	(a+i)Y	−	$A(1-m_a)$	−	$I(1-m_I)$
	demand for finished goods		domestic value added in agriculture		domestic value added in industry

It follows from the above formulation that for import-competing goods, the marginal propensity to import will be equal to the marginal propensity to spend; and, furthermore that domestic production will reduce imports by less than the value of the corresponding output, as long as an import component remains.

(c) Domestic price of import-competing goods:

$$P_d^{mc} = P_{CIF}^{mc} (1 + tm + ptm) + RTChg^{mc}$$

where P_d^{mc} = domestic retail price

$RTChg^{mc}$ = domestic retailing and transportation costs

Services

Services in Indonesia are very labor-intensive, and what capital or current inputs are needed can be imported at given world prices. Furthermore, capacity in the service sector can be expanded very rapidly even in the short run. (The exceptions, as usual, confirm the rule, as in the case of electricity generation.) Moreover, the supply of unskilled labor to the urban economy of Indonesia is infinitely elastic, given the country's substantial unemployment and underemployment. While skilled labor is in much scarcer supply, as is managerial capacity, unskilled labor can be trained rapidly, thus making the supply curve of skilled labor quite flat. In total, then, it is a good approximation to assume that the supply curve of services is horizontal in the relevant range. Thus, the quantity of services forthcoming in the economy is determined by the conventional interaction of an infinitely elastic supply curve with a downward-sloping domestic demand curve, as shown in Figure 7.3. The precise level of the supply curve is dependent on input costs, where such enter the production process, and on factor costs, with the latter determined largely by historical rates of pay, as modified from time to time in response to changes in the institutional environment and the average product of labor in agriculture, which affects the reservation price of labor to the urban sector. (See G. F. Papanek, "The Effect of Economic Growth and Inflation on Workers' Income" in this volume.) The price of services is thus supply- (and tradition-) determined; the quantity produced is demand-determined.*

---

*Note that this also means that when demand shifts to the left, the capital stock becomes idle along with labor. In effect we have an ex-post clay production function, with no factor substitution.

FIGURE 7.3

The Domestic Market for Services

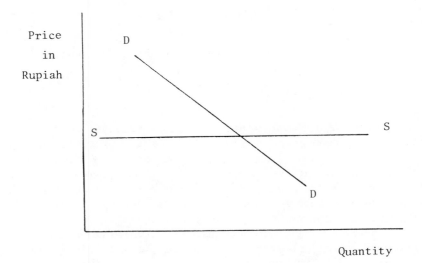

Nontraded Goods

This category consists principally of the construction trades. The markets are fully competitive, with prices and quantities determined jointly by supply and demand. As can be seen in Figure 7.4, the supply curve is fairly horizontal, then curves sharply upward as capacity in the relevant sectors is reached. A shift in demand for this kind of commodity therefore can produce increases in quantity as well as increase in price, depending on where the curves intersect. It should be noted, however, that capacity in these sectors has been expanding very rapidly, and the tendency has been to respond to shifts of the demand schedule through increases in output rather than increases in price, although the latter have taken place.

Summary and Implications

In the major commodity-producing sectors of the Indonesian economy (export and import-competing commodities), the level of domestic output is determined in the short run without regard to the level of domestic demand. Rather, domestic output is determined by the interaction between domestic supply conditions and world prices, as modified by the relevant taxes and port and other trading costs. Similarly, domestic prices in these sectors are determined by world price levels, as modified by import and export taxes and port and other trading costs. The role of domestic demand is to determine, on the one hand, the quantity of the export products in fact available for export and, on the other, the amount of imports required to close the gap between quantities demanded and supplied domestically.

FIGURE 7.4

The Domestic Market for Nontraded Goods

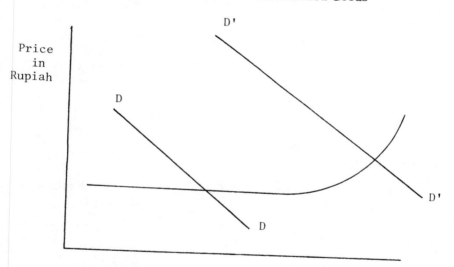

The service sector's output is fully demand-determined in the sense of responding with infinite elasticity to whatever quantity is demanded. Nontraded goods behave similarly to services but show a slower output response. Thus, for these last types of goods, increases in the quantity demanded transitorily show an increase in prices together with increase in output. Over time, however, capacity expands and the quantity demanded is forthcoming. In view of this capacity-enlarging behavior, the nontraded goods sector and the service sector will henceforth be grouped together for modeling purposes.

The implications of these market structures for the short-run macroeconomic behavior of the economy are very significant. In the first place, the supply-determined nature of major commodity production reverses the usual order of causation. Rather than "demand creating its own supply," we have a situation of "supply creating its own demand"—that is, commodity production generates income, which in turn signifies demand for commodities. Second, the supply-determined nature of commodity production means that a major portion of national income is exogenously determined in the short run and only a minor portion—services and nontraded output—is determined by the usual income-expenditure adjustment mechanism. If it is borne in mind that many services are directly complementary to commodity production, the scope of endogenous income determination is reduced even further. Third, the residual nature of major components of export supply and import demand makes the balance of trade very sensitive to changes in income and demand, thus reflecting the great openness of the Indonesian economy. Fourth, this openness causes the stock of money to become endogenous and very closely connected to the balance of payments as changes in the reserve position expand or contract the domestic monetary base. Fifth, the close link of domestic to world prices signifies that world inflation is imported unless world price increases are offset by changes in import levies. Domestically originated inflation is possible, however, if the trade taxes, port charges, or other trading costs change in the appropriate direction.

It is also possible for an increase in the international price of wage goods—specifically rice—to cause inflation of and by itself through an increase in the wage component of importing costs of commodities (stevedoring costs, transportation wages, importers' wage bills, wholesalers' and retailers' labor costs), which signifies a rise of all import-competing prices (through $\Delta RT\,Chg^{mc}$). Furthermore, it should be noted that as increases in domestic demand cause commodities to cease being exported and become import-competing instead, price rises equal to the difference between c.i.f. and f.o.b. prices plus domestic transport and selling revenues and trade taxes will ensue.* Finally, a ratchet effect may be exerted on prices if an increase in demand temporarily drives up prices of import goods until expanded supplies can be ordered and imported. This, in turn, can lead to lasting wage increases, which are then reflected in higher importing costs.

———————

*Note that in a time of rising international food prices, the drying up of exports of cassava in late 1972 paved the way for substantial price increases in this commodity.

THE MODEL

In the preceding section it was argued that domestic prices in Indonesia depend on four elements: world prices, trade taxes, port charges and other importing costs, and wages. This section explores how the domestic level of income is determined, and how it interacts with the balance of payments and with the monetary system. For this purpose it is assumed that world prices are given and constant; that trade taxes are given and constant; that port charges and other importing costs do not change; and that wages are and stay at their supply-determined level. These assumptions are not implausible approximations of reality, given Indonesia's size in the world markets (that is, it is a price taker) and given the level of unemployment and underemployment in the economy (which means a wage determined largely by the supply of labor). Moreover, trade taxation is not normally a tool of short-run economic management and importing costs are largely determined by wages. In sum, these assumptions mean that prices are given from outside the model.

Income and Expenditure Functions

The basic identity of income with the sum of private and government expenditure and the net balance of trade is valid for Indonesia, as it is for other countries. Thus we have

$$Y \equiv E + G + \Delta ST + X - M \tag{1}$$

where Y represents income, E represents private expenditure, G represents government expenditure, ΔST represents expenditure on increased food stockpile, X stands for exports, and M stands for imports.*

Private expenditure is equal to the sum of private expenditure for consumption and for investment. The latter itself is the sum of investment expenditures by nationals and by foreigners. Equations (2) and (3) show this in symbolic form:

$$E = C + IV \tag{2}$$

$$IV = IV^n + FPI \tag{3}$$

---

*For a full set of symbols used see the list at the end of this chapter.

where C is consumption, IV is investment, IV^n is investment by nationals, and FPI is foreign private investment.

Consumption and investment expenditure by nationals is the composite result of decisions by two different groups of households. One group owns their own businesses and the second does not.

The business households have the option of spending only their own income or of borrowing in order to raise expenditure above current income. On the other hand, they are required to surrender some of their income as taxes, and they have the option of spending their remaining available resources on consumption goods, on investment goods for their own business, on other "store of value" real assets (such as gold or real estate), or of increasing their stock of liquidity through raising their holdings of money or acquiring savings or time deposits in the banking system. Since investment in their own businesses yields a much higher rate of return than is obtainable from deposits in the banking system, the business households have little incentive to save in monetary form except to satisfy their liquidity needs or to build up collateral for borrowing. Furthermore, since much credit from the banking system is subsidized,* business households will attempt to borrow as much as possible from the banks, and invest the proceeds in their businesses. As a result, business households spend on consumption and on investment in their own businesses their total income plus whatever they are able to borrow, less taxes and any increases in holdings in money or time deposits that they may need for liquidity or collateral purposes. In symbols:

$$(C + IV^n)_{bh} = Y_{bh} + \triangle CRP_{bh} + \triangle CRF_{bh} - T_{bh} - \triangle CMD_{bh} - \triangle L^d_{bh}$$

where the subscript refers to business households and T is taxes, CMD is time deposits, L^d_{bh} is liquidity demanded, CRP is credit from the Indonesian monetary system (Bank Indonesia plus banking system), CRF is direct credit from abroad, and $\triangle$ signifies an increase.

By comparison, the options open to the pure (nonbusiness) households are fewer. By definition they do not have the option of investing directly in a business, and thus typically invest their savings in the banking system as either savings or time deposits. Furthermore, they do not usually have access to subsidized credit,

---

*This is particularly true of "investment credits." Working-capital credit carries a higher rate, although it is probably still below the private rate of return on investment.

and thus are not normally borrowers from the banking system. As a result pure households typically spend only for consumption and only out of their own income. What they do not spend for consumption goes into savings or time deposits. In symbols:

$$C_{ph} = Y_{ph} - T_{ph} - \triangle CMD_{ph}$$

where the subscript refers to pure households.

Equation 4 sums these relations for both types of households:

$$C + IV^n = Y - T - \triangle CMD - \triangle L^d + \triangle CRP + \triangle CRF \tag{4}$$

where, again, T stands for taxes, CMD represents domestically owned quasi money (savings and time deposits owned by residents of Indonesia), L^d represents liquidity demand, CRP is credit from the Indonesian monetary system (Bank Indonesia plus banking system) to the private sector, CRF is direct credit to the private sector from abroad, and $\triangle$ signifies an increase.

To the extent that the accumulation of domestically owned quasi money, $\triangle CMD$, reflects savings behavior of pure households, we can define a marginal or average propensity* to save in the banking system; to the extent that $\triangle CMD$ reflects accumulation of collateral by business households, which in turn is related to their income, a similar coefficient would be appropriate. Defining sb as the marginal (= average) propensity of all households to save in the banking system, we can write:

$$\triangle CMD = sbY \tag{5}$$

Furthermore, desired liquidity can be related to transactions needs and income; thus:

$$L^d = kY \tag{6}$$
$$\triangle L^d = k\triangle Y \tag{6a}$$

where k is the transactions liquidity needed per unit of income, which in turn will depend on the real interest rate(s) in the economy and on the degree of monetization.

---

*Throughout the model the marginal and average propensities are set equal for algebraic simplicity. However, the coefficients vary across time as a function of various elements, as noted in "Calibrating the Model."

Government in Indonesia aims at maintaining a balanced cash budget. Thus it plans to spend precisely what it expects to collect. Nonetheless, operating surpluses and deficits do occur, which are financed by the monetary system. In addition, government spends in excess of its tax revenue to the extent that it receives foreign aid. This situation is expressed in equation (7):

$$G = \overline{T} + \Delta CRG + AID \tag{7}$$

where $\overline{T}$ represents expected tax revenue, ΔCRG represents government borrowing from the monetary system, and AID is foreign aid, consisting of program aid and project aid.

Tax collections in Indonesia are based on a target system, which assigns to each regional and provincial tax collector an amount of taxes that he is expected to collect from the taxpayers in his area. These targets are determined on the basis of the historical experience of tax collections under existing rates, in conjunction with desired changes in enforcement. Tax collectors will usually collect the amount targeted for them, unless the tax bases on which the rates are levied have varied substantially from their forecast values. At the same time, the tax target is adjusted during the tax year as collections or other indicators give evidence that the base is significantly different from the intial forecast corresponding to it. As a consequence of this system, the elasticity of tax revenue to changes in the base depends fundamentally on revisions in the targets. This revenue function is expressed by equation (8):

$$T = \overline{T} + t\,(Y - \hat{Y}) + t'\,(M - \hat{M}) \tag{8}$$

where t and t' are the average tax rates on domestic income and imports, respectively, and the "hatted" variables represent the estimated values on which the tax targets have been constructed. Moreover,

$$\hat{Y} = Y + E_y$$
$$\hat{M} = M + E_m$$

where E_y and E_m are the errors in forecasting the base, which are reduced by a process of successive approximations during the collection year.

The export and import functions can be taken directly from the discussion in "The Markets for Goods and Services" with regard to the nature of the market for export and import-competing products. Equation (9) shows realized exports as the difference between an exogenous level of production of export goods and an income-dependent consumption of these products.

$$X = PX = xY \tag{9}$$

In turn, imports equal the difference between domestic production of and domestic demand for agricultural and industrial commodities plus the import component of domestic output and of foreign private investment, and any desired stockpiling of agricultural goods that may take place under the Food Logistics Board's (BULOG) stockpile program.* These relationships are captured in equations (10) and (11):

$$M = (A^d - A) + (I^d - I) + m_a A + m_i I + m_f FPI + m_x PX + \Delta ST \tag{10}$$

$$M = (a + i)Y - A(1 - m_a) - I(1 - m_i) + m_f FPI + m_x PX + \Delta ST \tag{11}$$

where a equals the marginal (= average) propensity to absorb agricultural goods; i equals the marginal (= average) propensity to absorb industrial goods; A and I are the levels of domestic production of agricultural and industrial goods, respectively (measured at c.i.f. prices); m_a, m_i, m_f, and m_x are the import components of domestic production of agricultural and industrial goods, foreign private investment, and exports, respectively; and ST is the level of the BULOG stockpile of agricultural goods.

Income and Expenditure Equilibrium

We can now develop the equations for equilibrium income and expenditure by substituting equations (2) through (11) in equation (1). First, however, it is useful to note that with income in equilibrium, according to equation (6a), $\Delta L^d = 0$; that is, with income stable, liquidity will be at the desired level. Furthermore, with income stable, estimated income and imports ($\hat{Y}$, $\hat{M}$) in equation (8) will be equal to the equilibrium values of income and imports, and tax

---

*Notice that the expansion of the equation of "The Markets for Goods and Services" to include imported inputs into exports, foreign private investment, and the stockpile follows from the wider perspective that we are now dealing with. It should also be pointed out that an import component of government expenditure is omitted because of lack of data on its magnitude.

collections will be precisely equal to the tax target. Carrying out the substitutions, collecting terms, and solving for the equilibrium income level, we obtain the following expression:

$$\overline{Y} = \frac{1}{sb + x + a + i} \; [PX(1 - m_x) + A(1 - m_a) + I(1 - m_i)$$

$$+ \; FPI(1 - m_f) + \triangle CRP + \triangle CRF + \triangle CRG + AID] \tag{12}$$

This expression for equilibrium income can be recognized as an analog to the conventional Keynesian formulation of autonomous expenditures multiplied by an income multiplier. Indeed, in this equation the multiplier is the reciprocal of the sum of the marginal propensities to save in the form of bank deposits (sb), to absorb exports (x), and to absorb import-competing commodities $(a + i)$. In turn, the exogenous expenditures consist of the domestic component of production of export goods $\{PX(1 - m_x)\}$, the domestic component of agricultural and industrial production $\{A(1 - m_a) + I(1 - m_i)\}$, the domestic component of foreign private investment $\{FPI(1 - m_f)\}$, the increase in credit to the business households $\{\triangle CRP + \triangle CRF\}$ and government $\{\triangle CRG\}$, and foreign aid $\{AID\}$.

Equation (12) reveals in symbolic form a characteristic of the Indonesian economy already noted at the end of "The Markets for Goods and Services": the exogenous nature of goods production $\{PX(1 - m_x) + A(1 - m_a) + I(1 - m_i)\}$, which determines income, rather than being determined by it. Demand for services, however, is endogenous and is the basis for the existence of a multiplier.

Moreover, the nature of the multiplier can be further clarified if it is noticed that the propensities in its denominator sum to 1 minus the propensity to spend on services and nontraded goods. Thus the multiplier is the inverse of the propensity to spend within the economy. Therefore it is analogous to the Keynesian multiplier, which is the inverse of 1 minus the propensity to spend for consumption. The difference arises from the recognition that leakages in Indonesia are not only into savings but also into imports, which at the margin means all demand for goods, and from the recognition that expenditure on domestic output for investment purposes is not a leakage. Thus the substitution of propensity to consume by propensity to spend, and by the addition of the caveat that the expenditure stay within the economy, use of the propensity to spend on services and nontraded goods.

Equilibrium imports can be derived by inserting equation (12) into equation (11), with the following outcome:

$$\overline{M} = \frac{a + i}{sb + x + a + i} \; [PX(1 - m_x) + A(1 - m_a) + I(1 - m_i)$$

$$+ \; FPI(1 - m_f) + \triangle CRP + \triangle CRF + \triangle CRG + AID]$$

$$- \; A(1 - m_a) - I(1 - m_i) + m_f FPI + m_x PX + \triangle ST \tag{13}$$

which can be reduced to the following:

$$\overline{M} = \frac{a + i}{sb + x + a + i} \; [\triangle CRP + \triangle CRF + \triangle CRG + AID]$$

$$- \; \frac{sb + x}{sb + x + a + i} \; [A(1 - m_a) + I(1 - m_i)]$$

$$+ \; \frac{a + i + m_f(sb + x)}{sb + x + a + i} \; FPI + \frac{a + i + m_x(sb + x)}{sb + x + a + i} \; PX + \triangle ST$$

$$\tag{14}$$

Imports are seen to be directly related to the level of production of export goods, the increase in credit, the increase in stockpiling, the level of foreign private investment, and the level of foreign aid. They are negatively correlated with the level of domestic output of import-competing agricultural and industrial goods. Each of these variables, however, affects equilibrium imports with different intensity, depending on the manner in which it acts directly on the level of imports and indirectly on that level through influence on the equilibrium level of income.

In turn, equilibrium exports are equal to production of export goods less domestic demand for these goods. The corresponding equation can be derived by inserting equation (12) into equation (9), with the following result:

$$\overline{X} = PX - \frac{x}{sb + x + a + i} \; [PX(1 - m_x) + A(1 - m_a) + I(1 - m_i)$$

$$+ \; FPI(1 - m_f) + \triangle CRP + \triangle CRF + \triangle CRG + AID] \tag{15}$$

which can be simplified to the following reduced form:

$$\overline{X} = \frac{sb + a + i + xm_x}{sb + a + i + x} \; PX - \frac{x}{sb + x + a + i} \; [A(1 - m_a)$$

$$+ \; I(1 - m_i) + PFI(1 - m_f) + \triangle CRP + \triangle CRF + \triangle CRG + AID]$$

$$\tag{16}$$

In like manner we can derive the equilibrium level of the increase in domestically owned quasi money, which is a constant fraction of the equilibrium level of income. The equation is as follows:

$$\overline{\triangle CMD} = \frac{sb}{sb + x + a + i} \; [PX(1 - m_x) + A(1 - m_a) + I(1 - m_i)$$

$$+ \; FPI(1 - m_f) + \triangle CRP + \triangle CRF + \triangle CRG + AID] \qquad (17)$$

We can now calculate the equilibrium value of the balance of trade by taking the difference between equilibrium levels of exports and imports, as follows:

$$\overline{BT} = \overline{X} - \overline{M} = \; PX(1 - m_x) - \frac{x}{sb + x + a + i} \; [EXOG]$$

$$- \; \frac{a + i}{sb + x + a + i} \; [EXOG] + A(1 - m_a) + I(1 - m_i)$$

$$- \; m_f \; FPI - \triangle ST \qquad (18)$$

where

$$EXOG = PX(1 - m_x) + A(1 - m_a) + I(1 - m_i) + FPI(1 - m_f)$$

$$+ \; \triangle CRP + \triangle CRG + AID$$

Collecting terms, simplifying, and using (17) leads to

$$\overline{BT} = \overline{X} - \overline{M} = \overline{CMD} - FPI - \triangle CRP - \triangle CRF - \triangle CRG - AID$$

$$- \; \triangle ST \qquad (19)$$

Note that capital inflows have a negative effect on the balance of trade (but not the balance of payments, see equation [20] below). This occurs because these inflows increase imports either directly (for instance, import content of foreign private investment) or indirectly (via increased domestic income and expenditure). Such a result signifies that the capital inflow is effectively transferred to the economy in the form of real goods, and does not remain a mere paper transaction. Domestic credit creation ($\triangle CRP$, $\triangle CRG$) also has a negative effect, because it has an expansionary internal effect and hence raises imports. The increase in savings and time deposits, by comparison, has the opposite effect, because it reduces domestic expenditure. Finally, the increase in the food stockpile

(ΔST) raises food imports directly, hence its negative effect on the balance of trade.

Reserve changes will reflect the balance of trade and net capital flows:

$$\overline{\Delta ITL} = \overline{B} = \overline{BT} + \Delta CRF + FPI + AID = \overline{\Delta CMD} - \Delta CRP$$

$$- \Delta CRG - \Delta ST \qquad (20)$$

where ITL means official international reserves of the banking system.

It follows that Indonesia will run a positive balance of payments and accumulate reserves as long as the increase in domestically owned quasi money exceeds the increase in autonomous credit expansion and the increase in the food stockpile.

At this point it is worth noting that foreign-exchange reserves and the commodity stockpile are alternative ways for the economy to hold foreign assets. Moreover, the institutional manner in which funding of the stockpile occurs causes these two alternatives to exchange on a one-for-one basis with no macroeconomic cost to the economy. Hence the division of the country's foreign assets into currency and rice reserves can proceed unhampered by concerns for side effects on the domestic macroeconomic balance.

Finally, the equilibrium level of liquidity is derived by inserting equation (12) into equation (6) to obtain

$$\overline{L} = \frac{k}{sb + x + a + i} [PX(1 - m_x) + A(1 - m_a) + I(1 - m_i)$$

$$+ FPI(1 - m_f) + \Delta CRP + \Delta CRF + \Delta CRG + PGM + PJC] \qquad (21)$$

The Monetary System

The Indonesian monetary system consists of the central bank, Bank Indonesia, and the commercial banking system in which the state commercial banks have overwhelming importance. Schematic balance sheets of Bank Indonesia, the consolidated commercial banking system, and the monetary system are shown in Table 7.1.

A few things should be pointed out. The first of these is that due to Indonesia's free foreign-exchange market, commercial banks are allowed to offer accounts in foreign exchange to their clients. A certain number of Indonesian residents have chosen to do so. Item FL2D which appears in the consolidated balance sheet of commercial banks reflects foreign-exchange liability to the Indonesian public. In turn, FL2F reflects the foreign-exchange deposits of

TABLE 7.1

Indonesia's Monetary Accounts

Assets			Liabilities
		Monetary Authorities	
Net foreign assets	ITL	CUR1	Currency issued
Net domestic assets	CR1	RDP	Demand deposits of commercial banks
Net credit to government	CR1G	DD1	Demand deposits of others
Net credit to BULOG	CR1B		
DICS	DICS		
Net credit to private sector (direct and through banks)	CR1P		
Other net	CR1O		
Total assets	SAS1	SLB1	Total liabilities
		Commercial Banks	
Rupiah reserves	RES2	DD2	Demand deposits
Currency	CUR2	CM	Savings and time deposits
Demand deposits in Bank Indonesia	RDP	CMD	Owned by residents
		CMF	Owned by nonresidents
Foreign assets	FA2	FL2	Foreign exchange deposits
Required reserves	RFA2	FL2D	Owned by residents
		FL2F	Owned by nonresidents
Domestic assets	CR2		
Net credit to government	CR2G		
Credit to private sector			

Net credit to private sector gross credit in rupiah less Bank Indonesia funds	CR2P	
Credit in foreign exchange	VFA2	
Net others	CR2O	
Total assets	SAS2	SLB2 Total liabilities

Monetary System

Foreign assets	NFA	MO	Money supply
Bank Indonesia	ITL	CUR	Currency in hands of public
Commercial banks	FA2	DD	Rp. demand deposits
Net domestic assets	CR	DD1	Bank Indonesia
Net credit to government	CRG	DD2	Commercial banks
Bank Indonesia	CR1G	FL2	Foreign exchange deposits
Commercial banks	CR2G	FL2D	Owned by residents
Less: Treasury cash	CURT	FL2F	Owned by nonresidents
Credit to BULOG	CR1B	CM	Quasi money: savings/time deposits
Credit to private sector	CRP	CMD	Owned by residents
Bank Indonesia	CR1P	CMF	Owned by nonresidents
DICS	DICS		
Commercial banks rupiahs	CR2P		
Commercial banks foreign exchange	VFA2		
Other net	CRO		
Total assets	SAS	SLB	Total liabilities

Source: Compiled by the authors.

nonresidents. On the asset side of the balance sheet, it should be noted that commercial banks are entitled to lend in foreign exchange both inside Indonesia and abroad and thus an item for voluntary foreign-exchange investment, VFA2, appears on the asst side of the balance sheet. Since most of the lending in foreign exchange is to resident business, it is appropriately grouped with rupiah lending to the private sector, rather than being shown as part of net foreign assets, as is customary in the conventional International Monetary Fund presentation. Finally, it should be noted that Bank Indonesia extends credit to the private sector through various mechanisms, including rediscounts to the banks. The item Net Credit to the Private Sector (CR1P) summarizes these operations. A special kind of Bank Indonesia loan, the DICS, arises from the liquidation of accounts of enterprises previously expropriated, which are now made available gradually to new foreign private investors.

In addition to the normal balance sheet identities, a number of functional relationships hold within the accounts of the monetary system.

A principal relationship refers to the reserve requirements. Commercial banks are required to hold reserves against their demand, savings, and time deposits. They may hold these reserves in the form of currency or demand deposits in Bank Indonesia. Equation (22) expresses this relationship. (For definitions of the symbols in equation (22), refer to Table 7.1.)

$$RES2 = (RMO)\,DD2 + (RCM)CM + XRES2 \tag{22}$$

Where RMO is the percentage reserve requirement on demand deposits, RCM is the percentage reserve requirement on other rupiah deposits (time deposits and savings), and XRES2 is excess rupiah reserves held voluntarily by the banking system. The corresponding equation for foreign-exchange assets is given by the following expression:

$$RFA2 = (RFL)\,FL2 \tag{23}$$

where RFL is the percentage reserve requirement for foreign-exchange liability to the public. Note that banks can invest the part of their foreign-exchange deposits that they are not compelled to hold as reserves in foreign exchange, creating VFA2, or they may convert that foreign exchange into rupiah and use it to expand credit in local currency. From the above two equations it can be deduced that credit from commercial banks will be equal to that part of rupiah deposits not segregated for required reserves or kept in voluntary excess reserces, plus that part of the foreign-exchange liability not used for foreign-exchange reserves. This result is summarized in equation (24):

$$CR2 = (1 - RMO)DD2 + (1 - RCM)CM - XRES2$$
$$+ FL2(1 - RFL) \tag{24}$$

In terms of borrowers, commercial bank credit can be divided between credit to the government and to the private sector. Thus:

$$CR2 = CR2G + CR2P + VFA2 \tag{25}$$

(Credit to others, CR2O, is included in CR2P for reasons of simplicity.)

The monetary system also has functional relationships with the real system. The first of these arises from the definition of liquidity. It will be recalled from equation (6) that liquidity is demanded in proportion to income. We now note that liquidity is constituted by money (rupiah demand deposits and currency), plus foreign-exchange deposits owned by residents. Furthermore, we shall assume that at given interest rates, the public wishes to hold currency in a given proportion to rupiah demand deposits. It should be noted that in many economies, foreign-exchange deposits have more the nature of quasi money, being used primarily as an interest-bearing store of value. It is felt that in Indonesia they are used primarily by business households as a ready means for making payments abroad. This information is summarized in equations (26) and (27).

$$L = MO + FL2D = CUR + DD2 + FL2D \tag{26}$$

$$CUR = \alpha MO \tag{27}$$

A second link of the financial system to the real system arises from the freeing of blocked rupiah accounts resulting from earlier expropriation of foreign enterprises. Under the DICS system, the central bank makes rupiah funds available to foreign private investors. The amount of periodic disbursement is very dependent on particular negotiations, so no specific equation for this item is posited.

Further direct functional relationship between the financial and the real systems arises from the operations of BULOG. This agency is entitled to draw on a central bank account to finance its purchasing operations during the harvest season. It repays the loans as it sells its stockpiles. The net change of BULOG debt to the central bank, year to year, is equivalent to the increase in its stockpile and any new net losses (or gains) that may have arisen from its operations. Note that the existence of an annual BULOG loss financed by Bank Indonesia is a constant expansionary influence, and requires inclusion in equation (1) alongside the increase in stockpile, ΔST. This relationship is given expression by equation (28).

$$\Delta CR1B = \Delta ST + \Delta LOSBUL \tag{28}$$

Finally, the change in quasi money in the monetary system is, by definition, the result of changes in holdings of quasi money by Indonesian residents plus changes in quasi money owned by foreigners. The first of these is directly related to income, thus constituting a further link between the monetary and real systems:

$$\Delta CM = \Delta CMD + \Delta CMF = sbY + \Delta CMF \tag{29}$$

It should be noted that under the government's policy of a balanced cash budget, changes in net credit to the government from year to year are intended to be null. An accumulated stock of credit from the monetary system to the government naturally exists, and the government does borrow for transitory cash needs during the year. This notwithstanding, the policy is to keep expenditures down to the level of revenues and to repay all current borrowings from the monetary system.

Aggregate Equilibrium

The next step is to integrate the real and monetary sides of the economy into an overall equilibrium that encompasses the income and expenditure equilibrium and the financial equilibrium of the monetary system.

The monetary variables affecting the equilibrium values shown in equations (12)-(21) are the increases in credit to the private sector and to the government. In turn, the increase in credits to the private sector is determined in part by other variables of the financial system as well as of the real system.

From the consolidated balance sheet of the monetary system, we know that the increase in credit to the private sector is the sum of new lending from the central bank and the commercial banks. The former includes lending to the resident private sector and to foreign private investors. Equation (30) summarizes this equality:

$$\triangle CRP = \triangle CR1P + \triangle DICS + \triangle CR2P + \triangle VFA2 \tag{30}$$

Increase in lending to foreign investors (DICS) is a function of foreign private investment, but with such variability as to be better taken as exogenous. Commercial bank lending to the private sector is endogenous, depending on the banking system's level of deposits, the required reserve ratios, and banks' wishes regarding excess reserves. These determinants are shown in equation (24) in combination with (25).* Inserting the relevant first-difference forms of these equations into equation (30), we obtain the following:

$$\triangle CRP = \triangle CR1P + \triangle DICS + (1 - RMO) \triangle DD2 + (1 - RCM) \triangle CM$$

$$- \triangle XRES2 + (1 - RFL) \triangle FL2 - \triangle CR2G \tag{31}$$

We know from equation (6) that with income in equilibrium, ($\triangle Y = 0$), changes in liquidity will be zero as well ($\triangle L = 0$). Given a set of stable interest rates, it follows further that the different liquid assets held by the public will also be in equilibrium. That is, the ratio of currency to demand deposits and the ratio of each of these to foreign-exchange deposits is constant. Hence $\triangle DD2 = \triangle FL2D = \triangle CUR = 0$. Finally, equilibrium implies for the banking system that the level of excess reserves and the distribution of assets are at the desired level. Hence $\triangle XRES2 = 0$. Inserting these values in equation (31) and making use of equation (29), we observe that the increase in credit to the private sector is equal to the sum of increase in central bank credit to the domestic private sector and to foreign private investors, plus that part of the increase in savings and time deposits not required to be kept in the form of reserves and not lent to the government:

$$\triangle CRP = \triangle CR1P + \triangle DICS + (1 - RCM) (sbY + \triangle CMF)$$

$$+ (1 - RFL) \triangle FL2F - \triangle CR2G \tag{32}$$

Inserting this result in equation (12) and noting the comment preceding (28) gives us an expression for the equilibrium level of income as a function of exogenous real and monetary variables:

---

*To keep the expression manageable in size, the reserve ratios are assumed constant. If one wishes to calculate the effect of changes in these ratios, the full difference form must be written out.

equilibrium income	$\overline{Y}$
equals	$=$
multiplier	$\dfrac{1}{(RCM)sb + x + a + i}$
times	
real output levels	$[PX(1 - m_x) + A(1 - m_a) + I(1 - m_i)$
+	
foreign private investment	$+ FPI(1 - m_f)$
+	
credit to the private sector	$+ \Delta CR1P + \Delta DICS + \Delta CRF$ $+ (1 - RCM)\Delta CMF + (1 - RFL)\Delta FL2F$
+	
central bank and foreign lending to the government	$\Delta CR1G + AID + \Delta LOSBUL]$ (33)

Contrasting equations (33) and (12), two important changes can be noted. First, the income multiplier has changed, reflecting the fact that as a result of the functioning of the financial system, not all the funds put in savings and time deposits are lost from the income stream. Indeed, the part of those funds not required to be held by the banking system as reserves flows back into the income stream in the form of credit to the private sector, which is spent on consumption and investment. Hence, one of the leakages from the income stream has been partially plugged and the multiplier is now larger.

Second, the exogenous variables have changed with the removal of part of bank credit. On the other hand, they now include that part of foreign monies flowing into rupiah-denominated time deposits that are not sterilized by regulation in the form of required reserves against these deposits. Furthermore, discretionary lending by the central bank appears explicitly, as do government finance from the central bank and foreign aid.

Expressions corresponding to the equilibrium level of imports and exports, accumulation of savings and time deposits, and stock of liquidity developed on the basis of equation (33) are shown in equations (34) through (37):

$$\overline{M} = \Delta ST + \frac{a + i}{(RCM)sb + x + a + i} [\Delta CR1P + \Delta DICS + \Delta CR1G$$

$$+ \Delta LOSBUL + AID + \Delta CRF + (1 - RCM) \Delta CMF$$

$$+ (1 - RFL) \Delta FL2F] + \frac{(RCM)sb + x}{(RCM)sb + x + a + i} [A(1 - m_a)$$

$$+ I(1 - m_i)] + \frac{(a + i) + m_f[(RCM)sb + x]}{(RCM)sb + x + a + i} FPI$$

$$+ \frac{a + i + m_x [(RCM)sb + x]}{(RCM)sb + x + a + i} PX \qquad (34)$$

$$\overline{X} = \frac{(RCM)sb + a + i + xm_x}{(RCM)sb + x + a + i} PX - \frac{x}{(RCM)sb + x + a + i} [A(1 - m_a)$$

$$+ I(1 - m_i) + FPI(1 - m_f) + \Delta CR1P + \Delta DICS + \Delta CRIG$$

$$+ (1 - RCM) \Delta CMF + (1 - RFL) \Delta FL2F + \Delta LOSBUL$$

$$+ AID + \Delta CRF] \qquad (35)$$

$$\overline{CMD} = \frac{sb}{(RCM)sb + x + a + i} [PX(1 - m_x) + A(1 - m_a) + I(1 - m_i)$$

$$+ FPI(1 - m_f) + \Delta CR1P + \Delta CRF + \Delta DICS + \Delta LOSBUL$$

$$+ \Delta CRIG + AID + (1 - RCM) \Delta CMF + (1 - RFL) \Delta FL2F] \qquad (36)$$

$$\overline{L} = \frac{k}{(RCM)sb + x + a + i} [PX(1 - m_x) + A(1 - m_a) + I(1 - m_i)$$

$$+ FPI(1 - m_f) + \Delta CR1P + \Delta DICS + \Delta CRIG + AID + \Delta LOSBUL$$

$$+ \Delta CRF + (1 - RCM) \Delta CMF + (1 - RFL) \Delta FL2F] \qquad (37)$$

The equilibrium change in the balance of trade can be determined by taking the difference between the equilibrium levels of exports and imports as given by equations (34)–(35). The resulting value is shown in equation (38):

$$\overline{BT} = \overline{X} - \overline{M} = (RCM) \overline{\Delta CMD} - FPI - \Delta CR1P - \Delta DICS$$

$$- \Delta CRIG - \Delta LOSBUL - AID - \Delta CRF - \Delta ST$$

$$- (1 - RCM) \; \Delta CMF - (1 - RFL) \Delta FL2F \qquad (38)$$

Comparing this expression with equation (19), it can be seen that including the effects of the monetary system in the general equilibrium results in a substantial deterioration of the annual balance of trade. In the first place, only the part of the increase in domestic savings and time deposits that is held for required reserves contributes to generating a surplus. In the second place, the tendency toward deficit is aggravated by the lending of commercial banks out of foreign-capital inflow into time deposits $[(1 - RCM) \Delta CMF]$ and foreign-exchange deposits $[(1 - RFL)\Delta FL2F]$. This deterioration in the balance of trade is, however, offset by additional inflows on capital account. Equations (39), (40), (40a), and (41) provide alternative expressions for the equilibrium change in the overall balance of payments.

$$\overline{B} = \overline{BT} + FPI + \Delta CMF + \Delta FL2F + AID + \Delta CRF \qquad (39)$$

$$\overline{B} = (RCM) \, (\overline{\Delta CMD} + \Delta CMF) - \Delta DICS - \Delta CR1P - \Delta ST$$

$$- \Delta CR1G - \Delta LOSBUL + RFL(\Delta FL2F) \qquad (40)$$

$$\overline{B} = (RCM) \, (\overline{\Delta CMD} + \Delta CMF) + RFL(\Delta FL2F) - (\Delta DICS$$

$$+ \Delta CR1P + \Delta CR1B + \Delta CR1G) \qquad (40a)$$

$$\overline{B} - (RCM) \, (\overline{\Delta \dot{CMD}} + \Delta CMF) + RFL(\Delta FL2F) - \Delta CR1 \qquad (41)$$

From equation (41) we see that in equilibrium the balance of payments will equal the net difference between the accumulation of required reserves in the banking system and the expansion of central bank credit.

The international reserves of the monetary authorities will increase by only a part of the surplus on the balance of payments; the remainder will be retained by the commercial banks as foreign assets. The allocation between Bank Indonesia and the commercial banks is a function of the reserves against foreign-exchange liabilities that the banks are required to deposit in Bank Indonesia. Thus,

$$RFL(\Delta FL2F) = RFLBI \, (\Delta FL2F) + (RFL-RFLBI) \, (\Delta FL2F)$$

with only the first term on the right-hand side of the equation accruing to official reserves. Incorporating this into (41), we obtain

$$\Delta \overline{ITL} = RCM \, (\overline{\Delta CMD} + \Delta CMF) + RFLBI \, (\Delta FL2F) - \Delta CRI \qquad (42)$$

Comparison of equation (42) with equation (20) shows that inclusion of the financial system results in an equilibrium change in international official reserves arising from the difference between the equilibrium level of increase in required reserves held by the banking system against increases in time deposits, savings deposits, and nonresident foreign-exchange deposits, on the one hand, and the increase in central bank credit, on the other.

It follows that if the latter is held to zero, the system will steadily accumulate international reserves. By the same token, equation (42) can be used to derive the equilibrium level of central bank credit that can be sustained for any desired equilibrium accumulation of international reserves.

Summary

The Indonesian macroeconomic system is characterized by the interaction of two types of productive sectors: those whose output is supply-determined (export production, agricultural and industrial import-competing production) and those whose output is demand-determined (services and nontraded goods). The existence of the second type of sector gives rise to the operation of a multiplier.

Financial elements enter into the determination of income in Indonesia through two channels: credit increases the level of expenditure of both the private sector and the government, thus expanding the level of activity of the demand-determined sectors; accumulation of financial assets, mainly time and savings deposits, represents a leakage from the income stream and thus affects the size of the multiplier. However, to the extent that greater bank deposits lead to an increase in credit, the leakage from financial asset accumulation is reduced. Hence the reserve requirement becomes an element in the multiplier.

In summary terms, equilibrium income can be written as follows:

$$\overline{Y} = \lambda \, [EXOG]$$

where λ is the multiplier and [EXOG] represents the independent variables generating autonomous expenditure.

The multiplier is the reciprocal of the sum of the leakages. These are the propensities to absorb exports (x), absorb agricultural goods (a), absorb industrial goods (i), and hold bank reserves ([RCM]sb). Thus

$$\lambda = \frac{1}{x + a + i + (RCM)sb}$$

The autonomous elements are of two kinds: real and financial. Thus

$$EXOG = PX(1 - m_x) + A(1 - m_a) + I(1 - m_i)$$
value added in export, agriculture, and industry

$$+ \triangle CR1P + \triangle DICS + \triangle CR1G + \triangle LOSBUL$$
central bank credit to the private and public sectors

$$+ \triangle CRF + FPI(1 - mf) + AID$$
foreign private and public capital inflow

$$+ (1-RCM)\triangle CMF + (1 - RFL)\triangle FL2F$$
bank lending of foreign deposits in the banking system

It follows that financial flows, say foreign capital inflow, will have an immediate short-run effect on the nation's income level, as determined by the reserve requirements and the multiplier. It also follows that different kinds of autonomous expenditures are substitutes for each other, thus offering scope for income stabilization measures. For example, a fall in export production can be offset through increased aid. It also follows that apparent gains in efficiency may have macroeconomic costs. Thus, a smaller loss on BULOG's operations will cause a reduction in autonomous expenditure and a decline in national income. This contradictory result becomes plausible when we realize that a reduction in BULOG's loss signifies either a higher rice price to consumers or a lower one to growers, and thus withdraws purchasing power from the population. Such reduction in real income must lead to lower real expenditure and a downward adjustment through the multiplier. However, a lower $\triangle LOSBUL$ can easily be offset by greater central bank credit elsewhere, thus reestablishing the original macrobalance.

The balance-of-payments result is the outcome of an adjustment mechanism with income fluctuations as the main element. However, since the output of traded goods is given, the marginal propensity to import is equal to the marginal propensity to spend on traded goods. This feature reflects the great openness of the economy and allows demand pressure to spill very quickly into the balance of payments. As one might expect under such circumstances, the net payments result depends on the balance between the accumulation of reserves against domestic financial assets and the expansion of central bank credit. Thus

$$\overline{B} = (RCM)(\Delta\overline{CMD} + \Delta CMF) + RFL(\Delta FL2F) \quad - \quad \Delta CR1$$

reserves against rupiah   reserves against   central bank
savings and time deposits   foreign-exchange   credit
                                  deposits

While this balance-of-payments result is the same as one obtains from the monetary models of the balance-of-payments mechanism, it should be emphasized that the model here differs from the monetary models in one important respect: in this model there is an income-adjustment mechanism resulting from the existence of demand-determined productive sectors; in the monetary models all sectors are supply-determined.

From a policy point of view, the balance-of-payments conclusions are quite conventional: tighter money will increase reserves, looser money will do the opposite. However, one element is novel: the system accumulates reserves when income is in equilibrium, since the increase of domestically owned time deposits is positive under such circumstances. Thus the maintenance of stable international reserves is compatible with a measure of central bank credit expansion.

THE QUASI DYNAMICS OF THE MODEL

The model as developed so far is static, showing the equilibrium states for its different endogenous variables. For its concrete application, be it as a forecasting tool or for policy analysis, it is necessary to introduce modifications to make it applicable to real Indonesian situations, where no variables are ever at stationary equilibrium.

The time period used has an important bearing on the applicability of the model. Ideally, one would wish to have a quarterly model, but the existing data base totally precludes this. The most plausible unit of time is the calendar year. This imposes some limitations on the model use, particularly for very short-run forecasting, but it coincides well with the annual budgeting and planning effort that is undertaken.*

---

*The question can still be raised whether the 12-month period should be the calendar year or the fiscal year, which currently do not coincide. The decision on this is of course related to the particular uses to which one wishes to put the model, as well as to the

From a pure modeling point of view, two considerations are particularly relevant to the question of the applicability of a quasi-static approach. First, whether the time period used as a basis for analysis is long enough for the various multiplier effects to work themselves out. Fortunately, this is settled by the choice of the annual period. The 12 income periods that generally appear to exist in a normal year in Indonesia are sufficient to guarantee that virtually the whole multiplier effect will be felt within the 12-month period. This is not to say that events occurring at the end of one year will not have their impact in the next year, but only that within 12 months of the first impact of any particular change in an exogenous variable, all the secondary effects should have been felt.

Second, the accumulation of liquidity during the movement from one static equilibrium to another is obviously not incorporated in the model as developed in the preceding section. This needs to be included in order to make the model fully applicable to the situation for which it is designed. At the same time, it is also desirable to include the possibility of changes in velocity and incorporate their effect into the model. A "quasi-dynamic" model follows, making extensive use of the static equations developed earlier.

The Quasi-Dynamic Equations

The first five equations of a static model are preserved unchanged and reproduced below:

$$Y \equiv E + G + X - M + \triangle ST + \triangle LOSBUL \tag{1}$$

$$E = C + IV \tag{2}$$

$$IV = IV^n + FPI \tag{3}$$

$$C + IV^n = Y - T - \triangle CMD - \triangle L^d + \triangle CRP + \triangle CRF \tag{4}$$

$$\triangle CMD = sbY \tag{5}$$

---

availability of data on each variable. The decision in this case has been to adopt the calendar year as base, although it would have been possible to choose the fiscal year as well, provided the national income accounts, which are estimated on the calendar year, could be suitably adjusted by interpolation or other means.

Liquidity is defined as before (equation [6]). However, the increase in liquidity is now taken as the sum of the increases due to changes in income and changes in velocity, and the product of the two. The corresponding equation is labeled (6*).

$$L^d = kY \tag{6}$$

$$L^d = k\Delta Y + \Delta kY + \Delta k\Delta Y \tag{6*}$$

The functions for government expenditures, exports, and imports are taken over unchanged from the static model:

$$G = \bar{T} + AID + \Delta CRG \tag{7}$$

$$X = PX - xY \tag{9}$$

$$M = (a + i)Y - A(1 - m_a) - I(1 - m_i) + m_f FPI + m_x Px + \Delta ST \tag{11}$$

Income and expenditure equilibrium can be derived by substituting these various equations in each other, in a fashion precisely analogous to a static case. The result will be the expression for the quasi-dynamic equilibrium level of income:

$$Y = [sb + x + a + i + \Delta k]^{-1} [PX(1 - m_x) + A(1 - m_a)$$
$$+ I(1 - m_i) + FPI(1 - m_f) + \Delta LOSBUL + \Delta CRG + AID$$
$$+ \Delta CRP + \Delta CRF - (k + \Delta k)\Delta Y] \tag{43}$$

When comparing the quasi-dynamic equilibrium level of income and expenditure with the static analog shown in equation (12), it will be noticed that two differences exist. First, the multiplier has become smaller by inclusion of a term for increases in demand for liquidity, Δk, in its denominator. Second, the exogenous term has decreased with the subtraction of a term involving the level of and changes in velocity as well as changes in the level of income, $(k + \Delta K)\Delta Y$. Both these elements reflect the restrictive impact of accumulation of liquidity during the move from one equilibrium to another.

To incorporate the monetary system into the model, we adopt equation (31) unchanged from the static model:

$$\Delta CRP + \Delta CR1P + \Delta DICS = (1 - RMO)\Delta DD2 + (1 - RCM)\Delta CM$$
$$- \Delta XRES2 + (1 - RFL)\,\Delta FL2 - \Delta CR2G \tag{31}$$

We now expand the terms for increases in demand deposits and in foreign-exchange deposits by making use of equations (26), (27), and (6*):

$$\Delta DD2 = (1 - \alpha)\alpha'(k\Delta Y + \Delta kY + \Delta k\Delta Y) \tag{44}$$

$$\Delta FL2 = \Delta FL2F + (1 - \alpha')(k\Delta Y + \Delta kY + \Delta k\Delta Y) \tag{45}$$

where: $\alpha' = MO/L$ (46)

We also make use of equation (29):

$$\Delta CM = sbY + \Delta CMF \tag{29}$$

Substituting equations (44), (45), and (29) into equation (31) yields the following:

$$\Delta CRP = \Delta CR1P + \Delta DICS - \Delta CR2G + (1 - RMO)(1 - \alpha)\alpha'$$
$$(k\Delta Y + \Delta kY + \Delta k\Delta Y) + (1 - RCM)(\Delta CMF + sbY)$$
$$- \Delta XRES2 + (1 - RFL)\Delta FL2F + (1 - RFL)(1 - \alpha')$$
$$(k\Delta Y + \Delta kY + \Delta k\Delta Y) \tag{47}$$

Comparing this equation with equation (31), it can be seen that the amount of credit to the private sector is modified by lending from additional holdings of liquidity against which only fractionary reserves are required.

Substituting equation (47) into (43), collecting terms, and simplifying, we obtain the following expression for the quasi-dynamic aggregate equilibrium level of income:

$$Y = \lambda_1[PX(1 - m_x) + A(1 - m_a) + I(1 - m_i) + FPI(1 - m_f)$$
$$+ AID + \Delta CR1 + \Delta CRF + (1 - RCM)\Delta CMF + (1 - RFL)\Delta FL2F$$
$$- \Delta XRES2 - (k + \Delta k)\left\{[\alpha + (1 - \alpha)RMO]\alpha' + (1 - \alpha')RFL\right\}\Delta Y] \tag{48}$$

where $\lambda_1 = \dfrac{1}{sbRCM + x + a + i + \Delta k\left\{\alpha'[\alpha + RMO(1 - \alpha)] + RFL(1 - \alpha')\right\}}$

Comparison of equation (48) with equation (43) shows incorporation of the remaining effects resulting from the increase in various kinds of bank liabilities. In turn, comparing (48) with equation (33), the aggregate equilibrium analog of (48) in the static case, we can see that the difference resides in the addition to the multiplier and to the exogenous term of values reflecting changes in velocity and in level of income. It might be noted parenthetically that in the same way that the coefficient sb, denoting propensity to save in banks, is multiplied by its reserve requirement, the term in brackets that multiplies Δk in the multiplier and is also found reproduced in the exogenous grouping of variables, represents the net reserve requirement against changes in liquidity. It is, as one might expect, composed of reserves required to be held against the part of liquidity that is denominated in foreign exchange $[RFL(1 - \alpha')]$, plus the reserves held against the part of liquidity denominated in local currency (α'), which in turn is composed of currency in circulation (α) and reserves against demand deposits $[RMO(1 - \alpha)]$.

With the quasi-dynamic aggregate equilibrium level of income specified, the definition of exports and imports is a straightforward matter, requiring merely the substitution of equation (48) into equations (9) and (11), respectively. In turn, the balance of trade is the difference between the values of exports and imports. Carrying out this difference, substituting appropriately, and collecting terms, we obtain the following simplified expression for the balance of trade:

$$
\begin{aligned}
BT = {} & RCM(\Delta CMD + \Delta CMF) + RFL\Delta FL2F + \Delta XRES2 \\
& + \left\{ \alpha'[\alpha + RMO(1 - \alpha)] + RFL(1 - \alpha') \right\} [\Delta kY + k\Delta Y \\
& + \Delta k\Delta Y] - \Delta CR1 - FPI - AID - PJC - \Delta CRF - \Delta CMF \\
& - \Delta FL2F
\end{aligned} \tag{49}
$$

In turn, summing capital flows to the balance of trade yields the overall balance-of-payments result:

$$
\begin{aligned}
B = {} & RCM(\Delta CMD + \Delta CMF) + RFL\Delta FL2F + \Delta XRES2 \\
& + \left\{ \alpha'[\alpha + RMO(1 - \alpha)] + RFL(1 - \alpha') \right\} [\Delta kY + k\Delta Y \\
& + \Delta k\Delta Y] - \Delta CR1
\end{aligned} \tag{50}
$$

To calculate the change in official international reserves, we further need to separate out the increase in foreign assets of the commercial banks:

$$
\Delta ITL = B - \Delta RFA20 \tag{51}
$$

where RFA20 is required reserves against foreign-exchange liabilities held outside of Bank Indonesia. Using the required reserves at Bank Indonesia, we have:

$$
\Delta RFA20 = RFL\Delta FL2 - RFLBI\Delta FL2 \tag{52}
$$

$$\triangle RFA20 = (RFL - RFLBI) (1 - \alpha') [\triangle kY + k\triangle Y + \triangle k\triangle Y] \tag{53}$$

Substituting in (51)

$$\triangle ITL = B - (RFL - RFLBI) (1 - \alpha') [\triangle kY + k\triangle Y + \triangle k\triangle Y] \tag{54}$$

Expanding:

$$\triangle ITL = BT + FPI + AID + \triangle CRF + \triangle CMF + [1 - RFL$$
$$+ RFLBI] \triangle FL2F - (RFL - RFLBI) (1 - \alpha') (\triangle kY$$
$$+ k\triangle Y + \triangle k\triangle Y) \tag{55}$$

Using (49) and simplifying:

$$\triangle ITL = RCM(\triangle CMD + \triangle CMF) + RFLBI \quad \triangle FL2F$$
$$+ \triangle XRES2 + \{ \alpha'[\alpha + RMO(1 -\alpha)]$$
$$+ RFLBI(1 -\alpha') \} \ [\triangle kY + k\triangle Y + \triangle k\triangle Y] - \triangle CR1 \tag{56}$$

Equation (56) bears comparison with equation (42) from the static system. It will be noticed that only two differences stand out. First, changes in excess reserves of the banking system are shown explicitly as contributing to the level of international reserves when they increase. This is not surprising, since an increase in excess reserves means curtailed lending and, therefore, curtailed domestic demand. Second, the by now familiar term of reserve requirements held against changes in liquidity appears, again causing no surprise, since the accumulation of these reserves also has a deflationary impact on domestic demand, and hence should lead to the accumulation of international reserves.

Comparative quasi dynamics can be analyzed in this model by applying the same kind of procedure to these equations as has been applied in Appendix A to the static model.

Summary

Recognition that the Indonesian economy is not in static equilibrium requires introduction into the model of the consequences of changes in liquidity and in velocity. As a result, the specification of the equations for the income level and the balance-of-payments outcome are somewhat modified. However, the basic relationships in the economy and the basic adjustment mechanisms do not change.

Income is still determined by the interaction of a multiplier and some exogenous expenditure variables. The multiplier still is the reciprocal of the sum of all the leakages. However, these leakages no longer consist only of the propensities to spend on exportables and import-competing goods and the p ropensity to hold bank reserves against savings and time deposits; they also include the increase in idle financial assets due to changes in velocity. This last term is a complex one, since changes in velocity cause modifications in the amounts held of demand deposits, currency, and foreign-exchange deposits; and each of these has a different reserve requirement affecting it.* The multiplier expression now is as shown below.

$$\lambda_1 = \frac{1}{x + a + i + (RCM)sb + \triangle k \left\{ \alpha'[\alpha + RMO(1 - \alpha)] + RFL(1 - \alpha') \right\}}$$

where the last term in the denominator is the addition resulting from changes in desired liquidity holdings.

The autonomous elements now also need to include the accumulation of liquidity: changes in excess reserves in the banking system, and changes in desired liquid balances due to changes in the level of income. Note that this second item is different from a change in velocity, which enters the multiplier. We therefore have the following list of autonomous expenditures:

EXOG = $PX(1 - m_x) + A(1 - m_a) + I(1 - m_i)$
value added in export, agriculture, and industry

$+ \triangle CR1$
central bank credit

$+ \triangle CRF + FPI(1 - m_f) + AID$
foreign private + public capital inflow

$+ (1 - RCM)\triangle CMF + (1 - RFL)\triangle FL2F$
bank lending out of foreign deposits in the banking system

$- \triangle XRES2$
increase in excess reserves of the banking system

$- \left\{ \alpha' [\alpha + RMO(1 - \alpha)] + (1 - \alpha')RFL \right\} (k + \triangle k) \triangle Y$
reserve requirement against increased liquidity holdings caused by a higher income level

---

*In fact, no part of currency holdings can be relent, since by definition currency in the hands of the public is not in the banks. As a result, the implicit reserve requirement on currency is 100 percent.

The balance-of-payments result is still the difference between required reserves and central bank credit expansion, but once again increases in desired liquidity play a role. Thus

$$B = RCM(\Delta CMD + \Delta CMF) + \quad RFL\,\Delta FL2F \quad - \qquad \Delta CR1$$

reserves against rupiah	reserves against	central bank
savings and time deposits	foreign-exchange	credit
	deposits	

$$+ \text{XRES2} + \left\{ \alpha\,'[\,\alpha + RMO(1 -\alpha\,)] + (1 -\alpha')RFL\right\} [\Delta kY + k\Delta Y + \Delta k\Delta Y]$$

excess   reserves against new liquidity holdings
reserves

CALIBRATING THE MODEL

Observations on four calendar years, 1969 to 1972, have been used to estimate functions corresponding to the different parameters. Only 1970-72 have been used for testing the tracking ability for the model; 1969 was excluded from the simulation exercise because of the partial use of first differences, which causes loss of one year of observation.

Since only four observations were available, no conventional econometric estimation could be employed. Instead, the functions have been fitted by inspection, in an attempt to minimize the deviation of the estimated from the observed values. Although no explicit statistical theory underlies the estimates, the logic employed is the same as that underlying least-squares estimation. The lack of underlying probability theory implies, however, that it is not possible to establish confidence intervals around the estimates and in that way assess their quality. Nonetheless, it is possible to compare the estimated values with the observed values, and assess the quantitative importance of the observed differences between them. The overall quality of the calibration can be assessed by comparing the estimated values for the endogenous variables with the realized values in the years 1970-72. The absolute and percentage differences between estimated and observed values give a clear indication of the quality of the calibration, and are an indication of the reliability of the forecasts undertaken with the model.

It is important to emphasize the pitfalls in quantitative analysis with existing Indonesian time series. Unfortunately, the information content of many series is an open question. For many of them both the underlying indicators and the procedures of construction are very questionable. For other variables, more than one series exists, and each has its own and different value. Furthermore, it is not uncommon that the announced content of a series as given, say, by its title diverges from the meaning of the data that can be derived from the manner in which it is constructed. For example, it is well known that national income and expenditure data are of dubious accuracy, that the balance-of-payments figures, even for the values of exports and imports, are likely to entail substantial error, and that even the figures on the banking system have deficiencies that raise serious questions about the extent to which they reflect the underlying magnitudes.

The traditional argument that the available data are the best there are, that policy decisions must be made, and that forecasts for this purpose are necessary, does indeed apply to Indonesia. However, where such significant and well-known biases exist in the data, it is unclear to what extent the analysis of existing series throws light on reality or merely misleads the observer. Hence quantitative estimates derived from the existing data base should be used with the greatest caution.

The data for the model are given in Appendix B, where sources, quality, and compromises adopted are discussed.

Estimation of the Functional Relationships

Table 7.2 shows the estimating equations for the parameters that the model requires for projection purposes, as well as the fit of those functions.

For three of the functions—the propensities to spend on export goods (x), the liquidity coefficient (k), and the currency ratio (α α'), simple functions of time provided a very adequate fit. This finding is very plausible.

In the case of the propensity to spend on export goods, it is to be expected that as the economy grows, it will use domestically more of its own raw materials and, hence, of its export goods. The variable "time" in the equations thus represents the secular trend toward consuming or otherwise utilizing more of the country's primary output internally within the economy. Its sign should be, and is, positive.

It is to be expected that the liquidity coefficient should also rise over time as the economy becomes more monetized. At issue is a secular trend affected, but not determined, by the real interest rate as long as that is within some reasonable range. Holdings of financial assets are interest-elastic, but this elasticity is contributed primarily by time and savings deposits, while the holdings of demand deposits respond only to extreme changes in the interest rate or to very substantial and sustained inflation.

TABLE 7.2

Parameter Estimations for the Model, 1969–72

	1969	1970	1971	1972
Average propensity to spend on export goods (x)				
Observed values	.0183	.0283	.0306	.0327
Equation: $x = .0284 + .0022t$, for $t = 0$ in 1970 (estimated values)	.0262	.0284	.0306	.0328
Average propensity to spend on agricultural and industrial goods (a + i)				
Observed values				
Total imports (rp. billion)		599.1	690.7	985.6
$- m_f FPI - m_x PX - \triangle ST$		171.1	213.3	169.8
Domestic-income-dependent imports		428.0	477.4	815.8
+ domestic supply: $A(1 - m_a) + I(1 - m_i)$		1,658.5	1,753.2	1,902.2
Total supply		2,086.5	2,230.6	2,718.0
Y		3,340.2	3,697.3	4,223.8
a + i = total supply / Y		.6247	.6033	.6435
Estimate used: average of 1970 and 1971		.614	.614	.614
Liquidity coefficient (k)				
Observed values	.0582	.0681	.0812	.0959
Equation: $k = .068 + .014t$, for $t = 0$ in 1970 (estimated values)	.054	.068	.082	.096

Currency ratio (cur/liq = α α')				
Observed ratio	.596	.586	.579	.573
Equation: α α' = .585 − .006t, for t = 0 in 1970				
(estimated values)	.591	.585	.579	.573
Propensity to save in banks (sb)				
Gross of interbank deposits				
Observed values	.013	.007	.013	.008
Real interest rate on time deposits (percent/year)	24.2	11.05	19.15	14.95
Equation: sb = .013 + .0004 $\Sigma_t \Delta_i$, for t = 0 in 1969				
(estimated values)	.013	.007	.013	.008
Net of interbank deposits				
Observed values	.01232	.00594	.0107	.00604
Equation: $sb_t = sb_{t-1} \dfrac{i_t}{i_{t-1}}$; $sb_{1969} = .12$				
(estimated values)		.00548	.0095	.00743
Foreign-exchange deposit ratio: Foreign-exchange deposits/liquidity = 1 − α'				
Observed values		.0755	.0815	.086
Equation: 1 − α' = .0755 + .0055t, for t = 0 in 1970				
(estimated values)		.0755	.0810	.0865

Source: Prepared from data in Appendix B of this chapter.

229

The currency ratio is expected to decline over time, as checks and other mechanisms for the transfer of money come into use and supplant currency. The estimation equation reflects this secular trend by showing a negative sign on the coefficient associated with the "time" variable.

The average propensity to spend on agricultural and industrial goods was derived by taking averages of the realized values for 1970 and 1971. No particular reason for a trend seemed to exist and the 1972 data appeared to be still preliminary, particularly as regards agricultural value added. The resultant parameter of .614 is plausible, in the sense that a 60/40 split of expenditures between goods and services is not unreasonable.

Finally, functions were fitted to two different series of the propensity to save in domestically owned time and savings deposits: gross of interbank deposits and net of these deposits. In both cases the coefficient was regarded as affected by the real rate of interest. The better fit is obtained for the equation using gross deposits, but the more relevant equation for the model is that using net values. This equation has by far the worst fit of all those estimated, and it is unclear at this point whether this is due to misspecification of functional form; lack of a sufficiently long series of observations originating in an essentially stable environment; or imperfect sorting of domestic-owned from foreign-owned deposits in the underlying data. Fortunately the impact of these parameters on the endogenous variables other than time deposits themselves is rather minor.

Calibration of the Model 1970-72

The parameters estimated above have been used, together with data on the exogenous variables (Appendix B), to test the quality with which the model can reproduce the observed developments from 1970 to 1972.

Table 7.3 develops the estimators used by the model: the multiplier and the exogenous variables. It will be noticed that the multiplier is about 1.5 and decreases slightly from 1970 to 1972. This is the result of changes in each of its components, many of which are a function of time.

The exogenous variables are the observed values of the respective items for the period under estimation. It will be noted that no information is included for the value of credit extended abroad to Indonesian enterprises. This is due to a lack of reliable information on this point.

TABLE 7.3

Estimators of the Model, 1970-72

Multiplier: $\lambda^{-1} = sbRCM + x + a + i + \Delta k\,[\alpha'\,\alpha(1 - RMO) + RMO]$

		1970	1971	1972
Propensity to save in banks x reserved requirement thereon	sbRCM	.0006	.0003	.0007
Propensity to spend on nonexport goods	a + i	.614	.614	.614
Propensity to spend on export goods	x	.0284	.0306	.0328
Required reserves against increases in liquidity holdings	$\begin{cases}\Delta k(\alpha'\,\alpha)\ (1 - RMO) \\ \Delta k\ (RMO)\end{cases}$	— —	.0057 .0042	.0058 .0042
Inverse of multiplier	λ^{-1}	.6430	.6548	.6575
Multiplier	λ	1.555	1.527	1.521

Exogenous variables: EXOG

		1970	1971	1972
Domestic value added of export production	$PX(1 - m_x)$	406.9	462.1	597.4
Domestic value added of agric. prod.	$A(1 - m_a)$	1,346.7	1,415.3	1,504.1
Domestic value added of ind. prod.	$I(1 - m_i)$	311.8	337.9	398.1
Domestic component of foreign private invest.	$FPI(1 - m_f)$	6.4	11.7	42.4
Increase in credit of Bank Indonesia	$\Delta CR1$	17.3	49.7	6.1
Increase in credit out of foreign-owned rupiah time deposits	$\Delta CMF(1 - RCM)$	6.3	16.4	9.3
Foreign aid	AID	99.7	104.7	150.9
Increase in credit out of foreign-owned dollar demand (D) and time (T) deposits	$\begin{cases}\Delta FL2FD(1 - RFLD) \\ \Delta FL2FT(1 - RFLT)\end{cases}$	12.0 10.6	10.9 6.4	50.5 43.2
Change in excess reserves of banks	$' -\Delta XRES2\ Rp$	5.3	5.4	-10.0
Increase in credit from abroad	ΔCRF	n.a.	n.a.	n.a.
Change in food stockpile	$-\Delta ST$	-15.9	+.1	+23.5
EXOG		2,207.1	2,420.6	2,815.5
ΔEXOG		369.6	213.3	394.9

n.a. = not available.

<u>Source:</u> Prepared from data in Appendix B of this chapter.

Using the multiplier and exogenous variable values of Table 7.3 to estimate the different endogenous variables gives results that, on the whole, closely approximate actual values. (For the computational approximations used in obtaining these values, see Appendix C.) The corresponding magnitudes are shown in Table 7.4.

Gross domestic product (GDP) estimates in all three years come admirably close to the realized values: within less than 1.5 percent. The error declines in size from 1970 to 1972, reaching a low of 0.1 percent in 1972. Furthermore, in 1970 the model overestimates the GDP, whereas it underestimates it in the later years.

The export estimation is even better; the errors in the estimation of exports are all less than 0.4 percent. Imports of goods and services are estimated with a very acceptable degree of accuracy, the largest error being 3.1 percent. 1971 and 1972 import figures are slight overestimates; 1970 is an underestimate. However, a small percentage change is equivalent to a substantial absolute amount. For example, a 3 percent error in the estimated imports for 1971, while small, equals approximately U.S. $50 million.

The estimate for domestically owned savings and time deposits is very unsatisfactory, with the largest error amounting to 23 percent. Furthermore, some serial correlation in the errors is apparent, with 1970 and 1971 being underestimated and 1972 showing an overestimate. The absolute magnitudes involved in this case are fairly small, being of the order of $10 million or less.

The estimates for domestically owned liquidity (currency plus rupiah and dollar deposits) show very small margins of error. The largest error is 1.2 percent, for 1970. The estimates for domestically owned foreign-exchange deposits are also highly satisfactory, ranging from 1.8 percent to 0.3 percent, with small absolute magnitudes.

The estimate of the current account in the balance of payments is derived by taking the difference between estimated exports and estimated imports. In consequence, any errors in each of these estimates risk being cumulated. Furthermore, since the difference between two large numbers is involved, any error that is a small percentage of either exports or imports can loom large as a percentage of the difference between the two. The errors in the estimates range from 6.9 percent to 12 percent and from $11 million to $30 million.

The estimate for the change in international reserves of the monetary authorities is built up from the estimate of the current account and the known capital inflows. It thus cumulates the error of both its components and adds them to the smallest residual in the balance-of-payments accounts. As one might expect, the estimates produced by the model are considerably off the mark, from

$45 million to $192 million. However, the errors and omissions entry in the official balance of payments is large as well. When both errors are compared, the model is seen to do almost as well as the official balance of payments in 1970 and 1971, but considerably worse in 1972.

In summary, the model calibrates amazingly well for GDP, exports, imports, and liquidity. It does poorly on domestically owned time deposits and on the two residuals of the balance of payments, the current account and the change in international reserves. However, for the last of these it does almost as well as the official balance-of-payments estimates.

POLICY ANALYSIS WITH THE MODEL

Three types of policy analysis can be carried out with this model. One category consists of investigating the implications of the structure of the economy for a particular policy concern—that is, what happens if benign neglect is practiced and no particular policy measure is adopted. This category, usefully called "structural analysis," will be illustrated by exploring the management of the international reserve position.

A second category, which might be called "post-audit," consists of ascertaining the quantitative structure of the cause of an event that has already taken place, in order to determine whether policy was operating in the appropriate direction and with the right magnitude. This will be illustrated by examining the causes leading to the steep rise in imports in 1972.

The third category, calculating the consequences of a given policy, might best be called "policy evaluation." It will be illustrated by examining the consequences of imposing a tax on interest earned by nonresidents on bank deposits in Indonesia.

Structural Analysis: Management of the International Reserve Position

The fundamental question for the management of the international reserve position is whether the growth of the economy "automatically" provides the reserves that are needed, or whether an explicit contractionary central bank policy is needed to provide these reserves, or, conversely, whether there is room for an expansionary central bank policy without depleting the reserves below an adequate level. Central bank action in this context will be regarded as neutral if its total loan portfolio is maintained at a given

TABLE 7.4

Estimates and Actual Figures for the Model, 1970–72

	1970	1971	1972
Gross domestic product			
$\hat{Y} = \lambda$ EXOG $- \lambda^2$ kΔEXOG$[\alpha'\alpha(1 - RMO) + RMO]$			
λ EXOG	3,432.0	3,696.3	4,282.4
λ^2 kΔEXOG$[\alpha'\alpha(1 - RMO) + RMO]$	-43.1	-28.8	-61.4
$\hat{Y}$	3,388.9	3,667.5	4,221.0
Y realized	3,340.2	3,696.3	4,223.8
Absolute error of estimate: $\hat{Y}$ - Y	48.7	-28.8	-2.8
Percentage error of estimate: $100(\hat{Y}/Y - 1)$	1.5	-.8	-.1
Exports			
$\hat{X}$ = PX - x$\hat{Y}$			
PX	538.6	631.6	866.4
x$\hat{Y}$	-96.2	-112.2	-138.4
$\hat{X}$	442.4	519.4	728.0
X realized	444.0	518.4	728.3

Absolute error of estimate: $\hat{X} - X$ -1.6   1.0   -.3

Percentage error of estimate: $100(\hat{X}/X - 1)$ -.4   .2

Imports of goods and services

$M = (a + i)Y - A(1 - m_a) - I(1 - m_i) + m_f FPI + m_x PX + \Delta ST$

$(a + i)Y$	2,080.8	2,251.8	2,591.7
$A(1 - m_a)$	-1,346.7	-1,415.3	-1,504.1
$I(1 - m_i)$	-311.8	-337.9	-398.1
$m_f FPI$	23.5	43.9	62.1
$m_x PX$	131.7	169.5	269.0
ΔST	15.9	-.1	-23.5
$\hat{M}$	593.4	711.9	997.1
M realized	599.2	690.7	985.6

Absolute error of estimate: $\hat{M} - M$ -5.8   +21.2   +11.5

Percentage error of estimate: $100(\hat{M}/M - 1)$ -1.0   +3.1   +1.2

Domestically owned savings and time deposits

$\Delta \widehat{CMD} = sb\hat{Y}$	18.6	34.8	31.4
ΔCMD realized	19.9	39.6	25.5

Absolute error of estimate: $\Delta \widehat{CMD} - \Delta CMD$ -1.3   -4.8   +5.9

Percentage error of estimate: $100(\Delta \widehat{CMD}/\Delta CMD - 1)$ -6.5   -12.1   +23.1

(continued)

Table 7.4, continued

	1970	1971	1972
Liquidity = domestically owned currency, Rp. and $ dem. deps.			
$\hat{L} = k\hat{Y}$	230.4	300.7	405.2
L realized	227.7	300.4	405.3
Absolute error of estimate: $\hat{L} - L$	+2.7	+.3	-.1
Percentage error of estimate: $100(\hat{L}/L - 1)$	+1.2	+.1	—
Domestically owned foreign-exchange deposits			
$\widehat{FL2D} = (1 - \alpha')\,L$	17.4	24.3	35.0
FL2D realized	17.1	24.5	34.9
Absolute error of estimate: $\widehat{FL2D} - FL2D$	+.3	-.2	+.1
Percentage error of estima te: $100(\widehat{FL2D}/FL2D - 1)$	+1.8	-.8	+.3
Current account of balance of payments			
$\hat{BT} = \hat{X} - \hat{M}$	-151.0	-192.5	-269.1
BT realized	-155.2	-171.8	-256.5
Absolute error of estimate: $\hat{BT} - BT$	4.2	-20.7	-12.6
Percentage error of estimate: $100(\hat{BT}/BT - 1)$	2.7	-12.0	-4.9
Absolute error in $ million	11.1	-52.3	-30.3

236

International reserves of the monetary authorities

$$\widehat{\text{ITL}} = \widehat{\text{BT}} + \text{FPI} + \text{AID} + \text{CMF} + (1 - \text{RFL} + \text{RFLBI})\ \text{FL2F}$$

$\widehat{\text{BT}}$	-151.0	-192.5	-269.1
FPI	29.9	55.6	104.5
AID	99.7	104.7	150.9
ΔCMF	6.9	16.9	10.3
0.8 ΔFL2F	22.2	17.5	92.3
$\widehat{\Delta\text{ITL}}$	7.7	2.2	88.9
ΔITL realized = monetary movements - spec. draw. rts.	-9.4	-35.1	168.5
Absolute error of estimate $\widehat{\Delta\text{ITL}}$ - ΔITL	17.1	37.3	79.6
Absolute error in $ million	45.2	94.1	191.8
Errors and omissions acct. in bal. of paymts. ($ million)	31.0	95.0	83.0
Excess of estimated error over errors/omissions account	14.2	-.9	108.8

level ($\triangle$CR1 = 0); contractionary if the loan portfolio is reduced ($\triangle$CR1 < 0); expansionary if it is increased ($\triangle$CR1 > 0).

The analysis can conveniently start from equation (56), which shows the factors determining reserve accumulation in the quasi-dynamic model:

$$\triangle ITL = RCM(\triangle CMD + \triangle CMF) + RFLBI \, \triangle FL2F + \triangle XRES2$$
$$+ \left\{ \alpha ' \left[\alpha + RMO(1 - \alpha) \right] + RFLBI(1 - \alpha') \right\} \, (\triangle kY$$
$$+ k\triangle Y + \triangle k\triangle Y) - \triangle CR1 \tag{56}$$

This equation tells us that if Bank Indonesia keeps its portfolio constant ($\triangle$CR1 = 0), then the international reserves of the monetary authorities will rise by the amount of required reserves against increases in rupiah time and demand deposits, plus the amount of reserves required to be deposited in Bank Indonesia against foreign-exchange deposits, plus any increase in excess reserves. Since it expresses the amount of reserves that will be forthcoming in any given situation, equation (56) may well be referred to as the supply-of-reserves function.

Some of the variables appearing in this equation are themselves endogenous ($\triangle$CMD, Y, $\triangle$Y). Replacing them with their determinants leads to a "reduced form" that expresses the supply of reserves as a function of the exogenous variables in the model. This is done in equation (57), which says exactly the same thing as equation (56) but expresses everything in terms of the variables that are exogenous to the model, and therefore is more useful for estimation and evaluation purposes.

$$\triangle ITL = RCM\triangle CMF + RFLBI \, \triangle FL2F + \triangle XRES2 + \left\{ RCMsb \right.$$
$$+ \triangle k \, \alpha ' \left[\alpha + RMO(1 - \alpha) \right] + \triangle k \, RFLBI(1 - \alpha') \right\} \left\{ \lambda \, [EXOG] \right.$$
$$- \lambda^2 (k + \triangle k) \, A[\triangle EXOG] \right\} + (k + \triangle k) \left\{ \alpha'[\alpha + RMO(1 - \alpha)] \right.$$
$$+ RFLBI(1 - \alpha') \right\} \left\{ \lambda \triangle EXOG - \lambda^2 (k + \triangle k)A \, \triangle^2 EXOG \right\} \tag{57}$$

Having examined the supply of reserves, we must now examine the demand for these assets. The demand for international reserves arises from two sources. On the one hand, reserves are held in order to maintain the smooth flow of imports in the face of fluctuating foreign-exchange receipts. On the other, reserves are maintained for liquidity reasons against the liabilities of the banking sector to foreigners, mostly rupiah-denominated time deposits.

With regard to the demand for reserves arising from the fluctuation of foreign-exchange receipts, no clear standard exists for the appropriate relationship between the reserve position and the level of imports. Traditionally, Indonesia has aimed for the bench mark of the IMF: two to three months of imports. Desired reserves can be defined on this basis as a proportion of imports; and these, in turn, depend on all the exogenous variables in the system. For convenience the import equation of the quasi-dynamic system is reproduced here:

$$M = (a + i)\{ \lambda [EXOG] - \lambda^2 (k + \triangle k) A[\triangle EXOG]\} - A(1 - m_a)$$
$$- I(1 - m_i) + m_f FPI + m_x P_x + \triangle ST \tag{11}$$

Some multiple of M thus defined, say 2/12 or 3/12, measures this element of the demand for reserves.

The demand for reserves originating from liabilities of the banking system to foreigners depends essentially on the volatility of those liabilities. As long as foreigners are content to keep their money in rupiahs and in Indonesia, no drain of foreign exchange will result, and therefore foreign reserves will not be necessary. It is only against a "run on the bank" that reserves are held. Therefore, no precise formula can be given to link the requirement of reserves to volume of liabilities. Furthermore, since the liabilities are exogenous, no equation for them is available.

To ascertain whether the system automatically provides sufficient reserves against imports, we must compare the response of reserves to changes in the exogenous variables specified in (57) with the response of imports specified in (11). Suppose, for example, that value added in exports production increases by Rp. 1 billion ($25 million). The relevant changes for $\triangle ITL$ and M would be the following:

For reserves:

$$\frac{\triangle^2 ITL}{\triangle PX(1 - m_x)} = \{RCMsb + \triangle k \alpha'[\alpha + RMO(1 - \alpha)] + \triangle kRFLBI$$
$$(1 - \alpha')\}\{\lambda - \lambda^2(k + \triangle k) A\} + (k + \triangle k)$$
$$\{\alpha'[\alpha + RMO(1 - \alpha)] + RFLBI(1 - \alpha')\}$$
$$\{\lambda - \lambda 2 (k + \triangle k) A\} \tag{58}$$

which on further simplification becomes:

$$\frac{\triangle^2 ITL}{\triangle PX(1 - m_x)} = \{RCMsb + (k + 2\triangle k) [(1 - \alpha'\alpha)RMO + \alpha'RMO$$
$$+ RFLBI (1 - \alpha')]\}\{\lambda - \lambda^2(k + \triangle k)A\} \tag{59}$$

where

$$A = \alpha' \alpha (1 - RMO) + RMO$$

Evaluating this expression numerically with the parameters found in "Calibrating the Model" for 1972, we obtain:

$$\frac{\Delta^2 ITL}{\Delta PX (1 - m_x)} = \{.0511\}\{1.366\} = .07$$

That is, for each rupiah of new value added in export production, reserves will increase by Rp. 0.07. Correspondingly, Rp. 1 billion of such new output will yield Rp. 70 million of new reserves.

For imports:

$$\frac{\Delta M}{\Delta PX(1 - m_x)} = (a + i)[\lambda - \lambda^2 (k + \Delta k)A] = (.614)(1.366)$$
$$= .84 \tag{60}$$

That is, imports will rise Rp. 0.84 per Rp. 1 of increased generation of value added in export goods. Correspondingly, Rp. 1 billion of such new value added will generate Rp. 840 million of new imports.

The automatic provision of reserves can now be clearly seen: against new imports of Rp. 840 million, new reserves of Rp. 70 million have been generated. That is, one month's worth of imports are automatically added to reserves as a result of growth in production of exportables. Therefore, if Indonesia wishes to achieve the conventional ratio of maintaining reserves equal to two-three months of imports, it cannot expect the economy automatically to generate such reserves as exports expand. Deliberate policy action would be required.

The situation may well be different for other exogenous variables. For example, a similar analysis for increases in value added in import-competing agricultural and industrial production yields the following:

For reserves:

$$\frac{\Delta^2 ITL}{\Delta[A(1 - m_a) + I(1 - m_i)]} = \frac{\Delta^2 ITL}{\Delta PX(1 - m_x)} = .07$$

For imports:

$$\frac{\Delta M}{\Delta[A(1 - m_a) + I(1 - m_i)]} = (a + i)[\lambda - \lambda^2 (k + \Delta k)] - 1$$
$$= .84 - 1 = -.16$$

As can be seen, in this case imports actually fall while reserves rise. An appropriate combination of growth of exports and import substitutes may, thus, generate an automatic growth of reserves of sufficient magnitude. For a complete analysis, changes in all the exogenous variables must be summed together.

The evaluation of the adequacy of reserve growth vis-à-vis short-term liabilities to nonresidents cannot be approached directly, since no demand function for such reserves is available. However, we can evaluate the supply of reserves provided by Rp. 1 of capital inflow and assess its sufficiency in general terms. To this end equation (57) must be differentiated with regard to one of the exogenous capital-inflow variables. The impact of inflow into time deposits, for example, is as follows:

$$\frac{\Delta^2 \text{ITL}}{\Delta^2 \text{CMF}} = \text{RCM} + \left\{ \text{RCMsb} + (k + 2\Delta k) \left[(1 - \alpha'\alpha) \text{RMO} \right.\right.$$
$$\left.\left. + \alpha' \text{RMO} + \text{RFLBI} (1 - \alpha') \right] \right\} \left\{ 1 - \text{RCM} \right\}$$
$$\left\{ \lambda - \lambda^2 (k + \Delta k) A \right\} \tag{61}$$

Numerical evaluation yields

$$\frac{\Delta^2 \text{ITL}}{\Delta^2 \text{CMF}} = .1 + \left\{ .0511 \right\} \left\{ .9 \right\} \left\{ 1.366 \right\} = .163$$

that is, capital inflow into rupiah time deposits automatically generates a reserve of some 16 percent of the inflows.

Taken by itself, a 16 percent liquidity reserve seems somewhat low; but when the system is evaluated as a whole, it may well be that some of the reserve creation of the other exogenous variables makes up the difference between this 16 percent and some more desirable level, such as 30 or 40 percent. Indeed, if import substitution is strong enough, it may free up enough reserves from covering imports to raise the reserves available for liquidity purposes.

Post-Audit: The Rise of Imports in 1972

Table 7.4 shows that imports rose by approximately Rp. 300 billion in 1972 compared with their 1971 level. Previous annual increases were much more modest—for instance, Rp. 100 billion in 1971. Since 1972 also was a year in which prices began to rise sharply, considerable interest attaches to breaking down this increase quantitatively by cause.

The analysis naturally starts from the import function, equation (11), which can be used to express the difference between imports in 1972 and 1971:

$$M_{72} - M_{71} = \text{Rp. } 300 \text{ billion}$$

We now write the explicit import function for each year:

$$(a + i)_{72} \{ \lambda [EXOG] - \lambda^2 (k + \triangle k)A[\triangle EXOG] \}_{72} - A(1 - m_a)_{72}$$

$$- I(1 - m_i)_{72} + m_f FPI_{72} + m_x PX_{72} + \triangle ST_{72}$$

$$- (a + i)_{71} \{ \lambda [EXOG] - \lambda^2 (k + \triangle k)A[EXOG] \}_{71} \llcorner$$

$$+ A(1 - m_a)_{71} + I(1 - m_i)_{71} - m_f FPI_{71} - m_x PX_{71}$$

$$- \triangle ST_{71} = \text{Rp. } 300 \text{ bil.} \tag{62}$$

For simplicity's sake, let us assume that in both years the following were equal: λ, k, $\triangle k$, A, m_f, m_x, a + i. Then we can collect terms as follows:

$$(a + i) \{ \lambda [EXOG_{72} - EXOG_{71}] - \lambda^2 (k + \triangle k)A[\triangle EXOG_{72}$$

$$- \triangle EXOG_{71}] \} - [A(1 - m_a)_{72} - A(1 - m_a)_{71}] - [I(1 - m_i)_{72}$$

$$- I(1 - m_i)_{71}] + m_f(FPI_{72} - FPI_{71}) + m_x(PX_{72} - PX_{71})$$

$$+ \triangle ST_{72} - \triangle ST_{71} \tag{63}$$

We can now group the variables in three categories:

Endogenous demand:

$$(a + i) \{ \lambda [EXOG_{72} - EXOG_{71}] - \lambda^2 (k + \triangle k) A[\triangle EXOG_{72}$$

$$- \triangle EXOG_{71}] \}$$

Exogenous demand:

$$m_f(FPI_{72} - FPI_{71}) + m_x(PX_{72} - PX_{71}) + \triangle ST_{72} - \triangle ST_{71}$$

Supply:

$$- [A(1 - m_a)_{72} - A(1 - m_a)_{71}] - [I(1 - m_i)_{72} - I(1 - m_i)_{71}]$$

Table 7.4 allows us to put values on these categories:

	ΔM Caused
Endogenous demand	+ Rp. 340 billion
Exogenous demand	+ Rp. 94 billion
Total demand effect	Rp. 434 billion
Supply	− Rp. 149 billion
Net effect	Rp. 285 billion

These figures show that approximately one-quarter of the new gross demand for imports was exogenous, and hence not directly controllable with macro policy. Furthermore, virtually one-third of the increased gross demand for imports was offset by new import-substituting production.

Endogenous demand obviously can be broken down further by taking the change of each exogenous variable separately:

$$\sum_i (a + i)\lambda \quad (EXOG_{72} - EXOG_{71})_i - \sum_i (a + i)\lambda^2 (k + \Delta k)$$

$$A(\Delta EXOG_{72} - \Delta EXOG_{71})_i = Rp.\ 340\ \text{billion} \qquad (64)$$

Evaluating the parameters at their 1972 values, we have $(a + i)\lambda = .93$, $(a + i)\lambda^2 (k + \Delta k)A = .095$. Using Table 7.3, we have:

	Δ M Caused
Demand originating from increased income in the productive sectors: $PX(1 - m_x)$, $A(1 - m_a)$, $I(1 - m_i)$	Rp. 251.7 billion
Demand originating from direct foreign private investment: FPI	Rp. 26.2 billion
Demand originating from foreign capital inflow into the banking system: ΔCMF, $\Delta FL2F$	Rp. 58.3 billion
Demand originating from foreign aid disbursements: AID	Rp. 39.1 billion
Demand originating from Bank Indonesia Credit*: $\Delta CR1 - \Delta ST$	Rp. −12.3 billion

*Note that Bank Indonesia credit to finance the stockpile (ΔST) does not go through the domestic income stream. Hence it is subtracted from $\Delta CR1$ and taken into account as part of exogenous import demand.

Demand originating from changes
in excess reserves: $\triangle$XRES2   Rp. <u>-12.8 billion</u>
    Total effect   Rp. 350.2 billion
    Diff. due to assumption
    of constant parameters   Rp.   10.2 billion

The breakdown of increased demand into its components shows the following interesting facts: the monetary system had an exogenously "contractionary" effect; reductions in Bank Indonesia credit, combined with increases in excess reserves, dampened import demand by some Rp. 25 billion; the expansionary effect of private capital inflow into the banking system completely overshadowed this restrictive effect, causing close to Rp. 60 billion worth of import demand; foreign private investment and aid together contributed another Rp. 65 billion worth of import demand; all of the foregoing were small compared with the major determinant on the demand side, which was the growth of the productive sectors, amounting to Rp. 250 billion of demand.

The overall post-audit of the 1972 import growth can be said to have shown that this growth was largely the result of exogenous factors, not controllable directly by macro policy. The monetary system played a minor role, sterilizing at best a quarter of the expansion originating from foreign investment and foreign aid. The implication that emerges is that changes in central bank (Bank Indonesia) credit alone cannot be expected to bear the whole burden of balance-of-payments stabilization.

Policy Evaluation: Tax on Interest Earned by
Nonresidents on Bank Deposits in Indonesia

Our post-audit of 1972 import developments showed that demand for imports originating from capital inflow into the banking system accounted for close to Rp. 60 billion worth of increased demand for imports—that is, about one-sixth of the increase in endogenous import demand and one-seventh of the increase in all import demand. The importance of the inflow makes it relevant to analyze policies that might stem it. One such policy could be a tax levied on the interest earned by nonresidents on their accounts in the banking system.

Any evaluation of this policy should cover determination of the effect of the tax on the level of inflow, and determination of the effects on the economy of the change in that level of inflow. The model has nothing to say about the first and, indeed, not much is known with precision about the interest sensitivity of "portfolio" capital inflow into Indonesia. The model can shed considerable light on the second, however.

From equation (48) we can derive the effect on income of a change in inflows and evaluate it with the 1972 parameters:

$$\frac{\Delta Y}{\Delta^2 CMF} = (1 - RCM) \{ \lambda - \lambda^2 (k + \Delta k)A \} = (.9)(1.366)$$

$$= 1.2294 \tag{65}$$

Thus, a reduction in ΔCMF of **Rp.** 1 would cause a fall of GDP of Rp. 1.23.

The impact on exports and imports is as follows:

$$\frac{\Delta X}{\Delta^2 CMF} = -x \frac{\Delta Y}{\Delta^2 CMF} = -(.03)(1.23) = -.07 \tag{66}$$

$$\frac{\Delta M}{\Delta^2 CMF} = (a + i) \frac{\Delta Y}{\Delta^2 CMF} = (.614)(1.23) = .75 \tag{67}$$

That is, a Rp. 1 reduction in inflow would cause an increase in exports of Rp. 0.07 and a decrease in imports of Rp. 0.75.

The impact on the current account of the balance of trade can be derived from (49) or taken from (66) and (67).

$$\frac{\Delta BT}{\Delta^2 CMF} = \frac{\Delta Y}{\Delta^2 CMF} - \frac{\Delta M}{\Delta^2 CMF} = -.07 - .75 = -.82$$

Thus a Rp. 1 reduction in inflow will improve the balance of trade by Rp. 0.82.

Notice that a reduction in inflow causes an improvement of the current account because as GDP declines, imports decline and exports rise.

Finally, the change in the total balance of payments is equal to

$$\frac{\Delta BT}{\Delta^2 CMF} + 1 = -.82 + 1 = +.18 \tag{68}$$

Hence a Rp. 1 reduction in inflow will worsen the balance of payments by Rp. 0.18.

In turn, the Bank Indonesia reserve change will be a bit smaller, as calculated in (61), which yielded 0.163—that is, a reduction in inflow will cause a loss of reserves equivalent to 16 percent of that reduction. (Note that banks also hold international reserves. These would decrease by .025 per rupiah of reduced inflow.)

With these estimates in hand, the policy evaluation can proceed in terms of the desirability or acceptability of the various consequences. For example, a fall of aggregate demand (GDP) may well be desirable, if there is already demand pull. On the other hand, reserves may or may not be urgently needed. The evaluation of these questions obviously falls outside the scope of the model.

FORECASTING WITH THE MODEL

One of the obviously useful applications of the model is forecasting the endogenous variables. In principle, this is no different from the calibration exercise undertaken earlier, except for the availability of data on the exogenous variables. Whereas in the calibration case, figures for these data obviously were available, forecasting requires estimating the values that the exogenous variables might take. One would expect a model-generated forecast to be "better" than a set of direct estimates of all the desired figures because the model will assure that the forecasts are consistent, and the relationship between the variables forecast by the model will correspond at least reasonably to what we know about the macroeconomic structure of the Indonesian economy.

Table 7.5 shows estimates for the exogenous variables based on plausible guesses of knowledgeable people made in mid-1973. Table 7.6 contains the parameter projections. Note that the real interest rate is negative as a result of inflation; thus the propensity to save in banks has consequently turned negative as well.

The forecast (Table 7.7) shows a GDP growth in current prices of 20 percent that includes the assumption of price increases (on a yearly average basis) of 10 percent and 38 percent in agriculture and industry, respectively. Exports are up very significantly, reflecting primarily the increase in the value of oil that had already taken place or was foreseeable in mid-1973. Imports are up approximately 90 percent, of which between one-third and one-half is accounted for by price increases and much of the rest reflects the food crop situation. International reserves were estimated to be some $200 million higher, a figure already appearing conservative in mid-1973.   The inflation eroded the real interest rate; hence savings in banks are down but liquidity needs are up, due in large part to the price rises, and liquidity is shown rising by about 50 percent.

TABLE 7.5

Estimated Values of the Exogenous Variables, Calendar 1973

	Billions of Rp.
1. Exports and attendant domestic expenditure	
Oil	
Domestic sales	168
Export sales ($1,607 million)	667
Total	835
Imports of goods and services	415
Net domestic expenditure	420
Timber	
Gross exports	236
Imports of goods and services	151
Net domestic expenditure	85
Rubber	
Gross production	151
Export sales	145
Domestic sales	6
Other exports	245
Summary	
Production: PX	1,467
Import component: $m_x PX$	566
Net domestic exports: $PX(1 - m_x)$	901
Domestic use: xY	174
2. Import-competing agricultural output	
Value added in agriculture, forestry, and fishing: $A(1 - m_a)$	2,091[a]
Less: production of rubber, export timber, other agricultural exports[b]	531
Import-competing agricultural output	1,560

(continued)

Table 7.5, continued

	Billions of Rp.
3. Import–competing output of industry	
Value added in industry: $I(1 - m_i)$	621^c
4. Foreign private investment	
Gross disbursement: FPI	208
Import component: m_f FPI	137
Net domestic expenditure: $FPI(1 - m_f)$	71
5. Bank Indonesia credit: $\triangle CR1$	34
6. Net foreign aid disbursement: AID	183
7. Foreign portfolio capital inflow	
Into rupiah time deposits / into foreign-exchange deposits $\Big\{ \triangle CMF + \triangle FL2F$	21
Reserve requirement: 30 percent	
Relendable foreign portfolio capital inflow: $RCM(\triangle CMF + \triangle FL2F)$	15
8. Others	
Change in	
Excess reserves: $\triangle XRES2$	0
Direct borrowing abroad: $\triangle CMF$	0
Food stockpile: $\triangle ST$	0
9. Total: EXOG	3,385
$\triangle EXOG$	570

[a]Assumes a quantity increase of 4.2 percent and a price increase of 10 percent over 1972.

[b]Other agricultural exports are assumed to be approximately 40 percent of other exports, or Rp. 100 billion.

[c]Assumes a quantity increase of 12.9 percent ahd a price increase of 38 percent over 1972.

Source: Compiled by the author.

TABLE 7.6

Estimated Value of the Multiplier, Calendar 1973

1. $sb_{73} = sb_{72} \dfrac{i73}{i72}$

   $sb_{72} = .00743$ $\qquad$ $i_{73} = -10\%$ $\quad$ $i_{72} = 15\%$ $\quad$ $sb_{73} = -.005$

2. $RCM = .1$ $\qquad\qquad$ $RMO = .3$ $\qquad$ $RFL = .3$

3. $a + i = .614$

4. $x = .0284 + .0022t$ $\qquad\qquad$ $t = 3$ $\quad$ $x = .035$

5. $k = .068 + .014t$ $\qquad\qquad$ $t = 3$ $\quad$ $k = .119$ $\quad$ $\triangle k = .014$

6. $\alpha \, \alpha' = .585 - .006t$ $\qquad\qquad$ $t = 3$ $\quad$ $\alpha \, \alpha' = .567$

7. $\alpha'\alpha(1 - RMO) + RMO = .6969$

8. $(1 - \alpha') = .0755 + .0055t$ $\qquad\qquad$ $t = 3$ $\qquad$ $1 - \alpha' = .092$

9. $\lambda^{-1} = sbRCM + x + a + i + \triangle k[\alpha'\alpha(1 - RMO) + RMO]$

   $sbRCM$ $\qquad\qquad\qquad\qquad = -.0005$

   $x + a + i$ $\qquad\qquad\qquad = .649$

   $\triangle k[\alpha'\alpha(1 - RMO) + RMO] = \underline{.0098}$

   λ^{-1} $\qquad\qquad\qquad\qquad = .6583$ $\qquad\qquad$ $\lambda = 1.519$

10. $\lambda^{2}k[\alpha\alpha'(1 - RMO) + RMO] = .1913$

Source: Compiled by the author.

249

TABLE 7.7

Model-Generated Values of the Macroeconomic Variables, Calendar 1973
(billion Rp.)

---

1. Gross domestic product

$$\hat{Y} = \lambda \, EXOG - \lambda^2 \Delta k [\, \alpha \alpha'(1 - RMO) + RMO] \, \Delta EXOG$$

$$\hat{Y} = 1.519(3,385) - .1913(570) = 5,032.8$$

2. Exports

$$\hat{X} = PX - xY$$

$$\hat{X} = 1,467 - .035(5,032.8) = 1,291 \ (\$3.110 \text{ million})$$

3. Imports

$$\hat{M} = (a + i)Y - A(1 - m_a) - I(1 - m_i) + m_f FPI + m_x PX$$

$$\hat{M} = .614(5,032.8) - 1,560 - 621 + 137 + 566 = 1,612 \ (\$3.883 \text{ million})$$

4. Balance of trade

$$\hat{BT} = \hat{X} - \hat{M}$$

$$\hat{BT} = 1,291 - 1,612 = -312 \ (\$773 \text{ million})$$

5. Liquidity

$$\hat{L} = k\hat{Y}$$

$$\hat{L} = .119(5,032.8) = 598.9$$

6. Domestically owned foreign-exchange deposits

$$\widehat{FL2D} = .092\hat{L} = 55.1$$

7. Domestically owned savings and time deposits

$$\widehat{\Delta CMD} = sbY$$

$$\widehat{\Delta CMD} = -.005(5,032.8) = -20.2$$

8. International reserves of the monetary authorities

$$\widehat{ITL} = \hat{BT} + FPI + PGM + PJC + \Delta CMF + \Delta FL2F \, (1 - RFL + RFLBI)$$

$$- (RFL - RFLB1) \, \Delta FL2D$$

$$\widehat{ITL} = -321 + 208 + 183 + 11 + 8 - 4 = +85 \ (\$205 \text{ million})$$

Source: Compiled by the author based on Tables 7.5 and 7.6.

To complement the forecast of macro variables, an attempt was made to forecast the changes in the consolidated balance sheet of the monetary system (Table 7.8). Apart from a significant error in the estimate figure, what stands out in this table is the extent to which the liquidity needed in the economy appears ex-post as generated by the balance of payments. For 1973 almost half the increase in liabilities of the system is "accounted for" by the increase in international reserves. Causality, it should be noted, runs the other way. The system accumulates a high proportion of reserves in relation to liquidity because of the high currency ratio, which has an effect on reserve accumulation analogous to a 100 percent reserve requirement on demand deposits.

The discussion of this forecast must end on a cautionary note. The reader should not be misled about the information content of all these numbers. The underlying data are weak, as was noted in the section "Calibrating the Model," and the technique for fitting the model was, appropriately, not probabilistic. The apparent neatness of numbers (almost) adding up is fundamentally a construct. This writer believes the model to be qualitatively accurate; the quantitative results do not have more information content than the numbers that went into estimating them. Finally, it should be noted that the forecast presented here cannot simply be compared with the realized series in order to test the model's forecasting ability, for the inputs to the model were separately estimated. Thus a proper test would require at least replacing the estimates of the exogenous variables with their realized values, then recomputing the model estimates and comparing them with recorded outcomes.

CONCLUSIONS

In the preceding pages an attempt has been made to capture the essence of the macroeconomic system of Indonesia in a limited number of equations, with the objective of making it possible to answer a number of policy questions. In so doing, it has been necessary to depart extensively from conventional macromodel formulations in order to come closer to the apparent functioning of the Indonesian economy.

Three main features distinguish Indonesia's macroeconomic system and are central to the model: First is the existence side by side of sectors with quite opposite mechanisms for determining their levels of output: supply-determined-output sectors, which account for most of export production, and agricultural and industrial import-competing production; and demand-determined output

TABLE 7.8

Projection of Changes in Consolidated Balance Sheet of the
Monetary System, Calendar 1973

Assets			Liabilities	
International reserves (ΔITL)	+ 85		(ΔMO + ΔFL2D) Liquidity	+ 193.9
Commercial bank foreign exchange reserves (RFL – RFLBI)ΔFL2	6		(ΔCMD) Domestic savings and time deposits	– 20.2
Domestic assets (ΔCR)	91.5	182.5	(ΔCMF) Foreign savings and time deposits	21.0
			(ΔFL2F) Foreign exchange	
Error of estimate (6.3%)	12.2			
Total assets	194.7		Total liabilities	194.7

Note: ΔFL2D   20.1
      ΔFL2F (by assumption)   10.0
      ΔFL2   30.1

Sources: ΔITL, ΔMO + ΔFL2D, ΔCMD—Table 7.7, items 5–7; ΔCMF + ΔFL2F—Table 7.5, item 7;
ΔCR = ΔCR1 + (1 – RMO)(1 – α)α' ΔL + (1 – RCM)ΔCM – ΔXRES2 + (1 – RFL)ΔFL2F
= 34 + .7(.433)(193.9) + (.9) (–9.2) + (.7)(10) = 91.5.

252

sectors, which account for most of the production of services and nontraded goods. The first group of sectors behaves in non-Keynesian fashion; the second group gives rise to a Keynesian multiplier. Supply in this second group is infinitely elastic for a range, because of Indonesia's very high rate of underemployment. However, it should be noted that it is also assumed that capital is not fully utilized in the short run.

The second feature is the interplay of real and monetary variables in determining the level of economic activity. Expenditure in any period is augmented by new debt: money creation and foreign-capital inflow both raise the level of expenditure above income. But since expenditure determines the level of activity in part of the economy, financial variables directly affect real output. Furthermore, a constant fraction of current savings is deposited in the banking system, thus constituting a leakage from the system and contributing to the determination of the multiplier. However, not all savings are a leakage: the major part flows directly into investment expenditure, since in many instances savers and investors are the same economic units (business households).

The third feature is the degree of openness of the economy, which finds its expression in a number of different ways. First, prices of traded goods are given, in large part, from outside the economy, although increases in nominal wages may cause price rises by raising the importing and distribution charges on traded goods. Second, the marginal propensity to import is very high, since the output of tradables is unresponsive to demand. Thus, all increases in demand for tradables spill directly into the balance of payments, and the marginal propensity to import equals the marginal propensity to spend on agricultural and industrial goods. Third, exogenous expenditures flow directly out through the balance of payments, except as dampened by higher real output in services and by the accumulation of financial assets in the banking system.

The features noted are not characteristic only of Indonesia. Rather, they typify the small, open economy of a country in the early stages of industrialization and without a well-developed capital market. For all countries of this kind, a mixed Keynesian-classical, real-monetary model of the type developed would appear to be appropriate.

Some aspects of reality have not been built into the model. The major omission in this regard refers to several situations in which domestic prices do not remain stably linked to world prices: when demand increases so rapidly that inventories of imported goods are drawn down due to delays in ordering or shipping, or overburdening of the import infrastructure; when products that traditionally were exported are completely absorbed by domestic use and eventually become import-competing; when import duties are raised or prohibitions are imposed. In all these cases domestic prices rise independently of the behavior of world prices; and if such increases feed back on the wage level, a limited domestic wage-price spiral becomes possible.

Another major element not explicitly modeled is the reaction of the economy to a devaluation, however such an event can be directly taken into the model in the form of exogenous price increases of traded goods, with the accompanying exogenous adjustment in the supply price of nontraded goods. Finally, a rising supply curve of rice to the country also has not been explicitly considered. Given a policy to maintain the domestic rice price, however, such a supply curve simply means greater BULOG losses, greater finance of these losses by the central bank, and the consequent effect on international reserves, interrelations that the model fully captures.

The price adjustment elements not built into the model, as well as other aspects of the Indonesian economy not captured in the equations as they stand, can, of course, be introduced by suitably expanding the model. Likewise, the model parameters can be updated by use of more recent information. Laying bare the basic macroeconomic flows of the economy, as done in the model, is a necessary prelude to such additional work and by itself constitutes a very significant step ahead in developing a macro framework for understanding the functioning of economies at Indonesia's state of development and of Indonesia's structural characteristics.

The policy uses of this kind of model are numerous, and four of them have been illustrated in the two preceding sections. The model can be used to answer the question of where to intervene. Thus, with "structural analysis," the model can be used to explore the extent to which the economy responds automatically to certain problems. The example shown concerned the accumulation of foreign-exchange reserves. The model can also be used to assess the effect of policy. Using "post-audit," the crucial element is determining the share of any outcome that is due to policy variables. The example explored concerned the increase in the level of imports. Furthermore, the model can be used for predicting the consequences of certain policies. Under "policy evaluation," the emphasis in this case is on assessing the quantitative consequence of adopting a particular policy action. The example explored was the adoption of a tax on interest income of foreigners. Finally, of course, the model can be used to forecast developments in the next period(s). This also has been illustrated for the full range of endogenous variables and for the monetary balance sheet.

In sum, the model summarizes a wide range of aspects in the behavior of the Indonesian economy, providing potential answers for many policy questions (see Figure 7.5). It also has applicability to other countries with similar economic structure, although naturally the numerical values of the parameters are not transferable.

LIST OF SYMBOLS USED

Y	Gross domestic income
E	Private expenditure
G	Government expenditure
ΔST	Increase of food stockpile
X	Exports
M	Imports
C	Consumption
IV	Investment
IV^n	Investment by nationals
FPI	Foreign private investment
Δ	Increase
CRP	Credit from the Indonesian banking system to the private sector
CRF	Credit to the private sector from abroad
L	Liquidity
CMD	Domestically owned savings and time deposits
T	Taxes
sb	Marginal (= average) propensity to save in banks
CRG	Government borrowing from the monetary system
AID	Program and project aid
PX	Production of export goods
x	Marginal (= average) propensity to consume export goods
A	Value of agricultural output
I	Value of industrial output
m_a	Import component of agricultural output
m_i	Import component of industrial output
m_f	Import component of foreign private investment
m_x	Import component of exports
a	Marginal (= average) propensity to absorb agricultural goods
i	Marginal (= average) propensity to absorb industrial goods
RMO	Reserve requirement against rupiah demand deposits
RCM	Reserve requirement against rupiah time and savings deposits

FIGURE 7.5

Interrelations in the Short-Run Macroeconomic Adjustment Mechanism of Indonesia

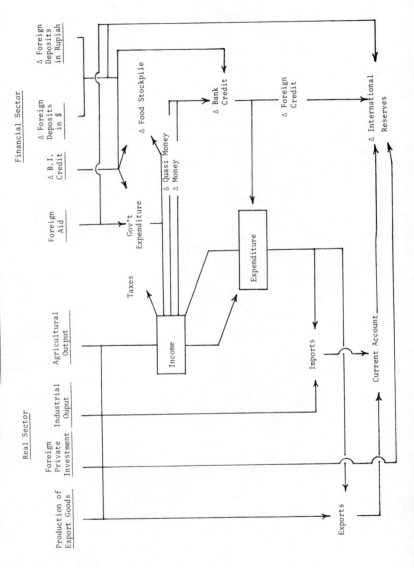

RFL	Reserve requirement against foreign-exchange deposits
RFLBI	Reserve requirement against foreign-exchange deposits that must be held at Bank Indonesia
DD_2	Demand deposits in rupiah
CMF	Nonresident-owned time deposits
XRES2	Excess reserves
FL2	Foreign-currency liabilities of commercial banks
FL2F	Foreign-currency liabilities of commercial banks to nonresidents
FL2FD	Foreign-currency demand deposits in commercial banks owned by nonresidents
FL2FT	Foreign-currency time deposits in commercial banks owned by nonresidents
FL2D	Foreign-currency liabilities of commercial banks to residents
CR2	Commercial bank credit
RFA2	Required reserves against foreign-exchange liabilities
CR2G	Commercial bank credit to the government
CR2P	Commercial bank credit to the private sector
α	Ratio of currency to money
α'	Ratio of money to liquidity
CR1B	Bank Indonesia lending to BULOG
LOSBUL	BULOG's annual loss
CR1	Bank Indonesia lending
CR1P	Bank Indonesia lending to the private sector
DICS	Bank Indonesia lending to foreign private enterprise
VFA2	Commercial bank lending in foreign exchange to residents

APPENDIX A: THE COMPARATIVE STATICS OF THE MODEL

This appendix examines the effect that permanent changes in the level of exogenous variables have on the equilibrium values of the various endogenous flow and stock variables.

Effects on Equilibrium Levels of Flows

Differentiation of equations (33) through (42) yields the impact of lasting changes in the levels of exogenous variables on the equilibrium levels of income, imports, exports, domestic quasi money, liquidity, balance of trade, and change in international reserves. Writing λ for the income multiplier, this procedure can be illustrated for the impact on the equilibrium level of income of the various exogenous variables in the following manner:

$$\lambda = \frac{1}{(RCM)sb + x + a + i} \tag{A.1}$$

$$\frac{d\overline{Y}}{dPX} = \lambda (1 - m_x) \tag{A.2}$$

$$\frac{d\overline{Y}}{dA} = \lambda (1 - m_a) \tag{A.3}$$

$$\frac{d\overline{Y}}{dI} = \lambda (1 - m_i) \tag{A.4}$$

$$\frac{d\overline{Y}}{dFPI} = \lambda (1 - m_f) \tag{A.5}$$

$$\frac{d\overline{Y}}{d\triangle CR1P} = \frac{d\overline{Y}}{d\triangle CR1G} = \frac{d\overline{Y}}{d\triangle DICS} = \frac{d\overline{Y}}{dAID} = \frac{d\overline{Y}}{d\triangle LOSBUL}$$

$$= \frac{d\overline{Y}}{d\triangle CRF} = \lambda \tag{A.6}$$

$$\frac{d\overline{Y}}{d\triangle CMF} = \lambda (1 - RCM) \tag{A.7}$$

$$\frac{d\overline{Y}}{d\triangle FL2F} = \lambda (1 - RFL) \tag{A.8}$$

It can be noticed immediately that the impact of the various exogenous variables on the equilibrium level of income depends on which part of the change in value of the exogenous variable finds its way directly into the income stream. For example, in the case of production of export goods, only the part that is domestic value added enters the income stream, not the part that is import component. Thus λ has to be multiplied by $1 - m_x$. This is shown by equation (A.2). In a similar manner the impact of increases in agricultural or industrial production and in foreign private investment are reduced by the respective import components, as shown by equations (A.3) through (A.5). Outright expansion of central bank credit to the private or public sector flows fully into the income stream, and thus its impact is given directly by λ, as shown in equation (A.6). The same effect obtains for aid inflows and direct borrowing abroad. Finally, changes in the inflow of foreign quasi money generate the requirement to hold reserves against such deposits; thus the proportion 1-RCM flows into the income stream [equation (A.7)], whereas inflows into foreign-exchange-denominated deposits have their own reserve requirement [equation (A.8)]. It follows that the impact of a rupiah worth of change in the exogenous variables will have a differential impact on the income level according to what proportion stays in the domestic income stream and what proportion flows into imports or into reserves.

A similar analysis for each of the other exogenous variables can be undertaken, and is left to the reader.

Use of Comparative Static Analysis

Analysis of the comparative statics of the equilibrium level of imports yields some interesting results. For example, one can compare the impact on the equilibrium level of imports of an expansion in production of exportables and an expansion in production of import substitutes—agricultural goods, for instance. The respective equations are shown below both for the values of output and for the values of domestic value added.

$$\frac{d\overline{M}}{dPX} = \lambda \{ a + i + m_X [(RCM)sb + x] \} \tag{A.9}$$

$$\frac{d\overline{M}}{dPX(1 - m_X)} = \frac{\lambda}{1 - m_X} \{ a + i + m_X [(RCM)sb + x] \} \tag{A.10}$$

$$\frac{d\overline{M}}{dA} = \lambda (1 - m_a) [(RCM)sb + x] \tag{A.11}$$

$$\frac{d\overline{M}}{dA(1 - m_a)} = \lambda [(RCM)sb + x] \tag{A.12}$$

It can be noticed immediately that the impact on imports of a rupiah worth of value added in production of export goods is greater than that of the rupiah worth of additional output in import substitution. This is more formally shown in equation (A.13), which explicitly relates the impact on imports of increases in value added in export production and in agricultural production.

$$\frac{d\overline{M}}{dPX(1 - m_X)} = \frac{d\overline{M}}{dA(1 - m_a)} \quad \frac{m_X}{1 - m_X} + \frac{\lambda(a + i)}{1 - m_X} \tag{A.13}$$

It should be noted, however, that the impact of a rupiah worth of additional value added in each of these activities on the balance of payments and on the equilibrium change in international reserves is identical. Equations (A.14) and (A.15) derive the changes in equilibrium increases in international reserves arising from changes in the values of these outputs, and equation (A.16) shows the equality of these two impacts per rupiah of domestic value added.

$$\frac{d\overline{\Delta ITL}}{dPX} = RCM \frac{d\overline{\Delta CMD}}{dPX} = RCM \, \lambda \, sb(1 - m_x) \qquad (A.14)$$

$$\frac{d\overline{\Delta ITL}}{dA} = RCM \frac{d\overline{\Delta CMD}}{dA} = RCM \, \lambda \, sb(1 - m_a) \qquad (A.15)$$

$$\frac{\overline{d\Delta ITL}}{dPX(1 - m_x)} = \frac{\overline{d\Delta ITL}}{dA(1 - m_a)} \qquad (A.16)$$

It should be pointed out that intuitive first reactions would lead one to expect (correctly) that imports would increase more when export production is expanded than when import substitution is expanded, and also that (incorrectly) the impact of these changes on international reserves would be different. The explanation of the equality arises from the nature of the aggregate equilibrium. Import substitution raises the level of income until the induced demand for imports and for local use of exportables absorbs the foreign exchange made available. Additional export production also raises the level of income, and causes imports and domestic use of exportables to rise until the foreign exchange made available is spent. However, one should not lose sight of the fact that the levels at which the balance of payments will be equilibrated in either case are different. The total volume of trade with an increase in volume of export production will be greater than with import substitution. Thus, although the balance-of-payments and reserve situations will be identical, the total value of trade will differ and presumably desired reserves will differ as well.

A further interesting implication from the comparative static analysis can be drawn for the use of import propensities derived from statistical time series. A time-series regression of imports on income is a sophisticated way of comparing the change over time of imports with the change over time of income. This is summarized in the equation (A.17):

$$STAT \; MPM = \frac{\Delta M}{\Delta t} \bigg/ \frac{\Delta Y}{\Delta t} \qquad (A.17)$$

In comparison, the theoretical definition of the marginal propensity to import is a partial derivative of imports with regard to income, which from equation (11) can be seen to equal the marginal propensity to spend on agricultural plus industrial goods. This is stated in equation (A.18):

$$MPM = \frac{\Delta M}{\Delta Y} = (a + i) \tag{A.18}$$

If we now take differences of the import function, equation (11), with regard to time, we find a fairly lengthy expression:

$$\frac{\Delta M}{\Delta t} = (a + i)\frac{\Delta Y}{\Delta t} - (1 - m_a)\frac{\Delta A}{\Delta t} - (1 - m_i)\frac{\Delta I}{\Delta t} + m_f \frac{\Delta FPI}{\Delta t}$$
$$+ m_x \frac{\Delta PX}{\Delta t} + \frac{\Delta \Delta ST}{\Delta t} \tag{A.19}$$

It can immediately be seen that dividing through equation (A.19) by $\Delta Y/\Delta t$ yields an expression substantially different from the value we are trying to find—namely, $a + i$, as shown in equation (A.18). Indeed, the statistical results could conceivably be larger or smaller than the number we are trying to determine. However, agricultural and industrial value added is large in comparison with the import components of foreign private investment, export production, and increase in stock accumulations. Therefore, it is very likely that the statistical measure underestimates the true marginal propensity to import. It follows that uncritical acceptance of statistically estimated marginal propensities to import would lead to underestimation of import requirements generated by specific policy options or specific paths of development.

It is also worth pointing out the conclusions that emerge from the behavior of quasi money as a function of foreign inflow into such deposits. Partial differentiation of equation (36) shows us that an inflow of foreign quasi money has an impact on the equilibrium level of domestically owned quasi money. Thus inflow of such foreign funds affects quasi-money liabilities of the domestic banking system, not only directly but also in multiplied fashion as a result of the impact on domestic income streams, and therefore on the domestic holdings of quasi money. Equation (A.20) shows the expression pertaining to this result:

$$\frac{d\Delta CM}{d\Delta CMF} = 1 + \lambda sb(1 - RCM) \tag{A.20}$$

Inflows of foreign funds into savings and demand deposits also affect equilibrium levels of the balance of trade and international reserves, as can be seen from equations (A.21) and (A.22):

$$\frac{\overline{dBT}}{d\Delta CMF} = [(RCM) \lambda sb - 1] (1 - RCM) \tag{A.21}$$

$$\frac{d\overline{\Delta IT} L}{d\triangle CMF} = (RCM) \ [1 + \lambda \ sb \ (1 - RCM)] \tag{A.22}$$

It is interesting to note that the impact on the equilibrium changes in international reserves of an increase in the constant inflow of foreign funds into rupiah-denominated time and savings deposits is far smaller than the amount of those flows. The implications of this for the management of the reserve position are dealt with in the section "Policy Analysis with the Model."

Effects on Equilibrium Stocks

The effect of changes in the exogenous variables on the equilibrium levels of stocks of liquidity, money, currency, quasi money, and international reserves ranks as equal in interest with the effects that changes in the exogenous variables have on the various flows analyzed previously. Some of these changes in stocks can be derived quite easily; others are more complicated.

The effect of changes in the exogenous variables on the equilibrium stock of liquidity can be derived by starting from equation (6) and inserting in it the expression for the equilibrium level of income [equation (33)]. This is done in equation (A.23). Differentiating the right-hand side of equation (A.23) with regard to the exogenous variables yields equation (A.24), which tells us that changes in the exogenous variables affect the equilibrium stock of liquidity in proportion to the income multiplier and the liquidity coefficient.

$$\overline{L} = k\overline{Y} = k\lambda \{ EXOG \} \tag{A.23}$$

$$\frac{d\overline{L}}{d \ \{EXOG\}} = k \lambda \tag{A.24}$$

where

$$EXOG = PX(1 - m_x) + A(1 - m_a) + I(1 - m_i) + FPI \ (1 - m_f)$$

$$+ \triangle CR1P + \triangle DICS + \triangle CR1G + AID + \triangle LOSBUL$$

$$+ \triangle CRF + (1 - RCM) \ \triangle CMF + (1 - RFL) \triangle FL2F$$

The effect on the monetary stock is derived from equation (26), which shows the relation between the monetary stock and liquidity. As can be seen in equation (A.25), the impact on the money stock of changes in the exogenous variable depends not only on changes in liquidity resulting from changes in the exogenous variables, but also on changes in the amount of liquidity that the public wishes to hold in the form of foreign-exchange deposits.

We can, however, derive a straightforward relationship for the money supply if we are willing to assume a simple proportional relationship between the stock of money and the stock of liquidity. Equation (A.25) shows the more general situation, and equation (A.26) shows the specifics of the proportional relationship. Substituting appropriately yields equation (A.27), in which the change in equilibrium stock of money pursuant to change in the exogenous variable can be seen to be the product of the proportionality relationship of money to liquidity, the liquidity coefficient, and the income multiplier. Naturally, any one element within the exogenous group will affect the money supply differently as it is itself multiplied by various coefficients of domestic value added or domestic expenditure. In a sense the situation is no different from that described for the impact of any one of the exogenous variables on the level of income.

$$\frac{dMO}{d[EXOG]} = \frac{dL}{d[EXOG]} - \frac{dFL2D}{d[EXOG]} \qquad (A.25)$$

$$MO = \alpha'L \qquad (A.26)$$

$$\frac{d\overline{MO}}{d[EXOG]} = \alpha' \frac{d\overline{L}}{d[EXOG]} = \alpha'k\lambda \qquad (A.27)$$

Changes in the equilibrium level of the stock of currency, pursuant to changes in the exogenous variables, can now be directly derived by combining equations (A.27) and (27). The result is shown to be the following:

$$\frac{d\overline{CUR}}{d[EXOG]} = \alpha' \frac{d\overline{MO}}{d[EXOG]} = \alpha \alpha'k\lambda \qquad (A.28)$$

Deriving the changes in the level of quasi money in the economy is more complicated, because in equilibrium, quasi money is changing all the time, as shown by equation (36). In consequence, the magnitude that it is interesting to estimate is the change in quasi money over a given time period. Equation (A.29) shows this change to be the sum of the changes in domestically owned quasi money and changes in foreign-owned quasi money. The former is a function of the level of income, as per equation (5). The latter variable is exogenous.

$$\sum_{t=j}^{n} \Delta CM_t = \sum_{t=j}^{n} \Delta CMD_t + \sum_{t=j}^{n} \Delta CMF_t = sb \sum_{t=j}^{n} Y_t + \sum_{t=j}^{n} \Delta CMF_t \tag{A.29}$$

To derive the change in international reserves over a given period of time, we begin from the identity of the monetary-system balance sheet shown in Table 7.1 and reproduced in equation (A.30) below:

$$\Sigma \Delta ITL \equiv \Sigma \Delta MO + \Sigma \Delta CM + \Sigma \Delta FL2 - \Sigma \Delta CRO - \Sigma \Delta CR2P$$

$$- \Sigma \Delta CR1P - \Sigma \Delta DICS - \Sigma \Delta CR1B - \Sigma \Delta CRG$$

$$- \Sigma \Delta FA2 - \Sigma \Delta VFA2 \tag{A. 30}$$

Making repeated use of equations (24), (26), (A.23), (A.26), and (5), and assuming that increase in credit to other domestic borrowers and to BULOG is zero, we arrive by straight substitution at the following equivalent expression for the increase in international reserves over a given period:

$$\Sigma \Delta ITL = \alpha 'k \Sigma \Delta Y + sb\Sigma Y + \Sigma \Delta CMF + (1 - \alpha ') k\Sigma \Delta Y$$

$$+ \Sigma \Delta FL2F - 0 - \Sigma \Delta CR1 - \Sigma [(1 - RMO)\Delta DD2$$

$$+ (1 - RCM) \Delta CM - \Delta XRES2 + \Delta FL2(1 - RFL)]$$

$$- 0 - \Sigma \Delta RFA2 \tag{A.31}$$

Further collection of terms and simplifications lead to equations (A.32) and (A.33):

$$\Sigma \Delta ITL = k \Sigma \Delta Y \{ \alpha ' [RMO(1 - \alpha) + \alpha] \} + RCM [sb\Sigma Y$$

$$+ \Sigma \Delta CMF] + \Sigma \Delta XRES2 - \Sigma \Delta CR1 \tag{A.32}$$

$$\Sigma \Delta ITL = \Sigma \Delta Y[\frac{CUR}{Y} + RMO (\frac{DD}{Y})] + RCM [sb\Sigma Y + \Sigma \Delta CMF]$$

$$+ \Sigma \Delta XRES2 - \Sigma \Delta CR1 \tag{A.33}$$

This last equation tells us that the increase in stock of international reserves over a given period of time will be the result of the increase in the level of income over that time, multiplied by the ratio of currency to income plus the reserve requirement on demand deposits multiplied by the ratio of those demand deposits to income; plus reserves held against any increase in the stock of quasi money that has occurred over the period; plus any increase in excess reserves that has occurred over the period; minus any increase in central bank credit over the period.

It should be noted that increase in income observed between two periods in equation (A.33) can be derived from the changes in equilibrium level of income shown in equations (44) through (49), provided the period of adjustment to equilibrium income levels is short enough in comparison with the period over which the change in international reserves is being computed.

APPENDIX B: DATA BASE FOR THE MODEL

The data used for calibrating the model are shown in Tables 7.B.1.-7.B.3.

The figures for oil are very similar to those used in the balance of payments for gross and net oil exports. The difference is due to the treatment of oil sold to the domestic market. In the balance of payments, the foreign-exchange expenditure of the oil sector is subtracted from the foreign-exchange revenues arising from oil exports. But in the context of this model, we are interested in the import component of total production (domestic use of oil plus exports). In consequence, the value of domestic expenditure arising from the oil sector is greater than the net oil figure in the balance of payments by the value of the domestic sales of oil.

In the case of timber, there is no traditional computation of gross and net foreign exchange, despite the fact that in this sector the difference between the two concepts is at least as large as for oil. Furthermore, the registered export of timber understates the true value on several accounts. First, the actual exports are taken at the official checkprice, which has systematically lagged behind the market value. Second, the companies substantially understate the number of cubic meters exported. Thus underreporting and undervaluation combine to reduce the registered value of exports. On the other hand, a substantial part of the true value of timber exports is transferred out of Indonesia in the form of profits and other remittances, with the amounts staying in Indonesia corresponding principally to taxes and wages paid by the companies exploiting the timber concessions. Since the taxes are based on the volume or value of goods registered as exported, the underreporting and undervaluation affect the amount retained within Indonesia. As a result, the error on net timber is smaller than the difference between the registered and true values of gross timber exports. In Table 7.B.1. an attempt has been made to estimate the amount of domestic expenditure arising from the timber sector in Indonesia,

TABLE 7.B.1

Production of Exportables and Their Import Component, Domestic Use of Exportables, 1969–72
(billion Rp.)

	1969	1970	1971	1972
Exchange rate for conversion	326	378.5	378.5–414	415
Oil				
Domestic use	45.9	86.3	102.1	124.0
Exports	119.3	164.3	205.3	363.6
Gross production	165.2	250.6	307.4	487.6
Less: imports (c and f)	31.3	38.6	49.1	74.5
Less: services (excluding freight)	61.3	78.0	84.5	152.2
Domestic expenditure	72.6	134.0	173.8	260.9
Import component	.56	.46	.44	.46
Export-type timber				
Domestic use	.9	4.2	7.4	10.6
Exports	8.5	38.1	66.8	95.5
Gross production	9.4	42.3	74.2	106.1
Less: imported inputs	4.0	15.1	35.9	42.3
Less: profit, other remissions	5.4	27.2	38.3	63.8
Domestic expenditure				
Import component	.42	.36	.48	.40
Rubber				
Domestic use	3.0	4.1	3.7	3.5
Exports	71.9	98.4	87.3	81.1
Gross production	74.9	102.5	91.0	84.6
Less: imported inputs				
Less: profit, other remissions				
Domestic expenditure	74.9	102.5	91.0	84.6

Mining (excluding oil)				
Tin exports	17.2	23.5	25.4	27.6
Less: profits, other remissions	n.a.	n.a.	n.a.	n.a.
Domestic expenditure, tin mining	17.2	23.5	25.4	27.6
Other mining	n.a.	n.a.	n.a.	n.a.
Copra, palm oil, palm kernel exports				
Copra exports	6.0	11.1	5.7	1.6
Palm oil exports	7.2	13.8	18.5	17.5
Palm kernel exports	1.3	1.9	2.2	1.5
Total	14.5	26.8	26.4	20.6
Other exports				
Agriculture (excluding timber, rubber, copra)	38.9	56.7	47.7	108.7
Nonagriculture (excluding oil, timber, rubber, mining)	54.2	36.2	59.5	31.2
Total	93.1	92.9	107.2	139.9
Total production of exportables (PX)				
Oil gross production + timber gross production + rubber gross production + tin exports + total copra etc. + total other	374.3	538.6	631.6	866.4
Total domestic use (xY)				
Oil domestic use + export timber domestic use + rubber domestic use	49.8	94.6	113.2	138.1
Proportion to spend on exportables (x): domestic use oil, export timber, rubber ÷ Y	.0183	.0283	.0306	0.327
Import component (absolute)	96.6	131.7	169.5	269.0
Oil imports + oil services + timber imported inputs + timber profits + rubber imported inputs + rubber profits + tin profits				
Import proportion (m_X): above imports and profits ÷ 7	.258	.245	.268	.310

n.a. = not available.

Notes: Gross production = domestic use + exports. Domestic expenditure = domestic use + exports. Domestic expenditure = gross production − imports − services. Domestic use of export-type timber = 10 percent of gross production = 1/9 exports. Domestic use of rubber = 4.0-4.2 percent of gross production.

Sources: Dir. of Oil Tax; balance of payments, May 31, 1973; Bank Indonesia Weekly Report, July 12, 1973; Bank Indonesia Weekly Report, July 19, 1973.

267

taking into account the adjustments necessary to revalue exports (note, however, that the official export total has been left unchanged), an allowance for domestic use, and the repatriations on account of profits and depreciation. Thus the figure shown for domestic expenditure compensates, at least conceptually, for all the omissions in the data. It must be realized, however, that this is a figure constructed by "expert" sources rather than from official data. The accuracy is deemed to be reasonably good, particularly for 1972.

In the case of rubber, an estimate has been made of domestic use of rubber in order to add it to exports and obtain gross production. Furthermore, it was assumed that the import component of rubber production is nil, and hence domestic expenditure was taken as equivalent to gross production.

For the remainder of the export products, domestic expenditure was taken as equivalent to exports. Furthermore, production was taken as equal to exports. These two assumptions together signify that the value of output is wholly domestic value added, and that there is no domestic consumption of these goods. The latter assumption is surely incorrect for the agricultural exports, particularly copra and palm oil. In the absence of underlying estimates for the domestic production and consumption of copra, it is preferable to assume the existence of a separate "export" copra sector and a separate "domestic" copra sector, with the former included in the production of exportables and the latter in the production of import-competing agricultural goods. If data are available, it would be desirable to reconstitute a single copra sector to be handled in much the same way as oil, timber, and rubber.

It should be noted that the proportion-of-import component of exports is very unstable. (See last row of Table 7.B.1.) Hence it is preferable to work directly with the absolute values of net domestic expenditure as an exogenous variable in the model instead of building this magnitude up from the total value of production of exportables minus the import component. It should also be noted that total domestic use reflects only domestic use of oil, timber, and rubber. Furthermore, in the case of timber, only domestic use of the export types of timber is reflected, with all other types of timber being included directly in import-competing agriculture production.

Table 7.B.2 shows the data on the production of import-competing output, GDP, direct foreign private investment, and foreign aid. The domestic expenditure of import-competing production of agriculture, forestry, and fishery is taken equal to the registered value added of these sectors less the gross production of the export agriculture sectors. The remaining net value added is assumed to be import-competing. It should be noted that the

Central Statistical Bureau's (BPS) value for agricultural output is an understatement of the true magnitude to the extent that Kalimantan timber output is underestimated. There may be other sources of understatement as well. These are compensated for by keeping these values and those of industry in domestic prices, rather than deflating to c.i.f. prices as required by the specification of the model.

The domestic expenditure of manufacturing output is taken as equal to the quoted value added of this sector. Total GDP, which is not used as an exogenous variable but is estimated endogenously, is shown for reference in these tables according to the values recorded by BPS.

Table 7.B.3. shows the relevant elements of the monetary system. Increase in Bank Indonesia credit has been taken as equal to the increase in credit from the monetary authorities. The total has been increased by the net of other items in the monetary balance sheet, since central bank activities on any account increase or contract the monetary base.

Nonresidents' deposits in foreign exchange are computed as the difference between foreign liabilities of deposit money banks and deposits of residents, which have been taken to equal the counter-value in rupiah of foreign-exchange-denominated demand deposits in commercial banks. These demand deposits are assumed to constitute working balances of resident firms. Furthermore, the gross foreign-currency deposits of nonresidents have been subdivided into time deposits and others, a division that is necessary because of the difference in the reserve requirements.

The increase in foreign-owned deposits has been derived on the basis of the sum of the state banks' time deposits outstanding to foreign banks and the time deposit liabilities of branches of foreign banks. This figure underestimates the total amount of foreign money in rupiah time deposits, since it does not include the deposits made by individuals directly in the state banks. There is some offset to this, however, insofar as Indonesian residents deposit rupiahs in the branches of foreign banks. On balance, however, it is to be assumed that more foreigners make deposits in the Indonesian state banks than residents do in branches of foreign banks. Thus the figure shown in Table 7.B.1 is almost certainly an understatement.

The data referring to savings and time deposits appearing in the consolidated balance sheet of the banking system, published in the Bank of Indonesia Bulletin, does not net out interbank deposits. Hence it is in fact a series resulting from summation, rather than consolidation. An appropriate correction is made in Table 7.B.3 and shown as "Adjustment for double-counting of interbank deposits."

TABLE 7.B.2

Production of Import-Competing Goods, 1969-72

(billion Rp.)

	1969	1970	1971	1972
Exchange rate for conversion	326	378.5	378.5-414	415
Total agriculture/forestry/fishing				
Value added	1,339.3	1,575.0	1,654.6	1,824.1[a]
Less: production of rubber	-74.9	-102.5	-91.0	-84.6
Less: production of export-type timber	-9.4	-42.3	-74.2	-106.1
Less: export of copra, palm oil	-14.5	-26.8	-26.4	-20.6
Less: other agricultural exports	-38.9	-56.7	-47.7	-108.7
Import-competing	1,201.6	1,346.7	1,415.3	1,504.1
Manufacturing				
Value added	250.7	311.8	337.9	398.1[b]
Gross domestic product	2,718.3	3,340.2	3,697.3	4,223.8[c]
ΔGDP	621.6	621.9	357.1	526.5
Percent ΔGDP	29.6	22.9	10.6	14.2

Direct foreign private investment (DFPI)			
Inflow	8.8	29.9	55.6	104.5
Less: imports of DFP investors	7.5	23.5	43.9	62.1
Domestic expenditure of DFPI	1.3	6.4	11.7	42.4
Import component of DFPI (m_f)	.89	.79	.78	.59
Foreign aid net of repayment				
Program aid (PGM)	100.4	107.1	121.3	150.0
Project aid (PJC)	3.8	18.3	26.3	44.7
Less: repayment and interest	-14.3	-25.7	-42.9	-44.0
Net aid disbursement	89.9	99.7	104.7	150.9
Change in government (BULOG) food stockpile	15.9		-.1	-23.5

[a] 3.5 percent real growth, 6.5 percent price increase.
[b] 10.6 percent real growth, 6.5 percent price increase.
[c] 7.2 percent real growth, 6.5 percent price increase.

Sources: BPS; Table 7.6; balance of payments; rev. IBRD.

Domestic transactions balances are composed of rupiah and foreign-exchange balances, thus differing from the conventional definition regarding foreign-exchange balances as quasi money. As argued before, the definition used in the model seems more appropriate to current Indonesian conditions.

The required reserve ratios against rupiah and dollar liabilities shown in Table 7.B.3 are the statutory required ones. It should be noted, however, that the effective reserve ratios with which the banks operate differ somewhat from the required ones, due to specification of the liquid assets in which required reserves can be held. Only one-third of the required reserves must be held at Bank Indonesia; the remainder can be held in currency or in demand deposits in other banks. In the case of rupiah deposits, there can be multiple credit expansion arising out of subsequent deposits from one bank in another, which can significantly reduce the effective reserve requirement. Whether such an erosion in fact takes place can be ascertained only by a detailed analysis of the use of interbank deposits, which exceeds the scope of this paper. The impact of the foreign-exchange reserve requirement is equally complicated, since deposits can be placed in banks abroad and then redeposited back by those banks, while the original deposit may be included in the reserve computation.

It should be noted that the underlying information on the execution on foreign private investment projects is very poor, due to lack of reporting by foreign private investors to the Foreign Investment Board on the execution of the projects. Furthermore, there is some evidence that a portion of what is in fact foreign private investment has used the legal channel of the Domestic Investment Board, and hence has not been reported as foreign investment. Thus there is an unknown degree of error in the estimate of realized inflow because of direct foreign private investment. Likewise, the imports attributed to foreign private investors are estimated from customs declarations under the import duty exemption regulations of the foreign investment law. However, a significant portion of imports is delivered directly to mining and oil enterprises; the corresponding amount should, but does not appear to be, fully captured by the statistics. Thus, it is reasonable to expect the net domestic expenditure of foreign private investment shown to be significantly wide of the mark. Unfortunately, however, it is impossible, without much more detailed analysis, to assess precisely where the bias lies or what its order of magnitude is.

The disbursement of foreign aid, as well as the corresponding repayment and interest items, taken from World Bank (IBRD) sources, differs somewhat from those in the balance of payments. Furthermore, in the case of program aid there is a significant

TABLE 7.B.3

Financial Variables, 1969–72

		1969	1970	1971	1972
1.	Bank Indonesia credit (= credit from monetary authorities)				
(i)	Claims on government	120.3	111.7	104.1	100.8
(ii)	Claims on official entities	73.8	68.3	70.3	105.8
(iii)	Claims on business, individuals	13.6	28.4	33.4	21.5
(iv)	Claims on deposit money banks	70.2	111.8	142.5	149.4
(v)	Claims on other banks	9.3	1.0	1.0	1.0
(vi)	Subtotal	287.2	321.2	351.3	378.5
(vii)	Net other items (other costs – counterpart – capital – other liabilities)	-19.4	-36.1	-16.4	-37.5
(viii)	Total Bank Indonesia credit	267.8	285.1	334.9	341.0
(ix)	△Claims on the sectors (subtotal)	4.7	34.0	30.1	27.2
(x)	△Bank Indonesia credit (total Bank Indonesia credit) = △CR1	30.9	17.3	49.7	6.1

Source: Bank Indonesia Monthly Bulletin, Table 1b.

2.	Deposits in foreign exchange from abroad				
(i)	Foreign liabilities of deposit money banks	56.8	83.5	118.3	243.6
(ii)	Less: foreign-currency deposits of residents	17.7	16.6	30.5	39.4
(iii)	Gross foreign-currency deposits of nonresidents	39.1	66.9	88.8	204.2
(iv)	Time deposits	.9	11.5	17.9	61.1
	Demand deposits	38.2	55.4	70.9	143.1

Source: (i) Bank Indonesia Monthly Bulletin, Table 1g, line 18; (ii) and (iv) Bank Indonesia "Assets & Liabilities of Commercial Banks."

(continued)

Table 7.B.3, continued

	1969	1970	1971	1972
3. Deposits in rupiah from abroad				
(i) State bank time deposits outstanding to foreign banks	—	—	9.3	20.0
(ii) State bank time deposits outstanding to branches of foreign banks	1.2	5.0	13.7	19.0
(iii) Time deposits of branches of foreign banks	2.5	9.4	17.0	26.6
(iv) Total rupiah deposits of nonresidents (state bank time deposits outstanding to foreign banks + time deposits of branches of foreign banks)	2.5	9.4	26.3	36.6
(v) ΔRupiah deposits of nonresidents	1.9	6.9	16.9	10.3

Source: Bank Indonesia Monthly Bulletin: (i) and (ii) Table 2k, (iii) Table 1d.

	1969	1970	1971	1972
4. Domestic savings and time deposits				
(i) Time deposits in deposit money banks	49.8	80.0	145.3	190.2
(ii) Less: rupiah deposits of nonresidents	2.5	9.4	26.3	36.6
(iii) Savings and time deposits of residents	47.3	70.6	119.0	153.6
(iv) ΔSavings and time deposits of residents	35.9	23.3	48.4	34.6

Source: Bank Indonesia Monthly Bulletin, Table 1g.

	1969	1970	1971	1972
4a. Adjustment for double-counting of interbank deposits				
(i) Savings and time deposits of residents [4 (iii) above]	47.3	70.6	119.0	153.6
(ii) Less: interbank deposits	2.6	6.0	14.8	23.9
(iii) Net savings and time deposits of residents	44.7	64.6	104.2	129.7
(iv) ΔNet savings and time deposits of residents	33.5	19.9	39.6	25.5

Source: Bank Indonesia Monthly Bulletin, Table 2b, line 2.

5. Domestic transactions balances				
(i) Currency in hands of the public	114.2	152.8	195.5	269.0
(ii) Rupiah demand deposits in deposit money banks	65.7	88.3	117.1	201.8
(iii) Foreign-currency deposits of residents	17.7	16.6	30.5	39.4
(iv) Total domestic transactions balances (currency + demand deposits + foreign-currency deposits)	197.6	257.7	343.1	510.2
(v) Total domestic transactions balances (average of year ends)	158.4	227.7	300.4	405.3
(vi) Currency in hands of the public (average of year ends)	94.5	133.5	174.2	232.3

Source: (i), (ii) Bank Indonesia Monthly Bulletin, Table 2a.

6. Excess reserves				
(i) Increases in excess reserves of deposit money banks		-5.3	-5.4	10.0

Source: Bank Indonesia Monthly Bulletin.

7. Required reserve ratios (percent)				
(i) Rupiah demand deposits	30	30	30	30
(ii) Rupiah time savings deposits	30	9	3	10
(iii) Foreign-exchange demand deposits	30	30	30	30
(iv) Foreign-exchange time and savings deposits	0	0	0	0

Sources: Bank Indonesia, Monthly Bulletin (various issues).

275

difference between the balance-of-payments and IBRD figures and those in the government's budget. Part of the discrepancy seems to arise from the treatment of the exchange rate at which tied aid is utilized; another part seems to derive from the subsidies attached to some of the commodity aid. The balance of payments of course shows these amounts gross of special subsidies, whereas the budget shows them after deduction of subsidies. From the point of view of macro analysis, it is the gross value that is relevant, since the government subsidy is akin to any other kind of government expenditure. Thus the concept underlying the balance-of-payments and IBRD figures is the appropriate one for the use in the model. The IBRD figures were chosen because they represented more recent revisions than the balance-of-payments figures.

APPENDIX C: COMPUTATIONAL APPROXIMATIONS
FOR MODEL CALIBRATION

In order to simplify the computations, two approximations have been adopted. RMO has been assumed to be equal to RFL. This is correct for demand deposits, but not for foreign-exchange time deposits; hence its approximate character. The simplification of this assumption allows the following:

$$\alpha ' [\alpha + RMO(1 - \alpha)] + RFL(1 - \alpha') = \alpha'\alpha + RMO(\alpha' - \alpha'\alpha + 1 - \alpha')$$

$$= \alpha'\alpha + RMO(1 - \alpha'\alpha) = \alpha'\alpha(1 - RMO) + RMO$$

The equation for the quasi-dynâmic equilibrium level of Y includes a term in ΔY. This has been substituted out by successive approximation, and then truncated after the second term.

The precise operation is the following:

define A $= [\alpha'\alpha(1 - RMO) + RMO]$

EXOG $= Px(1 - m_x) + A(1 - m_a) + I(1 - m_i) + FPI(1 - m_f)$

$\qquad + PGM + PJC + \Delta CR1 - \Delta ST + \Delta CRF$

$\qquad + (1 - RCM) \Delta CMF + (1 - RFL) \Delta FL2F$

$\qquad - \Delta XRES2$

$\lambda = [sbRCM + x + a + i + \Delta k \quad A]^{-1}$

then $Y = \lambda EXOG - \lambda (k + \Delta k)A\Delta Y$

$\qquad \Delta Y = \lambda \Delta EXOG - \lambda (k + \Delta k)A\Delta^2 Y$

$$\Delta^2 Y = \lambda \Delta^2 EXOG - \lambda (k + \Delta k) A \Delta^3 Y$$

hence $Y = \lambda EXOG - \lambda^2 (k + \Delta k) A \Delta EXOG + \lambda^3 (k + \Delta k)^2$

$$A^2 \Delta^2 EXOG - \ldots \div \ldots$$

Taking $\lambda \approx 1.5$, $A \approx .7$, $k + \Delta k \approx .1$, we have

$$\lambda^2 (k + \Delta k) A \approx .16$$

$$\lambda^3 (k + \Delta k)^2 A^2 \approx .016$$

Considering that $\Delta^2 EXOG$ is also likely to be relatively small, truncation after the term in λ^2 appears to be justified.

8
INTERGOVERNMENTAL FISCAL RELATIONS
G. K. Shaw

Intergovernmental finance is an important issue for Indonesia because of the geographical nature of the archipelago, the great diversity and history of its peoples, and the recognition of the need for coordinated regional planning to promote economic development.

Meaningful discussion of central/provincial finance presupposes a political model able to delineate the respective areas of national and subnational government, and to specify the objective function of the central government with regard to the degree of autonomy to be conferred upon the provinces. The first issue concerns the division of tasks to be allocated between central and local governments; the second deals with the degree of discretion accorded to local authorities with respect to expenditures.* This distinction, while often overlooked, is fundamental to the question of intergovernmental finance. For example, it is commonly assumed that increasing the number of tasks to be undertaken by the local authorities implies an increase in the degree of local autonomy and vice versa. However, the central government may assign tasks to the provinces, and so dictate the nature of the service to be provided and its conditions of operation, that no discretionary power of expenditure remains to the local authorities. In this case the provincial government is acting merely as fiscal agent for the central government.

---

*Discretion with respect to revenue raising is neither a necessary or a sufficient condition for regional autonomy. Control of expenditures may be so severe as to negate the impact of discretionary revenue powers, while autonomy in expenditures does not in principle require discretionary revenue powers.

Provincial autonomy, defined here to mean discretionary power over expenditures by the local authorities, may be desired on a number of grounds. It may, for example, improve the overall allocation of resources, to the extent that the peoples of a particular region or province may possess preference patterns distinct from those of the taxpayer at large. In this way, by raising the assessment of benefits received from public outlays, provincial autonomy may increase the degree of fiscal compliance with regard to both central and local government taxes. Moreover, provincial autonomy may be an essential prerequisite in the attraction of high-caliber personnel into local government service, which in turn may be important to the effective coordination of central government development outlays. Finally, the closer contact between project undertakings and provincial (as opposed to central) decision-making authorities may be expected to raise overall efficiency, and in particular to avoid misallocations that may hinder the development effort (in particular, by generating a better time horizon with respect to related investment projects).

Discretionary power over expenditures need not, in principle, imply discretionary power over tax revenues. The central government may simply provide a block grant and allow the provincial authorities to utilize it as they see fit. In practice, however, autonomy with respect to expenditures is likely to require at least some discretionary power over revenues. This arises from the fact that the central government, as representative of the taxpayer, will have an understandable desire to see that such monies are used wisely and not squandered. Such a concern will usually lead to detailed specification of the precise ways in which central government funds may be spent, which ultimately will conflict with the desire for meaningful provincial autonomy. Consequently, expenditure autonomy is easier to effect if there is also autonomy with respect to revenue raising.

This issue is of some importance to central/provincial fiscal relations in Indonesia, for while provincial autonomy in expenditures may be desirable on a number of grounds, it is not so clear that a similar case can be made with respect to taxing powers. Indeed, it has been forcefully argued that the provinces are generally poor agents of taxation and that the taxing powers they have commanded in the past have produced perverse results for the national economy.

Finally, it should be noted that the central/provincial fiscal relations are but one aspect of intergovernmental finance—albeit an important one—and that any proposals for reform implicitly presume something about the nature of financial relationships between other layers of government. In particular it would be pertinent to consider the financial relationships between the central government and the kabupatens (governmental level below the province, often likened to a county or shire), and between the kabupatens and the provinces, in any discussion of central/provincial government finance.

THE NATURE OF THE GRANT SYSTEM

It has been argued that the extent of provincial expenditures should be determined by the division of tasks between central and local government and by the politically determined degree of local autonomy, although there may be limitations imposed on the extent of provincial government taxation. It follows that there is no clear reason for subnational expenditures to be self-financing. Indeed, if it is conceded that the central government legitimately seeks to establish minimum standards in service provision—for example, in health and education—and that there are sizable regional disparities with regard to revenue capacities, then the revenue/expenditure dichotomy is reinforced. Hence the need for some form of intergovernmental transfers. The questions that remain then concern the nature of the grant system to be imposed, its rationale, and its mode of operation, in particular:

The criteria to be adopted in determining the extent and allocation of such transfers

The manner in which such transfers are to be effected—of particular importance here is the need to avoid any disincentive impact upon local revenue raising

The control to be exercised over the expenditure of such transfers, a question fundamental to the issue of provincial autonomy.

Prior to 1971-72, Indonesian central government grants were allocated according to a formula determined by Parliament (Law no. 32), which specifically attempted to take account of relevant economic considerations. Thus, for example, grant allocations would differ according to population, road mileage, irrigation projects, and so forth. Unfortunately, the actual operation of the system was extremely complex; provincial governments were uncertain of the amount of central government aid they could expect, and in some cases the formula operated in such a manner that certain provinces were unable to meet the salary payments of the government officials they were obliged to employ in order to carry out the tasks assigned to them. It was generally conceded that the grant system was inequitable and ill-suited to aid the development of the regions, and the program was finally terminated in the fiscal year 1971-72.

Ultimately a new system will emerge, sanctioned by Parliament; and the present measures, which are intended to serve only as a temporary stopgap, will be abolished.

The existing system is administered by the Ministry of the Interior and employs criteria similar to those used formerly. However, there are two important differences that make the present method far superior. First, whereas the previous formula determined the percentage of central government taxes that would be returned to each province, the present system determines the absolute lump sum that each province will receive. Second, under the existing arrangements the dominant element is the number of officials, including teachers, employed by the province. In effect, the Ministry of the Interior provides 100 percent of the money wage bill of local government employees and approximately two-thirds of the wages paid in kind (mainly rice allowances).* Consequently the Mininstry of the Interior meets the vast bulk of the routine budget and effectively guarantees that the provincial governments are able to pay their officials. At the same time, it necessitates that the Ministry of the Interior should exercise effective control over additional appointments to provincial government service.

The provincial governments have alternative sources of revenue. In particular, they receive timber and mining royalties and a fixed payment from the central government in lieu of the proceeds arising from the tax on exports (called the changed ADO). These reimbursements are paid directly from the Ministry of Finance. In addition the provinces possess their own local tax sources, over which they have the power to vary the rate of tax. Finally, they receive 10 percent of the levy on land (IPEDA). In general, reimbursements from the Ministry of Finance are specifically assigned to the development budget of the provincial government. The provinces are thus dependent upon their own power to raise local taxes to meet any routine expenditures not covered by the general grant, although provision does exist, in the event of a shortfall, for the transfer of up to 10 percent of the development funds to the routine budget.

---

*Thus providing an incentive to "clean wages" in the provincial government service. It will be noted that fluctuations in the price of rice will impart a variable element into the routine budget unless the provincial authorities are able to purchase at guaranteed prices.

ASPECTS OF PROVINCIAL GOVERNMENT FINANCE

Even a superficial survey of the existing grant system, together with other sources of provincial revenues, highlights a number of key issues. The most pertinent—from the viewpoint of potential reform—would appear to be the following.

First, the provinces are overwhelmingly dependent upon the
central government subsidy to carry out the functions assigned to
them, since their taxing powers are extremely limited (97 percent
of all fiscal revenues are paid directly to the central government).
Moreover, with very few exceptions, taxes assigned to the provincial governments are decidedly income-inelastic, being levied upon
specific activities and not upon the basis of value added. While provincial authorities possess the power to determine the actual rates
of tax, their discretion is limited by the nature of the taxes (nui-
sance taxes), which impose very high marginal collection costs upon
attempts to raise revenue yields, whether by changes in the rate
structure or by increased collection efforts. Finally, there is some
evidence to suggest that provincial tax yields may be interdependent,
so that increasing the yield of one tax may reduce yields elsewhere.
A study of the cost effectiveness of provincial tax revenue sources,
with a view to scrapping or consolidating many minor taxes, would
be highly desirable, and logically should precede any attempt to reform the central/provincial relationship.

Second, this highly centralized system of finance is reinforced
by a strict system of budgetary control. Provincial governments
are compelled to submit their budgets to the central authorities for
approval and the latter require strict adherence to a balanced budget.
While provincial assemblies do debate local budgets and make amend-
ments to the overall financial plan outlined by the governor, the predetermined central government subsidy and the balanced budget principle severely limit the freedom of maneuver. One consequence is
that in the event of a revenue shortfall, often the only possible recourse is to curtail existing local development projects, at high cost
and with a considerable waste of resources.

Third, an undeniable feature of the existing system of intergovernmental finance is a good deal of resentment by the provinces
toward the central government. In part, this springs from the limitations imposed upon provincial taxing and spending powers, but it
is also possible to identify a number of more specific factors. In
some provinces there is the belief that they are being "exploited" by
being compelled to make net financial transfers to the central authorities. In many cases this sense of exploitation is misplaced, and
springs from the failure to distinguish between the taxes that are
collected within a province and those that are actually paid by the

residents of that province. For example, regional data on revenues
collected will include import duties levied upon goods at the port of
entry, even though the goods are destined for consumption in other
provinces. Assuming normal patterns of behavior with regard to
incidence, it is clear that the amount of revenue collected within the
province will exceed that actually paid by the population of the province.* A further source of resentment frequently encountered stems
from the conversion of the ADO tax in 1969-70. Prior to that year
the ADO revenues, levied upon exports from the province,† were
returned to the province for its own development use. Now, however, the ADO transfers to the provinces have been converted to an
absolute figure equal to 105 percent of the 1969-70 figure. Thus a
revenue source that expanded along with export growth has been
transformed into a fixed receipt, the real value of which is declining under the pressure of inflation. Moreover, since the receipts
returned to the provinces were based upon export proceeds in dollars,
the subsequent devaluation of the dollar has intensified the resentment. Finally, a common source of complaint arises from the fact
that local tax revenues, raised to promote local development projects, are often diverted to expenses for the maintenance and purchase of the infrastructure associated with the employment of central government employees. Although the Ministry of the Interior
effectively meets the wage bill of central government officials employed in the provinces, it does not necessarily meet all the atten-
dant costs, with the result that locally raised revenue has to be
transferred from the development budget to the routine budget.

---

*This sense of exploitation is reinforced by the failure to im-
plement the financial edict of 1955, which expressly states that 90
percent of revenues collected by the central government should be
returned to the provinces from which they originate. Such a stipulation is, of course, clearly unworkable, unless the government is
going to resort to inflationary increases in the money supply, for it
entirely ignores the allocation of centrally provided services (including defense) among the provinces.

†The ADO receipts are returned to the province from which
export occurs, not the province where the production of the exported product occurs. Together with the point made previously,
this implies that a province with extensive import/export activity,
owing to natural geographical advantages, would appear to be making a larger fiscal contribution than it is in fact, and would also be
receiving a larger amount of central government assistance than
would appear logically defensible.

Fourth, a striking characteristic of the existing system is the absence of any linkage between grant allocations and provincial tax effort. Superior tax effort is not rewarded by superior grant allocations. The only tax with any incentive feature is the IPEDA land levy, assessed by the central authorities but collected at the kabupaten level. Exceeding the target figure results in increased per capita aid to the kabupaten program. The system also contains no incentive to cooperation between provincial governments. One may look askance at a system of intergovernmental finance that has no relevance for the coordination of development expenditures between provinces that form natural economic regions.

Fifth, and perhaps the most fundamental defect of the existing system of intergovernmental finance, is the fact that the total amount of central government assistance to the provinces is not correlated with any relevant economic criteria. This springs directly from the division of authority between the Ministry of the Interior, responsible for grant allocations, and the Ministry of Finance, responsible for the reimbursements of royalties, export taxes, and so forth. The net effect is for total central government assistance to be channeled to the provinces in an essentially haphazard way, so there is no necessary relationship between the amount of aid received and the level of income per capita—or any other indexes of need. Indeed, it is possible for the richest or fastest-growing provinces to qualify for the largest amount of aid, either because their greater infrastructure will be accompanied by higher levels of public-sector officials and IPEDA contributions or because of export royalties denied less fortunate provinces.

ATTITUDES TO REFORM OF CENTRAL/PROVINCIAL FISCAL RELATIONSHIPS

Considerable interest and controversy, particularly in government circles, has been aroused by the need to formalize intergovernmental fiscal relations in a manner consistent with planned development. A survey has indicated wide discrepancies in the budgetary practices of the various provinces, which renders financial comparisons difficult to make. There is a general lack of uniformity in the preparation of budget statements, and in some cases inconsistencies exist between the revenue and expenditure accounts of a provincial budget.* These exploratory studies have raised a number of inter-

---

*For example, the revenue side of the budget accounts may be prepared on a cash basis, while the expenditure side may be drawn

esting issues, but no consensus has emerged with regard to reform of the system.* It is, however, possible to identify a number of diverse, and on occasion conflicting, viewpoints concerning the optimal system of central/provincial government finance. It is striking how much the opinions differ according to the vantage point of the interested party.

Increased Provincial Autonomy in Expenditures

A considerable body of opinion favors an increase in the degree of provincial autonomy over expenditure decisions. The provinces are virtually united in believing that the existing system of control and the specific assignment of revenues to particular tasks lead to serious waste and resource misallocation. Combined with the prohibition on debt financing, such strict control leads not infrequently to the termination of development projects until new funds can be obtained. These interruptions raise costs, occasion delays through the need for retendering of bids, and jeopardize consistent employment policies. Other officials argue that central government control of minor development projects is too distant and remote, and performs poorly, especially in relation to the timing and coordination of investment expenditures. A contrary view suggests that greater provincial autonomy might conflict with the aims of regional planning in cases where investment in infrastructure (particularly with respect to communications) is seen as encompassing several provinces. According to this viewpoint, the provinces are often too small to be viable economic units and coordinated planning is essential to secure potential economies of scale.

Provincial Autonomy in Taxation

Considerable skepticism was expressed with regard to increased taxing powers in the provinces. Provinces with very low levels of

---

up on an authorization basis—a procedure that, given the stipulation of nondeficit finance, generally leads to underutilization of available revenues. Adoption of an accrual basis with respect to revenues would appear to be a preferable alternative.

*One point of agreement, however, is recognition that reform of financial relationships need no longer be constrained by fears for the political unity of the nation. The sizable differences—racial, religious, and linguistic—that gave rise to separatist movements in the past have lessened in importance.

income per capita and lacking skilled personnel expressed the view that increased taxing authority would be an inadequate solution to their most pressing problem: lack of finance. In their view, the only solution was an increased allocation of central government aid specifically geared to their income levels and development needs.

One extreme view argued that provincial governments should be stripped of their taxing powers entirely. There existed no tax that was logically a provincial tax, and taxes assigned to the provincial government in the past often generated perverse incentives or income distributions. In support of this contention, reference was made to the operation of the former export tax, whereby 10 percent of the tax was returned to the province of export. One result was a serious distortion in transportation patterns as each province sought to avoid using ports in other provinces. (West Java, for example, sought to avoid Jakarta and channel all exports through Tjirebon.) In a similar vein, it was argued that the vehicle transfer tax is extremely inequitable. A large percentage of the proceeds accrue to Jakarta, where the formal transfers are primarily carried out, although the vehicle will often be used elsewhere. Finally, it was argued that provincial revenue authorities have a natural tendency to exploit high-yielding revenue sources, or those easy to collect, without regard to whether their effects are consistent with national priorities. One example cited was the frequent recourse to cesses imposed upon interisland trade, raising interisland transportation costs and weakening national economic unity. Provincial revenues by their nature are often divorced from any economic rationale, since the provinces are political entities created without regard to their economic potential.

An alternative view was that some provinces could handle certain central government taxes as effectively as, if not more effectively than, presently administered. This raises a very delicate issue: Is uniformity among provinces in the assignment of taxing powers between central and local units of government a necessary requirement for a rational system of intergovernment finance? Could not superior tax effort by certain provinces be rewarded through an increase in their taxing autonomy? And is it not possible that a tax deemed consistent with national policy objectives in one province may be considered unwise in another province?

Finally, when discussing the issue of provincial autonomy, whether in respect to taxation or to expenditures, it should be noted that considerable autonomy does exist with regard to expenditures or revenues in kind—particularly gotong royong (cooperative self-help) forms of resource utilization. Such activity, essentially a quasi-voluntary form of the French corvée, admittedly is primarily of importance at the village, as opposed to the provincial, level.

Nonetheless, it is a form of investment activity able to raise the standard of provincial infrastructure generally, and to promote linkage effects working through improvements in communications.

Global Provincial Finance

The need for a financial structure that would promote economic development while meeting the legitimate needs of the poorer provinces provided the rationale for the advocacy of global provincial finance. In this view, supported predominantly by economists responsible for the overall development and planning of the national economy, and therefore possibly unsympathetic to the provincial view, there should be but one form of central-government support— a general subsidy—the amount of which would be determined by a single formula based upon economic criteria including income per capita. Advocates of the global view were concerned with the impact of the fiscal structure upon overall economic development, and argued that an attempt should be made to assist the producing regions in order to provide rural employment and hasten transmigration to less densely populated islands.

In contrast, fiscal edicts that lend support to the consuming regions (for example, the imposition of additional taxes on gasoline) are held to be in conflict with national economic objectives. The adoption of a global approach to central government aid would permit the establishment of criteria for grant allocations in line with national economic policy objectives. Advocates of the global view tend to oppose the granting of increased taxing autonomy to the provinces, on the ground that it would lead to a proliferation of taxes easy to administer and collect but inconsistent with national priorities. The remaining sections of this paper will be concerned with establishing the criteria by which such a global system of finance might be allocated among the provinces.

AN IDEALIZED GRANT ALLOCATION FORMULA

It is taken as axiomatic that there is a need to modify the grant system so that the total of central-government aid to the provinces can be justified by reference to economic criteria. At the present time the division of responsibility between the Ministry of the Interior and the Ministry of Finance, with the former making grant contributions independently of the financial reimbursements made by the latter, lends a capricious element to the notion of central government subsidy, and is certainly hard to defend in terms of equity considerations. Admittedly the adoption of any system of global finance would raise delicate questions of shifts in ministerial power, but this is logically part of the price to be paid for rationalizing intergovernmental fiscal relationships.

To formulate a program of central government aid to the provinces, it will be assumed that the provinces receive no financial support from the central government other than that outlined by the grant allocation formula. The provinces would retain their existing taxing powers, providing they were deemed compatible with the national interest.

The total grant allocation would be divisible into two main parts, the first to meet the essential needs of the province and the second to provide additional incentives to desired provincial behavior. In the first component there would be provision for the essentials of the routine budget: wages of public-sector employees and the maintenance of infrastructure, especially provincial roads and irrigation systems. In addition there would be provision for minimum standards in such services as education, health, and possibly housing and employment opportunities. This would suggest the need to prescribe basic national standards—for example, the number of school places or hospital beds per thousand population. Provinces with services falling below the minimum would receive additional finance in order to attain the desired standard within a specified period. The first part of the grant, G_1, would be represented by the formula

$$G_1 = W + u(aR + bI) + \frac{(N - E)}{Y}$$

where W is the provincial public-sector wage bill approved by the Ministry of the Interior, R the provincial road mileage, I the existing number of hectares of irrigated land, N the national minimum standard of service provision, E the existing provincial standard of provision (both N and E expressed in monetary terms), Y the number of years over which the required adjustment is to be made, a and b monetary constants (so many Rp. per mile/hectare), and u the index of the area of the province (since one would normally associate higher maintenance costs with the greater dispersion of infrastructure).

Three comments are in order. First, implicit in such a formula is the need for finance to be effectively tied to expenditures in line with the justification underlying its allocation. Consequently, under this part of the grant at least, there is little scope for increased provincial autonomy. Second, for the Ministry of the Interior merely to underwrite the public-sector wage bill would generate inefficiency in the form of superfluous employees, or employees employed at higher wage rates, unless the ministry were to exercise such strict control as to impose inflexibility upon the hiring policies of the provincial governments. To meet this objection it could be specified that the provincial wage bill would be met in full only if the total number of public-sector employees per thousand population did not exceed a certain figure and the average wage did not exceed a certain multiple of the consumer price index. In addition, there could be a financial incentive to the provinces for reducing public-sector employees. The provinces could utilize revenues on nonessential services, in the belief that any shortfall in essential services would be made good by the central government. For this reason, payment of the grant could be made dependent on adequate performance in closing the gap between the standard and the actual provision of essential services in the previous year.

The second component of the overall grant, G_2, would provide incentives to improve provincial performance on local revenues, export production, and population control, with due allowance being made for migratory movements, and to coordinate investment outlays among provinces forming a natural economic region. Ideally, when linking grants to improved performance, allowance should be made for relative per capita income levels, since it is normally easier for high per capita regions to modify their behavior in line with the fiscal stimulus than for the lower per capita income regions, where the freedom of maneuver is more limited. Hence, the second part of the grant allocation formula, G_2, might take the form

$$G_2 = \left[\frac{cT + dX + epA}{P + M} \right] \cdot \left[\frac{y_n}{y_p} \right]$$

where T and X are the annual percentage increases in tax revenue and exports, respectively; A is the amount of approved coordinated regional investment expenditure;* p is the percentage undertaken by the province in question; and c and d are monetary constants, expressed in Rp. The actual value of the coefficient might vary with the absolute magnitude of taxes and exports.† A is also a monetary

---

*Presumably to qualify for assistance, such investment outlay would require the approval of those charged with supervising regional planning. Criteria might include the degree of labor intensity, in the interests of employment creation.

†On the ground that it might be judged easier to effect a given percentage increase from a low absolute base than from a comparatively high one.

aggregate, expressed in Rp., and e is thus a coefficient indicating the fraction of coordinated regional expenditure undertaken by the province that is financed by the central government.*

Thus, the province would obtain additional central-government assistance as it increased exports, increased tax revenues, and undertook approved coordinated regional investment expenditure. The ratio y_n/y_p is simply the ratio of national income per capita to the income per capita of the province in question, thus ensuring that aid received is correlated inversely with the amount of income per capita. P is the percentage increase in population (natural), and M is the net inward migration with respect to Java, Madura, Bali, and provinces generally considered overpopulated (and the net outward migration in all other cases). A system of differential weighting might be attached to M, reflecting the differences in the potential for transmigration in the various provinces. It will be noted that it is necessary to impose the restriction that $P + M \neq O$, in order to derive a meaningful result from the grant allocation formula.

Potential provincial benefits are thus reduced by natural population increase or by transmigratory policy deemed inconsistent with the national interest. It would be a simple matter to modify the coefficient d to reflect the national government's priorities with regard to exportables; thus a higher subsidy might be payable to, say, increased rubber production and a lower one to increased copra production if the former were to confront more favorable world market conditions.

Finally, since the second component of the grant, G_2, is paid for improved performance, the incentive impact would be strengthened if the provincial authorities were able to utilize such monies as they see fit. The result would be a grant structure geared partly to the provision of basic services and amenities, which would be subject to strict central-government control, and partly as a reward for improved performance, which justifies enhanced provincial autonomy. Having outlined an idealized grant allocation formula, as a conceptual aid in the approach to Indonesian intergovernmental fiscal relations, we now turn to a more feasible formulation.

---

*Thus, for example, if A is Rp. 500 million, half of which is undertaken by the province in question, and e is, say one-third, then the province would receive approximately Rp. 83 million.

A PRACTICAL GRANT ALLOCATION FORMULA

The foregoing specifically abstracts from the difficulties of implementation and assumes no data limitations.* In practice, of course, the data limitations would be considerable, especially with regard to annual estimates of population increase and per capita income levels. Moreover, simplification of the basic formula would be desirable, if only because it would extend the range of comprehension.

The first component of the formula presents no undue difficulty. Most of the required information is in the official census and related surveys; and since central government officials presently carry out the assessment of the IPEDA land levy, it would be a relatively simple matter to conduct sample checks upon the extent of roadways, irrigated land, and so forth. In the interests of simplicity, it would be advisable to make the maintenance subsidy uniform, as opposed to differentiating by class of road, land use, or other relevant criteria. It is the second part of the formula that would require modification. The use of annual population figures and per capita income figures for each province is clearly a nonstarter; apart from any other consideration, the administrative work involved would present an intolerable burden to both central and local government officials.† Family planning clinics could serve as a proxy for effort in this field, and provinces receiving migrants might receive a special incentive in the grant allocation formula.

While the use of exact per capita income ratios also would not be feasible, it should be relatively simple to divide the provinces of Indonesia into relatively high, median, and relatively low per capita

---

*Also, as mentioned, it assumes the abolition of the ADO receipts and royalty payments. The eventual abolition of the ADO receipts would appear to be but a matter of time, now that it is progressively declining in real terms. Royalty payments present a much more difficult problem. In some cases they are the major source of provincial revenue and have been expanding rapidly, the prime example being East Kalimantan, which retains 70 percent of the timber royalty. Moreover, an economic case can be made for their continuance, to ensure that producing regions are able to finance needed infrastructure.

†It is generally conceded that existing estimates of income per capita are probably unreliable, influenced in part by the extent of tax evasion, which exerts a feedback effect upon estimates of gross national product.

income regions (α, β, and γ). The total government grant could then be weighted by such indexes of income per capita. A practical grant allocation formula would then reduce to

$$G = \left[W + u(aR + bI) + \frac{(N - E)}{Y} + cT + dX + epA \right] \left[\alpha , \beta, \text{ or } \gamma \right]$$

where

$\alpha < 1$

$\beta = 1$

$\gamma > 1$

The foregoing, it should be emphasized, is intended to provide no more than a conceptual framework; but the formula would appear to possess the virtue of decomposing central-government assistance into two parts, the first meeting the routine needs of the provinces and the second providing incentives to improve performance in the light of national objectives.

PROVINCIAL GOVERNMENT AND DEBT FINANCE

Provincial governments are specifically prohibited from re-sorting to debt finance. This restriction, understandable in the light of past inflationary experiences, imposes a real burden upon the poorer provinces and, by generating inflexibility in local investment projects, is often responsible for serious waste. This suggests two possible ways by which such a restriction might be relaxed.

First, there appears to be no sound reason for prohibiting interprovincial debt. Provinces with surplus funds could lend to those in deficit. The principle of overall balance of provincial bud-gets would be unaffected, yet a certain amount of flexibility would be introduced into the system. Provinces suddenly experiencing an unanticipated revenue shortfall would at least be allowed to seek al-ternative funds before being compelled to curb existing activities.

Second, the existence of royalty payments to provincial gov-ernments and the political difficulty involved in terminating them completely suggest alternative means of diminishing the discrepancy between richer and poorer provinces. If provinces enjoying royalty payments were compelled to accept, say, 10 percent of any receipts in the form of guaranteed government bonds, redeemable at some later date and paying a nominal rate of interest, the central govern-ment would be able to lend such money to the poorer provinces. There could be the stipulation that loans be spent on revenue-raising infrastructure, so as to ensure eventual repayment. (For example, bus stations and similar infrastructure are natural tax handles.) Such a system really amounts to a form of forced saving imposed upon the richer provinces combined with the provision of cheap credit to the poorer.

KABUPATEN FINANCE

The kabupatens obtain revenue from four principal sources.

First, they retain 80 percent of the IPEDA land levy that they collect after assessment by the central authorities. The remaining 20 percent of the tax is divided equally between the central and provincial governments. The tax is defective in that assessment is often based upon land classification long out of date; review and reform of the assessment procedure would render the setting of tax target figures more realistic and would also be required in the context of any relevant grant allocation formula. There appears to be no rationale for the 10 percent IPEDA contribution from the kabupaten to provinces (which in some cases is not effected), which benefits the rich provinces more than the poor, making a rational grant allocation system more difficult to operate by equity criteria. By concentrating resources upon IPEDA, and especially by increasing the number of personnel involved in assessment procedures, it should be possible to obtain significant increases in net yield.* Moreover, improved assessment procedures would be essential to the smooth functioning of a grant allocation formula, as outlined earlier in this essay, if provincial roadways, irrigation schemes, and such are to be among the relevant criteria.

Second, they receive per capita income payments from the central authorities under the existing kabupaten program plus a bonus payment in the event of the IPEDA tax target figure being exceeded, the target being set in relation to the currently assessed land values plus arrears.

Third, they possess numerous small local taxing powers, such as the dog tax, bicycle tax, and radio tax. The striking features of such taxes are their comparatively low yield, their inelastic

---

*The attitude of provincial authorities may influence the amount of IPEDA actually collected. For this reason, even if the provincial governments no longer have any share in the IPEDA revenue, it might be still beneficial to make the tax incentive reflect IPEDA collections.

response to income growth, and their relatively high collection costs. The proliferation of such taxes is a source of concern; it is inimical to standards of fiscal compliance and a possible source of tax evasion. There is a definite need to abolish many nonproductive taxes and also to terminate taxes having perverse effects, such as those levied upon interkabupaten and interprovincial movement of goods. Limiting local taxes to a few clearly defined sources would be conducive to greater fiscal compliance and would lower collection costs.

Fourth, they may receive financial assistance from the provincial governments, sometimes in the form of failure by the latter to collect the 10 percent of the IPEDA levy due to them. In addition, the provinces are the vehicle through which the central-government subsidy is paid to maintain government officials employed within the kabupatens and, officially at least, the provinces are charged with the formal responsibility of maintaining certain kabupaten infrastructure. Partly owing to the failure of the provincial governments to meet this commitment, the kabupatens are now required to use 40 percent of their overall revenues on the maintenance of existing infrastructure.

The above recommendations come very close to terminating specific financial links between provincial and kabupaten levels of government. This would appear to be logically sound; both look to the central government for their main sources of revenue, and it is extremely unlikely that this financial dependence could be lessened in the near future. By dealing directly with the central government, the relationship between the central and other levels of government is greatly simplified and the rationale of a grant allocation formula is more readily perceived. Nor does this in any way diminish the extent of local autonomy, which, it is now argued, is dependent upon discretionary power over expenditures, and is ultimately to be determined through the political process.

9
JAPANESE INVESTMENTS IN INDONESIA: OWNERSHIP, TECHNOLOGY TRANSFER, AND POLITICAL CONFLICT

Yoshi Tsurumi

For some years developing nations have been trying to harness multinational firms as engines of development. Many developing nations regard multinational firms as expedient sources of necessary ingredients for economic development: technology, access to foreign markets, investment capital, and entrepreneurship and managerial skill. At the same time developing nations ideologically advocate "self-reliance"—relying on their own people and resources to meet development goals. To strike a balance between their competing desires, developing nations seek ways in which these items can be obtained without paying the high political costs of foreign ownership and continued presence of expatriate managers and engineers.[1]

This balance always remains tenuous. As often is the case with Japanese subsidiaries in Indonesia, the idiosyncrasies of Japanese ownership patterns and technologies require temporary but ubiquitous presence of Japanese expatriates.[2] And this political visibility of Japanese investments often invites adverse publicity from two local sources.

First, when foreign investments draw political protests from students, the urban unemployed, and mass media, the Japanese investments are likely to be singled out as the most visible "proxy target" for all foreign investments, and sometimes even for the host government. This point was most dramatically illustrated by the anti-Japanese demonstration that was triggered by Prime Minister Kakuei Tanaka's visit to Jakarta in January 1974.[3] Second, as foreign investors from such less industrialized nations as Korea, Taiwan, India, Singapore, and Hong Kong learn to produce the kind of standard manufactures that Japanese investors first transplanted to Indonesia, adverse publicity about Japanese businesses is often fanned by these new competitors. When Japanese firms attempt to upgrade their goods into more sophisticated product groups that are often dominated by European and American investors, Japanese investors again encounter adverse publicity generated by their new competitors. Thus the image of "ugly Japanese" is perpetuated.

This article was prepared in 1973, on the basis of an extensive field survey completed during the first quarter of 1973 in Indonesia. A major question that I pursued was whether the relative bargaining strength of Indonesia vis-à-vis Japanese investors in particular, and foreign investors in general, was changing in Indonesia's favor. As I look back now, I find that factual information about transfer of Japanese technologies and other aspects of Japanese businesses still holds true. Furthermore, subsequent years have upheld rather well a number of predictions and deductions that I made in 1973 about rising trends of foreign investors from less-industrialized countries overtaking the least technology-intensive and the least brand-conscious segment of the product market.[4] And I still stand by the policy recommendations that I made in 1973 for the Indonesian government.

SCOPE OF JAPANESE DIRECT
INVESTMENTS IN INDONESIA

By the end of 1972, Japan was the leader in terms of the number of approved foreign investment projects, and second only to the United States in terms of the value of approved investments (Table 9.1). By the first quarter of 1973, all but five investment projects authorized for Japanese firms had actually begun operations, with an average period of 18 months between the receipt of a permit from the government and the commencement of operation (of actual production, in the case of manufacturing subsidiaries). (See Table 9.2.) The reported $311 million of paid-in capital by Japanese subsidiaries is around 90 percent of the total value of approved Japanese investment during the period 1967-72.

A comparison with other foreign investments shows a heavier Japanese concentration in manufacturing industries and a more rapid implementation. The Indonesian government and a Japanese source (for selected industries) estimated the actual amount of investment (Table 9.3). As of the end of 1971, an average of some 16 percent of approved investments had been spent. By the end of 1972, the figure was approximately 23 percent. For the manufacturing sector alone, the actual investment reached 41 percent. The ratio of actual to approved investments in 1973 went beyond the 50 percent mark. From September 1971 to the end of 1972, approximately $260 million was actually invested, the bulk in imported capital equipment.

TABLE 9.1

Approved Foreign Investments in Indonesia, End of 1972

Investing Country	Number of Projects	Approved Investments			
		Percent of Total	Value (million U.S. $)	Percent of Total	
America					
United States	97	17.8	922.5	40.7	
Others	85	15.6	813.4	35.9	
	12	2.2	109.1	4.8	
Asia					
Japan	313	57.8	1,164.9	51.4	
Others	100	18.5	344.9	15.2	
Oceania*	187	34.5	701.6	30.9	
	26	4.8	118.4	5.3	
Europe	133	24.4	177.6	7.9	
Netherlands	33	6.0	48.5	2.1	
Great Britain	30	5.5	32.4	1.4	
West Germany	24	4.5	29.5	1.3	
Others	46	8.4	67.2	2.3	
Total	543	100.0	2,265.0	100.0	

*Australia and New Zealand.

Source: Compiled from "Approved Foreign Investments," Foreign Investment Board, Jakarta, March 1973. Mimeographed.

TABLE 9.2

Japanese Direct Investments in Indonesia
as of March 31, 1973

Industry	Number of Investment Projects in Operation	Equity Capital[a] Paid in (thousand U.S.$)	Ratio to Total (percent)
Manufacturing	65	184,008	59
Mining	3[b]	75,930[b]	23
Forestry	11	21,500	7
Agriculture	5	6,590	3
Fishery	9	14,206	5
Real estate and construction	6	5,800	2
Transportation	4	3,200	1
Total	103[c]	311,234	100

[a]For each investment project (a Japanese subsidiary) the amount of paid-in capital was obtained. However, the location of the cash funds or the amounts of capital equipment that have not arrived in Indonesia were not disclosed. Accordingly this figure tends to overestimate actual amounts of capital spent or actually held by each subsidiary.

[b]One of the three subsidiaries in an international consortium consisting of Sumitomo Mining (Japan), Newmont Mining (U.S.A.), American Smelting and Refining, and United States Steel Corporation. The total equity capital of this international consortium was not known.

[c]This figure is greater than the number of approved investments for Japan reported by the Indonesian government as of the end of 1972. This is because a number of Japanese subsidiaries "officially" commenced operations during the first quarter of 1973. Prior to their approval, "trial-run" operations of these manufacturing subsidiaries were often conducted under the guise of "free technical assistance" to the Indonesian partners' plants.

Source: The checklist was compiled by the author from the records of the Japanese embassy. Their operation was ascertained as existing either by author's actual visits or by telephone interview.

TABLE 9.3

Amounts Approved and Invested: Foreign Direct Investments in Indonesia, 1967–72
(million U.S.$)

Industry	From 1967 to September 30, 1971			From 1967 to the End of 1972		
	Amount Approved	Amount Invested	Percent Invested	Amount Approved	Amount Invested	Percent Invested
Agriculture	74.7	3.9	5.2	80.5	N.A.	N.A.
Forestry	402.0	69.0	17.1	446.0	101.0	22.6
Mining	541.1	30.8	5.6	860.5	N.A.	N.A.
Manufacturing	459.1	131.8	28.7	654.2	270.0	41.3
Construction	35.1	9.0	25.6	38.3	N.A.	N.A.
Hotel and trade	51.4	5.1	9.9	97.9	N.A.	N.A.
Transportation and communication	12.0	6.8	56.6	15.1	N.A.	N.A.
Entertainment and services	15.6	4.8	30.7	72.5	N.A.	N.A.
Total	1,591.0	261.2	16.4	2,265.0	523.0	23.0

N.A. = not available.

Note: The amounts invested were estimated from custom clearance records of Indonesia and expenditure records of DICS Rp. The latter comprised merely 3 percent of total amounts invested.

Sources: Foreign Investment Board, a mimeographed data sheet (Jakarta: the Board, March 1973); Tokei Geppo (Statistics Monthly) Toyo Keizai, Tokyo (May 1973): 26.

While 59 percent of Japanese approved investments were in the manufacturing sector, only 28 percent of all foreign investments were in this sector. Furthermore, actual Japanese investment in manufacturing was about 68 percent of all such investments (as of the end of 1972), indicating that Japanese subsidiaries dominated manufacturing.

THE ROLE OF TRADING FIRMS

The first quarter of 1973 may well be marked as the time at which careful observers of Japanese investors could detect three major developments. First was the more rapid expansion of Japanese manufacturing subsidiaries. Second was their newly expanded vistas, particularly in the exploration of export possibilities. Textiles and fishing led the way in exporting operations. Among new investments being contemplated by Japanese firms, there were plans to manufacture apparel, plastic sandals, and canvas shoes solely for export to markets outside Indonesia, specifically in the United States and even in Japan.

The third development was the beginning of a changed role for the trading companies. Japanese subsidiaries in Indonesia are still dominated by leading Japanese trading companies (sogo shosha) when compared with other Japanese subsidiaries abroad.[5] In Indonesia these trading companies are most visible in manufacturing. Of all Japanese manufacturing subsidiaries abroad in 1967-72, only 28 percent were controlled by Japanese trading firms.[6] In Indonesia, however, 66 percent of subsidiaries engaged in manufacturing activities (43 out of 65) were organized through the initiative of trading firms (Table 9.4).

Many Japanese manufacturing firms that formerly exported to Indonesia wanted to manufacture in that country before entry was blocked by the Indonesian government or preempted by their competitors. In many cases exports had been handled through Japanese trading firms. These trading companies helped Japanese manufacturers to find suitable local partners and, in general, to overcome their unfamiliarity with local conditions, their lack of managerial talent seasoned in a different culture and language, their lack of worldwide communication networks (telex, for example), and even their lack of experience in international financing.

At first, Japanese manufacturing subsidiaries were established in Indonesia merely to avoid tariff and other import barriers. The timing of their entry was determined mainly by each investor's fear of being preempted by Japanese competitors. The rivalry among leading Japanese trading firms encouraged speculative entry into manufacturing activities in Indonesia. When the competition is fierce, as in the case of synthetic fibers, one firm's move to enter Indonesia was immediately followed by its competitors. Trading firms, eager to obtain the manufacturers' technologies at a bargain price, fanned the rivalry among competing manufacturing firms in Japan to enter Indonesia.

TABLE 9.4

Trading Companies in Japanese Manufacturing Subsidiaries in Indonesia, by Product Group, 1967-72

Product	Total Subsidiaries	Trading Company Subsidiaries
Textiles	16	15
Galvanized iron sheets	5	5
Plastic sandals, plastic soles, foam, films	3	3
Steel and iron pipes, structures, wire, nails, tools, aluminum sheets	10	9
Bicycles, parts	2	2
Electric and electronic appliances, batteries, dry batteries	4	0
Foods, food additives	5	1[a]
Pharmaceuticals, cosmetics	4	0
Jute bags, zippers, gloves	4	0
Miscellaneous[b]	12	8
Total	65	43

[a]This is the Coca-Cola bottling operation in Jakarta.

[b]Trading companies are involved in cigarette filters, printing, leather tanning, charcoal making, stationary and marine diesel engine assembly, and furniture. They are not involved in automobile sales and assembly, sheet glass, printing ink, and one logging mill.

Source: The author's field work in Indonesia, 1973.

Trading firms are also actively involved in the subsidiaries engaged in developing natural resources, fishing, and agriculture. The dominance of trading companies in these subsidiaries is explained by their long experience in seeking natural resources and agricultural products on a worldwide basis. They established a global logistics network to service their customers in Japan, which provided an important advantage.

Trading firms are now beginning to invest directly in subsidiaries that mine, log, fish, and grow various commodities. In addition to their own captive sources of timber, trading firms will continue to purchase timber from logging firms belonging to investors from the United States, Korea, the Philippines, and Malaysia; and their plans to grow corn in Indonesia will, at best, supply less than one-tenth of the future needs of Japan. Accordingly, in terms of trading firms' needs to procure food and natural resources for Japan, Indonesia's natural resources remain peripheral and are seen in these terms. On logging a typical comment (reflecting the outlook of all three Japanese logging operations in Kalimantan) was:

> We still continue to buy 80-90% of the tropical timbers we ship to Japan from independent [other foreign] logging firms. However, the fact that we are also in the logging operation itself gives us a good chance to develop friendly feelings with independent firms, through industry-wide meetings and joint negotiations with the government. Besides, we now can estimate the logging cost of timber with a fair degree of accuracy. This gives us an additional edge in negotiating with independent firms.
>
> . . . Besides, Malaysia and the Philippines have already over-cut their tropical timbers. For all practical purposes, Indonesia is the only place left now.

On growing corn and tobacco, the manager of the large pilot farming projects run by a leading Japanese trading firm in Sumatra had this to say:

> The U.S. still practically has a monopoly of these commodities in the world market. Rather than being totally at the mercy of the U.S. suppliers, we intend to have our own source of supply that will eventually produce enough to enable us to hold off our purchase feelers to the U.S. until their offering terms become more acceptable.

. . . Indonesia needs to develop her agricultural cash commodities. Japan can provide capital, know-how, and a ready market for Indonesian farmers.

Particularly in the logging operations, the Japanese trading firms are hiring the necessary skills from Japan and elsewhere (Malaysia and Singapore) in order to run their operations. The trading companies provide finance, managerial personnel, and international logistics. Their widespread contacts with manufacturers in Japan and in other parts of the world enable them not only to provide markets for exports but also to organize finance, manpower, technology, and management for their overseas ventures.

Recently, however, the involvement of trading companies in manufacturing activities abroad in general, and in Indonesia in particular, has been developing along two distinct lines.

First, despite the short history of Japanese direct investment in Indonesia, the relative bargaining strength between trading companies and manufacturers is shifting in favor of the latter when the success of a venture depends on a continuous flow of production know-how from the manufacturing parent in Japan, or when the manufacturing parent contemplates including Indonesia in its strategy for worldwide cross-hauling of products among its own affiliates.

Of the products produced in Indonesia by Japanese subsidiaries, automobiles and electric and electronic products have avoided trading firms' control, as have foods, pharmaceuticals, and cosmetics. This is mainly because the successful export of these products requires customer services, such as repair shops or sales promotion. Trading companies simply do not possess either manufacturing expertise to provide customer services or marketing expertise to deal with consumers. Thus, it is only in the textile industry that the decline of the trading company's influence can be measured. As textile parents move to establish integrated operations of dyeing, bleaching, weaving, and spinning, and further move to integrate the making of synthetic yarn and filament, with a possible view to worldwide cross-hauling of products among their affiliates, the trading company's role is often reduced from that of initial organizer of the joint venture to that of shipper of raw materials or finished products under the manufacturer's direction.

Second, in other situations, in which the necessary technology can be procured from many sources, trading firms dominate the operations of Japanese subsidiaries in Indonesia. Examples are plastic sandals, foam rubber, bicycles, galvanized iron sheets, and leather products. Since technologies for these standard products can be obtained from many sources, the trading firm's dependence on specific Japanese manufacturers becomes less critical.

OWNERSHIP PATTERNS AND SELECTION
OF INDONESIAN PARTNERS

It is widely assumed by host governments that local equity participation not only assures local influence in the management of the joint ventures, but also facilitates local absorption of the manufacturing skills and managerial talents of the multinational partners. The Indonesian government has generally demanded equity participation by Indonesian nationals in manufacturing investments. In the past Indonesia's low estimate of its bargaining strength vis-à-vis likely foreign investors, and its eagerness to attract foreign investments, have discouraged the government from demanding a sizable minority position, let along a 50-50 or majority position for Indonesian partners. The government does insist, however, that joint-venture agreements include a clause to increase Indonesian equity ownership up to, say, 50 percent over a 15-year period.

A "typical" Indonesian partner in a Japanese venture is an individual Indonesian of Chinese ancestry, who used to be an importer of Japanese goods, and who has paid for a 10-20 percent ownership in a joint venture in cash, in kind (plant sites, building, or the cash value of "good will"), or with funds borrowed from a Japanese partner. Out of 87 Indonesian partners, 61 (70 percent) paid for their equity share either in cash or in kind. The remainder, whose equity shares had been financed by Japanese partners, were involved in larger ventures, whose average equity was approximately 2.3 times as great as that of subsidiaries whose Indonesian partners paid in cash or in kind. This may well indicate a future trend as the Japanese subsidiaries expand further; financially hard-pressed Indonesian partners may need either to have Japanese (and other foreign) partners lend them ever increasing amounts or resign themselves to seeing their relative equity position in Japanese (foreign) subsidiaries decline.

It is interesting to ponder whether the characteristics of the Indonesian partners shown in Tables 9.5-9.7 are unique to Japanese investments. It is probable, on the basis of research so far, that investments by other nationalities show similar backgrounds for their Indonesian partners, but solid evidence is lacking.

The ethnic bias in the choice of local Indonesian partners for Japanese subsidiaries can be attributed to the concentration of Japanese investments in manufacturing. Historically, Indonesians of Chinese ancestry have dominated commercial activities. It was logical that these former importers of Japanese goods sought to maintain their connection with the source of supply by joining the newly formed manufacturing subsidiaries of former exporters of goods from Japan. The Japanese partners preferred to continue

TABLE 9.5

Ownership of Japanese Subsidiaries in Indonesia

Japanese Partner(s)' Equity Share (percent)		Number of Subsidiaries
51–95		80
50		5
49		2
	Total	87

Note: The ownership of Japanese partners is combined; over two-thirds of Japanese subsidiaries have more than one Japanese parent.

Source: The author's field work in Indonesia, 1973.

TABLE 9.6

Indonesian Partners' Methods of Paying for Their Equity Share

Source	Number of Subsidiaries	Average Size of Subsidiary Equity (million U.S.$)
Lent by Japanese partners*	26	2.3
Paid in kind	21	1.0
Paid in cash	40	0.9

*Included is a product-sharing agreement in which the Indonesian partners have their debt amortized by supplying the joint venture with the goods they produce.

Source: The author's field work in Indonesia, 1973.

TABLE 9.7

Backgrounds of Indonesian Partners of Japanese Subsidiaries

Background	Number of Subsidiaries
Chinese-Indonesian (former importer agents)	35
Chinese-Indonesian (manufacturers)	22
Indonesian (manufacturers)	2
Indonesian (with government contacts)[a]	28[b]
Total	87

[a]Government-owned businesses and government-related groups (for instance, organized by retired navy officers) are included, as well as those Indonesians who had concessions for natural resources.

[b]These subsidiaries are engaged in mining, logging, and fishing.

Source: The author's field work in Indonesia, 1973.

dealing with their former distributors, whom they knew and who could assure them of an extensive, well-managed distribution system.

According to the interim findings of the Multinational Enterprise Project at the Harvard Business School, for 1,210 overseas subsidiaries of Japanese firms as of January 1, 1971, only 35 percent had Japanese partners owning over 51 percent of equity. In Indonesia over 91 percent of the Japanese subsidiaries have a Japanese partner(s) owning over 51 percent of equity. A complete explanation of this difference requires elaborate comparisons of ownership patterns that are beyond the scope of this essay. But one factor is the weakness of indigenous competition, which allows Japanese and other foreign firms to obtain a majority equity. More important, by the time Japanese firms began to invest in Indonesia around 1970, they had realized the possible gains available from cross-hauling products among their own manufacturing subsidiaries and world markets. With this in mind, they insisted on majority ownership. The days are past when Japanese firms limited their equity to a minority position, or preferred to share the risks of "untested" ventures abroad with other Japanese firms, because this presumably reduced learning costs. [7]

INDONESIAN PARTNERS' INFLUENCE
ON MANAGEMENT

The notion that a joint venture makes the subsidiary more "Indonesian" than the fully owned subsidiary of foreign parents presupposes the active involvement of Indonesian partners in making and implementing the key decisions. But, with some notable exceptions, Indonesian partners are generally not involved in the management of the foreign subsidiaries. More often than not, the following comment, made by a European expatriate manager of a leading pharmaceutical firm, describes the situation:

> He [the Indonesian partner] is given the major job of distributing our products as our distributor-agent. He put up hardly any cash when he thought the manufacturing subsidiary was not going to pay dividends at least for three years. Meanwhile he is happy to make substantial wholesale commissions as our distributor.

His comment was echoed by other expatriate managers of diverse manufacturing operations. Similar comments by Japanese investors rationalize the notable absence of their Indonesian partners' influence in management.

Some foreign managers maintain that this silent partnership of Indonesian equity holders may be partially attributed to their commercial mentality, which is accustomed to quick recovery of capital. In an economy where the best lending rate of the leading banks is 1.5 to 2.0 percent per month, an Indonesian investor's reluctance to freeze any capital for a few years, without the prospect of immediate return, is understandable. Others cling to the view that their Indonesian partners' unfamiliarity with manufacturing operations and their lack of experience in running a modern plant inhibit their active participation in the management of the foreign subsidiaries.

There are a few instances in which positive and strong entrepreneurial responses from indigenous manufacturers have resulted in their substantive participation in joint ventures. Such instances are few and concentrated in Japanese subsidiaries in which Indonesian partners hold an above-average equity share—40 percent or more. The Indonesian partners had at least one of the following attributes prior to their entry into these joint ventures:

The Indonesian partner was already engaged in manufacturing, and
   actively sought Japanese partners as he moved to diversify into
   products then imported into Indonesia in great quantities.
He had been engaged in manufacturing similar products under licensing agreements from the Japanese manufacturer. In order to upgrade his technological capability, he and the Japanese licenser
   formed the joint venture.
He had been producing goods similar to those of the Japanese firm.
   In order to obtain outside capital, design capability for new
   products, and stable sources of processing materials, he entered into the joint venture with the Japanese partner(s).

In the instances mentioned above, it was not unusual for Indonesian managers to return to exclusively Indonesian parent firms
once they became familiar with management techniques of the joint
ventures. Thus, the management skills of a foreign subsidiary
would be diffused to an independent local firm through alert Indonesians who were loyal to their former employers and acted as the
transfer agents.

However, in view of the fact that there are not too many accomplished local industrial entrepreneurs in Indonesia, it remains
important that Indonesian employees of foreign subsidiaries be increasingly promoted to supervisory and managerial positions. This
may create conflicts between Indonesian and foreign partners.
Among Indonesian manager candidates hired by foreign partners,
there is some fear of the increase in the Indonesian partners' influence in joint ventures. They are afraid that once Indonesian partners gain a voice in personnel policies, they may distrust the Indonesians hired, trained, and promoted by foreign partners.

TRAINING AND PROMOTION OF
INDONESIAN EMPLOYEES

It is frequently rumored throughout Southeast Asia that Japanese investors are slow to promote non-Japanese to managerial
positions. Sensitive as this issue is, it requires more than allega-
tions and hearsay evidence to establish whether Japanese investors
are slower in promoting local nationals than other foreign investors
in comparable situations; and what factors determine the number of
expatriate Japanese. The prevailing assumption is that the smaller
the number, the better, in part because Indonesian nationals in key
managerial and engineering positions, like Indonesian partners, will
help to safeguard the national interest.

Size of firm (Table 9.8) does not appear to be significant in the number of Japanese expatriates of all categories, or in the number of engineers and technicians relative to total employment. However, even a slight difference in the complexity of the technology affects the number of Japanese expatriates (Table 9.9). Integrated textile mills are eliminated from the sample, but they would merely reinforce the conclusions. Based on field observation of Japanese subsidiaries in Indonesia, the following additional factors are suspected to affect the need for Japanese expatriates: operator-instructors' breadth of skills and their teaching capability; learning aptitude of local trainees; communication patterns between subsidiaries and parents; number of years of operation of local subsidiary.

TABLE 9.8

Average Number of Japanese Expatriates per Manufacturing
Subsidiary in Indonesia, First Quarter of 1973

Number of Employees	Average Number of Japanese Expatriates (to nearest whole number)	
	All Categories	Engineers and Technicians[a]
100 or less	6	3
101–200	5	3
201–400	6	4
401–800	8	6
801–1,000+	25[b]	18

Note: Sample size = 42 firms.

[a]Technicians and instructors of machine operators are included in this category.

[b]This jump in the average number of Japanese managers and engineers is strongly influenced by the presence of large integrated textile mills.

Source: The author's field work in Indonesia, 1973.

TABLE 9.9

Number of Japanese Expatriates per Manufacturing
Subsidiary, by Product Group,
First Quarter of 1973

Product Group[a]	Modal Number of Japanese Expatriates (all categories)[b]
I. Simple products	
Instant noodles, charcoal making, saw-mills, plastic sandals, plastic film and bags, dry batteries, leather products, furniture, cigarette filters, bicycle assembly	2-3
II. Less simple products	
Galvanized iron sheets, steel and iron pipes and structures, drugs, cosmetics, diesel engine assembly, fishing nets, monosodium glutamate, stretch nylon yarns, electronic and electric appliances, modern printing operations	7-8

[a]A more rigorous test of the complexity of manufacturing processes can be used, such as recording the number of production processes involved and the required degree of machine operations. But the field observations of these product groups, and of the required degree of product quality control in the process, are adequate for the purpose of this paper.

[b]The difference in this modal value does not change significantly even if a few simpler products in Group II, such as assembly of small stationary diesel engines, are reclassified into Group I.

Source: The author's field work in Indonesia, 1973.

Two other points that may distinguish Japanese from other foreign investors need to be stressed. First, the specific nature of Japanese manufacturing processes, especially the narrow range of skills of Japanese engineers, technicians, and even managers, often makes it necessary for the investing firm to send in a team of Japanese "instructors." Second, subsidiaries with more than one Japanese partner are likely to let each Japanese partner send his own man to Indonesia. This may explain why Japanese subsidiaries have a larger number of expatriate managers, especially at the out- set of their operation, than other foreign ventures do.

There may also be differences between Indonesia and other countries in the region. The investment in machinery equipment may be especially high because power plants and other infrastruc- ture investments are, in many cases, absolute necessities. In- vestors then attempt to maintain a high degree of machine utiliza- tion through running three shifts or continuous operations. In order to reduce the risk of breakdowns, many Japanese firms send in a "start-up" team consisting of a full contingent of plant managers, engineers, technicians, and machine operator-instructors, whose task is to train Indonesian employees on a man-to-man basis, as well as to be ready to step in and keep machines running if neces- sary. This, of course, increases the number of Japanese.

The number of foreign managers and engineers also depends upon the specific manufacturing processes selected by foreign par- ents. The choice of less labor-intensive technology by a foreign subsidiary might mean the presence of fewer expatriate managers. In the future the choice of specific manufacturing technologies for Indonesia by foreign investors might well be analyzed in the light of its impact on the number of foreigners involved, as well as the jobs created.

CHOICE OF TECHNOLOGIES

The decision-making process, related to the selection of tech- nology for a typical Japanese firm, is summarized in Table 9.10. It is important to note that once an entry decision is made, the product and product quality of the prospective subsidiary are deter- mined mainly by corporate strategy and concern with competition, the constraints identified in decision step 2. This is all the more important because Japanese parents have limited choices of tech- nology alternatives if they are to manufacture products of a prede- termined quality. Even when alternative technologies are available from other countries or firms, parents often prefer to work with their own technologies because they are familiar with them.

TABLE 9.10

A Japanese Parent Firm's Decision Process in Selecting
Manufacturing Technologies for Indonesia

Decision Step	Key Decision Maker and Relevant Information	Crucial Constraints of Decision
1. Entry decision	Parent's top management evaluates economic and political information on the target country	Target country's trade policy Japanese competitors' moves Parent's worldwide strategy
2. Selection of product, its quality, and production scale	Parent's middle management decides on the quality and the product that will not damage the firm's brand image	Corporate strategy of the sub-sidiaries (domestic-market-oriented vs. export possibility)
3. Decision on manu-facturing techmolo-gies and processes: plant location, plant buildings, and layout of machinery and equipment	Parent's engineers design plant and production scales to meet the quality of product that commands a premium price in Indonesia	Difficulty of product imitation by indigenous firms Local labor's work habits Local availability of maintenance and repair services for equipment Market uncertainty

312

That Japanese investors are very conscious of present and future competition cannot be stressed too strongly. For Japanese investors in manufacturing activities in Indonesia, their competitors are often other foreign firms. In the weaving and dyeing branches of the textile industry, in which indigenous firms could offer serious competition, Japanese firms choose the products and processes that are most difficult for indigenous firms to imitate. In this fashion Japanese subsidiaries also attempt either to preempt the market from other foreign subsidiaries, or to avoid price competition from indigenous firms.

Japanese investors' preoccupation with avoiding competition both from foreign investors and from indigenous firms results in two distinct biases in the selection of product quality and production scale: a preference for high-quality products and, for latecomers, a notch higher quality than that of the existing competitors; and plans for a higher production capacity than the initial market warrants. Both biases are caused by the investors' desire to hedge against the risk of being outproduced by future competitors in terms of product quality and supply capability. Each investing firm is very conscious of what has happened in Taiwan, Thailand, Singapore, and Malaysia, especially as the result of competition among Japanese subsidiaries. It is familiar with histories of Japanese investors being prevented by latecomers from upgrading their product quality, or of being squeezed out by latecomers who outproduced the early settlers' firms. In Indonesia the investing firm is trying either to repeat its success or to avoid its mistakes elsewhere.

For the complicated operations required for high-quality products, plant engineers rely heavily on semiautomatic and continuous processes rather than risk production breakdowns and deterioration of product quality by using unskilled workers. The dyeing processes of textile mills, for example, use automatically controlled, continuous processes rather than manually controlled batch systems. The latter require a skilled artisan's know-how to produce a quality product. This preference for automatic processes is not unique to foreign subsidiaries. Indigenous textile mills were switching over to automatic processes once management had decided to upgrade product quality.

Once product quality and production scale are determined, the parent engineers and cost accountants take over the specific decisions on final selection of technologies and equipment. They are influenced by the following considerations, reported as reflecting their experience.

Local Labor's Work Habits

Even when the jobs assigned to workers require that work flow in sequence from one worker to the next, the Indonesian worker's attitude of "minding one's own business" tends to cause bottlenecks. Instead of helping a fellow worker who lags behind, a faster worker simply rests. Supervisors often fail to prod workers to maintain a quick pace and continuous flow of work, perhaps out of strong reluctance to antagonize fellow Indonesians. As a result, many foreign plants have decided to install conveyor belts and semiautomatic machines to handle vital flows of materials. Even when labor-intensive methods of operation are feasible with the extensive use of simple manual tools (knives, for example), initial attempts to employ them are often abandoned when tools keep disappearing. Foreign managers tend to solve these control problems by using machine-paced production processes. Thus, they substitute machinery (capital) for their lack of training and supervisory skills.

A common rule of thumb that plant engineers use is to expect of the Indonesians 50-60 percent of the work accomplished by their Japanese, Korean, and Singaporean counterparts in the same amount of time, for simple man-and-machine interactions or simple manual work. Compared with their Thai counterparts, foreign investors use a 70-80 percent rate for Indonesian recruits. This assumption by plant engineers initially leads them to assign more Indonesian workers per piece of equipment or per operation than is usual in other countries. After 12 to 18 months of work experience and closely supervised training, Indonesian workers' efficiency is said to reach, on the average, 80-90 percent of their Japanese, Korean, and Singaporean counterparts (still for simple man-and-machine and manual operations). This means that the learning effect can be substantially exploited in Indonesia.

Local Availability of Maintenance
and Repair Services

Like other developing countries, Indonesia is characterized by severe scarcity of skilled maintenance and repair technicians, and of independent maintenance and service workshops. As a result, foreign engineers and technicians need to train and develop Indonesian maintenance crews inside their own plant, and to maintain and repair their own equipment. These circumstances invariably lead foreign plant engineers and technicians to select the processes and machinery with which they are most familiar.

Of 74 manufacturing subsidiaries the author investigated, the choice in all but one case echoed the comment of one engineer who was responsible for designing a textile weaving plant:

No, we did not bring the newest model machines available in our country or elsewhere. We picked the second or third newest models which we know inside-out. We can fix these models blind-folded. More importantly, we can anticipate the breakdowns and prevent them on the basis of our experience with them back home.

More often than not, the equipment and processes thus chosen require more man-hours per machine than the newest models, and are geared to a lower volume of production per machine. Consequently the manufacturing processes that are moved to Indonesia tend to be more "labor-intensive" than those in parent countries. It is important to note, however, that the foreign plant engineers' concern with equipment maintenance precludes their attempting to readjust their familiar machines to fit other local conditions, such as the abundance of untrained workers eagerly seeking jobs.

The preoccupation with maximum utilization of expensive capital means that it is costly to have a long downtime on key machinery or delayed production of key parts or intermediate materials. As a result, the key machinery processes always have at least one identical back-up machine. The overall capital/labor ratio in foreign subsidiaries in Indonesia is therefore definitely greater than in places where maintenance and repair services are readily available.

Market Uncertainty

When market conditions are full of uncertainties, firms are willing to pay a premium for flexibility in production. Labor-intensive processes, with complicated firing or reassignment procedures, generally lack flexibility in adjusting production volume or varieties. Foreign managers who prefer to avoid, almost at all cost, any possibility of antagonizing labor, government officials, or politicians of the host country are prone to prefer machines to labor intensity.

All of the preceding indicate the need for Indonesia's government to counteract the general preference for capital-intensive processes on the part of foreign investors. It might well explore sources of technology other than the developed nations.

ALTERNATIVE SOURCES OF TECHNOLOGY

In terms of the ability to play one prospective foreign investor off against another, Indonesia now has alternative ways of obtaining the necessary technology for various products. The fierce competition among Japanese trading firms in itself often ends up assisting the rapid development of indigenous firms to compete with Japanese subsidiaries.

This intensive competition among leading trading companies of Japan causes those who lose in the race to establish manufacturing subsidiaries in Indonesia to search for Indonesian businessmen who can be persuaded to begin manufacturing under the Domestic Investment Law. They are approached by Japanese trading companies to purchase machinery, manufacturing know-how, and the necessary intermediate goods, often on liberal deferred-payment schedules. The rapid growth of Indonesian weaving and dyeing in and around Bandung is a result of such activities by Japanese trading companies. The sudden appearance of "Indonesian-owned" plants manufacturing galvanized iron sheets also results from trading company influence.

Furthermore, Japanese trading companies are now looking for local suppliers of standard chemical and plastic products for the manufacturing subsidiaries in Indonesia in which they have equity interest. For example, in order to provide their plastic sandal plants with plastic compounds and sponge rubber, trading firms supply resins and other chemicals to locally owned producers of plastic compounds. These producers are guaranteed the purchase of all their output by the trading companies that operate the plants using the intermediate products made by these captive local suppliers.

On the other hand, a number of Japanese manufacturers of electronic items, electrical appliances, and automobiles are concluding technical licensing agreements with local producers who import C.K.D. (complete knock-downs) parts and other necessary supplies from the Japanese licensers. The licensers provide technical assistance, including plant design and training of local personnel. The assembled products are often sold back to the joint venture sales subsidiary formed between the licenser and the licensee, whose job it is to direct marketing and customer service activities in Indonesia. Commercial success for these products requires extensive marketing activities, such as repair services, and advertising. Accordingly, Japanese firms have chosen to control marketing activities while contracting out manufacturing activities to the fully Indonesian-owned manufacturing plants of their Indonesian partners in the marketing subsidiary.

Of late, Taiwan, Hong Kong, Singapore, and Korea have become the suppliers of technology for a wide range of standard industrial and consumer products. These countries have for some time absorbed technology from Japan by way of Japanese direct investment, through licensing agreements with Japanese firms, or by direct imitation of standard Japanese products.

When the entrepreneurs from Taiwan, Hong Kong, Singapore, and Korea seek to learn further product and process technologies from Japan, they send one or two technicians on a training tour of duty into small-to-medium-size firms in Japan. More often than not, six to twelve months in these plants is deemed sufficient by Chinese and Korean technicians to round out their experience and skill. By combining Japanese technologies they know with the imitations of standard Japanese machines made in Taiwan and Hong Kong for half the cost of the Japanese, these non-Japanese Asian industrialists are ready to set up a manufacturing subsidiary in Indonesia.

Some alert Japanese manufacturers and trading companies have realized the economic advantage of using the "Chinese method" described above, and are now exploring ways to establish their own manufacturing subsidiaries in Indonesia through the same means. The Japanese firms provide a joint-venture partner from, say, Hong Kong, with capital and technology. The Chinese partner supplies Chinese managers, engineers, technicians, and machinery. Together they establish a plant in Indonesia.

The products involved in direct or indirect non-Japanese Asian investment include rubber belts, rice-hulling machines, water pumps, plastic sandals, dry batteries, iron bars (made from scrap iron), glutamatic acid (MSG food seasoning), polystyrene resins and foams, steel rolling mills, and integrated textile mills and sawmills.

Hong Kong's share in the dollar value of approved investment increased over 14 times the annual average for all of Asia in 1967-68 to 1971-72; Japan's increased only 8.7 times (Table 9.11). The year 1972 signaled the beginning of Taiwanese expansion into Indonesia. Over half of the approved investments as of the end of 1972 were held by Asian countries. Within Asian investments the average dollar value (size) of the approved investments of Japan, Hong Kong, and Singapore were about equal by 1971-72 (Table 9.12).

A cursory look at the list of foreign investors and their products authorized by the government during the first quarter of 1973 suggests that competition among manufacturers from Japan, the United States, Europe, Australia, Hong Kong, and Taiwan will be intensified. The positions that Japanese subsidiaries have held in manufacturing will be challenged from below and above. From below, Indonesian and other Asian investors will move into the product ranges characterized by less technology-intensive processes. As Japanese manufacturers move into products more complicated than those that they have been manufacturing, they will inevitably feel strong resistance and competition from above.

As the Japanese synthetic-textile mills integrate backward to the production of chemical materials like nylon and polyester polymers and filaments, they are likely to run into competition from petrochemical producers in the United States and Europe. From

TABLE 9.11

Approved Investments in Indonesia by Asian Countries, 1967–68 to 1971–72

| | Annual Average of Approved Investments for Two-Year Period | | | | | | | | | |
| | 1967–68 | | 1968–69 | | 1969–70 | | 1970–71 | | 1971–72 | |
	No.	Mil. $	No.	Mil. $	No.	Mil. $	No.	Mil. $	No.	Mil. $
Asian investors' total	15.5	46.9	38.0	251.3	65.5	268.6	73.0	169.3	63.0	201.2
Japan	5.0	10.1	11.5	58.6	21.5	74.4	27.0	78.4	23.5	88.0
Non-Japan	10.5	36.8	26.5	192.8	44.0	194.2	46.0	90.9	39.5	113.2
South Korea	0.5	24.0	0.5	24.0	1.5	2.4	1.5	2.5	1.0	2.3
Hong Kong	5.0	4.3	9.0	11.8	15.5	17.6	19.5	45.9	18.0	61.6
Taiwan	—	—	—	—	—	—	—	—	1.0	8.7[a]
Singapore	3.0	3.3	7.5	17.4	11.0	28.9	8.5	19.3	6.0	16.9
Malaysia	0.5	0.5	3.0	8.0	9.0	14.6	11.5	13.4	8.0	11.3
Thailand	—	—	2.0	1.6	2.5	1.9	3.0	7.0	2.5	6.7
Philippines	1.5	4.7	4.5	130.0[b]	4.5	128.8[b]	2.0	2.7	3.0	5.7
Japan's share in $ value (percent)		21.5		23.3		27.6		46.3		43.7
Hong Kong's share in $ value (percent)		9.1		4.6		6.5		27.1		30.6

[a]Taiwanese investments actually appeared in 1972, amounting to $17.3 million for two projects.

[b]Investments in logging operations that amounted to $255 million in 1969 contributed to this marked increase.

Source: Compiled from Foreign Investment Board, mimeographed data (Jakarta: the Board, March 1973).

the construction industry, in which they now hold a strong position, Japanese investors will move into cement production, and run into competition from American firms contemplating similar moves. In bicycle and pedicab (betjak) tires, Japanese firms contemplating new moves will have to take on Goodyear (United States). In the sewing machine field, Singer (United States) has long established its position in Indonesia. In diesel engines, Siemens (Germany) will resist Japanese attempts to enter the field. For sheet glass, glass bottles, bottle caps, and bottle crowns, Australian and American firms have already begun operations in Indonesia. In paints, nonorganic chemicals, fertilizers, baby foods, and dairy products, competition among foreign investors will increase. In pharmaceutical products, three Japanese firms will take on the multinationals from the United States and Europe. All this competition among would-be investors in Indonesia serves to increase alternative sources of manufacturing and management skills for Indonesia.

TABLE 9.12

Approved Investments in Indonesia: Asian Share
and Average Dollar Value, 1967-68 to 1971-72

	1967-68	1968-69	1969-70	1970-71	1971-72
Asian share (percent)	22.9	52.6	55.5	74.5	60.4
Dollar value per investment (million U.S. $)					
Japan	2.02	5.09	3.46	2.90	3.74
Hong Kong	0.86	1.31	1.13	2.35	3.42
Singapore	1.10	2.32	2.62	3.37	2.81

Source: Compiled from Foreign Investment Board, mimeographed data (Jakarta: the Board, March 1973).

CONCLUSIONS

The scope of the study on which the conclusions have been drawn has been limited, but one can conclude that the benefits Indonesia expects from foreign direct investments are by no means automatically guaranteed.

Further Growth of Japanese Investment and Tax Incentives

As of the first quarter of 1973, Japanese subsidiaries in Indonesia were estimated by the author to employ a total of 40,000 Indonesians. Over 70 percent of this employment was in the manufacturing sector, with the textile industry leading others by a great margin. According to the expansion plans of interviewed firms for the years 1973 and 1974, the capital invested and the number of employees hired by Japanese subsidiaries would increase by some 50 to 60 percent in two years or so.

Aside from export-oriented investment in natural resources, fishing, and agriculture, this expansion will still be oriented to the domestic markets of Indonesia. As long as this orientation continues, the present corporate tax exemptions for foreign investments will not be necessary for the growth of foreign investment. Even in the past, the tax incentives appeared to have had little influence on Japanese entries into Indonesia.

Like other foreign investors in manufacturing from 1967 on, the Japanese rushed in to obtain "approvals" for two economically related but administratively different reasons: to capitalize on the gap between domestic demand and supply, and to avoid being shut out of Indonesia, especially of West Java, by applying too late. Under these circumstances, tax exemptions played at best a marginal role in determining the timing of Japanese investors' requests for investment approvals. Japanese manufacturing subsidiaries would have started production, even without tax concessions, as long as they were able to benefit from high prices in the protected market of Indonesia.

Now that the initial gap between supply of and demand for various standard products appears to be filled, the question is how the government can induce foreign manufacturers to expedite expansion of existing operations and prod potential investors with "approved" projects to begin their promised operations on the promised scale. In view of the fact that competition among potential foreign investors is likely to be intensified, the Indonesian government can demand that foreign investors increase the "Indonesian content" of their products. Rather than tax incentives, for instance, administrative priorities for "rapid customs clearances" of imported materials might be granted to firms, both domestic and foreign, that meet the targets of "Indonesian content."

Export Orientation of Japanese Manufacturing Subsidiaries

Exports of manufactured goods can be important to expand Japanese manufacturing operations beyond what is currently contemplated, in order to increase employment; to increase foreign-exchange availability not subject to the political uncertainties attached to aid; and to turn domestic manufacturers' attention to the world outside Indonesia.

Three product groups can become immediately exportable from Indonesia through the multinational market contacts of Japanese parent firms: footwear (plastic sandals and canvas shoes), apparel, and textiles (cotton and polyester blends). These are not now exported, mainly because high tariffs on the intermediate materials and high international transportation costs make their production more expensive in Indonesia than in other parts of Asia.

Furthermore, the foreign firms now are usually barred from making new entries into such standard products as canvas shoes, plastic sandals, and apparel. The Indonesian government wants to keep these products for firms fully owned by Indonesians. However, export markets can be separated from domestic markets by "offshore" (bonded treatment of import materials and export-only operations of plants) production. Japanese trading firms are particularly adept at these export-oriented operations.

Once foreign markets are alerted to Indonesia as a source for standard industrial goods, it is likely that they will contact domestic Indonesian firms with similar products. And these "exporting" domestic firms can be provided with full reinvestments of tariffs paid by them on imported materials, on a pro rata basis of exports to total production.

Reporting Obligations of Foreign Subsidiaries to the Indonesian Government

Earlier it was pointed out that the government does not know the extent of actual foreign investments (as opposed to approved plans). It also was stated that joint-venture arrangements, or the formal promotion of Indonesians into high positions, does not guarantee either adequate domestic knowledge of foreign subsidiaries or the subsidiaries acting in Indonesia's interests.

It is therefore important for the Indonesian government to enforce the reporting obligations of foreign subsidiaries now contained in their investment agreements with the government, and to monitor closely employment practices, transfer price agreements with parents, and other operations of foreign subsidiaries.

The Indonesian government's need to grasp better foreign subsidiaries' operations, and the latter's need to reduce the uncertainties of various government regulations, such as those associated with tax negotiations and customs clearances, may well be met at the same time, if and when the regular reporting and spontaneous disclosures of foreign subsidiary operations are rewarded by the government's acceptance of such reporting as a basis for tax payments and by the speedy, perhaps preferential, customs clearance of goods. Random auditing of these reports would be sufficient to maintain a reasonable degree of accuracy of reports about a firm's operations if any violations or tax evasions can be prosecuted retroactively for five to seven years.

In short, the bargaining position of the Indonesian government vis-à-vis would-be and existing foreign investors has improved, and is likely to improve further as potential competition among foreign investors intensifies. Accordingly, in order to enhance Indonesia's bargaining position, the government may well benefit a great deal if it invests time and some funds in obtaining necessary information on the economic and political environments of foreign investors that are motivating them to come to Indonesia. Improved knowledge of potential and existing investors would be an obvious place to start. Improved knowledge on worldwide structures of manufacturing industries and resource-oriented industries would be useful if Indonesia wished to reassess its current and future bargaining positions with other developing countries as well as with industrialized countries. After all, what is happening to foreign investments in Indonesia reflects what is happening to worldwide competition among the manufacturing industries based in industrialized and emerging countries. Without an accurate grasp of such global knowledge and specific behaviors of firms based in various countries, Indonesia may be forced to bargain upon "hunch," rather than upon facts, with existing and would-be foreign investors.

Last, it should be pointed out that this essay purposely left out detailed analyses of the political implications of the increased Japanese presence in Indonesia. However, the facts and analyses contained in this essay lead one to predict political problems ahead for Japanese investors in Indonesia. As of the end of the first quarter of 1973, one can easily conclude that the concentration of Japanese investment in manufacturing industries oriented to Indonesian consumers makes the Japanese highly visible. This political visibility of Japanese investments predictably can lead to the singling out of Japanese investments as the surrogate for all foreign investments. If Indonesian sentiment ever rises against "foreign investors" in general, it will be the Japanese investors who will bear the brunt of their protests. When this happens, such popular criticism of Japanese firms' behavior as the "ubiquitous presence of Japanese expatriates," deeper technological causes of which this essay pointed out, will be quoted liberally as the proven evidence of the evils committed by Japanese perpetrators.

NOTES

1. For relative changes in bargaining strength between multinationals and developing nations, see Yoshi Tsurumi, Multinational Management (Cambridge, Mass.: Ballinger, 1977), pp. 267-80.

2. See Yoshi Tsurumi, The Japanese Are Coming (Cambridge, Mass.: Ballinger, 1976), ch. 7.

3. For political reactions of developing nations to Japanese investments, see Yoshi Tsurumi, "The Multinational Spread of Japanese Firms and Asian Neighbors' Reactions," in The Multinational Corporation and Social Change, ed. David Apter and Richard Goodman (New York: Praeger, 1976).

4. See Donald Lecraw, "Direct Investment by Firms from Less Developed Countries," Oxford Economic Papers 29, no. 3 (November 1977); Louis Wells, "Foreign Investments in Third World," Columbia Journal of World Business (Spring 1978).

5. There are about 5,000 trading firms in Japan, but the leading ten firms account for approximately 80 percent of sales volume. Japanese trading firms have recently diversified themselves into direct investments abroad in fields ranging from service-oriented ventures and manufacturing operations to large-scale natural-resource developments. See Tsurumi, The Japanese Are Coming, ch. 5; and Sogoshosha, the Institute for Research on Public Policy, Montreal, 1980.

6. Based on data collected by the author for the Multinational Enterprise Project of the Harvard Business School. For a detailed analysis, see Tsurumi, The Japanese Are Coming.

7. For detailed analysis, see ibid., ch. 8.

10

THE COMMUNIST COUNTRIES OF EUROPE AND INDONESIAN TRADE: A CRUCIAL DECADE

Francis Seton

This essay consists of extracts from a much more substantial report written for the Indonesian government in 1972, with the object of making detailed recommendations for the economic appraisal of bilateral trade agreements—for instance, those that might be offered by the Soviet Union (USSR) or Eastern Europe. No doubt the essay still bears the imprint of this original purpose.

INTRODUCTION

Owing to the vast extent of the USSR, the Communist countries of Europe cover nearly one-sixth of the globe's surface, although their population is little more than 10 percent of humanity. By 1980 it will probably be under 8.5 percent, but still 50 percent larger than that of the next most populous unit among Indonesia's industrialized customers, the enlarged European Economic Community (EEC).

As a consumer of Indonesian exports, however, Eastern Europe has consistently and substantially underperformed in relation to its size. During the 1960s it bought well under 6 percent of Southeast Asian exports—less than a quarter of the purchases of either Japan or Western Europe from that part of the world. Its consumption of natural rubber, though much more commensurate with its size, scarcely exceeded half the level achieved by the rest of Europe in the period 1950-70.

This underperformance is due partly to the lower real incomes of Eastern Europe and partly to its traditional bias against dependence on foreign trade.

East European figures for national income per head cannot easily be compared with those of Western countries or Japan, owing to important discrepancies in underlying methodology. The latest independent inquiry into relative levels—that of the United Nations Secretariat in the mid-1960s—suggests that the average per capita income of Eastern Europe (corresponding roughly to that of the USSR) was about 20 percent below the Japanese level, nearly 40 percent below Western Europe, and 60 percent below that of the United States. Soviet authorities, on the other hand, claim that the lag behind the United States was only 52 percent in 1965 and had decreased to 48 percent by 1971.

By far the major cause of Eastern Europe's underperformance as a trading partner is the long-established preference of the regimes concerned for closed, and as nearly as possible autarchic, economies. This has its origin in the policy of the dominant country—the USSR. It derives in part from ideology and the traditional concept of a siege economy under "capitalist encirclement," and in part from the practice of centralized planning, whose undisturbed implementation demands a sharp reduction in the influence of all economic forces that tend to escape from national control.

Although some "opening" of East European economies has occurred in recent years, the role of the Communist world (including China) in international trade must still be described as puny in relation to its size. In 1971, for instance, the countries concerned accounted for about one-third of world industrial output, but furnished barely 10 percent of total world trade—most of which was trade among themselves.

The importance attaching to foreign trade in particular countries may be gauged from their trade ratios, defined as the ratio of turnover (the arithmetic mean of exports f.o.b. and imports c.i.f.) to gross national product (GNP). Although certain differences in coverage and definition impair the strict comparability of this statistic between one country and another, it is doubtless the most revealing single indicator in its general order of magnitude. In 1970 its average value stood at 18.4 percent for the nine countries of the enlarged EEC and at 9.7 percent for Japan. In Eastern Europe, on the other hand, it barely exceeded 5.2 percent on average—although this figure concealed variations from 2.6 percent (USSR) to 21.7 percent (Yugoslavia). When intrabloc trade is excluded, the trade dependence of Eastern Europe appears even smaller, compared with other trading areas (Table 10.1).

While the ratios obviously are largely a function of the country's size, very significant differences can also be observed between countries and blocs of roughly equal sizes. Thus Eastern

Europe's trade dependence on countries outside its own confines is scarcely more than half that of the United States, and well below a quarter of Western Europe or Japan. Its dependence on trade with developing countries is barely one-sixth that of Western Europe, and hardly more than one-eighth that of Japan.

TABLE 10.1

Trade Ratios in 1970
(percent)

	Total Foreign Trade	Trade with Areas Outside Bloc	Trade with Developing Countries
Bulgaria	18.8	4.8	1.1
Czechoslovakia	12.1	4.3	0.9
East Germany	13.8	4.5	0.6
Hungary	16.3	6.2	1.0
Poland	8.8	3.2	0.6
Romania	8.2	4.2	0.7
USSR	2.6	1.2	0.4
Yugoslavia	21.7	16.0	1.8
Eastern Europe (av.)	5.2	2.2	0.5
Western Europe (av.)	18.4	9.5	2.9
United States	4.2	4.2	1.0
Japan	9.7	9.7	3.2

Note: The GNPs of Communist countries have been adjusted to include services, for better comparability with other countries.
Source: Compiled by the author.

Thus, comparative income levels and low trade dependence have combined to reduce Eastern Europe's role as a trading partner of developing countries far below the level that its size, industrial potential, and population would have led one to expect. Comecon Europe (excluding Yugoslavia), in fact, took less than 5 percent of these countries' imports during the 1960s, while Japan—with scarcely more than a quarter of Comecon's population—took nearly 9 percent; at the same time the United States took nearly 20 percent and Western Europe over 40 percent. The proportions have, of course, varied slightly from year to year.

Table 10.2 shows the relative importance of Comecon Europe and the other main trading partners to the less-developed world as a whole and to specific areas within it. Unfortunately, the statistics available classify Yugoslavia with the rest of Europe and do not permit a comparative analysis of Eastern Europe properly so called, which we would have preferred. While this is regrettable, it is hardly likely to affect the general orders of magnitude involved.

The table shows that up to 1965, Comecon Europe treated Indonesia somewhat better as a supplier of imports than it did the underdeveloped world as a whole, though the margin of favored treatment diminished sharply after 1962 and turned into the reverse in the second half of the 1960s. The reasons for this were no doubt largely political, but the similar (albeit less pronounced) behavior of the United States suggests that other forces, possibly on the supply side, may also have contributed. It is interesting to note a very strong opposite tendency in the case of Japan. Western Europe, on the other hand, appears to have placed consistently less reliance on Indonesian than on other, traditionally more closely associated areas of the underdeveloped world. Malaysia and Singapore, in spite of their smaller populations, bulked consistently larger in Comecon imports than did Indonesia.

While the size of per capita incomes and low trade dependence combine to reduce Eastern Europe's role as a trading partner far below the level that its size and population would warrant, this does not mean that a policy of expanding trade relations with that area, even at the expense of other markets, could not yield handsome dividends to a developing country ready to pursue it in a systematic and circumspect manner. In the first place, such a policy could help to diversify export markets and lessen dependence on one or a small number of customers where this is felt to be excessive. In the second place, East European markets might be faster-growing in capacity, particularly as buyers of staple exports, than the more established and fully developed markets of the West. In the third place, the economies of Eastern Europe, being centrally planned and relatively unaffected by the business cycle, might offer stabler markets whose performance could be relied upon to follow more foreseeable patterns in the short run. Last, the unsatisfied demand for simple consumer durables in Eastern Europe might promise the less-developed trading partner an outlet for the products of an infant manufacturing sector on which future industrialization plans might have to rely as a "pump primer" for development.

The attractions that such arguments might hold certainly have not gone unnoticed by East European advocates of expanding trade with less-developed countries. They have seized on the fourfold benefits of diversification, faster growth, increased stability, and

TABLE 10.2

The Importance of Comecon Markets to Indonesia and
to Other Less-Developed Countries, 1960–70
(percent, based on dollar values f.o.b.)

Percentage Distribution of Exports from to	Indonesia			Malaysia and Singapore			All LDCs		
	1960	1965	1970	1960	1965	1969	1960	1965	1970
World	100.0	100.0	100.0	100.0	100.0	100.0	100.0	100.0	100.0
United States	23.0	21.6	15.3	9.5	10.0	13.2	21.8	18.5	18.2
Japan	4.1	15.9	48.7	16.0	10.6	10.8	5.1	7.6	11.3
Non-Comecon Europe	25.1	30.5	24.2	33.4	10.3[a]	17.6[a]	40.9	41.1	40.0
Comecon Europe	4.4	5.7[b]	2.1[c]	6.4	6.8	5.5	3.5	5.1	3.9

[a]Western Europe and Great Britain only.

[b]The peak occurred in 1962, when 7.2 percent of Indonesian exports went to Comecon Europe.

[c]The figure for 1971 appears to have fallen below 1 percent.

Sources: Indonesia computed from Bank Indonesia, Monthly Bulletin (April 1972), and data from the Central Statistical Office, Jakarta; Indonesia 1970 from International Monetary Fund and World Bank, Direction of Trade 1966–70, p. 276, supplemented for Soviet-type countries from data of the Central Statistical Office, Jakarta; Malaysia and Singapore 1960 includes Federation of Malaya plus North Borneo, data from International Monetary Fund and World Bank, Direction of Trade, 1958–62, pp. 347, 349; and U.N., Commodity Trade Statistics, ser. D, 15, no. 27, pp. 6759, 6664; Malaysia and Singapore from U.N., Economic Survey of Asia and the Far East 1969, pp. 251, 253 (1969 refers to first half of year only); all LDCs from U.N., Yearbook of International Trade and Development Statistics, 1972, p. 46.

manufacturing outlets as siren calls to those prepared to trade with them, and have done so with great insistence and single-mindedness. It would be foolish to dismiss these claims as mere propaganda, but equally foolish to accept them at face value. A careful examination of the record, however difficult, is certainly in order.

Table 10.3 is a preliminary, and admittedly impressionistic, summary of the past performance of Comecon countries in respect to size and growth, and to some extent stability, in their role as markets for Southeast Asia. In addition, the last section of the table provides some evidence on their role as manufacturing outlets. In each case the performance is compared with that of rival trading partners of a similar size. The comparison is greatly deepened in the more detailed sections of our original report, where improved measures of growth and stability are used, the time horizon is expanded, and the focus is narrowed on the specifics of Indonesia and Indonesian products. In the present essay, however, the larger canvas of Southeast Asia can serve as a testing ground for which standard data of the required degree of comparability are readily available.

Focusing on the average annual growth rate for the 1960s as a whole (second row of each section), it appears that in spite of its small initial size, Comecon Europe does not make good its claim to be the fastest-growing market for any major commodity group other than food, drink, and tobacco. It lags behind Japan, and even behind the United States, for total imports, despite the latter's large initial size. In the various subcategories its growth performance is second only to Japan, though only marginally better than that of the United States. As far as Southeast Asia as a whole is concerned, therefore, the growth claims of Comecon can partially be justified. (Within the Comecon bloc the USSR was slightly lagging in growth performance, except as an importer of crude materials, oils, and fats.)

A glance at the two subperiods of the 1960s (third and fourth rows of each section) suggests, however, that the claim to relative market stability is somewhat further from the truth—at least as far as quinquennial periods are concerned. The growth rate of world imports from Southeast Asia more than doubled between the first and the second half of the 1960s, as did imports into the United States; that of Comecon Europe approximately halved. Japan's performance was slightly steadier; that of the USSR was considerably less so. As an importer of food and drink, the growth rate of Comecon Europe dropped from record levels to near stagnation, an about-face exceeded in abruptness only by the countries of socialist Asia (although Japan came pretty near it). As an importer of crude materials, Comecon Europe as a whole did not change tack as

TABLE 10.3

Size and Growth of Markets for Southeast Asian Exports, 1961–70
(percent, based on dollar values f.o.b.)

| | World | United States | Japan | West Europe[a] | Comecon Europe[b] | Of Which | |
						USSR	Socialist Asia
All imports							
Relative share (average)	100.0	19.4	13.6	22.6	5.6	3.5	1.4
Average annual growth rate	6.3	11.0	12.0	2.7	9.5	8.6	2.1
Of which: first half	3.9	6.9	9.2	1.3	12.6	15.2	2.5
second half	8.8	15.2	15.0	4.2	6.4	2.4	1.7
Food, drink, and tobacco[c]							
Relative share (average)	100.0	15.6	11.7	24.3	5.9	3.5	0.8
Average annual growth rate	2.6	5.7	10.1	-1.9	10.7	7.0	-13.3
Of which: first half	5.2	7.4	18.7	0.0	21.6	14.6	33.8
second half	0.1	4.0	2.2	-3.8	0.7	0.0	-43.8
Crude materials, oils, fats[d]							
Relative share (average)	100.0	13.2	22.1	26.6	8.9	5.7	3.5
Average annual growth rate	1.4	-1.2	7.4	-2.6	2.6	3.9	6.4
Of which: first half	-2.0	-7.2	3.8	-2.9	4.4	10.2	2.6
second half	4.9	5.1	11.2	-2.2	0.9	-2.0	10.3
Manufactures[e]							
Relative share (average)	100.0	29.4	2.5	23.0	3.6	2.4	0.3
Average annual growth rate	13.2	21.1	38.5	12.6	22.4	21.0	-21.8
Of which: first half	10.4	18.9	34.8	12.0	29.3	33.6	-4.4
second half	16.0	23.4	42.3	13.3	15.8	9.6	-36.1

First half = 1961–65; second half = 1966–70.
[a]Includes Yugoslavia.
[b]Excludes Yugoslavia.
[c]SITC (Standard International Trade Classification) 0 + 1.
[d]Excludes fuels (i.e., SITC 2 + 4).
[e]Excludes metals (i.e., SITC 6 + 8, excluding 67 and 68).
Source: United Nations, Handbook of International Trade Statistics (New York: 1972).

330

radically as the remaining trading areas outside Western Europe; but the USSR reversed growth into decline at a time when the world as a whole (and the United States) changed in the opposite direction and Japan greatly accelerated its growth. Finally, as an outlet for manufactures, the countries of Comecon almost halved their growth rate between the early and the late 1960s (the USSR reducing it by nearly three-quarters), while Western countries and Japan accelerated theirs. It must be stressed, however, that the Comecon growth performance in the early years of the decade had been three times as great as that of the world as a whole; it even rivaled that of Japan—which, however, continued at a greatly accelerated rate in the late 1960s. The overall impression produced by the Comecon bloc is thus one of comparative market instability rather than of stability, superimposed on small, rapid, but fitful growth.

THE EXPERIENCE OF THE 1960S

To what extent does past experience support the claims of Comecon countries regarding their capacity, superior growth performance, and relative stability as trading outlets for developing countries? Ideally one would like to focus on those aspects of the claims that are of the greatest relevance to Indonesian decision making: the trade between Comecon and Indonesia. Unfortunately, however, such a direct approach is practicable to only a limited extent, and cannot by itself yield completely reliable conclusions. This is so because historical trade series involving Indonesia—whether taken from indigenous or foreign sources—are normally too aggregative and subject to distortion by entrepôt trade, falsified pricing, and the omission of extralegal trade flows (contraband).

Table 10.4 shows that as a trading outlet for the Third World as a whole, Comecon Europe rose from insignificance in the mid-1950s to minor importance (4.5 percent) in the following decade, then fell back to under 4 percent in 1970. The USSR, which initially accounted for less than half of these exports, increased its share to well over 70 percent by 1970.

Southeast Asia was slightly more favored by Comecon Europe than the Third World as a whole, with about 5.5 percent of its exports going to Comecon during the 1960s. Its manufactures, however, were considerably less favored than the staple exports—particularly agricultural raw materials, of which the bloc took 9–10 percent. In fact, little more than 4 percent of manufacturing exports from Southeast Asia found their way to Eastern Europe. Even this, however, represented some progress over the mid-1960s, when these trade flows were virtually nonexistent.

TABLE 10.4

Importance, Growth, and Stability of Markets Relevant to Indonesia
(percent, based on f.o.b. dollar values)

	Share in Total			Annual Growth Rate[a] (instability coefficient[b])			
	1955	1960s[c]	1970	1955–60	1961–65	1966–70	1955–70
All Imports from Less-Developed Countries							
World	100.0	100.0	100.0	2.3 (3)	8.0 (2)	9.5 (3)	5.6 (10)
United States	23.3	19.1	18.2	1.1 (2)	4.4 (2)	8.3 (3)	3.6 (11)
Japan	4.1	8.7	11.3	6.0 (9)	17.0 (7)	17.1 (5)	13.7 (24)
West Europe[d]	40.2	41.1	39.6	2.5 (3)	7.8 (2)	8.8 (3)	5.6 (8)
Comecon Europe[e]	1.7	4.5	3.9	19.2 (8)	11.0 (7)	4.4 (5)	12.5 (8)
Of which: USSR	0.7	2.6	3.0	29.7 (13)	10.7 (11)	10.8 (14)	15.6 (13)
Socialist Asia	0.7	0.9	0.7	10.2 (9)	17.6 (18)	0.7 (2)	6.6 (22)
All Imports from Southeast Asia							
World	100.0	100.0	100.0	1.6 (6)	5.9 (2)	10.5 (4)	4.8 (11)
United States	15.6	19.4	23.7	2.3 (7)	8.5 (6)	17.9 (3)	8.0 (22)
Japan	8.3	13.6	16.7	4.8 (12)	12.9 (8)	15.4 (6)	10.3 (19)
West Europe[d]	29.0	22.6	19.0	0.0 (8)	3.9 (3)	4.6 (3)	2.1 (6)
Comecon Europe[e]	1.3	5.6	5.4	29.6 (14)	12.0 (3)	8.2 (8)	13.8 (9)
Of which: USSR	0.4	3.5	3.1	46.8 (25)	11.6 (5)	4.4 (6)	15.5 (13)
Socialist Asia	1.9	1.4	1.3	4.2 (4)	9.4 (2)	8.3 (2)	1.2 (18)
Imports of Crude Materials, Oils, and Fats[f] from Southeast Asia							
World	100.0	100.0	100.0	0.7 (11)	1.0 (2)	5.8 (8)	0.6 (8)
United States	19.6	13.2	12.2	-3.0 (12)	-4.1 (3)	7.0 (10)	-3.2 (12)
Japan	10.1	22.1	26.8	8.4 (13)	6.0 (8)	8.1 (5)	7.8 (10)
West Europe[d]	38.3	26.6	23.5	-3.2 (11)	0.8 (2)	0.2 (10)	-2.1 (8)
Comecon Europe[e]	1.8	8.9	8.1	35.1 (19)	1.3 (10)	1.4 (11)	10.3 (21)
Of which: USSR	0.3	5.7	4.9	66.9 (41)	0.7 (17)	-0.8 (8)	15.7 (29)
Socialist Asia	2.4	3.5	5.1	9.2 (8)	16.5 (14)	15.7 (38)	2.9 (25)

	Imports of Manufactures (excluding metals)[g] from Southeast Asia[h]						
World	100.0	100.0	100.0	6.9[i]	11.2 (5)	17.4 (5)	12.9 (11)
United States	10.8	29.4	37.2	23.1[i]	19.5 (9)	28.1 (5)	20.9 (21)
Japan	0.7	2.5	4.0	5.3[i]	36.9 (7)	42.2 (4)	38.0 (37)
West Europe[d]	17.9	23.0	21.6	12.1[i]	14.1 (7)	12.3 (8)	12.9 (7)
Comecon Europe[e]	—	3.6	4.1	—	30.4 (23)	12.4 (11)	24.2 (14)
Of which: USSR	—	2.4	2.4	—	35.3 (25)	2.4 (9)	24.9 (18)
Socialist Asia	0.9	0.3	..	11.4[i]	0.3 (71)	-48.8 (72)	-8.8 (78)

[a]Continuous exponential growth rates per year (e^g-1), obtained by fitting the function Ae^{gt} to the time series (t = time in years, e = base of natural logarithms).

[b]The figures in brackets are the root-mean-square deviations (i) from the linear trend expressed as a percentage of mean values; that is,

$$i = 100 \left[\frac{1}{n-2} \sum (x-\hat{x})^2 \right]^{\frac{1}{2}} \div \bar{x},$$

where n is the number of years, and x, $\bar{x}$, and $\hat{x}$ are actual, mean, and linear-trend values of imports, respectively.

[c]Average of ten years (1960–69).

[d]Including Yugoslavia, Finland, and Greece.

[e]All Comecon countries in Europe (excluding Yugoslavia).

[f]Excludes fuels, that is, SITC 2 + 4.

[g]SITC 6 + 8, excluding 67 and 68.

[h]For period 1961–65 and 1955–59 read 1960–65 and 1960–69, respectively.

[i]Average annual growth rate from 1955 to 1960.

Source: Computed from United Nations, Handbook of International Trade Statistics (New York: 1972), pp. 46, 56, 82, 154, and annex tables.

333

On the other hand, Comecon's growth performance in Third World trading was second only to Japan's, with an annual growth rate of 12.5 percent, the Soviet Union leading this meteoric rise with a rate of over 15.5 percent per annum. This long-term average, however, conceals sharp declines of growth rates in three successive quinquenniums, dipping from the spectacular rate of 19 percent in the late 1950s (nearly 30 percent in the case of the Soviet Union) to a mere 4.5 percent ten years later. Moreover, the rise started from abysmally low levels.

In Southeast Asian trade, Comecon's growth performance was even more spectacular, and undoubtedly put the bloc at the head of the league table. This is true of all the major commodity flows involved, including manufactures. Again, however, the rates declined very sharply from each five-year period to the next, and ended up at or near the bottom of the league table in the late 1960s. In almost every case the long-term growth rates owe their astonishing levels predominantly to the explosive movements of the 1950s, when the merest trickle of trade burst into a minor stream. The only exception to this is the trade in food, drink, and tobacco, in which the fastest expansion occurred in the early 1960s. In the later years of the decade, the Comecon countries were in general slow growers and in some cases—notably agricultural raw materials—even diminished their Southeast Asian imports from year to year in absolute terms.*

As far as stability is concerned, Western Europe has been a stabler trading partner to the Third World and Southeast Asia than Comecon in all respects except food. The United States, while highly unstable in total imports, was no less stable than Comecon in manufacturing imports and very considerably stabler in its purchases of crude materials, oils, and fats. Japan marred its spectacular growth performance by a record level of instability, due mainly to erratic movements in food imports; but its purchases of crude materials from the region, though slower-growing, exhibited much more stability than those of Comecon Europe.

On the whole it may be said that the overall stability performance of Comecon in its purchases from the Third World is excellent. It is, however, very much below par in manufacturing imports, and downright bad in the commodities of special interest to Indonesia: crude materials, oils, and fats.

---

*The Soviet Union did not differ very markedly from other Comecon countries in its growth performance. It marginally outperformed them in global terms, but lagged behind them to some extent in the growth of food imports from Southeast Asia.

We may now sum up the position and performance of Eastern Europe in the league table of the four major trading areas of relevance to Indonesia (United States, Japan, Western Europe, and Comecon):

First, its importance as an outlet for exports of less-developed countries was uniformly inferior to that of any of the others during the 1960s. This applied to Southeast Asian and Indonesian exports, as well as to Third World exports as a whole. It was only as an outlet for individual commodities, particularly rubber and coffee, that it occupied a more important place.

Second, Comecon's long-run growth performance between 1955 and 1970, while slightly inferior to that of Japan in global terms, was well in the forefront of the league as far as imports from Southeast Asia and Indonesia are concerned. It outdistanced the other trading areas by a particularly large margin in the importation of rubber—in which, indeed, it was the only one of Indonesia's trading partners to show an upward growth trend in the period under review. In every case, however, the superior growth performance of Comecon was due to the exceptional spurt with which it burst out of its former insignificance in the mid-1950s.

The stability of Comecon imports was also good over the long term, placing it at the head of the league table, in close competition with Western Europe. It was, however, markedly bad in the case of commodities of special interest to Indonesia—raw materials and rubber—even if noticeably better in the case of coffee.

Third, in the short run (two five-year periods in the 1960s) Comecon's growth performance was distinctly less impressive. As a trading outlet for the Third World as a whole, it yielded pride of place to Japan in the early 1960s and, together with Western Europe, occupied the last place in the growth stakes as a declining market for rubber. In the second half of the 1960s, it was the slowest grower among the four. As a market for Southeast Asia it started the decade well, usually occupying second place in the growth stakes after Japan, but it finished near the bottom in the late 1960s. As an outlet for Indonesian exports, Comecon's growth performance was worse than the rest of the league in the early 1960s, when it was the only declining market among the four. In the late 1960s, however, its decline, though greatly accelerated, was slightly less precipitous than that of Western Europe. It remains true, moreover, that rubber imports from Indonesia into Comecon Europe declined less rapidly than those into the United States and Japan after 1965.

The short-run stability of Comecon imports makes a considerably worse showing than their stability in the longer term. As a trading outlet for the Third World as a whole, it comes at or near the bottom of the league in both halves of the 1960s. This is true also for Comecon imports from Southeast Asia. As an importer from Indonesia, Comecon's stability performance demoted the bloc from the first to the last place as the 1960s wore on.

On the whole, therefore, the growth performance of Comecon markets may be described as impressive, but distinctly uneven in the short run. Their much-vaunted superior stability cannot be substantiated from past experience. Their long-run performance in this respect, while very good in global terms, was not particularly promising for the commodities that are of greatest concern to Indonesia. At the same time it left much to be desired in the short run. We cannot, therefore, recommend market stability as a positive argument for expanding trade with Comecon. On the other hand, performance in this respect was not bad enough (in comparison with other trading partners) to justify a recommendation in the opposite direction. Certainly no developing country wishing to expand its trade with Comecon on other grounds should be discouraged from doing so on this particular score.

COSTS AND BENEFITS OF COMECON TRADE

A considered judgment on the degree to which trade with Eastern Europe might be beneficial to Indonesia must depend in part on the extent to which such trade is likely to be additional to trade with other areas and the degree to which it may be a mere diversion from established outlets. Unfortunately, these are very difficult facts to establish, let alone quantify. This is so on both statistical and conceptual grounds.

Conceptually, a distinction must be drawn between "mechanical" and "economic" diversion. The first type occurs when a new trading partner imports Indonesian goods merely in order to reexport them to Western countries that might otherwise have bought them from Indonesia directly. More rarely, perhaps, it occurs when the new partner starts buying goods from Indonesia that it previously acquired as reexports from a Western country. In both cases the proximate effect is increased trade with the East and reduced trade with the West; but this is merely a lengthening or shortening of an already established "chain of trade" between producer and ultimate consumer through the insertion or elimination of an intermediate link.

"Economic" diversion, on the other hand, implies a net rise of demand for Indonesian products by the new trading partner, either because it increases its total requirements or because it switches from other original producers to Indonesia. It occurs when the goods or resources needed for this new demand cannot be released in

Indonesia without reducing those available for other customers, and supplies are therefore "diverted" from one ultimate consumer to another. The conceptual difficulty here stems from the fact that one cannot reasonably assume a fixed pool of goods or resources. A proper estimate of economic diversion therefore presupposes a judgment on the degree to which the new pattern of trade results in activating previously idle resources (or freezing previously active ones), and thereby enlarges the pool from which both old and new customers may be supplied. Such a judgment, however, requires some hypothesis on the path that the economy would have taken if the new trade flow had not occurred. This in turn must depend heavily on assumed extrapolations of some arbitrarily chosen economic variables, such as production or market shares; and this, in the last analysis, can never amount to more than speculation.

Mechanical Diversion

The effects of any kind of trade diversion on the old and new trading partners will vary greatly with the market shares they enjoyed before the diversion takes place. Since trading links and natural resources tend to be branch-specific, this will depend crucially on the commodities involved. Although the matter is largely one of simple arithmetic, it will be useful to illustrate the effects in question on a sample of commodities important to Indonesia in potentially competing markets. With this in view we show, in Table 10.5, the relative importance of Indonesia's four major trading partners as direct buyers of selected exports, when all other trading outlets are disregarded.

Table 10.5 may be used to measure the relative impact of given percentage rises in East European exports on the volume or value of the corresponding trade flows to other markets, on the assumption that total supplies are constant. Thus, a 10 percent rise in rubber exports to Eastern Europe in 1970 would have entailed a 3.5 percent fall in those to Western Europe, or a 28.9 percent fall in those to Japan, or a 4.7 percent reduction in those to the United States. (The percentages can be computed by simple division of the relevant shares in the table. For Western Europe, .10 x 15.9/45.0 = .035.) If spread evenly over all three of them, it would have entailed a fall by 1.9 percent in the exports to each—that is, .10 x 15.9/(100-15.9) = .0189.

The commodities listed in the table, with the exception of tea and palm oil, are clearly of the type for which an expansion in East European trade would make a noticeable impact on at least one of the major competing markets that might be chosen to bear the brunt of it, unless the expansion had a "trade-creating" effect in itself.

TABLE 10.5

Relative Importance of Four Main Markets for Indonesian Commodities:
Percent Shares in Total Exports to All Four Main Markets, 1963-70

	United States	Japan	West Europe	East Europe	United States	Japan	West Europe	East Europe
	Natural Rubber (based on volume)				Palm Oil (based on volume)			
1963	25.8	1.4	54.3	18.4	9.2	20.2	63.5	7.1
1965	45.1	13.6	27.7	13.6	2.8	11.6	82.1	3.4
1967	35.9	14.8	37.0	12.3	6.1	16.2	76.1	1.5
1970	33.5	5.5	45.0	15.9	41.2	39.1	19.7	—
	Coffee (based on volume)				Spices (pepper) (based on value)			
1963	6.0	1.8	91.1	1.1	18.4	0.2	80.4	1.0
1965	65.5	1.8	31.0	1.7	62.3	0.1	32.2	5.3
1967	28.6	53.4	17.4	0.6	30.0	31.4	31.3	7.3
1970	78.1	3.8	3.8	9.9	n.a.	n.a.	n.a.	n.a.
	Tea (based on volume)				Hides and Skins (based on value)			
1963	21.4	—	76.4	2.2	31.4	. .	35.3	33.3
1965	16.6	—	83.4	—	22.3	0.8	72.7	4.2
1966	20.4	—	79.6	—	10.1	3.5	73.0	13.3
1967	7.9	—	92.1	—	7.6	4.2	84.8	3.5

Note: For coffee, tea, and palm oil, West Europe = Britain, Netherlands, France, and West Germany (excluding Netherlands in 1970); for hides and skins and spices, West Europe = expanded EEC.

Sources: Calculated from Central Bureau of Statistics sources; Department of Trade, Jakarta, December 1972; and Ekspor Menurut Jenis Barang . . . 1963-1966, and 1967 (Jakarta).

The most frequent cases of "mechanical" diversion occur when Comecon countries engage in new purchases from a less-developed country and then resell them to third parties who would otherwise have bought them from the producer directly. This intermediate function has been a matter of considerable concern in most countries where trade agreements with Eastern Europe are in force.

It is generally known that most East European countries engage in such resales. In a broader interpretation of the term, we ought to include the export of domestically produced goods that, but for the importation of close substitutes from less-developed countries, would have been consumed at home.* In the nature of things, the extent of these operations is very difficult, if not impossible, to establish. East European countries do not regularly publish statistics of reexports as such; and even if they did, it would be difficult to trace the goods in question to their ultimate origins.

A cursory impression of the magnitude of Comecon exports of Indonesian-type goods or their nearest substitutes may be obtained from the import statistics of West European countries. This still leaves out possible reexports to non-European countries, and sometimes draws the boundaries of "substitutability" in uncomfortably loose and ill-fitting ways. It is, however, the only relevant information we are likely to obtain.

On the basis of this information we have estimated the following "diversion ratios" for the most important commodities, and derived a set of overall ratios for Indonesian trade by weighting, as shown below.

Reexports of Close Substitutes as Percent of Imports

	Rubber	Coffee	Spices	Hides and Skins	Tea	Weighted Average
All Comecon Europe	8.0	0.5	30.0	3.0	2.1	7.5
Of which:						
Soviet Union	2.8	0.1	0.5	3.0	3.0	2.5
Other countries	16.0	0.6	90.0	3.0	0.1	15.5
Assumed weights for averaging	.85	.10	.02	.02	.01	1.00

---

*The operative word is "close," since all imports are to some extent substitutes for exportables consumed at home. The "closeness" needs to be sufficient to be perceived by the ultimate buyer, leading to curtailment of former imports from the less-developed country.

Our estimates thus imply that 7.5 percent of Indonesian exports to Comecon countries are likely to be diverted to Western Europe, and that the proportion is as high as 15.5 percent in the case of the People's Democracies (non-Soviet Comecon Europe). Given that additional switching to countries outside Western Europe may occur, it would be wise to put the allowance for mechanical trade diversion somewhere between 7.5 and 10 percent for Comecon countries as a whole, with corresponding allowances within the ranges of 15-20 percent for the People's Democracies and of 2.5-5 percent for the Soviet Union.

How does this compare with the experience of other developing countries trading with Comecon Europe? In India it appears to be accepted in official circles that for commodities like tea, coffee, spices, jute goods, and gray cotton cloth, the percentage of exports to Eastern Europe diverted elsewhere is within the range of 5-10 percent.[1] In the case of Pakistan it has been estimated that at least 15 percent of ostensible exports to the Comecon bloc are currently finding their way to Western markets.[2] In the light of these figures, our own estimate of 7.5-10 percent for Indonesia does not seem implausible.

There remains the question of whether the same ratios that apply to average trade flows, as observed in the past or forecast for the future, would also be applicable to incremental flows that might occur in the wake of new trade agreements. In our view there is no firm basis for assuming any divergence between average and marginal diversion ratios, since most of past trade between the countries concerned has also been conducted under the umbrella provisions of trade agreements. The matter could, however, bear further investigation if time and resources can be made available.

The modalities of East European trade diversion and the concern with which it is viewed by the affected trading partners vary widely from one country to another and from commodity to commodity. Our knowledge of the subject is of necessity eclectic, but stray bits of information may well give a clue to the general situation.

In the case of Indian cashews, for instance, we are told that once placed on board a ship destined for Eastern Europe, they may be rerouted to Rotterdam or New York, where they are sold at a 5 percent discount on the world price. The American importer then opens a dollar credit for the East European country, which in turn opens a nonconvertible credit in favor of the Indian shipper. India has strongly protested such practices, which are in violation of trade agreements, and has achieved some compromise—with the Romanians, at least—whereby any commissions made on such reexports are partly credited to India.

Giving evidence to the Indian Estimates Committee, a Ministry of Trade official stated that India had entered a stipulation in various trade agreements with Eastern Europe to the effect that Indian exports under the agreement were intended exclusively for use in the country of ostensible destination. He went on to say, however, that it had been found impossible to enforce this, because trade statistics provided no concrete evidence of switching practices; but there was indirect evidence that Indian cashews, hides and skins, spices, coffee, tea, and jute goods had occasionally been resold through Hamburg, Antwerp, or Rijeka (Fiume). The Soviet Union was free from blame in this respect, but almost all other East European countries indulged in this practice. The Indian government had attempted to curb this by demanding landing certificates from the ostensible consignee, but had abandoned the stipulation because it could not be enforced and would, in any case, have smacked of discrimination. They were now invoking the provisions of the trade agreement in confidential letters between the parties concerned.[3]

Pakistan exports have also been diverted from stated destinations to a significant extent. Some evidence on this is provided by shipping bills recording unloadings of goods in transit to one particular country at more than one port of transshipment on the same journey. Multiple transshipments of this sort are said to have accounted for 23.5 percent of West Pakistan's exports to Eastern Europe in 1969-70.[4]

Prima facie, such reexports represent a hidden loss to the original supplier compared with the situation that the new trading venture with Eastern Europe may have led the supplier to expect. It is difficult to be convinced, however, that the loss is always as great as it appears at first sight. Some reexported trade may be instrumental in locating previously unsuspected demand, and some may provide indirect access to markets that the producing country could not penetrate if it had to rely on its own commercial know-how. Nor is it entirely clear that reexporting by Comecon countries should always be resisted, even to the extent that it is known to be damaging to the original supplier. The developing country concerned may wish to indulge in switching operations itself where its import obligations from Eastern Europe are concerned, and may gain from this more than it loses by allowing its trading partner the same privilege.

Economic Diversion

Apart from the "mechanical" diversion discussed so far, incremental exports from Indonesia to Eastern Europe may suffer from what we have termed "economic" trade diversion. This will

happen when the expanded demand strains existing supplies or resources, so that its satisfaction must bring with it some effect on
the export potential available for other destinations. The most important commodity to which this is likely to apply—indeed, the only
one we have found it practicable and worthwhile to investigate—is
natural rubber.

Even here, however, the pattern of historical development allows only very tentative conclusions. If there had been a prolonged
postwar period in which Indonesian rubber had gone exclusively to
nonsocialist countries, it might be possible to estimate the typical
movement in Indonesia's free-market share in the absence of Comecon trade. We could then investigate how this movement was affected
in some other period in which Comecon trade had expanded. As it is,
no suitable, completely "Comecon-free" period of sufficient length
appears to exist. We must therefore attempt to disentangle historical situations in which everything is found to change simultaneously.

It can, for instance, be established that during 1955-60, when
Indonesian rubber exports to Eastern Europe increased by 11.8 percent per year, the country lost, on average, 3.5 percent of its share
of all other markets from year to year. During the subsequent ten
years, by contrast, rubber exports to Eastern Europe increased by
only 1.9 percent per year and Indonesia's share of other markets
remained approximately stable. It is tempting—though hazardous—
to conclude that over longer periods (six to ten years), the first 2
percent or so of annual growth in rubber exports to Eastern Europe
is nondiversionary, but that anything in excess of this makes some
incursion into the growth of other export outlets that would otherwise
have taken place.

Initial Terms of Trade

Of crucial importance to the costs and benefits of Indonesian-
Comecon exchanges are the terms of trade that Indonesia receives,
that is, the ratio of its export receipts per unit of each commodity
to its import bill per unit of goods imported. Clearly that ratio,
when compared with the corresponding ratios achieved in exchanges
with the rest of the world, must be the proximate criterion of the
profitability of Indonesian-Comecon trade, and not the comparative
levels of export (or import) prices themselves. Higher-than-average
prices received on exports to the Soviet Union, for instance, would
be of little use to Indonesia if the prices of Soviet imports were kept
correspondingly high.

Statistical data, some of which are shown in Table 10.6, suggest that East European countries have consistently paid more per

TABLE 10.6

Unit Values of Indonesian Exports to Eastern Europe, 1955-71
(percent of world prices based on U.S. dollars per kg., f.o.b.)

	United States	Japan	West Europe	East Europe
Natural Rubber				
1955	98	115	106	135
1963	97	93	96	121
1965	86	96	67	128
1970	94	100	104	125
1971	102	97	101	119
Coffee				
1963	131	176	95	243
1965	92	142	111	183
1969	99	94	116	97
1970	102	88	88	103

	United States	Japan	West Europe	East Europe
Tea				
1963	95	—	100	143
1969	125	—	97	—
1970	98	—	101	106
Palm Oil				
1963	73	68	117	74
1965	103	100	99	123
1968	91	104	102	112
1969	101	91	99	—
1970	96	101	106	—
Palm Kernels				
1963	—	101	97	98
1965	—	102	97	110
1966	—	126	68	150
1968	—	—	100	100
1969	57	99	102	—
1970	144	100	93	—

Note: In the case of commodities other than rubber, the world price is taken to be the weighted average unit value of the four markets quoted.

Source: Computed from data supplied by the Indonesian Department of Trade, December 1972, partly through the courtesy of the Working Committee for Crumb Rubber.

unit weight for Indonesian exports than any other major trading partner. To some extent, of course, this impression may be deceptive.
It is known, for instance, that the rubber imports preferred by
Comecon countries are of better-than-average quality because of
the greater demands on the raw material that their less sophisticated processing equipment must make. On closer examination,
however, it turns out that this factor does not account for more
than 10-20 percent of the differential between world prices and those
paid by East European countries to Indonesia during the mid-1960s.
If the export composition of Indonesian rubber to the four major
markets had been the same as that of Singapore, one would expect
East European prices to have exceeded world prices by only 3.3
percent during 1964-67.* This would have accounted for less than
11 percent of the differential referred to. If further allowance is
made for the fact that the Indonesian quality mix might have been
even higher than that of Singapore, the excess above world prices
to be expected from East European customers might conceivably be
double that observed in Singapore—that is, 6.6 percent—and therefore some 21 percent of the terms-of-trade advantage that Comecon
trade seems to offer.

It does not appear that the remaining advantage in export
prices is outweighed by any compensating inflation of import prices.
What evidence there is, suggests that the latter are broadly comparable with Western or Japanese prices for goods of similar type.
Since much of what Comecon exports to less-developed countries
consists of machinery and equipment, price comparisons are subject to large margins of error, owing to differences in quality, design, and performance. Systematic studies therefore tend to shy
away from these all-important items and to concentrate on imports
of chemicals, fertilizer, and basic metals. An Indian study of this
sort concludes that during 1957-59 Comecon countries charged
prices no higher than other suppliers if the goods were of domestic
manufacture, but tended to inflate the price if they were reexports
from the West.[5] A study conducted by the Indian Institute of Foreign Trade arrives at similar conclusions for the period 1960-61-
1965-66.[6] This, however, applies only to 20-30 percent of India's
imports from Eastern Europe and leaves machinery and equipment
out of account.

Different conclusions in respect to Comecon raw material exports to Pakistan are offered by Michael Kidron, who reports that

---

*Those of the United States should have been about 4 percent
lower than world prices, those of Japan 2 percent higher, and those
of Western Europe about 1.5 percent lower.

zinc sold to the Pakistan Trading Corporation was priced nearly 11 percent higher when it came from Eastern Europe, and even exceeded the Western tied-aid prices in the last few years. [7]

Kidron has also studied a sample of machinery items, which shows an East European price 25 percent below the West European average for power transformers and 17 percent lower for substations, and a Soviet price for spinning machinery as much as 50-67 percent below Western offers. These, however, are stray items, and it would be only by the merest fluke that they might turn out to be representative of the machinery imports of relevance to Indonesia. We know that Indian government officials are on record as saying that East European prices for equipment have sometimes exceeded those of other suppliers by 10 to 30 percent; but since some of this equipment was financed by tied credits, the comparison with free-market prices in other parts of the world is not wholly valid. [8]

Even if Comecon prices for machinery and equipment could be broken down satisfactorily into their component parts, the comparison with rival products could easily be distorted by differences in quality. Kidron reports the Pakistan experience that East European equipment has generally been found satisfactory from a technological point of view, but rather poor as far as economic performance is concerned. [9] In the case of textile machinery, for instance, the Russian product was thought to be reliable and long-lasting, but suffering from relatively high running costs. Polish, Czech, and Yugoslav machinery, on the other hand, was described as excellent and in some instances technically superior to West European makes, without any loss in economic performance.

The Terms of Trade Through Time

While the formal terms of trade provided for in Comecon trade agreements with the most important Asian countries can thus be shown to be satisfactory in general, the same cannot always be said of the real barter terms as they are found to have operated ex post when the agreements have been in force for some time. Above all, the after-sales service offered by East European countries, and the Soviet Union in particular, is often deplorable. Lack of servicing and spare parts, and the inability to obtain them on reasonable notice from the manufacturers, has resulted in at least one Pakistani line of machine tools standing idle for two years and another for fully five years, for want of relatively small components. Much of this is apparently due to Comecon factories being unwilling to deal with small and ad hoc orders—for which, indeed, the machinery of planning is singularly ill-adapted. The same cumbrousness and preference for production in large lots frequently results in local conditions being ignored: Volga cars for West Pakistan have been known to arrive fitted with heaters instead of air conditioners, and Russian motorcycles for East Pakistan (now Bangladesh) have been found to seize up for want of tropicalization. Bureaucratic procedures are frustrating and time-consuming, and delivery lags "huge and unpredictable."

On price movements in the course of time, once commitments have been entered into, the evidence is contradictory. Some of Comecon's Asian trading partners were impressed by price discounts offered in the mid-1960s and by the fact that prices remained normal under long-term credits, "as against heavy price increases when such arrangements are entered into with the Western powers."[10]

In other cases, however, there are complaints that import prices initially fixed at competitive levels in barter agreements are subsequently scaled up. Spare parts are usually expensive, sometimes outrageously so, and frequently unusable due to changes in the design of models and lack of standardization.

All in all, it appears that the initial or ostensible terms on which Comecon exchanges have been on offer in the less-developed countries of Asia compared quite favorably with those offered by other trading partners. While there is no absolute unanimity in this, it is at least so on the best consensus available. Ex post experience with these exchanges, however, has often wiped out the presumed advantage and in some cases has converted it into the opposite.

The reasons for this pincer movement are not far to seek: Comecon trade officials, though commercially as expert as anyone else and acting under the usual motivation, do not always have the same network of personal contacts as Western traders. They are less well or less promptly informed of price movements that offer advantages, and more impeded by bureaucratic constraints on decision taking. In some cases they may agree to pay higher prices simply to use up reserves of particular currencies they happen to hold or to balance an account in a trade agreement at the right time. All this easily results in a drift toward more favorable initial terms for their trading partners. Add to this a certain degree of overproduction of machinery and equipment, induced by an early enthusiasm for industrialization at all costs, and the willingness to part with these surpluses without exacting high prices becomes explicable. Nor can we disregard the possibility that some Comecon countries may wish to gain entry into a given market on semipolitical grounds, simply to "establish a presence." This probably applies to the Soviet Union with much more force than to other Comecon countries, but will apply to all of them in some degree. Once the "entry fee" has been paid and local knowledge acquired, one can expect a certain withdrawal of the favors initially offered, whether in terms of price changes, less favorable delivery dates, or servicing and spare parts.

It follows from this that, apart from the diversion discounts and the allowances for initially favorable terms of trade, Indonesia would do well to apply a separate discount for the notional deterioration in the terms of trade that usually follows implementation of long-term trade agreements with Comecon countries. It is difficult to say how large this discount should be, but it almost certainly ought to rise with the proportion of machinery and equipment in the import mix offered by the Comecon trading partner.

De Facto Inconvertibility

Unfortunately the list of necessary discounts does not end here. Foreign currency becoming available from Comecon countries, even if paid in convertible exchange, is by virtue of the trade agreement committed to be spent on specified imports that cannot be replaced, delayed, or abandoned without cost. As long as the trading partner insists on balancing its trade with Indonesia at set intervals, or is likely to exert pressure to secure such balancing, the currency receipts from Indonesia's exports to that partner cannot be valued on a par with foreign exchange that is freely disposable. A discount should therefore be applied to these receipts to reflect this restriction.

The costs of de facto inconvertibility used to be continuously assessed in a market in which unwilling holders of Comecon currencies met international switch traders offering convertible exchange at a switch premium. These premiums varied with the commodities that the currency holders would have had to import from their Comecon trading partners in the absence of the switch deal, and that the switch trader would therefore have to sell to other buyers. With such ready-made estimates of the real costs of de facto inconvertibility (d.f.i.), it is a simple matter to compute the "d.f.i. discount"; for even if the switch premiums contain a brokerage component, this is hardly more than the cost (in terms of time, trouble, and expertise) of locating and persuading third parties to take the goods that Indonesia preferred not to import.

Switch trading is a device to which Indonesia might well wish to resort, and therefore should be thoroughly understood. Its function is to transfer excess balances (unplanned surpluses) arising from trade agreements between Comecon countries and others from their (unwilling) owners to third parties that wish to use them.

Suppose Hungary has not fully used its bilateral import entitlements from, say, Ghana, and therefore has a book balance of $100,000 standing to its credit (possibly in terms of "clearing dollars"). A Swiss trader may wish to buy this balance for convertible dollars (at a discount), for resale to, say, a French firm that wants to purchase the Ghanaian exports the Hungarians failed to take. The French firm can get these goods below world market prices because it obtained the clearing dollars at a discount (albeit at a smaller discount than the Swiss intermediary, who takes his own margin), while the Hungarians get convertible dollars in exchange for clearing dollars (at a premium), and are thereby liberated from their obligation to import unwanted goods from Ghana. The Ghanaians now find their exports switched from Hungary to France, while the Hungarians may wish to use their convertible dollars for imports from, say, Argentina without having a direct trade agreement with that country.

Such switch trading is not usually practicable without the ultimate, and probably tacit, connivance of Comecon countries themselves. It may not in any case be practicable except in marginal cases, and the switch premiums or discounts for clearing dollars may be too high. But possibilities of this sort should certainly be investigated.

It seems reasonable to assume that even if Indonesia found it impossible to switch unwanted Comecon imports, it should discount the face value of these imports by the putative cost of such switches and base its profitability calculations on this revaluation. It could thereby provide itself with much sounder criteria for the acceptance or rejection of proposed trade agreements with Comecon countries.

The following are examples of differential discounts that might be used to allow for d.f.i.:

5 percent for imports of raw materials, basic metals, or chemicals
10 percent for timber
15 percent for semifabricates, ball bearings, or roller bearings
20 percent for agricultural machinery and tractors
25 percent for other machinery, except machine tools
30 percent for machine tools.

These percentages, which correspond to the switch premiums charged by experienced Central European switch traders in recent years, can easily be applied to any given import mix. The phenomenon of d.f.i. arises even when payments are made in convertible currencies by the Comecon country, as long as the agreement stipulates that Indonesia must pay for its imports in like manner and that trade must be "balanced" at certain intervals. Even where the last stipulation is not explicitly made, Indonesia must expect periodic pressure to balance its trade, and will almost certainly be forced to spend convertible currency on items that it would not have chosen.

CONCLUSIONS—ECONOMIC RELATIONS WITH COMECON

The last half-century of history has played havoc with both the Western and the Leninist visions of economic development and with hopes for a convergence of standards between the developed and the underdeveloped worlds.

Capitalism did, of course, spread to many backward areas in pursuit of profit and investment opportunities. But in general it failed to penetrate beyond the enclaves of economic dependence that metropolitan powers and multinational companies had established for themselves, and left the vast hinterland of poverty and stagnation relatively unaffected, if not actually disabled by the internal barriers that a superior competitive power had erected. The gap between rich and poor nations signally failed to narrow, and the ancient claim of capitalism to be the automatic equalizer of fortunes remains unsubstantiated, if it has not actually been disproved.

Nor did the Marxist-Leninist vision fare any better. The Soviet Union, in a race against time to build up its own capital goods and defense industries against the presumed threat of militant Western capitalism and the actual onslaught of Nazi Germany, had nothing to spare in the way of help for the Third World. When Eastern Europe was absorbed into the Soviet bloc after the war, the first priority inevitably became the rebuilding of war-torn economies and the consolidation and development of the enclaves of advanced technology that already existed at home: defense industries, aerospace ventures, and their supporting power base in engineering, instrument making, and computer technology. With these preoccupations the desire to help the Third World, even where political self-interest pointed in the same direction, could be of little practical import. Where the political advantage promised to be overwhelming, the Soviet Union did step in with highly selective measures, and sought to secure its foothold by continuing trade and aid agreements. But all the evidence suggests that severe disillusionment with politically motivated trade soon set in,* and after 1959 or so the Comecon

---

*The marked disinclination to make economic sacrifices in support of Salvador Allende's regime in Chile appears to have sprung largely from a desire to avoid "the burden of another Cuba." It

advocates of closer relations with the Third World based their arguments on purely economic considerations of mutual advantage.

Such arguments are difficult to muster, and even more difficult to substantiate. To be sure, the theory of comparative costs—long decried by Communist ideologists as a weapon of capitalism—has been rediscovered and rehabilitated in Eastern Europe. Comecon countries now realize and proclaim that mutual advantage may arise from exchanges of sugar for steel with Cuba, of rubber for cotton fabrics with Malaysia, and of jute for machinery with India and Pakistan. But the complementarity between East European countries and the Third World is far weaker and more sporadic than that between the Third World and the developed countries of the West. Many of the Third World products traditionally needed by the West—petroleum, minerals, raw cotton—are relatively abundant in the Soviet landmass, while the traditional Comecon exports—timber, furs, and basic metals—have more obvious uses in the West than in the Third World. The equipment and machinery that Eastern Europe offers typically come in such large and indigestible lumps, demanding long-term commitment and auxiliary services, that the Third World is wary of accepting it, and the producing countries themselves are beginning to doubt their clients' absorptive capacity in their present stage of underdevelopment.

Nor have the internal dynamics of Comecon and Third World development contributed to the economic complementarity between the two sets of countries. The Third World needs capital-saving, rather than labor-saving, equipment, light industry products, plastics, and chemicals—in short, the fruits of the second phase of industrial development—in preference to heavy machinery, iron and steel, and industrial fuel, the products of the first phase. But Eastern Europe has barely started on the second phase. Its long and passionate commitment to the first phase under the sway of Stalinist "metal eaters" has caused it to miss out on or delay the technological revolutions that have transformed the West, and much as the post-Stalin reorientation of policy has tended to put it belatedly on the right road, it still has tremendous backlogs to make up.

This is being frankly recognized in the Soviet Union and other Comecon countries. What is needed above all is a rise in economic cooperation with the developed West, a prolonged period of technological renewal demanding massive imports of advanced equipment

---

resulted in the Communist party of Chile being regarded as the most right-wing element in the Allende coalition, bent on serving the interests of international Communism rather than those of Chile, as understood by the Unidad Popular.

and know-how from West to East, in exchange for exports of raw materials, minerals, and fuel and power resources in the opposite direction. The crucial exchange of highly fabricated for relatively "earthy" products, for so long regarded as the key to a symbiosis between South and North, is now to become the cornerstone of economic relations between East and West.

Where does this leave the South? It must be said at once that the recent about-face of the East toward the West was preceded by a relative turning away of the East from the South for at least a decade. Eastern Europe, even while importing raw materials from the Third World on an unprecedented scale, has never made a secret of its intentions to develop a raw material base of its own that would ultimately make it independent of its suppliers. The Soviet Union plans to expand its synthetic rubber and fiber industries to the point where imports of the natural products will cover smaller portions of its needs. It plans—along with other Comecon countries—to increase its own supplies of raw cotton, sugar, rice, wool, leather, metal ores, and tea—almost anything that the Third World traditionally supplied and that can be domestically produced. Far from steering their economies toward greater complementarity, Comecon and the Third World appear to be bent on a course toward greater independence of each other, and at the same time toward the greatest possible assimilation to the developed economies of the West. With a few notable exceptions (like the Soviet arrangements with Afghanistan and Iran for the exploitation of natural gas) there has been no move toward anything that could be called even a partial integration of Third World economies into the East European fold.

The great upsurge of Comecon trade with developing countries in the late 1950s and early 1960s was probably a once-for-all phenomenon unlikely to be repeated. Some of it was occasioned by the new-found independence of African colonies, which merely replaced intermediate trade through the metropolitan countries by direct trade with an expanded Third World; some was due to the Sino-Soviet rift, which redirected important trade flows into Third World channels; and some sprang from the economic reform movements in Comecon countries that by now may have spent their main impetus, at least as far as trade with the Third World is concerned. The great upsurge, in its later stages, fell short of the expectations raised at its inception; and the subsequent years of the 1960s disappointed expectation even more. Comecon trade with less-developed countries remained concentrated on the Indian subcontinent, Egypt, and Turkey. These trading partners, along with the entrepot trade with Hong Kong and Singapore, accounted for over three-quarters of Comecon's exchanges with the Third World.

Not only has the great upsurge largely spent itself, but Comecon attitudes to Third World trade have undergone important changes. Eastern Europe is evidently taking a long, cool look at what it has to gain and lose from longer-term commitments of this sort. The terms it is offering have been getting harder and more exacting. Developing countries are finding initially favorable terms of trade gradually eroding and new offers of technological transfers hedged with costly conditions. They cannot rely on any tenderness of heart from Eastern Europe when competing in third countries, and have been undercut in crucial export markets wherever this suited Comecon aims.

To be sure, the overall trade of Comecon countries will grow, and possibly even rocket, in the 1980s, and some of it will spill over into Third World channels. But all the impressions the author has been able to gather point to one thing only: Eastern Europe and the Soviet Union turn to the Third World mainly for those things they are unable to obtain from the West. It will benefit them greatly to save Western currencies, whenever possible, by offering the Third World the surplus machinery and equipment that cannot be sold in the West and by demanding traditional raw materials or very simple manufactures in return. For some time to come their prime concern will be the resumption of the race to catch up to and overtake the developed countries of the West, which was in abeyance during the 1960s. They will engage in this in a spirit of cooperation and interchange with the West, treating the Third World as a stopgap or an intermediary, but not as an independent partner in its own right.

In this sobering light it would appear unrealistic for a major developing country like Indonesia to place much faith in Comecon trade as a strategic weapon in its development policy. The prime mover and engine of economic transformation must be sought elsewhere, unless a very special and unprecedented relationship with Comecon countries can be forged.

The general considerations in favor of Comecon trade that are so often urged on developing countries—diversification, growth of markets, and stability—should be brought into play only if experience shows them to be operative in a significant, decisive way that leaves no doubt of their validity. This, as we have seen, is not the case.

The conclusion that this would seem to suggest is that Indonesia should be guided closely by the expected profitability that a given trade deal or arrangement can be shown to offer, without allowing itself to be swayed by the promise of intangible future advantage. This profitability should of course be assessed in the light of all foreseeable effects, direct and indirect, including trade diversion, loss of "multilaterality," and likely erosion of trade terms in the course of implementation.

Indonesian negotiators would do well to focus on the opportunities offered for the export or import of particular commodities and the commercial advantage that may be gained in specialized markets at particular conjunctions of demand and supply. The price—and other advantages so offered—can be embodied in the detailed cost calculation that we have recommended elsewhere. To perceive them and to negotiate accordingly is, however, the concern of specialists in marketing and commodity experts, and not a matter of grand design.

NOTES

1. Asha L. Datar, India's Economic Relations with the USSR (Cambridge: Cambridge University Press, 1972), p. 161.

2. Michael Kidron, Pakistan's Trade with Eastern Bloc Countries (New York: Praeger, 1972), p. 27.

3. Indian Estimates Committee, 153, pp. 223-34; M. Goldman, as quoted in Datar, India's Economic Relations with the USSR, pp. 161-62.

4. Kidron, Pakistan's Trade with Eastern Bloc Countries, p. 26.

5. Suvendra Dave.

6. Indian Institute of Foreign Trade, Unit Values of Selected Imports . . ., pp. 26-27, 69-76.

7. Kidron, Pakistan's Trade with Eastern Bloc Countries, pp. 53-54.

8. Datar, India's Economic Relations with the USSR, p. 176.

9. Kidron, Pakistan's Trade with Eastern Bloc Countries, pp. 51-52.

10. Y. H. Shirazi, president of the Karachi Chamber of Commerce, quoted in ibid., p. 53.

PART III

AGRICULTURE
AND
INDUSTRY

11

INDUSTRIALIZATION IN INDONESIA

Juergen B. Donges, Bernd Stecher, and Frank Wolter

Indonesia has experienced relatively rapid industrial growth during the post-Sukarno period. The rate of about 11 percent per annum (in real terms) from 1967 to 1977 is not only somewhat higher than for the rest of the economy, but it is also remarkable in the light of industrial stagnation in the early 1960s. However, manufacturing industry still plays a minor role if compared with other East Asian countries, and the industry mix reveals a preponderance of consumer goods that are largely produced for the domestic market.

Rapid industrialization can significantly improve the efficiency of Indonesia's agriculture, through the supply of inputs and the processing of the sector's output. It can help to deal with the problem of providing jobs at rising real wages for the large and rapidly growing labor force. Finally, industrial growth permits diversification of exports that may be required for a viable long-run balance-of-payments position. In order to have a proper perspective on the problems and prospects of industrialization in Indonesia, it is worth examining the main features and structural relationships underlying the country's manufacturing sector. The following essay attempts to serve this purpose. It focuses mainly on the period up to 1973, when the oil price was boosted for the first time, and is followed by a brief survey of more recent trends.[1]

We gratefully acknowledge the benefits of discussions with Ranadev Banerji, James Riedel, and William Tyler, and the helpful comments made by Mathias Bruch and Dean Spinanger.

PATTERN OF INDUSTRIAL DEVELOPMENT, 1960-72

The Production Record

Statistical information is, unfortunately, extremely scarce.*
If we look at the 1960-72 period, two phases of industrial performance are roughly distinguishable, clearly reflecting the policies
pursued under the Sukarno and the Suharto administrations. During
the first, the country witnessed considerable political instability,
persistent deficits in the government budgets, domestic inflation at
an exponential rate, growing balance-of-payments problems, extensive government intervention in the market system, proliferation of
government-aided manufacturing plants, and an increasing hostility
to foreign capital, eventually bringing the whole economy close to a
total collapse. Under such conditions it is not surprising to see
production of most industrial activities declining (Table 11.1). Only
the production of cotton yarn, coconut oil, and fertilizer showed an
upward trend during the early 1960s.

The administration that replaced Sukarno's at the end of 1965
introduced fundamental and drastic changes in general economic policy. Besides successfully combating hyperinflation, it shifted economic policy away from highly interventionistic practices to a
framework that relied much more on market forces and assigned
a leading role to the private sector in supporting industrial development. While the First Five-Year Development Plan, which was
launched in 1969-70, gave priority to increasing agricultural production, the government was also determined to achieve rehabilitation of productive capacity in the manufacturing sector and to re-
sume the process of industrialization that was import-substituting
in character. Credit and tax concessions to both domestic and
private foreign investment, as well as protection through investment
licensing and import tariffs, were widely used to help attain this
objective. The recovery of the manufacturing sector in the late
1960s and early 1970s is a good illustration of the positive response
of entrepreneurs, both domestic and foreign, to the new measures
implemented in a politically and socially stable environment. In
this phase Indonesia has witnessed a more rapid industrial growth

---

*Data from different sources differ considerably, are incom-
plete, and lack continuity. Differences are of a quite large and unknown magnitude. Therefore, all figures presented in this essay
should be interpreted with considerable caution; inconsistencies of
data are inevitable.

TABLE 11.1

Production Figures for Selected Items, 1960-72

Product	Unit	1960	1967	1971	1972	Compound Annual Growth Rate (percent)	
						1960-67	1967-72
Cotton yarn	thousand bales	64.0	93.1	240.0	278.0	5.5	24.6
Cotton fabric	million meters	377.0	225.0	650.0	816.0	-7.1	29.5
Cigarettes	billion items	21.2	7.0	13.9	17.0	-14.6	19.4
Matches	million boxes	470.0[a]	238.0[b]	354.3	441.0	-9.2	16.7
Soap	thousand tons	n.a.	108.0[b]	138.0	n.a.	n.a.	8.5[c]
Toothpaste	million tubes	n.a.	13.0[b]	13.9	30.0	n.a.	23.7
Coconut oil	thousand tons	217.0[a]	221.4	266.2	266.0	0.3	3.8
Cooking oil	thousand tons	n.a.	23.5[b]	27.3	29.0	n.a.	5.4
Paper	thousand tons	8.7	11.3[b]	27.1	38.0	3.3	35.0
Fertilizer	thousand tons	60.4	93.1	107.2	114.0	6.4	4.1
Salt	thousand tons	196.7	121.0	42.4	n.a.	-6.7	-23.0[c]
Oxygen	million cubic meters	n.a.	1.5	3.2	n.a.	n.a.	21.0[c]
Cement	thousand tons	387.0	312.0	543.7	609.0	-3.0	14.3
Tires for motor vehicles	thousand items	530.0	232.4	463.6	732.0	-11.1	26.0
Tires for bicycles	million items	3.8	2.7	1.86	n.a.	-4.7	-8.9[c]
Glass and bottles	thousand tons	12.7	5.7	6.2	12.0	-10.8	16.1
Galvanized iron sheets	thousand tons	n.a.	n.a.	34.5	n.a.	n.a.	n.a.
Sewing machines	thousand items	n.a.	5.5	32.6	n.a.	n.a.	60.0[c]
Automobiles	thousand items	n.a.	1.2	16.0	23.0	n.a.	80.0
Motorcycles	thousand items	n.a.	0.8	33.0	n.a.	n.a.	154.0[c]
Dry batteries	million items	n.a.	1.2	6.0	n.a.	n.a.	50.0[c]
Light bulbs	million items	n.a.	7.8	4.8	n.a.	n.a.	-11.4[c]
Radios	thousand items	n.a.	216.0	311.9	700.0	n.a.	26.7
Television sets	thousand items	n.a.	0.5	5.6	60.0	n.a.	126.8

n.a. = not available.
[a] 1961. [b] 1968. [c] 1967-71.
Source: Data provided by the Department of Industry.

than in any period of comparable length since national independence. Not surprisingly the degree of economic revitalization differs from product to product. Although it is generally believed (the absence of reliable data does not permit anything more than conjecture) that the Indonesian manufacturing sector as a whole had in 1970 reached the production level of the early 1960s, it is interesting to see that for some products—cigarettes, matches, salt, bicycle tires, glass, and bottles—the output in the early 1970s was still below that of a decade earlier.

Available estimates on both gross value of output and value added in the manufacturing sector differ widely, especially if small-scale industries* are included. Estimates of gross value of output for 1970 range from Rp. 723 billion to Rp. 1,251 billion, with value added between 20 and 35 percent; food manufacturing is the main contributor to these differences. Excluding small-scale industries— advisable, in view of the limited knowledge of their production—the degree of uncertainty remains substantial, with output figures ranging from Rp. 377 billion to Rp. 520 billion in 1970. For value added the range is similar to that for all industry. The manufacturing sector accounts for 10 or 11 percent of gross domestic product (GDP) at that time. With 1970 GDP at current prices estimated at Rp. 3,200 billion, value added (gross) of all manufacturing would then be on the order of Rp. 315-325 billion.

Manufacturing is dominated by nondurable consumer goods, particularly food products (Table 11.2). The pattern of production is what one would expect of a country in the early phase of industrialization (Tables 11.A.1 and 11.A.2). Compared with an international standard derived from cross-section regression estimates based on per capita income and population, some industries are relatively overdeveloped: food processing, textiles, clothing and footwear, and transport equipment (including repairs). On the other hand, virtually all intermediate and capital-goods industries are below the "typical" pattern. Among intermediate products the main development has been in building materials with a simple technology (such as walling and roofing materials). Little production of industrial chemicals exists, with the exception of nitrogenous fertilizer.

---

*According to the Indonesian definition, small-scale industries employ fewer than five workers. Medium-scale industries employ 10 to 99 workers without using power equipment, or 5 to 49 workers with power equipment. Large-scale industries have 100 or more workers without power equipment, or 50 or more workers with power equipment.

There are several small steel mills scattered throughout the country, producing mainly reinforcing or flat bars and galvanized sheets. Currently under construction are an integrated steel plant with an annual capacity of 2 million metric tons at Krakatau and a nonintegrated steel mill based on the use of electric furnaces for the direct reduction of iron ore at Cilegon. A capital-goods industry scarcely exists. Its development has been discouraged because the combination of low tariffs on capital goods and the overvaluation of the rupiah, resulting from the system of protection, has kept the price of imported investment goods below their scarcity value.

Virtually none of Indonesia's industries were oriented to the world market. Both the tariff structure and the implicit overvaluation of the rupiah resulting from this protection made exports appear unprofitable even in those industries that might have a comparative advantage. As a result, exports of manufactured goods (excluding such traditional items as palm oil, tea, and tapioca) are limited; in 1970 they accounted for 1.7 percent of total exports and 2.6 percent of nonoil exports. In spite of several attempts by government to encourage an export orientation of production in manufactures, the position of nontraditional exports is still negligible (4 percent in 1977). Obviously the abolition of various export levies on manufactures (April 1976) has not been very effective or has been counterbalanced by other factors. One of these might have been constant rumors about a devaluation of the rupiah, which could have made potential exporters reluctant to penetrate foreign markets. Furthermore, the overvaluation of the rupiah continued to be one of the major impediments to actual export activities even after the early 1970s. Since August 1971, when the rupiah was devaluated by 9 percent, its exchange value has been kept constant in terms of the U.S. dollar (until 1979); during the period 1970-75, however, the domestic price level in Indonesia rose four times faster than in the United States and Germany, and about two times faster than in other main trading partners.

Employment, Size of Plants, and Productivity

Manufacturing is dominated by nondurable consumer goods, in terms not only of output but also of employment (Table 11.2). In 1970 the food-processing industry alone employed almost one-third of the labor force in the large- and medium-scale manufacturing industry. Textile and tobacco were next in terms of employment. The contribution of most intermediate and capital-goods industries to total employment is as negligible as their contribution to total value added.

TABLE 11.2

Output, Employment, Wages, and Establishments of Manufacturing Subsectors as Percentage of Total Manufacturing, 1970

	Share of Output			Share of Employees			Share of Wages and Salaries[a]			Share of Establishments		
	Large	Medium	Total	Large	Medium	Total	Large	Medium	Total	Large	Medium	Total
Preparing, preserving meat	n.a.	0.3	0.1	n.a.	0.1	0.0	n.a.	0.2	0.1	n.a.	0.1	0.1
Dairy products, ice	0.7	2.0	1.0	0.2	1.7	0.7	0.7	6.1	1.8	0.7	2.0	1.9
Coconut oil, cooking oil, vegetable oil	6.2	11.0	7.1	1.8	1.8	1.8	2.8	4.0	3.1	3.6	1.9	2.1
Grain mill products	8.0	24.8	11.3	3.5	12.0	6.0	3.3	11.7	5.0	7.0	17.5	16.3
Sugar factories, refineries	12.5	0.1	10.1	13.5	0.3	9.6	13.3	0.0	10.6	2.9	0.4	0.7
Tapioca, sago flour	0.1	3.9	0.9	0.4	2.2	0.9	0.2	2.3	0.6	1.4	2.3	2.2
Tea processing, sorting, packing	2.2	1.1	2.0	9.4	1.4	7.1	7.5	1.1	6.2	3.2	0.9	1.2
Other food manufactures	2.4	5.2	2.9	3.7	8.1	5.0	2.8	5.8	3.4	6.7	9.1	8.8
Beverages	0.9	1.3	1.0	0.4	1.0	0.6	1.0	1.1	1.0	0.8	1.1	1.0
Tobacco	30.3	5.5	25.5	22.6	13.6	20.0	13.0	6.7	11.7	14.6	5.7	6.7
Yarns, threads	3.8	0.1	3.0	2.6	0.2	1.9	5.9	0.1	4.7	0.9	0.1	0.2
Weaving mills	4.2	7.2	4.8	9.7	19.3	12.5	8.2	12.4	9.1	16.3	18.6	18.3
Finished woven textiles	0.9	0.6	0.9	0.6	0.3	0.6	0.7	0.4	0.7	1.0	0.3	0.4
Knitting mills	0.5	0.6	0.5	1.2	0.6	1.0	1.2	0.5	1.1	2.5	0.4	0.7
Other textiles	0.4	0.0	0.3	0.8	0.0	0.6	1.1	0.0	0.9	0.5	0.0	0.1
Batiks	0.1	3.4	0.7	0.2	8.2	2.6	0.1	5.6	1.2	0.9	9.5	8.5
Wearing apparel	0.0	0.5	0.1	0.0	0.7	0.2	0.0	0.6	0.1	0.2	0.7	0.7
Carpets and rugs	0.3	0.0	0.2	0.4	0.1	0.3	1.4	1.4	1.4	0.5	0.1	0.1
Tanneries, leather finishing	0.2	0.2	0.2	0.2	0.4	0.2	0.2	0.4	0.3	0.5	0.4	0.4
Footwear	0.8	0.3	0.7	0.5	0.3	0.4	0.9	0.3	0.8	0.6	0.4	0.4
Wood, cork products	0.3	1.9	0.6	0.4	3.1	1.2	0.3	4.8	1.2	0.9	4.4	4.0
Furniture, fixtures	0.1	0.6	0.2	0.2	1.3	0.5	0.1	1.9	0.5	0.4	1.5	1.3
Paper, paper products	0.2	0.1	0.2	0.5	0.7	0.5	0.8	0.3	0.7	0.9	0.5	0.5
Printed matter	0.5	5.2	1.4	1.2	3.0	1.7	1.6	5.4	2.3	2.7	3.1	3.1
Basic industrial chemicals	0.1	0.2	0.1	0.5	0.1	0.4	0.3	0.2	0.3	0.6	0.1	0.2
Fertilizers, pesticides	0.8	0.1	0.6	0.3	0.2	0.2	1.3	0.1	1.0	0.2	0.1	0.1
Processing incense, resin	n.a.	0.1	0.0	n.a.	0.1	0.0	n.a.	0.1	0.0	n.a.	0.2	0.2

Other chemical products	3.8	2.3	3.5	1.6	1.8	1.7	3.4	2.3	3.2	1.6	1.8	1.8
Drugs, medicines	0.8	0.4	0.7	1.0	0.6	0.9	1.8	0.8	1.6	1.5	0.4	0.6
Rubber products	14.2	14.6	14.3	17.0	4.4	13.3	17.0	7.4	15.0	14.1	2.6	3.9
Plastic products	0.2	1.0	0.4	0.5	1.3	0.7	0.6	2.0	0.9	1.2	1.2	1.2
Nonmetallic mineral products												
products	0.1	0.0	0.1	0.1	0.1	0.1	0.3	0.1	0.2	0.1	0.1	0.1
Glass, glass products	0.2	0.1	0.2	0.4	0.4	0.4	0.4	0.2	0.4	1.1	0.2	0.3
Cement	1.4		1.1	0.6	0.4	2.6	2.6		2.1	0.2		0.0
Other nonmetallic mineral products	0.1	2.0	0.4	0.3	4.0	1.4	0.3	3.8	1.0	1.3	5.2	4.7
Cutlery, hand tools, general hardware	0.3	0.8	0.4	0.5	1.6	0.8	0.5	2.6	1.0	1.2	1.6	1.5
Metal furnitures, fixtures	0.1	0.0	0.1	0.1	0.1	0.1	0.2	0.1	0.2	0.2	0.1	0.1
Structural metal products	0.4	0.4	0.4	0.3	0.7	0.4	0.4	1.1	0.6	0.8	1.0	1.0
Metal products except other equipment, machinery	1.1	1.0	1.1	0.5	0.7	0.6	1.0	1.0	1.0	1.4	0.7	0.7
Agriculture machinery, equipment	0.0	0.0	0.0	0.0	0.0	0.0	0.1	0.0	0.1	0.1	0.0	0.0
Other machines	0.2	0.2	0.2	0.5	0.6	0.5	0.8	0.8	0.8	0.8	0.6	0.6
Radio, television, communication equipment	0.1	0.1	0.1	0.1	0.1	0.1	0.1	0.2	0.1	0.2	0.1	0.1
Electrical apparatus, appliances	0.2	0.1	0.2	0.3	0.2	0.3	0.5	0.3	0.5	0.6	0.2	0.3
Shipbuilding, ship repairing	0.1	0.0	0.1	0.3	0.1	0.2	0.5	0.1	0.4	0.5	0.1	0.1
Assembling of motor cars	0.4	0.1	0.4	0.3	1.3	0.6	0.5	2.1	0.8	1.0	1.8	1.7
Assembling of bicycles	n.a.	0.0	0.0	n.a.	0.1	0.0	n.a.	0.1	0.0	n.a.	0.1	0.1
Other transport equipment	n.a.	0.0	0.0	n.a.	0.0	0.0	n.a.	0.0	0.0	n.a.	0.0	0.0
Other manufactures	0.1	0.9	0.3	0.7	1.4	0.9	0.3	1.4	0.5	1.5	1.1	1.2
Total manufacturing[b]	100.3	100.3	100.4	99.9	100.2	99.9	100.0	99.9	100.2	99.9	100.3	100.2
Total (absolute figures)	311,307[c]	75,992[c]	387,299[c]	613,385	255,431	868,816	27,692,963[d]	7,035,631[d]	34,728,594[d]	1,918	14,769	16,687

n.a. = not available.

[a]Including in kind.

[b]Details do not necessarily add up to totals because of rounding.

[c]Rp. million.

[d]Rp. thousand.

Source: Calculated from Biro Pusat Statistik, Statistik Industri 1970 (Jakarta: the Bureau, 1972).

According to the 1970 industrial census, all medium- and large-scale enterprises employed a total of 849,000 workers, or about 3.7 percent of Indonesia's total labor force (7.7 percent if small-scale firms are included); in 1961 medium- and large-scale manufacturing had absorbed 5.7 percent of the labor force. It is not clear which factors caused the failure of Indonesia's manufacturing industry to maintain its role in providing employment. The deterioration in the economy, especially its modern sector, between 1961 and 1967 was a major factor. Another reason may be that the fringe benefits provided by the labor legislation inherited from the pre-1965 period (which make labor more expensive than it otherwise would be), combined with the artificial cheapness of physical capital brought about by the post-1965 incentives to investment may have encouraged activities using too little labor.

The manpower so far absorbed by the manufacturing sector (Table 11.3) is employed in 17,900 medium- and large-scale enterprises and in an uncertain number of small-scale firms of both nonfactory and factory firms (thousands of cottage and handicraft industries as well as manufacturing and repair workshops, particularly in food processing, clothing, footwear, wood manufacturing including furniture, nonmetallic minerals, and transport equipment).

Most of the medium- and large-scale firms are characterized by a relatively small scale of production by international standards. Large firms, which account for 11 percent of the establishments, employ an average of 302 workers; only 5 out of 26 industries (petroleum products; pottery, china, and earthenware; food processing; rubber products; tobacco manufactures) rank above this average. Medium-scale firms average almost 16 workers per plant, with 14 industries somewhat higher.

There is a wide range in the size of firms. Extreme cases are incense and resin processing (average size of firm is 12 percent of the average size in total manufacturing) and cement production (average size of firm is 2,450 percent of the average size in total manufacturing). There is a significant positive correlation between the average size of firm and physical capital intensity (as measured by energy used per employee); the Spearman coefficient of rank correlation is 0.49. This supports the view that the optimal size of establishment in labor-intensive activities is smaller than in capital-intensive ones.

There is no evidence that the size of medium- and large-scale plants has increased over time. It is not easy to determine the minimum plant size required for economic production. But the fact that many industries in Indonesia are operating at low productivity levels by international standards leads us to believe that production activities are still excessively fragmented.

The small-scale industries probably absorb more than 50 percent of total manufacturing employment. There are no data concerning their structural characteristics; hence it is difficult to ascertain whether these firms suffer from an inherent economic weakness. Some of the existing small-scale establishments possess sufficient advantage in such respects as greater flexibility, regional dispersion, or product specialization to more than compensate for their serious disadvantage of generally low productivity. Other firms may be incapable of withstanding the competition of medium- and large-scale firms because of deficiencies in such factors as management capability, availability of technical know-how (including product design), capitalization in equipment, provision with water, electricity, and transport, and ability to obtain international financing domestically or abroad. Indonesia's small-scale industries have hardly had access to official sources of finance. They have often had to borrow from private lenders at considerably higher interest rates than those charged by the state banks making medium-term credits available to larger firms. The inadequate access to finance, together with some of the factors mentioned above, might explain why small-scale industry grew at a substantially lower rate than medium- and large-scale industry (3.2 percent versus 15.3 percent, on average, in the period 1968-71 and in terms of real value added[2]).

Labor productivity is another important dimension of industrial development in Indonesia. The few available data (provided by BAPPENAS [National Development Planning Board] and Central Bureau of Statistics) suggest that during the decade 1961-71 labor productivity in industry declined by 0.5 percent annually, while the economy's overall productivity rose by 1.5 percent per annum. This is surprising, since one would normally expect that productivity in manufacturing grows faster than in the rest of the economy. This anomaly is due largely to the decline in employment in urban manufacturing of 0.3 percent annually compensated by an increase of 6.8 percent annually in rural areas. Decreasing employment in urban manufacturing probably results from increasing capital-intensiveness of production, displacing labor. The rapid growth of employment in rural manufacturing then may result from the role of (mainly) rural small-scale firms as absorbers of labor. Such absorption could take place only with declining labor productivity. Given the respectable weight of small-scale industries in total manufacturing, the decrease of productivity for industry as a whole is no longer surprising.

Output per employee is now about Rp. 510,000 in large-scale and about Rp. 300,000 in medium-scale industry (Table 11.3). In comparison with other major economic sectors, total manufacturing

TABLE 11.3

Average Size of Firms and Output per Employee in Manufacturing Subsectors, 1970

	Employees per Firm Branch as Percent of Employees per Firm in Total Manufacturing			Output per Employee (Rp. thousand)		Productivity Gap*
	Large	Medium	Large + Medium	Large	Medium	
Preparing, preserving meat	n.a.	182	60	n.a.	795	n.a.
Dairy products, ice	31	82	35	1,794	358	5.0
Coconut oil, cooking oil, vegetable oil	52	100	89	1,717	1,781	1.0
Grain mill products	50	71	37	1,224	731	1.7
Sugar factories, refineries	472	71	1,450	469	53	8.9
Tapioca, sago flour	26	100	42	166	525	0.3
Tea processing, sorting, packing	296	165	612	120	222	0.5
Other food manufactures	56	88	58	324	190	1.7
Beverages	57	88	58	1,069	399	2.7
Tobacco manufactures	155	241	296	682	121	5.6
Yarns, threads	273	141	840	754	97	7.8
Weaving mills	59	106	69	233	115	2.0
Finished woven textiles	62	124	150	739	614	1.2
Knitting mills	49	135	152	191	318	0.6
Other textiles	157	59	694	259	98	2.6
Batiks	23	88	31	151	128	1.2
Wearing apparel	23	94	33	132	243	0.5
Carpets, rugs	84	106	244	303	45	6.7
Tanneries, leather finishing	31	112	62	532	154	3.4
Footwear	75	94	108	846	261	3.2
Wood, cork products	44	71	29	371	224	1.7
Furniture, fixtures	45	94	39	152	147	1.0
Paper, paper products	55	141	102	233	45	5.2

Printed matter	45	100	58	227	507	0.5
Basic industrial chemicals	79	112	206	121	430	0.3
Fertilizers, pesticides	177	112	164	1,430	94	15.2
Processing incense, resin	n.a.	35	12	n.a.	407	n.a.
Other chemical products	104	100	94	1,171	388	3.0
Drugs, medicines	67	141	154	423	214	2.0
Rubber products	120	177	340	425	1,010	0.4
Plastic products	42	112	64	219	239	0.9
Stone, clay products	98	129	137	376	122	3.1
Glass, glass products	35	177	135	280	73	3.8
Cement	380	n.a.	2,340	1,206	n.a.	n.a.
Other nonmetallic mineral products	28	77	35	77	148	0.5
Cutlery, hand tools, general hardware	46	106	56	297	184	1.6
Metal furniture, fixtures	54	100	119	287	157	1.8
Structural metal products	34	71	42	691	173	4.0
Metal products except machinery, equipment	38	106	77	1,153	438	2.6
Agricultural machinery, equipment	59	106	144	540	63	8.6
Other machines	64	100	85	263	128	2.1
Radio, television, communication equipment	59	106	144	570	477	1.2
Electrical apparatus, appliances	60	88	115	270	146	1.9
Shipbuilding, ship repairing	59	141	204	292	336	0.9
Assembling of motor cars	30	71	35	887	191	4.6
Assembling of bicycles	n.a.	112	37	n.a.	36	n.a.
Other transport equipment	n.a.	59	19	n.a.	79	n.a.
Other manufactures	43	129	75	114	184	0.6
Total manufacturing	100	100	100	508	298	1.7

n.a. = not available.

*Output per employee of large establishments divided by output per employee of medium establishments.

Source: Calculated from Biro Pusat Statistik, Statistik Industri 1970 (Jakarta: the Bureau, 1972).

industry, including small-scale firms, has a relatively low level of productivity. According to estimates made by BAPPENAS, the manufacturing sector ranks behind mining; electricity, gas, and water; banking and finance; wholesale and retail trade; and construction. This presumably reflects the widespread underemployment in manufacturing industry.

There are marked differences in labor productivity between large-scale and medium-scale firms. In 33 out of 44 subsectors for which data are available, labor productivity is higher in large-scale than in medium-scale firms (Table 11.3). Outstanding examples include the important yarn industry. Structural adjustment problems may arise whenever the productivity gap in a particular branch is large, provided there is a similar gap in total productivity and assuming that large-scale and medium-scale firms do not produce entirely different goods. The medium-scale establishments will experience relatively strong competitive pressure from large firms, often so strong as to menace their very existence. In the course of development, this competitive pressure is likely to increase, because the improvement of transport and communication facilities will lower the natural protection that many medium-scale plants enjoy.

The discussion so far has been in terms of labor productivity. In a country like Indonesia, with abundant labor but scarce capital, growth of labor productivity is not the most meaningful criterion for assessing overall efficiency. It reveals only the productivity of those workers who are effectively employed. It would be more interesting to know the output, or value added, per unit of such scarce inputs as capital. If low labor productivity were a result of having spread a given capital stock over a large number of previously unemployed workers, the situation would not be bad, because per capita income of the whole labor force would have increased. Owing to the very weak data base, it is difficult to know whether capital productivity rose. But casual evidence suggests that capital productivity tended to be stagnant during the years 1965-74 and increased slightly from 1974 on (mainly as a result of better utilization of existing capacity). If this observation is correct, Indonesia's industry had the worst of both worlds: a declining labor productivity along with a more or less stagnant capital productivity.

Regional Distribution of Manufacturing Activities

Until the end of the mid-1970s there were no conscious policies with respect to the regional pattern of industrial development: no attempt was made to spread industry throughout the country nor to promote concentration of industries in major cities. Industrial development took place mainly in Java (Table 11.4), with 78 percent of medium- and large-scale firms and 86 percent of total manufacturing employment. With 53 workers per plant Java also has the highest scale of production. Jakarta accounts for 11 (8.6) percent of firms and 7 (6) percent of employment in Java (Indonesia). On the other islands there is also a concentration of industrial activities in the provinces with larger cities. At a glance, the degree of regional concentration of both firms and employment, as measured by the Gini-Hirschman index, does not appear to be excessively high in Indonesia. However, regional concentration of the manufacturing industry may be higher than the figures in Table 11.4 suggest, because investment since 1970 has been regionally quite concentrated, particularly in Java. And Jakarta and its surrounding area may not be far from the point where the social diseconomies of agglomeration become so oppressive that private industries are burdened with substantial additional private costs outweighing their private benefits accruing from that agglomeration.

It is not possible here to analyze in detail the factors that have brought about this concentration. Briefly, one should say, however, that Java owes its initial industrial development to historical factors. Since ancient times this island has been the political, cultural, and economic center of the archipelago. Efforts to build up, and subsequently to improve, public services such as ports, roads, water, power, and communications were concentrated on Java (although they did not keep pace with requirements). Public investment in the physical infrastructure of the other islands lagged behind. Once provincial authorities took steps to provide public services, they also intended to give priority to the urban centers. Thus, Indonesia's economic development, in common with what is observed in other countries, promoted urbanization and urbanization promoted regionally concentrated industrial growth. A relatively big market for sales, a ready availability of workers (including reasonably skilled labor and managerial personnel) and material supplies (particularly those from abroad), and the access to the credit system all represent external economies for industrial concentration. In addition, experience in other countries reveals that would-be entrepreneurs tend to seek the company of others and, therefore, prefer to locate their plants in cities where industrial development has already started. Finally, government regulations, particularly those related to private investment, competitive imports, and imported supplies, have been very important in Indonesia. There is, therefore, an advantage for manufacturers in being close to the seat of the central government or the provincial authorities.

TABLE 11.4

Structure of Manufacturing Industry
and Employment by Region, 1970
(percent)

	Food		Beverages		Tobacco		Textiles	
	Firms	Empl.	Firms	Empl.	Firms	Empl.	Firms	Empl.
Sumatra								
North Sumatra	3.5	2.2	6.2	1.7	1.8	2.8	0.4	1.4
West Sumatra	0.9	2.0	—	—	0.7	0.3	0.7	0.7
South Sumatra	1.7	0.4	5.1	2.7	—	—	0.1	0.4
Riau	3.0	0.6	2.8	0.7	—	—	0.0	0.0
Other provinces	3.9	2.5	4.5	1.8	0.1	0.0	0.0	0.0
Java								
D.C.I. Jakarta Raya	2.7	1.5	16.9	30.6	0.2	0.3	10.4	8.0
D.I. Jogjakarta	1.9	1.5	2.2	4.0	1.8	0.5	6.8	5.2
West Java	18.1	30.3	9.6	6.9	0.1	0.7	12.6	24.0
Central Java	13.7	19.1	16.3	14.6	26.0	34.6	56.8	43.8
East Java	28.1	35.0	27.0	34.0	66.3	58.9	10.9	14.1
Kalimantan								
West Kalimantan	2.4	0.4	3.9	1.1	—	—	—	—
Central Kalimantan	0.1	0.0	—	—	—	—	—	—
South Kalimantan	1.1	0.2	1.1	0.4	—	—	—	—
East Kalimantan	0.1	0.0	—	—	—	—	—	—
Sulawesi								
North Sulawesi	1.4	0.7	—	—	—	—	0.0	0.0
Central Sulawesi	0.5	0.1	—	—	—	—	—	—
South Sulawesi	14.7	2.2	1.7	0.4	0.3	0.0	0.5	0.8
Southeast Sulawesi	0.1	0.0	—	—	—	—	0.0	0.0
Other regions								
Bali	1.0	0.7	—	—	0.6	0.7	0.5	1.4
Nusatenggara	0.7	0.4	0.6	0.2	2.3	1.0	0.1	0.2
South Maluku	0.1	0.0	—	—	—	—	—	—
West Irian	0.2	0.0	2.2	0.8	—	—	—	—
Total (percent)*	100.0	100.0	100.0	100.0	100.0	100.0	100.0	100.0
Total (absolute figures)	6,048	285,054	178	5,298	1,174	134,600	5,049	174,434
Gini-Hirschman concentration coefficient	34	47	31	44	70	66	58	48

| Leather | | Wood | | Paper | | Chemicals | | Rubber | |
Firms	Empl.	Firms	Empl.	Firms	Empl.	Firms	Empl.	Firms	Empl.
2.1	0.8	9.9	7.3	6.2	5.5	8.3	8.6	11.1	15.4
—	—	0.3	0.2	2.7	2.0	0.4	0.3	1.3	2.5
0.7	0.1	10.9	5.8	2.1	1.1	1.4	2.8	4.1	3.6
—	—	4.9	3.4	0.6	0.3	0.3	0.0	9.4	1.6
—	—	4.6	3.2	1.0	0.7	0.7	0.6	6.9	6.3
32.9	59.4	8.6	8.4	20.4	28.0	26.9	25.1	2.7	1.2
4.9	3.6	3.0	2.5	2.5	4.0	1.4	0.5	0.1	0.0
9.8	4.9	5.6	6.2	11.3	13.0	8.0	9.1	31.6	38.2
15.4	10.2	11.2	13.3	16.7	13.6	14.5	12.3	2.8	4.2
30.1	20.0	25.8	27.4	29.6	24.8	34.1	39.8	15.6	20.4
1.4	0.3	2.9	8.7	0.5	0.2	0.6	0.1	8.9	2.0
—	—	0.2	0.1	0.2	0.0	—	—	0.4	0.4
—	—	3.6	4.4	0.5	0.3	0.1	0.1	4.2	3.8
—	—	0.3	0.3	—	—	—	—	0.3	0.1
—	—	0.3	0.2	1.3	0.6	0.1	0.0	—	—
—	—	—	—	—	—	0.1	0.0	—	—
2.8	0.7	4.9	3.9	3.0	5.0	1.3	0.4	0.3	0.1
—	—	0.1	0.2	—	—	0.1	0.0	—	—
—	—	0.1	0.1	0.5	0.4	0.4	0.0	0.3	0.1
—	—	1.6	1.7	0.8	0.5	0.7	0.1	—	—
—	—	0.1	0.5	—	—	0.4	0.1	—	—
—	—	1.3	2.2	0.2	0.1	0.1	0.0	—	—
100.0	100.0	100.0	100.0	100.0	100.0	100.0	100.0	100.0	100.0
143	5,976	1,003	17,533	628	20,730	715	32,355	711	108,600
45	62	28	28	38	37	42	46	34	44

(continued)

Table 11.4 continued

	Nonmetallic Mineral Products		Basic Metals		Nonferrous Metals		Metal Products	
	Firms	Empl.	Firms	Empl.	Firms	Empl.	Firms	Empl.
Sumatra								
North Sumatra	3.2	2.2	—	—	6.1	13.5	11.2	5.5
West Sumatra	1.1	7.8	—	—	—	—	0.9	0.6
South Sumatra	6.7	6.8	—	—	—	—	7.1	2.8
Riau	2.6	1.2	2.3	3.7	—	—	0.4	0.1
Other provinces	0.7	0.4	—	—	—	—	2.7	0.8
Java								
D.C.I. Jakarta Raya	8.8	7.9	16.3	28.1	36.4	41.5	22.8	34.8
D.I. Jogjakarta	3.4	2.0	—	—	39.4	12.2	0.9	1.6
West Java	26.0	18.7	7.0	34.6	—	—	7.8	7.6
Central Java	13.4	14.3	32.6	18.7	9.1	1.8	14.1	9.0
East Java	20.3	28.1	39.5	12.2	9.1	31.0	22.1	28.6
Kalimantan								
West Kalimantan	—	—	—	—	—	—	0.9	0.4
Central Kalimantan	—	—	—	—	—	—	—	—
South Kalimantan	0.2	0.1	—	—	—	—	0.2	0.1
East Kalimantan	—	—	—	—	—	—	—	—
Sulawesi								
North Sulawesi	0.1	0.1	—	—	--	—	1.1	0.9
Central Sulawesi	—	—	—	—	—	—	—	—
South Sulawesi	7.8	6.9	—	—	—	—	6.5	5.8
Southeast Sulawesi	0.1	0.1	—	—	—	—	—	—
Other regions								
Bali	0.5	0.4	—	—	—	—	—	—
Nusatenggara	3.9	2.0	2.3	2.7	—	—	1.3	1.3
South Maluku	0.1	0.2	—	—	—	—	0.2	0.0
West Irian	1.0	0.8	—	—	—	—	—	—
Total (percent)*	100.0	100.0	100.0	100.0	100.0	100.0	100.0	100.0
Total (absolute figures)	842	23,228	43	1,351	33	1,184	553	12,773
Gini-Hirschman concentration coefficient	33	33	51	46	51	51	31	42

Note: Large and medium establishments only.
*Details do not necessarily add to totals because of rounding.
Source: Calculated from Biro Pusat Statistik, Survey Perusahaan Industri 1970
(Jakarta: the Bureau, 1971).

| Machinery | | Electrical Machinery | | Transport Equipment | | Other | | All Manufacturing | | Population 1971 |
Firms	Empl.	Firms	Empl.	Firms	Empl.	Firms	Empl.	Firms	Empl.	(percent)
8.6	17.0	14.9	13.6	9.7	4.7	1.0	0.3	3.9	4.4	5.5
—	—	—	—	1.7	0.6	—	—	0.8	1.5	2.3
1.0	0.1	1.5	0.2	6.1	4.8	0.5	0.1	2.2	1.2	2.9
—	—	1.5	0.2	1.5	0.5	0.5	0.1	1.9	0.5	1.4
1.0	0.1	—	—	1.0	0.3	1.5	0.4	2.1	1.8	5.4
5.7	2.9	40.3	57.3	23.5	39.5	4.1	2.7	8.7	6.3	3.8
11.4	7.9	—	—	2.7	1.3	13.7	19.0	3.6	2.1	2.1
34.3	19.5	4.5	1.1	4.1	6.4	4.1	1.3	14.0	21.9	18.1
6.7	7.6	10.4	12.7	10.9	11.4	33.5	36.9	26.4	23.8	18.4
16.2	42.9	20.9	13.9	27.4	23.6	39.6	38.8	24.9	31.9	21.4
—	—	—	—	2.2	0.7	—	—	1.5	0.6	1.7
—	—	—	—	—	—	—	—	0.08	0.06	0.6
13.3	1.6	—	—	0.7	0.2	—	—	0.9	0.7	1.4
—	—	—	—	1.2	0.3	0.5	0.1	0.1	0.03	0.6
—	—	—	—	0.2	0.4	—	—	0.6	0.3	1.4
—	—	—	—	1.2	0.4	—	—	0.2	0.03	0.8
1.0	0.1	6.0	1.1	5.1	3.6	0.5	0.1	6.3	1.5	4.4
—	—	—	—	—	—	—	—	0.06	0.02	0.6
—	—	—	—	0.2	0.1	—	—	0.6	0.7	1.8
—	—	—	—	0.2	0.5	0.5	0.2	0.8	0.5	3.8
—	—	—	—	—	—	—	—	0.05	0.02	0.9
1.0	0.3	—	—	0.2	0.6	—	—	0.2	0.09	0.8
100.0	100.0	100.0	100.0	100.0	100.0	100.0	100.0	100.0	100.0	100.0
105	4,677	67	2,923	412	10,299	197	7,914	17,901	848,933	119,182,000
38	46	46	59	36	45	50	53	41	46	36

THE ROLE OF DOMESTIC AND FOREIGN INVESTMENT

Probably the area in which the most radical change has occurred since 1965 is that of private investment. While the Sukarno administration discouraged private investment, the Suharto government favored private investment in manufacturing as well as in other sectors of the economy. This change in attitude was demonstrated by the enactment of a new Foreign Investment Law in January 1967 and a new Domestic Investment Law in November 1968; they provide a remarkable package of fiscal and tariff incentives aimed at improving the profitability of private investments. As far as we can see, neither domestic nor foreign investment in manufacturing has been promoted according to social priorities (such as potential for employment creation, backward linkage effects, new exports, government revenue, external economies). Hence, it is hard to say whether the pattern of investment that has emerged since the two investment laws reveals important deviations from the targets. What can be said, however, is that the mixture of policies related to investment has given support to the more or less natural tendency of investors to move largely into import-substituting industries.

Data on actual investment still are quite limited, but there is information on investments approved by the government. Most large-scale domestic and all foreign investments require government approval. From November 1968 to December 1972, a total of 1,001 domestic investment projects in manufacturing were approved under the Domestic Investment Law, representing U.S. $1,067 million or Rp. 403 billion (Table 11.5). A relatively high foreign-exchange component, a marked sectoral and regional concentration, and small size of investment have been the salient features so far.

The high foreign-exchange component, an average of 76 percent, may reflect the fact that about 45 percent of intended investment was for rehabilitation and/or expansion of existing enterprises, and therefore required relatively more (imported) machinery and equipment than (locally available) land and buildings. There is also some overestimation of the capital-goods imports required. The investor conceals some imported products in the foreign-exchange component of approved projects, which benefit from tax and tariff concessions. This means that the real cost of machinery and equipment to the investor is not necessarily as high as recorded in Table 11.5, though the table accurately reflects the costs to the economy as a whole. It shows that many of the import-substituting industries remained import-dependent. This can be ascribed to the trade policy that allows imports of capital goods and intermediate products at relatively low tariffs.

TABLE 11.5

Development of Domestic Investment in Indonesia's Manufacturing Industry, 1968-72

Industrial Branch[a]	Number of Projects					Amount in Million U.S. $[b]					Foreign-Exchange Component (percent)	Sectoral Share in Total (percent)
	1968	1969	1970	1971	1972	1968	1969	1970	1971	1972	1968-72	1968-72
Food processing	2	12	55	87	80	0.2	11.2	17.7	59.7	81.3	78.5	15.94
Beverages	—	—	2	—	2	—	—	1.1	—	0.6	65.0	.16
Tobacco manufactures	—	3	4	2	5	—	3.5	1.6	0.5	15.3	74.3	2.05
Textiles	1	26	66	70	62	12.6	18.5	72.0	80.7	150.4	81.7	31.32
Footwear	—	—	2	1	2	—	—	2.0	0.2	1.1	87.0	.31
Wood products	—	—	4	3	6	—	—	1.7	8.9	11.2	63.1	2.04
Furniture	—	—	1	—	—	—	—	0.2	—	—		.02
Paper products	—	6	1	2	4	—	3.9	0.2	0.3	19.5	73.8	2.40
Printed matter	—	6	14	13	18	—	3.4	5.0	9.6	16.5	66.5	3.23
Leather products	—	1	—	2	4	—	1.1	—	0.5	8.9	58.4	.98
Rubber products	—	27	33	17	12	—	9.0	23.9	10.0	17.6	63.0	5.67
Chemicals	—	16	17	18	26	—	4.6	5.7	3.0	10.8	98.1	2.26
Plastic products	3	6	12	17	20	1.6	1.8	2.6	9.7	24.9	83.2	3.81
Petroleum products	—	1	—	—	—	—	0.1	—	—	—	72.6	.01
Pottery, china, earthenware	—	—	—	1	1	—	—	—	0.1	0.8	83.7	1.32
Glass, glass products	—	—	2	—	6	—	—	2.1	—	12.0		.08
Other nonmetallic mineral products	—	—	2	2	15	—	—	7.5	5.2	17.7	50.0	2.85
Iron, steel	—	—	11	8	12	—	—	72.4	10.7	36.7	82.8	11.23
Finished metal products	—	5	17	17	21	—	0.5	8.6	16.9	35.4	74.1	5.75
Nonelectrical machinery	—	—	1	2	2	—	—	0.0	1.8	1.1	63.7	.27
Electrical machinery	—	5	13	19	13	—	2.2	9.7	22.4	15.9	69.5	4.70
Transport equipment	—	—	2	2	3	—	—	8.6	0.6	2.8	90.6	1.12
Scientific equipment (including photographic, optical goods)	—	—	2	3	3	—	—	0.4	1.5	1.0	72.7	.27
Other manufactures	—	1	6	6	4	—	0.1	1.9	7.0	16.0	41.0	2.34
Total manufacturing	6	115	267	292	321	14.4	59.9	244.9	249.3	498.5	76.2	100.00
Total economy	7	152	340	410	429	15.2	104.5	336.8	642.5	734.5		

Note: Uses approvals beginning November 1968.

[a]According to ISIC (International Standard Industry Classification).

[b]Calculated on the basis of U.S. $1 = Rp. 378.

Source: Data provided by Domestic Investment Board.

Domestic investors focused largely on textiles, food processing, and iron and steel, which together account for 58 percent of total intended investment. The intended investments in footwear, furniture, and leather manufactures were disappointingly small, in terms of both the number of projects and planned expenditures.

Not surprisingly, in view of the relative importance of rehabilitation efforts, most of the intended investment was small. On average, the planned expenditure per project was on the order of U.S. $1 million.

Some 30 percent of the approved investment is for Jakarta. The major exceptions are sectors that depend heavily on domestic raw materials with substantial transportation costs (such as tobacco manufactures and rubber products).

Approved foreign private investment in manufacturing started with 12 approved projects involving an investment expenditure of U.S. $34.1 million by the end of 1967. Total approvals amounted to 314 (U.S. $654.2 million) for the period until December 1972 (Table 11.6).

About 75 percent of the approved foreign investments are joint ventures. Although the Foreign Investment Law does not explicitly prohibit investment in the form of wholly owned foreign companies, foreigners have found it easier to get approval if they take in an Indonesian partner. In Indonesia, as in other developing countries, the political tolerance of foreign investors is not unlimited; and/or foreign investors may expect economic benefits by sharing the management or ownership with indigenous entrepreneurs.

Almost 75 percent of total private investment in manufacturing industry was by investors from Japan, the United States, Hong Kong, and Singapore. European firms have been somewhat reluctant to invest. Investments from Japan and the United States were in all subsectors. The Japanese paid the greatest attention to the textile, metal, and glass industries. U.S. investors concentrated on chemicals, textiles, and rubber. Moreover, Japanese investment largely took the form of establishing new enterprises; U.S. investment was directed to a great extent toward rehabilitation and/or expansion of American companies that had been nationalized under the Sukarno administration but were returned to their former owners after 1965. Both Japanese and U.S. private investment was largely motivated by the Indonesian government's policy of substituting domestic production for imports. Compared with the amounts invested in new projects by Japanese and U.S. investors, investment from Hong Kong and Singapore is rather small. These Asian investors were mostly interested in consumer-goods industries where the capital-labor and capital-output ratios are in general lower than elsewhere.

Sixty-four percent of total foreign investment was planned for textiles, "other" chemicals (mostly pharmaceutical products), non-metallic mineral products (other than glass), food manufactures, and electrical machinery. This degree of concentration appears to be in balance with the comparative advantage Indonesia has or may easily develop. The average size of the project is greater than in domestic investment, and so is the concentration of foreign investment in the Jakarta area.

Since the peak of 1970, the upward trend in intended foreign investment has become less strong. The reasons are not quite clear. By 1972-73 the investment climate had not worsened, but after the first burst of investment during the late 1960s it may have become increasingly difficult to identify projects with not too long a payoff period.

Information about the implementation of approved projects is still extremely scarce, particularly as far as domestic investment is concerned. Investors are reluctant to provide the information because all reports to the Foreign and Domestic Investment Board are passed on to the Department of Finance, and therefore can be used against them by the Tax Office. There are additional advantages to a firm in not reporting that its project has been completed. As long as the government believes that the investment is continuing, the firm may be entitled to import privileges on goods that it can claim to be capital goods, privileges it would lose once the completion of investment is acknowledged. It is clear, however, that not all approved investments have been implemented. According to partial data available, actual disbursements on approved domestic investment thus far amount to about 60 percent and those on approved foreign investment to about 80 percent.

The reasons for the delay between approval and implementation of investment are manifold. As far as domestic investment is concerned, it seems that some applications are partly fictitious, designed to obtain easier access to state bank credits. However, the root of the problem may lie in the many procedural and legal difficulties that remain to be overcome even after an investment project is approved. They include obtaining land, electricity, and water permits from regional and local authorities and various central ministries, and completing a cumbersome legal procedure—all compounded by widespread corruption and weaknesses in physical infrastructure. Such difficulties exist in most (and not only in) developing countries. However, the situation of Indonesia is complicated by the deterioration of infrastructure, administration, and investment atmosphere prior to 1965. If potential domestic investors are not to be inhibited and potential foreign investors are to be attracted in the future, it will be advisable to smooth the investment

TABLE 11.6

Approved Foreign Investment, by Manufacturing Sector, 1967–December 1972

ISIC Industrial Branch	Number of Projects	Amount (million U.S. $)	Average Amount per Project (thousand U.S. $)	Sectoral Share in Total (percent)	Share of Jakarta Area (percent)
Food manufacturing	20	44.7	2,235	6.83	79.4
Manufacture of animal feed	8	5.4	675	0.83	50.0
Beverages	9	18.4	2,044	2.81	58.6
Tobacco manufactures	11	13.8	1,255	2.11	61.4
Textiles	29	225.6	7,779	34.48	19.7
Clothing	11	17.7	1,609	2.71	92.1
Footwear	2	1.3	650	0.20	76.9
Wood products	5	2.4	480	0.37	72.7
Furniture	1	0.3	300	0.05	100.0
Paper products	5	4.7	940	0.72	89.4
Printed matter	9	6.1	678	0.93	88.1
Leather products	1	0.5	500	0.08	100.0
Rubber products	9	17.6	1,956	2.69	2.1
Industrial chemicals	10	14.4	1,440	2.20	89.6

Other chemicals	59	61.5	1,042	9.40	69.7
Plastic products	8	12.9	1,613	1.97	100.0
Manufactures of pottery, china, earthenware	1	2.8	2,800	0.43	n.a.
Glass, glass products	5	18.7	3,740	2.86	100.0
Other nonmetallic mineral products	4	46.3	11,575	7.08	0
Iron, steel	8	15.7	1,963	2.40	71.4
Nonferrous metals	2	3.1	1,550	0.47	45.2
Finished metal products	31	35.7	1,152	5.46	67.5
Nonelectrical machinery	6	5.0	833	0.81	57.9
Electrical machinery	27	42.8	1,585	6.54	88.2
Transport equipment	10	17.4	1,740	2.66	100.0
Scientific equipment (including photographic, optical products)	3	2.6	867	0.40	96.2
Other manufactures	20	16.5	825	2.52	50.9
Total	314	654.1	2,083	100.00	50.5

n.a. = not available.

Source: Data provided by the Foreign Investment Board.

379

process. Fortunately there is a great desire in Indonesia to overcome investment impediments. The establishment of the Capital
Investment Coordination Board in June 1973 was a step in this
direction.

CHOICES FOR THE FUTURE

Over the medium and long terms the question arises whether
industries should produce predominantly for the domestic market,
the export market, or both. Inward-lookers will argue that in an
"infant industry" economy high costs, risks, imperfect competition
in the international economy, and the restrictive trading practices
of the industrialized countries are strong initial obstacles to start
manufacturing production for the world market. Import substitution
also has the advantage that investment areas are easily identified.
It would be much less clear how to begin with export activities. On
the other hand, import substitution typically requires protection
against foreign competitors, which very likely imposes misallocations of resources and distortions on the economy rather quickly.
This will dampen overall productivity growth, inhibit employment,
cause excess capacity, slow down industrial development, discriminate against agriculture, discourage exports, provoke persistent
balance-of-payments difficulties, and aggravate inequalities in income
distribution. Manufacturing specialization, according to the classi-
cal concept of comparative advantage, would involve development of
both import-substituting and exporting industries. However, in the
short run, manufactured exports cannot be expected to play a remarkable role in inducing rapid and self-sustained industrial growth.
Thus, it is most likely that import substitution will continue to be
the major source of growth for the time being.

Indonesia has plenty of mineral and forest resources; and it
possesses, more than most developing countries, relatively large
reserves of unskilled and low-skilled labor, although it is relatively
poor in qualified manpower and physical capital. Therefore, the
development of predominantly resource-based industries, or of
relatively labor-intensive industries, or of resource-cum-labor-
intensive industries should be rewarding, from the point of view of
efficient growth, employment creation, and distribution of industry
throughout the country, as well as from that of achievement of international competitiveness. The known stocks of timber, hides, agricultural crops, crude oil, gas, and various nonferrous metals define the broad range of processing activities that Indonesia should be
able to run efficiently. Taking agriculture and mining as resource-
supplying sectors, the resource intensity of existing industry is

particularly evident in food processing, tobacco, and wood and rubber manufacturing, though in the latter case to a lesser degree than one might have expected (Table 11.7).*

The relative abundance of labor in Indonesia means that it is rather cheap: Rp. 85-375 or U.S. $.20-.90 per day in 1973 for unskilled workers. Although statistical information on existing wage rates is incomplete and inconsistent, casual inquiry shows a distinct wage advantage for Indonesia compared with most of its Southeast Asian neighbors. This is true of unskilled and low-skilled workers as well as of medium-skilled clerical and administrative labor and of scientific and technical personnel. A number of fringe benefits provided by Indonesia'a labor legislation, combined with the fact that a large part of the working population is still poorly educated, may mean that its labor force is not so much cheap as it is low-priced. However, fringe benefits also exist in other developing countries. And there are efforts under way in Indonesia that aim at improving the educational system. Given the present (1973) employment situation and the prospective growth of labor force and productivity, it is unlikely that Indonesia will lose its labor cost advantage in the years to come, especially since trade unions are weak and workers accept even very low wages. The alternative often would be to have no regular job at all.

Labor is also cheap in comparison with capital. Although the price of capital does not fully reflect its scarcity value, it is not excessively low. Interest rates in 1972 ranged from a subsidized 12 percent per annum for fixed capital to over 25 percent per annum for working capital. As long as the rate of price increase is relatively low, as it was until 1972, the interest rates are also high in real terms. When inflation reappeared in late 1972, interest rates were further increased. The widespread exemptions from import duties on capital items reduce the cost of capital below its scarcity price, and the fiscal incentives to investment also may introduce a bias in favor of higher capital intensity.

The accurate identification of areas of comparative advantage is generally impossible because of serious statistical problems. Therefore, the question is usually approached in an indirect way.

---

*In some cases the resource intensity is hidden in intrabranch or even interbranch trade, either because a large part of the raw materials are still imported (yarns and threads for textiles, ingots for basic metals) or because the natural resources used are directly attributed to the branch in question (manufactures of beverages, processing of leather).

TABLE 11.7

Intermediate Input Structure of Indonesia's Manufacturing Branches, by Sector of Origin, 1969
(percent)

	Agriculture	Mining	Manufacture I[a]	Manufacture II[b]	Others	Total
Food products	76	0	8	3	13	100
Beverages	0	0	0	57	43	100
Tobacco manufactures	65	0	0	9	26	100
Textiles, clothing, footwear	28	0	31	17	24	100
Wood products	48	0	16	13	23	100
Furniture, fixtures	2	0	0	75	23	100
Paper, paper products	1	1	52	11	35	100
Printed matter	0	0	0	60	40	100
Leather products	0	0	43	38	19	100
Rubber products	18	0	17	34	31	100
Fertilizer	0	11	26	46	17	100
Petrochemical products	0	69	6	7	18	100
Other chemicals	10	37	7	18	28	100
Nonmetallic mineral products	0	16	11	34	39	100
Basic metals	0	5	37	8	50	100
Metal products	2	3	4	65	26	100
Nonelectrical machinery	0	0	53	30	17	100
Electrical machinery	0	1	65	24	20	100
Transport equipment	0	0	67	23	10	100
Miscellaneous manufactures	3	5	7	62	23	100
Total manufacturing	58	5	10	10	17	100

[a]Input of same manufacturing branch (intrabranch trade).

[b]Input of other manufacturing branches (interbranch trade).

Source: Calculated from Input-Output Project Team (LEKNAS/Kyoto University), Input-Output Table of Indonesia 1969.

The fundamental assumption is that the wage component of value added per employee in a particular branch, in relation to the industrial average, can be used as a proxy for skill intensity, because wages are expected to increase according to the qualification of the employee; the nonwage component can be used as an indicator of capital intensity.[3] Since there are no sufficiently disaggregated data for the Indonesian manufacturing industry, the value-added concept can be applied only in a rough form (Table 11.8). By examining value added per employee, such relatively labor-intensive branches as food processing, tobacco manufacturing, textiles, clothing and footwear, and wood products can be identified. Among these, food processing, tobacco manufacturing, and textiles are low-skill-intensive. Clothing and footwear and wood products use a relatively high degree of skilled labor.

We believe that the key to Indonesia's future industrial development is the promotion of three groups of manufacturing activities. First are resource-based industries. Apart from food manufactures, rubber, leather, and timber processing are the most obvious candidates. Productive employment opportunities would be created, not only in the urban but also in the rural areas producing agricultural raw materials and mining and forestry products. The promotion of resource-based industries also should increase exports. Although Indonesia is a latecomer in the market for resource-based manufactures, its raw-material endowment and low-cost labor give it a potentially strong position.

Second are engineering goods, mostly light engineering. Indonesia's engineering sector is still quite small, and consists to a considerable extent of repair activities; but it has proven ability to produce or assemble a number of items—metal furniture, diesel and gasoline engines, agricultural implements, sewing machines, concrete mixers, pumps, air conditioners, radio and television sets—at reasonably efficient levels. Most light engineering goods can be produced relatively labor-intensively; they are needed by domestic consumers; and, if properly designed, they can be exported. Moreover, this sector offers a great opportunity for integrating small-scale industries into the process of industrial development. Subcontracting with larger firms can increase the division of labor within the engineering sector, and hence its efficiency, and also make the process more labor-intensive.

Third are "foot-loose" industries to be established in free-trade areas. Indonesia should try to participate in the new avenue of international division of labor that has emerged since multinational business corporations started the transfer of a great number of labor-intensive activities to less-developed countries.[4] The benefits in terms of value added, employment generation (taking

TABLE 11.8

Indexes of Labor-Capital and Relative Skill Intensity for Indonesia's Manufacturing Industry, 1970

ISIC Industrial Branch	Value Added per Employee		Wages and Salaries per Employee					
			Large-Scale		Medium-Scale		Total	
	Index	Rank	Index	Rank	Index	Rank	Index	Rank
Food manufacturing	80	3	94	5	113	8	99	5
Beverages	241	17	220	17	118	9	169	17
Tobacco manufactures	67	2	57	2	49	1	59	1
Textiles	81	4	120	7	71	3	98	3
Clothing, footwear	97	6	177	14	89	4	137	10
Wood products	95	5	85	4	156	13	105	6
Furniture	122	10	76	3	148	12	98	3
Paper products	40	1	168	13	50	2	141	11
Printed matter	102	7	130	9	177	17	134	9
Leather products	106	8	130	9	110	7	112	7
Rubber products	121	9	100	6	167	16	113	8
Chemicals, petroleum products	331	18	206	16	125	10	195	18
Nonmetallic mineral products	161	12	248	18	95	5	161	16
Basic metals	130	11	n.a.		n.a.		n.a.	—
Finished metal products	178	13	153	11	156	13	142	12
Nonelectrical machinery	208	14	161	12	132	11	153	14
Electrical machinery	229	16	124	8	216	18	142	12
Transport equipment	215	15	180	15	157	15	155	15
Miscellaneous manufactures	n.a.		48	1	99	6	61	2
Total	100		100		100		100	

n.a. = not available.

Note: An index below 100 reflects relative labor intensity (in the case of total value added per employee) or relatively low skill intensity (in the case of wages and salaries per employee).

Sources: Calculated from W. A. G. Boucherie, "Some Preliminary Estimates Concerning the Present Structure of Indonesian Industry" (Jakarta, May 1971) (mimeographed); Biro Pusat Statistik, Statistik Industri 1970 (Jakarta: the Bureau, 1972).

account also of backward linkages), on-the-job training, and foreign exchange can be important.

Apart from these types of industries, there is much scope for import substitution in heavy manufacturing, particularly basic chemicals and metals, as well as technologically advanced industrial machinery (including electrical equipment). In these sectors Indonesia still depends heavily on imports. Major obstacles to expansion, however, are the facts that economies of scale are substantial for most of the products in each of these sectors, and that reasonably efficient manufacturing requires markets of a size much larger than what Indonesia can hope to provide for some decades to come. It will hardly be possible to escape the narrowness of the domestic market unless export outlets for these products can be found from the very beginning. Given the fact that the world market for these goods is dominated by big suppliers from industrialized countries, the only chance we can think of for Indonesia to move efficiently into heavy manufacturing is offered in the context of a regional integration scheme such as ASEAN (formed by Malaysia, the Philippines, Singapore, Thailand, and Indonesia). What is needed is an agreement among the member countries to assign Indonesia the allocation of some of these industries to produce for the whole regional market, the size of which is substantially larger (in terms of population and per capita income) than Indonesia's domestic market.

POLICIES FOR INDUSTRIALIZATION

The policy measures that the Indonesian government has adopted since 1967 in order to encourage industrialization and to influence its pattern have to some extent complemented each other. They also suffer, however, from a lack of coordination and an inadequate relationship to specific industrialization objectives.

One key issue is lack of industrial finance, as a result of low levels of savings and weak money and capital markets. This is likely to become of critical significance for Indonesia's manufacturing industry in years to come, as industrial investment is expected to rise considerably and its domestic component grows, while the capacity for self-financing of indigenous entrepreneurs is rather low. Financial help therefore has to be provided to entrepreneurs, but in a way that does not unduly encourage capital-intensive techniques, regional concentration, and discrimination against small-scale industries. This purpose can be served by rationalizing the relationship between interest rates for fixed investment and those for working capital (whose requirements per unit of output are particularly high in labor-intensive activities).

A second area of important policy intervention is the fiscal incentive system. At present, tax concessions in some cases appear too generous and nonselective, and in others seem inadequate for coping with special industrialization objectives. Tax concessions obviously do not have a zero opportunity cost. To reduce their cost and improve their effectiveness might involve the following:

1. Dropping the tax holidays because they are, to a high degree, redundant. As far as most foreign investments are concerned, they simply result in a transfer of revenue from Indonesia to the lending countries. It would make much more sense to spend the tax revenue now forgone on the improvement of infrastructure, which is still insufficient.

2. The present rule of accelerated depreciation could be combined with a loss-carry-forward provision over an indefinite period. All investments would benefit fully from such an incentive, regardless of when they become profitable. The government would have to bear only the cost of interest forgone on the uncollected taxes during the period of special depreciation.

3. Investment allowances could be linked with the job-creating capacity of a particular investment project and given as a direct subsidy (financed in a relatively neutral way), either as money or as tax-refund certificates.

4. A special fiscal incentive, which could take the form of negotiable tax refund certificates (as applied in Colombia and Peru) could encourage Indonesian entrepreneurs to produce for export.

5. Enterprises could be allowed to invest a part of their income-tax liability in projects of a type and in a location especially wanted by the government. Such a device, if properly complemented by an improvement of infrastructure and a cutting down of administrative requirements, should lead to a regionally more diversified pattern of investment.

A third crucial area is investment licensing, which in practice seems to play a very important role in Indonesia. The country's authorities try to restrict entry in cases where they see a danger of excess capacity, or where economies of scale are considered significant, or where the tolerance for foreign investments is limited. Restrictions on entry do not seem wise as long as the competent authority does not have the expert knowledge of the economic and technical characteristics of individual investment projects upon which sound decisions could be based. In Indonesia the criteria actually used for licensing investments are rather vague. In some cases the principle applied is that of "first come, first served"; in other cases the criterion seems to be the bargaining power of the would-be investor or the closeness of his connections to the administration. This tends, on the one hand, to discriminate against new and small firms, which typically are not able to cope with the administrative complexities and cannot afford the special payments sometimes required. On the other hand, established foreign firms tend to be sheltered from competition of other foreign firms that want to produce in Indonesia, so that, in fact, the profits of foreign shareholders are protected at the cost of domestic consumers.

For these reasons it seems advisable to leave the decision about investments to those who think that they can do it better and earn money in the business. If import tariffs are reduced, as will be suggested below, the competitive threat from abroad will be sufficient to prevent early investors from making profits high enough to attract additional investment when existing production capacity is adequate. If the government does not want to rely on market forces alone as the basis of investment decisions, it should consider the temporary suspension of incentives when there is obviously an excessive inducement to invest. This would be better than prohibitions, which, as the experience in other developing countries suggests, cannot easily be removed at a later stage because of the resistance of powerful vested interests.

The key policies affecting industrial growth are those related to trade. In Indonesia there has traditionally been strong reliance on import restrictions to encourage industrialization.* As in other countries, severe import restrictions have several drawbacks. If effectively implemented, they usually cause considerable cost to the economy in terms of misallocation and waste of resources, bias against the use of labor, discouragement of exports, and loss in output and, therefore, in savings. The industrialization process sooner or later comes up against both balance-of-payments and size-of-market constraints.

If severe import restrictions are, on the other hand, unenforceable, they become redundant, have no protective impact, and

---

*The principal instruments since 1966 have been tariffs. After several reductions they ranged in 1972 from zero to 100 percent, and are, on the average, highest for consumer goods, lower for intermediate products, and lowest for capital goods. These import tariffs are supplemented by a system of sales taxes (of a multiple-stage turnover type) on imports that range, according to the degree of essentiality, from zero to 20 percent of the c.i.f. value. In addition there are a number of import prohibitions.

mainly cause a loss of revenue to the government because customs duties either are not paid at all or are not paid in full. This does not mean that any commitment to protection is wrong or that free trade would be better. It does point to the necessity for a rational system of protection. While outright import prohibitions should be eliminated, import tariffs can be gradually reduced to a moderate level (say, 20 or 30 percent) and made more uniform, thus providing similar encouragement to all types of manufacturing activities without distorting the price system or causing adverse allocative effects (and yet continuing to be an important source of customs revenue).

A temporary exception from uniformity in rates of protection may be advisable in selected genuine "infant industry" cases for which the efficiency increase resulting from upscaling and learning by doing is expected to be exceptional. In order to give export industries and import-substituting activities the same chance to develop, the import tariff has to be matched by an equivalent subsidy for exports. In the event of an exchange rate that, although in equilibrium, is pushed too high by Indonesia's dynamic primary exports (such as oil and timber) to allow the emerging export industries to achieve competitiveness, a deliberate undervaluation of the rupiah, with a definite notice of termination, can help to solve the problem.

RECENT TRENDS IN INDUSTRIALIZATION

The Pattern of Industrial Development

Industrial growth, after having been relatively rapid during the second half of the 1960s, accelerated in the early 1970s, peaked in 1973-74, then continued on a lower, but still relatively high, level (see Table 11.9). Notwithstanding this growth, the Indonesian economy is still dominated by the primary sector (agriculture and mining). The share of manufacturing in GDP amounted to only about 12 percent in 1977 (see Table 11.10). In viewing the manufacturing industry on a more disaggregated level, in contrast with earlier periods (1960-67 and 1967-72), growth in production, expressed in physical units, during 1971/72-1977/78 was positive in all industries for which such data are available (see Table 11.11). Among key products substantial growth has been realized in the textiles, paper, cement, and tire industries and in the assembly of automobiles, motorcycles, and television sets.

This section is based on a draft prepared by our colleague Mathias Bruch.

TABLE 11.9

Real Annual Growth Rates of GDP and Manufacturing
Production, 1971-72 to 1976-77
(percent)

	1971-72	1972-73	1973-74	1974-75	1975-76	1976-77
GDP	9.1	11.3	7.6	5.0	6.9	7.5
GDP per capita	6.6	8.5	4.9	2.3	4.1	4.8
GDP of manufacturing origin	15.1	15.2	16.2	12.3	9.7	11.8

Sources: International Financial Statistics Yearbook 1979
(Washington, D.C.: International Monetary Fund), pp. 226-27;
Bulletin of Indonesian Economic Studies 14, no. 2 (1978): 33.

TABLE 11.10

Share of Manufacturing in GDP, 1971-77

	1971	1972	1973	1974	1975	1976	1977
Share	8.8	9.3	9.6	10.4	11.1	11.4	11.9

Source: Bulletin of Indonesian Economic Studies 14, no. 2
(1978): 33.

By contrast, direct employment seems almost to have stagnated in manufacturing establishments with 20 or more workers. *
This follows from a comparison of the 1970 and 1975 industrial
census figures and those of Donald Snodgrass.[5] According to Snodgrass most, if not all, additional jobs in the manufacturing sector in
the period 1970-76 were provided by small establishments, mostly
of the household and cottage industry type. This would imply that
the size structure of manufacturing became even more skewed in the

---

*There is a high amount of uncertainty with respect to Indone-
sian employment figures; hence only very tentative conclusions are
possible. Indirect employment creation may have been more important, but is difficult to assess.

TABLE 11.11

Production of Selected Manufactured Goods, 1972/73–1977/78

	Unit	1972/73	1973/74	1974/75	1975/76	1976/77	1977/78[a]	Compound Annual Growth Rates, 1972/73–1977/78 (percent)
Cotton yarn	thousand bales	262	316	364	445	623	678	20.8
Cotton fabrics	million meters	852	926	974	1,017	1,247	1,332	9.3
Cigarettes (white)	billion	17	20	21	20	24	23	6.2
Matches	million boxes	491	555	707	874	n.a.	n.a.	21.1[b]
Soap	thousand tons	n.a.	131	131	161	n.a.	n.a.	n.a.
Toothpaste	million tubes	30	32	46	64	276	276	28.6[b]
Coconut oil	thousand tons	265	264	265	265	276	276	0.8
Cooking oil	thousand tons	29	28	29	30	33	31	1.3
Paper	thousand tons	40	47	43	47	54	84	16.0
Fertilizer	thousand tons	170	241	n.a.	n.a.	n.a.	n.a.	n.a.
Salt	thousand tons	n.a.	n.a.	n.a.	147	560	786	n.a.
Oxygen	million cu. m.	722	819	829	1,241	1,979	2,879	31.8
Cement	thousand tons	857	1,351	1,704	2,432	1,884	2,339	22.4
Tires for motor vehicles	thousand	n.a.	5	6	7	n.a.	n.a.	n.a.
Tires for bicycles	million	16	40	n.a.	n.a.	n.a.	n.a.	n.a.
Glass, bottles	thousand tons	n.a.	n.a.	70	145	156	185	n.a.
Galvanized iron sheets	thousand tons	340	500	400	520	n.a.	n.a.	15.2[b]
Sewing machines	thousand	23	36	65	78	75	84	29.3
Automobiles	thousand	100	149	251	300	268	272	22.2
Motorcycles	thousand	130	132	144	510	n.a.	n.a.	58.2[b]
Dry batteries	million	12	16	n.a.	n.a.	n.a.	n.a.	n.a.
Light bulbs	million	700	900	1,000	1,071	1,100	1,000	7.3
Radios	thousand	60	70	135	166	213	482	52.1
Television sets	thousand							

n.a. = not available.

[a]Preliminary.

[b]1972/73–1975/76.

Sources: Economist Intelligence Unit, Indonesia, Annual Supplement 1976, 1979; Bulletin of Indonesian Economic Studies (various issues).

1970s, the bulk of intersectoral migrants having been absorbed in low-productivity informal jobs, while considerable capital deepening and output expansion occurred in the group of larger establishments. A glance at the size structure of the Indonesian manufacturing sector (Table 11.12) reveals that in 1974-75 the total manufacturing sector employed about 8.4 percent of the total labor force (estimated at 48 million), of which only 1.4 percent were employed in medium- and large-scale establishments (employing 20 or more workers). The latter, however, produced about three-quarters of the sectoral value added. This situation highlights the extreme dualism persisting in Indonesian manufacturing.

A comparison of individual branches between 1970 and 1975 with respect to their share in total manufacturing value added (see Table 11.13) suggests that the type of structural change typical of a prolonged phase of import substitution had been taking place. * While the share of food products and textiles declined, the share of chemicals and most intermediate and durable consumer goods increased. The 1975 figures for the basic metals and transport equipment industries are likely to be too low, taking into account scattered information on the development of these industries. For the latter industry also the 1970 figure seems too high, probably because repair and maintenance are included.

Protected against foreign competition by various measures, Indonesian manufacturing industries still are highly inward-oriented. During the last few years, however, it has become increasingly evident that the phase of "easy" import substitution has come to an end. Many traditional import-substitution industries had already reached the limit of the domestic market and were suffering from high excess capacity (for instance, the textile, fertilizer, cement, building steel, and automobile assembly industries). Therefore, it was considered necessary to undertake more efforts to attempt to follow the experience of other Southeast Asian countries and diversify exports. One step in this direction was the November 1978 devaluation of the rupiah by 50 percent. While the SITC classification of Indonesian exports in 1976 includes $126.8 million worth of "manufactured" goods, a large percentage of these were processed raw materials, such as leather and tin, or reexports of electrical, telecommunications, generating, and other equipment.[6] Industries

---

*Data on the 1975 industry structure are available only for medium- and large-scale establishments (employing 20 or more workers).

TABLE 11.12

Selected Statistics for Manufacturing Industry, by Size of Establishment, 1974–75

Size Category	Number of Establishments (thousand)	Percent Using Power	Employment (thousand)	Value Added (billion Rp.)	Value Added per Worker per Year (thousand Rp.)
Household and cottage industries (1–4 participants)	ca. 1,300	near zero	ca. 3,050*	87	29
Small establishments (5–19 workers)	48	0.7	343	53	154
Medium establishments (20–99 workers)	5.8	55.1	662	409	617
Large establishments (100 or more workers)	1.3	86.1			
All manufacturing	ca. 1,355	0.3	ca. 4,055	549	135

Note: These data are for similar but not identical time periods; the reference periods are August 1974–July 1975 for household and cottage industries; calendar year 1975 for small establishments; calendar year 1974 for medium and large establishments. Data for household and cottage industries have been inflated by 5 percent to allow for areas of the country omitted from the survey. The table excludes about 200,000 manufacturing workers on estates (some 150,000 in rubber processing and the remainder in tea and other estate products).

*This is the average monthly employment figure. About 4.1 million people were employed over a 12-month period. If this annual figure had been used in these calculations, value added per worker would have been Rp. 21,000 in household and cottage industries and Rp. 108,000 in all manufacturing; the estimate of total manufacturing employment would have been 5.1 million.

Source: Donald R. Snodgrass, Small-Scale Manufacturing Industries: Patterns, Trends and Possible Policies, Development Discussion Paper no. 54 (Cambridge, Mass.: Harvard Institute for International Development, 1979), p. 13.

TABLE 11.13

Industry Structure of the Manufacturing Sector, 1975

	Number of Establishments	Number of Persons Engaged	Value Added, in Factor Prices (million Rp.)	Percentage Share in Total Value Added		
				1975	1970	Change
Food	1,613	145,146	119,991	24.9	30.7	-
Beverages	78	6,356	11,812	2.5	2.3	+
Tobacco	1,069	133,453	65,731	13.6	10.2	+
Textiles	2,754	231,980	71,742	14.9	19.0	-
Clothing, footwear	151	9,996	12,920	2.7	1.8	+
Wood	487	33,615	16,615	3.4	1.6	+
Furniture	123	4,923	1,696	0.4	1.5	-
Paper	77	8,099	8,020	1.7	0.1	+
Printing	295	17,942	9,189	1.9	2.0	-
Leather	51	2,874	1,404	0.3	1.4	-
Rubber	97	9,395	8,602	1.8	0.4	+
Chemicals	585	53,031	63,100	13.1	7.7	+
Petroleum products	n.a.	n.a.	n.a.	n.a.	2.0	?
Nonmetallic minerals	653	33,470	25,697	5.3	2.9	+
Basic metals (iron and steel)	13	2,883	1,097	0.2	2.1	-
Finished metal products	282	22,434	16,889	3.5	1.0	+
Nonelectrical machinery	98	8,833	8,034	1.7	0.3	+
Electrical machinery	77	10,463	18,276	3.8	0.2	+
Transport equipment	118	19,354	20,274	4.2	12.7	-
Miscellaneous manufactures	73	5,052	1,268	0.3	n.a.	?
Total manufacturing industries	8,694	759,299	482,356	100.0	100.0	

Note: Applies to establishments with 20 or more workers.
n.a. = not available.

Sources: United Nations, The 1973 World Programme of Industrial Statistics. Summary of Data from Selected Countries. (New York: U.N., 1979); Table 11.A.1.

that already have started to export (though often still in a rather sporadic way), are cement, fertilizer, building steel, plywood, and textiles.

Shifts in Industrialization Policies

The slowdown of manufacturing growth in 1974–75 had internal as well as external reasons. The worldwide recession that set in after the 1973 oil price shock led many national and transnational enterprises not only to cut back overseas investment plans, but also to increase exports (thereby applying marginal-cost pricing procedures). Galloping inflation together with a constant exchange rate of the rupiah (with respect to the U.S. dollar), since 1971, caused domestic costs to rise faster than import prices, thus increasing import competition. Protective countermeasures could be only partially successful, as a considerable proportion of Indonesian imports find an unofficial way into the country. Furthermore, in the mid-1970s the "easy" investment opportunities in the traditional import-substituting industries began to be exhausted and, with the increasing overvaluation of the rupiah, excess capacities began to pile up.

An internal reason for the decline in foreign direct investment was the increasing hostility to foreign capital, which, after the riots in January 1974, resulted in a number of new regulations that formed the core of the "Indonesianization" policy. In 1974 the Capital Investment Law of 1967 was amended as follows:[7]

While the share of Indonesian capital in all foreign-investment manufacturing projects approved up to 1973 had been about 15 percent (on an average), it has to be increased to not less than 51 percent in all existing and new projects during a period not exceeding ten years. Moreover, new joint ventures can be undertaken only together with the government, with pribumi (Indonesian natives), or with pribumi-dominated corporate partnerships. Exceptions to this rule are granted only to labor-intensive "footloose" industries (such as electronics assembly) and very large projects.

Investment incentives have been largely reduced—they are to be granted only to "priority" projects. Several branches have been closed to further foreign investment. (General rules applied in investment licensing are, however, hard to detect.)

Foreign investors have been obliged to provide training programs for their Indonesian employees and, in general, to replace foreigners within three to five years.

The results of the deterioration in the investment climate—as a consequence of the above-mentioned developments, as well as of the 1975 Pertamina crisis and the renegotiation of the oil contracts—can be seen from Tables 11.14 and 11.15. Domestic private investment approvals, mostly in the manufacturing sector, peaked both in number and in value in 1973, slowed down in 1975, and began to show a rising tendency in 1977. Foreign private investment approvals declined sharply in 1975 in most industries, except in basic metals, where a huge project in aluminum production was initiated. Above all, investment approvals in the textile industry decreased significantly, since this industry had been closed to foreign investment in Java. It probably can be assumed that implementation ratios, and consequently private foreign-capital inflow, declined after 1974. Therefore, in February 1977 the government undertook measures to speed up the rather lengthy application procedures. Since then the potential foreign investor need deal with only one agency.

TABLE 11.14

Domestic Investment Approvals, 1968–77

	Number of Projects	Total Value (billion Rp.)
1968	2	0.6
1969	185	53.6
1970	334	186.1
1971	390	275.7
1972	375	212.2
1973	616	599.6
1974	249	221.3
1975	173	252.5
1976	146	278.2
1977	309	511.6

Source: Bulletin of Indonesian Economic Studies 14, no. 2 (1978): 29.

TABLE 11.15

Foreign Investment Approvals in Manufacturing, 1970/72-77
(million U.S. $)

	1970-72		1973-74		1975		1976		1977	
	Value	Share (percent)	Value	Share (percent)	Value	Share (percent)	Value	Share (percent)	Value	Share (percent)
Food processing	59	9.7	59	3.7	23.5	2.0	67.7	19.4	5.5	1.6
Textiles, leather products	271[a]	44.4	642[a]	40.2	31.2	2.7	24.2	6.9	84.7	24.2
Wood products	2	0.3	16	1.0	21.9	1.9	5.5	1.6	—	—
Paper	11	1.8	4	0.3	18.5	1.6	66.2	19.0	9.7	2.8
Chemicals, rubber products	82	13.4	306	19.2	60.4	5.2	35.7	10.3	81.5	23.2
Nonmetallic mineral products	77	12.6	180	11.3	99.6	8.6	72.0	20.7	99.0	28.2
Basic metals	29	4.8	277	17.3	875.6	75.5	11.9	3.4	20.8	5.9
Metal products	73	12.0	109	6.8	28.8	2.5	65.0	18.7	49.3	14.1
Other	6[b]	1.0	4[b]	0.3	—	—	—	—	—	—
Manufacturing	610	100.0	1,597	100.0	1,159.5	100.0	348.1	100.0	350.5	100.0
Total economy	1,296		2,154		1,756.6		449.4		421.7	

[a]Without leather.

[b]Includes wholesale trade, transport, and service industries.

Sources: Bundesstelle fur Aussenhandelsinformation, Indonesien, Wirtschaftliche Entwicklung 1977/78 (Cologne: 1978), p. 31; Bulletin of Indonesian Economic Studies 12, no. 3 (1976): 33.

A major change in the economic environment took place in November 1978, when the rupiah was devalued by 50 percent with respect to the U.S. dollar. The stated reason for this was not balance-of-payments problems, but the increasing need to improve the position of the traded goods sectors—that is, to reduce import competition from goods bypassing protective walls, and to facilitate exports. The impact of the devaluation on the economy, however, was partially offset by additional measures. First, effective protection of import-competing industries was likely to have been increased excessively, since tariffs on final products were left unchanged while tariffs on imported raw materials and components were reduced by 50 percent.[8] Second, certain (actual or potential) key export commodities were subjected to export quotas, in order to prevent increasing prices and shortages in the domestic market.

CONCLUDING REMARKS

Considering the catastrophic economic situation of Indonesia by 1965, the overall development record of manufacturing since then should be considered a remarkable achievement. Despite limited investment resources, enormous bottlenecks in the physical infrastructure, a relatively low literacy rate, a lack of local management and entrepreneurship, and an administration that had been largely destroyed, the economic policies following the 1965 events have made it possible for the country to move toward sustained economic growth.

This does not contradict the fact that important structural problems still exist in the manufacturing sector. Severest bottlenecks are the lack of spare parts, excess capacity, sometimes antiquated equipment, low productivity, lack of adequate electricity and water, and shortage of working capital. The principal reason that these problems remain is the fact that Indonesia is still underdeveloped. Nevertheless, the large size and natural richness of the country lead us to believe that an industrial sector, significant in terms of value added and employment creation, will emerge.

However, as has been pointed out, up to now this growth potential has not been exploited adequately. Although there are some industrial activities (such as fertilizers, cement, tires, yarn, dry batteries, reinforcing iron) that have been able to increase output significantly, the manufacturing sector as a whole has not yet become an engine of growth. This can mainly be explained by the fact that production is predominantly inward-looking, not very efficient because of the operation of too many small firms producing well below optimum scale in a limited market; high costs in these protected industries represent a misallocation especially of such scarce skills as entrepreneurial and manual talents, and indicate that the transition to export activities will be difficult. Additional problems have arisen from the recent decline in investment, which appears to have been caused by the general fall in private capital exports of industrial countries during the worldwide recession following the oil price shock, by the scaling back of overseas investment plans, by changes in investment decisions as a consequence of reduced confidence following the Pertamina debacle, and by confusion about the government's practical handling of foreign investment after the "Indonesianization" initiative. Within Indonesia excessive bureaucracy and a high rate of inflation are still major problems whose solution will affect the willingness of domestic and foreign entrepreneurs to allocate their capital to investment opportunities.

NOTES

1. The paper draws on the authors' study <u>International Development Policies for Indonesia</u> (Tubingen: J. C. B. Mohr, 1974). It is mainly based on fieldwork undertaken in Indonesia from January until May 1973, which included personal interviews with 45 firms in the food processing, wood manufacturing, rubber, leather, and textile industries in Java and Sumatra. Attempts to update the empirical basis of this paper have met limitations, since quantitative information about the manufacturing sector still is sparse, highly aggregated, and difficult to obtain outside Indonesia.

2. See S. Grenville, "Survey of Recent Development," <u>Bulletin of Indonesian Economic Studies</u> 9 (March 1973): 24.

3. This method was developed and empirically tested for the first time by H. B. Lary, <u>Imports of Manufactures from Less Developed Countries</u> (New York and London: Columbia University Press, 1968), chs. 2, 3.

4. For a recent analysis of this phenomenon, see G. K. Helleiner, "Manufactured Exports from Less Developed Countries and Multinational Firms," <u>Economic Journal</u> 83 (March 1973): 21 ff.

5. See Donald R. Snodgrass, <u>Small-Scale Manufacturing Industries: Patterns, Trends and Possible Policies</u>, Development Discussion Paper no. 54 (Cambridge, Mass.: Harvard Institute for International Development, 1979), p. 21.

6. See <u>Bulletin of Indonesian Economic Studies</u> 13, no. 3 (1977): 12.

7. For details see Indonesia Overseas Bank, <u>Economic Bulletin</u>, no. 18 (1974): 359-64.

8. See H. Dick, "Survey of Recent Developments," <u>Bulletin of Indonesian Economic Studies</u> 15, no. 1 (1979): 23.

TABLE 11.A.1

Actual and "Normal" Structures of Indonesian Manufacturing Sector, 1970

Industrial Branch	(million U.S. $)	Percentage Shares in Total Value Added		
		Actual	"Normal"	A - N
Processed food	207.2	30.7	10.7	+
Beverages	15.3	2.3	8.4	−
Tobacco manufactures	68.8	10.2	13.3	−
Textiles	128.3	19.0	12.3	+
Clothing, footwear	12.0	1.8	1.7	+
Wood products	11.0	1.6	2.7	−
Furniture	10.3	1.5	1.5	−
Paper products	0.8	0.1	1.7	−
Printed matter	13.6	2.0	2.4	−
Leather products	9.6	1.4	1.5	−
Rubber products	12.4	0.4	3.5	−
Chemicals	51.9	7.7	13.1	−
Petroleum products	3.8	2.0	6.5	−
Nonmetallic minerals	19.3	2.9	3.8	−
Basic metals	14.4	2.1	3.6	−
Finished metal products	6.7	1.0	3.9	−
Nonelectrical machinery	2.3	0.3	1.5	−
Electrical machinery	1.5	0.2	2.9	−
Transport equipment	85.8	12.7	5.0	+
Miscellaneous manufactures	n.a.			
Total	675.6	100.0	100.0	

Sources: Actual value-added figures are from W. A. G. Boucherie, "Some Preliminary Estimates Concerning the Present Structure of Indonesian Industry" (Jakarta, May 1971) (mimeographed). "Normal" shares (for a per capita income of U.S. $89 and a population of 120 million) have been calculated using the cross-section regression estimates given in G. Fels, K. W. Schatz, and F. Wolter, "Der Zusammenhang zwischen Produktionsstruktur und Entwicklungsniveau," Weltwirtschaftliches Archiv 106, no. 2 (1971): 256.

TABLE 11.A.2

The Indonesian Manufacturing Sector in Detail: Input, Output, and Value Added in 1970
(values in Rp. million)

Industrial Branch (1)	Size of Firms (2)	Number of Firms (3)	Output (4)	Profits of Work Done for Others and Their Manufactures (5)	Subtotal (4) + (5) (6)	Raw Material (7)	Other Aux. Materials and Packing (8)
Preparing, preservation of meat	L M Σ	8	193.9	0.1	194.0	142.6	10.2
Dairy products, ice	L M Σ	13 301 314	2,247.3 1,550.6 3,797.9	82.6 0.2 82.8	2,329.9 1,550.8 3,880.7	772.0	509.4
Coconut oil, cooking oil, vegetable oil	L M Σ	68 278 346	19,146.7 8,371.0 27,517.7	145.6 19.2 164.8	19,292.3 8,390.2 27,682.5	12,629.4 6,829.9 19,459.3	104.3 147.2 251.5
Grain mill products	L M Σ	134 2,582 2,716	24,990.2 18,840.6 43,830.8	1,421.2 3,653.9 5,075.1	26,411.4 22,494.5 48,905.9	17,146.1 14,515.8 31,661.9	197.7 1,375.8 1,573.5
Sugar factories, refineries	L M Σ	55 56 111	38,877.3 35.4 38,912.7	8.0	38,885.3 35.4 38,920.7	22,317.7 21.3 22,339.0	2,534.6 0.4 2,535.0
Tapioca, sago flour	L M Σ	27 342 369	376.6 2,972.3 3,348.9	8.4 8.4	376.6 2,980.7 3,357.3	300.8 1,956.8 2,257.6	8.4 90.7 99.1
Tea processing, sorting, packing	L M Σ	61 132 193	6,762.8 804.6 7,567.4	151.0 0.4 151.4	6,913.8 805.0 7,718.8	1,594.0 524.8 2,118.8	1,217.8 39.3 1,257.1
Other food manufactures	L M Σ	128 1,344 1,472	7,342.5 3,915.7 11,258.2	32.8 32.8	7,375.3 3,915.7 11,291.0	4,695.8 4,695.8	161.0 161.0
Beverages	L M Σ	15 159 174	2,907.0 976.5 3,883.5	0.6 0.6	2,907.6 976.5 3,884.1	432.4 432.4	320.3 320.3
Tobacco manufactures	L M Σ	280 845 1,125	94,391.0 4,179.2 98,570.2	60.4 30.6 91.0	94,451.4 4,209.8 98,661.2	55,410.3 2,788.5 58,198.8	2,925.8 164.4 3,090.2
Yarns, threads	L M Σ	18 19 37	11,723.5 44.5 11,768.0	126.6 6.2 132.8	11,850.1 50.7 11,900.8	5,956.7 32.5 5,989.2	213.6 3.5 217.1
Weaving mills	L M Σ	312 2,746 3,058	13,149.0 5,434.9 18,583.9	689.6 214.9 904.5	13,838.6 5,649.8 19,488.4	6,953.9 3,594.6 10,548.5	1,104.5 22.5 1,127.0
Finished woven textiles	L M Σ	20 42 62	2,846.3 460.2 3,306.5	57.3 82.6 139.9	2,903.6 542.8 3,446.4	2,232.0 416.9 2,648.9	115.5 1.6 117.1
Knitting mills	L M Σ	47 65 112	1,398.0 428.1 1,826.1	0.6 51.0 51.6	1,398.6 479.1 1,877.7	680.3 256.9 937.2	93.2 2.2 95.4
Other textiles	L M Σ	10 4 14	1,266.5 4.0 1,270.5	32.6 0.0 32.6	1,299.1 4.0 1,303.1	431.7 3.7 435.4	30.7 0.0 30.7

Notes: Only large- and medium-scale establishments covered. Industrial branches are according to Indonesia's Industrial classification scheme.

n.a. = not available.

L = large-scale; M = medium-scale; Σ = large + medium.

(-) = increase of stocks; (+) = decrease of stocks.

Fuel, Gas, Electricity (9)	Depreciation (10)	Change of Stocks of Goods in Process (11)	Maintenance and Repairs (12)	Administration and Distribution (13)	Taxes (14)	Miscellaneous (15)	Subtotal (7) – (15) (16)	Value Added (6) – (16) (17)
3.4	0.7	(–) 0.5	5.7	4.8	23.2	6.0	196.1	-2.1
92.9	104.8	(+) 1.3	62.3	80.8	91.6	98.1	1,813.2	516.7
69.8								
162.7								
467.0	190.4	(+) 16.2	242.5	143.4	102.8	596.0	14,492.0	4,800.3
115.6	50.8		95.8	57.2	127.7	197.2	7,621.4	768.8
582.6	241.2		338.3	200.6	230.5	793.2	22,113.4	5,569.1
247.4	17.8	(+) 726.1	86.2	280.5	288.1	987.7	19,977.6	6,433.8
302.6	105.6		153.8	119.5	193.3	856.9	17,623.3	4,871.2
550.0	123.4		240.0	400.0	481.4	1,844.6	37,600.9	11,305.0
1,530.5	838.0	(–) 11.0	2,980.1	781.6	1,701.0	5,324.7	37,997.2	888.1
3.1	2.5		1.8	0.1	0.4	0.8	30.4	26.7
1,533.6	840.5		2,981.9	781.7	1,701.4	5,325.5	38,027.6	914.8
18.2	4.4	(+) 31.6	1.9	10.6	5.2	11.8	392.9	-16.3
73.6	14.6		22.2	12.0	12.3	108.8	2,291.0	689.7
91.8	19.0		24.1	22.6	17.5	120.6	2,683.9	673.4
773.0	131.2	(–) 28.8	652.9	133.8	73.1	746.7	5,293.7	1,830.1
39.0	0.9		66.2	7.3	11.3	46.5	735.3	69.7
812.0	132.1		719.1	141.1	84.4	793.2	6,029.0	1,899.8
178.6	236.8	(–) 144.5	73.4	429.2	595.8	375.8	6,601.9	743.4
25.6								
204.2								
109.7	30.6	(–) 67.2	83.2	249.0	471.1	325.2	1,960.3	947.3
7.3								
117.0								
235.5	259.8	(–) 2.2	378.2	1,008.5	14,252.1	9,572.8	84,040.8	10,410.6
13.9	17.7		24.4	24.7	235.1	90.8	3,359.5	850.3
249.4	277.5		402.6	1,033.2	14,487.2	9,663.6	87,400.3	11,260.9
630.1	103.7	(–) 55.5	585.9	935.0	23.8	594.1	8,987.4	2,862.7
3.7	0.0		0.1	0.1	0.4	2.0	42.3	8.4
633.8	103.7		586.0	935.1	24.2	596.1	9,029.7	2,871.1
670.6	318.7	(+) 165.1	400.6	179.6	122.7	1,131.3	11,047.0	2,791.6
64.6	59.4		55.9	30.8	26.1	166.7	4,020.6	1,629.2
735.2	378.1		456.5	210.4	148.8	1,298.0	15,067.6	4,420.8
188.8		(+) 98.7	68.7	39.7	4.6	43.4	2,791.4	112.2
8.8	20.8		1.7	1.5	9.2	35.6	496.1	46.7
197.6			70.4	41.2	13.8	79.0	3,287.5	158.9
41.1	15.6	(+) 1.2	18.4	19.8	31.2	183.7	1,084.5	314.1
7.3	7.7		4.1	4.7	4.5	28.9	316.3	162.8
48.4	23.3		22.5	24.5	35.7	212.6	1,400.8	476.9
29.8	68.4	(+) 3.7	74.8	26.7	9.9	75.3	751.0	548.1
0.0						0.1	3.8	0.2
29.8						75.4	754.8	548.3

(continued)

Industrial Branch (1)	Size of Firms (2)	Number of Firms (3)	Output (4)	Profits of Work Done for Others and Their Manufactures (5)	Subtotal (4) + (5) (6)	Raw Material (7)	Other Aux. Materials and Packing (8)
Batiks	L	17	183.9	0.0	183.9	112.5	10.2
	M	1,398	2,611.9	66.2	2,678.1	1,915.9	48.6
	Σ	1,415	2,795.8	66.2	2,862.0	2,028.4	58.8
Wearing apparel	L	3	26.9	2.5	29.4	8.3	4.1
	M	109	387.0	31.6	418.6		
	Σ	112	413.9	34.1	448.0		
Carpets, rugs	L	10	813.5	0.0	813.5	11.8	0.8
	M	13	10.7	0.0	10.7		
	Σ	23	824.2	0.0	824.2		
Tanneries, leather finishing	L	10	529.9	0.0	529.9	277.1	53.2
	M	52	139.7	8.8	148.5		
	Σ	62	669.6	8.8	678.4		
Footwear	L	12	2,354.7	69.0	2,423.7	806.5	42.5
	M	51	217.1	0.3	217.4		
	Σ	63	2,571.8	69.3	2,641.1		
Wood, cork production	L	17	784.0	98.3	882.3	493.3	41.1
	M	651	1,485.1	284.0	1,769.1		
	Σ	668	2,269.1	382.3	2,651.3		
Furniture, fixtures	L	7	149.0	4.5	153.5	73.5	
	M	215	486.0	1.1	487.1		n.a.
	Σ	222	635.0	5.6	640.6		
Paper, paper products	L	17	690.0		690.0	250.2	
	M	72	75.1	2.7	77.8		n.a.
	Σ	89	765.1	2.7	767.8		
Printed matter	L	51	1,537.2	127.1	1,664.3	632.0	165.7
	M	460	3,932.8		3,932.8		
	Σ	511	5,470.0		5,470.0		
Basic industrial chemicals	L	11	335.6		335.6	43.7	28.6
	M	18	144.0	n.a.	144.0	105.2	2.8
	Σ	29	479.6		479.6	148.9	31.4
Fertilizers, pesticides	L	3	2,433.0		2,433.0	371.1	116.5
	M	22	38.1	1.3	39.4	17.9	2.2
	Σ	25	2,471.1		2,472.4	389.0	118.7
Processing incense, resin	L						
	M	34	83.5	n.a.	83.5	n.a.	n.a.
	Σ						
Other chemical products	L	30	11,679.0	0.1	11,679.1	3,549.0	3,631.5
	M	265	1,746.0		1,746.0		
	Σ	295	13,425.0		13,425.1		
Drugs, medicines	L	28	2,495.6	26.0	2,521.6	489.8	584.1
	M	66	334.9		334.9	100.8	23.1
	Σ	94	2,830.5		2,856.5	590.6	607.2
Rubber products	L	271	44,105.3	207.7	44,313.0	29,531.5	619.3
	M	383	11,068.2	351.5	11,419.7	6,242.1	52.8
	Σ	654	55,173.5	559.2	55,732.7	35,773.6	672.1
Plastic products	L	23	670.3	0.4	670.7	447.5	30.8
	M	171	786.2	1.8	788.0	328.7	68.5
	Σ	194	1,456.5	2.2	1,458.7	776.2	99.3
Nonmetallic mineral products	L	2	236.3		236.3	93.8	
	M	10	26.5	n.a.	26.5		n.a.
	Σ	12	262.8		262.8		

Fuel, Gas, Electricity (9)	Depreciation (10)	Change of Stocks of Goods in Process (11)	Maintenance and Repairs (12)	Administration and Distribution (13)	Taxes (14)	Miscellaneous (15)	Subtotal (7) – (15) (16)	Value Added (6) – (16) (17)
2.9	0.1	n.a.	0.7	0.4	1.6	0.3	128.7	55.2
64.0	3.7	n.a.	7.0	7.4	12.4	63.7	2,122.7	555.4
66.9	3.8	n.a.	7.7	7.8	14.0	64.0	2,251.4	610.6
1.6	8.7		0.4		1.3	0.7	25.1	4.3
1.7		n.a.		n.a.				
3.3								
20.9	0.4	(–) 23.2	0.4	7.9	2.6	44.0	65.6	747.9
0.0								
20.9								
13.7	21.4	(–) 3.7	16.7	6.1	10.5	70.5	465.5	64.4
4.8								
18.5								
32.6	26.1	(+) 16.3	5.0	1.3	10.1	57.6	998.0	1,425.7
0.8								
33.4								
28.0	3.6	5.2	4.3	9.7	1.4	5.7	592.3	290.0
41.7								
69.7								
6.0	1.1	10.3	1.6	4.8	6.0	22.7	126.0	27.5
75.8	28.1	(–) 18.7	52.3	65.7	6.5	10.2	470.1	219.9
0.2								
76.0								
44.0	165.9	(–) 18.3	63.1	162.3	67.2	326.3	1,608.2	55.6
38.7								
82.7								
22.4	20.6	(–) 0.5	34.0	66.2	17.2	48.5	280.0	55.6
2.0	0.7		2.8	1.1	4.3	3.0	121.9	22.1
24.4			36.8	67.3	21.5	51.5	401.9	77.7
404.5	560.0		212.7	192.8	60.1	114.8	2,032.5	400.5
1.1	0.1	n.a.	0.1	0.1	0.7	0.8	23.0	16.4
405.6	560.1		212.8	192.9	60.8	115.6	2,055.5	416.9
n.a.	n.a.	n.a.	n.a.	n.a.	n.a.	n.a.	n.a.	n.a.
184.9	387.3	(–) 65.9	277.8	982.4	195.7	318.2	9,460.9	2,218.2
7.4								
192.3								
39.5	92.8	(–) 20.3	131.7	161.8	46.7	198.5	1,724.6	797.0
7.8	11.1		12.5	13.8	9.6	16.8	195.5	139.4
47.3	103.9		144.2	175.6	56.3	215.3	1,920.1	936.4
1,763.9	680.3	297.0	1,325.6	1,845.3	1,798.9	4,172.8	42,034.6	2,278.4
319.0	105.8		70.5	117.5	480.3	1,223.2	8,611.2	2,808.5
2,082.9	786.1	297.0	1,396.1	1,962.8	2,279.2	5,396.0	50,645.8	5,086.9
29.1	32.7	159.2	10.4	35.3	28.0	148.3	921.3	–250.6
54.7	7.3		7.5	7.2	14.3	75.9	564.1	223.9
83.6	40.0	159.2	17.9	42.5	42.3	224.2	1,485.4	–26.7
50.0		0.5	3.4	16.6	50.0	0.7	215.0	21.3
0.4	n.a.							
50.4								

(continued)

Industrial Branch (1)	Size of Firms (2)	Number of Firms (3)	Output (4)	Profits of Work Done for Others and Their Manufactures (5)	Subtotal (4) + (5) (6)	Raw Material (7)	Other Aux. Materials and Packing (8)
Glass,	L	22	695.3		695.3	243.0	28.2
glass	M	24	49.2	3.2	52.4		
products	Σ	46	744.5	3.2	747.7		
Cement	L	3	4,401.1		4,401.1	271.9	386.3
	M	—		n.a.			
	Σ	3					
Other nonmetal-	L	24	165.2	0.6	165.8	50.5	15.7
lic mineral	M	763	1,497.1		1,497.1		
products	Σ	787	1,662.3		1,662.9		
Cutlery, hand	L	22	927.9	34.0	961.9	370.0	52.3
tools, general	M	230	614.4	128.4	742.8	121.0	15.8
hardware	Σ	252	1,542.3	162.4	1,704.7	491.0	68.1
Metal furniture,	L	4	198.0	1.4	199.4	62.4	16.8
fixtures	M	10	11.4	15.4	26.8	5.5	0.2
	Σ	14	209.4	16.8	226.2	67.9	17.0
Structural	L	16	1,097.3	98.0	1,195.3	603.9	100.3
metal	M	149	266.4	48.0	314.4	150.5	6.7
products	Σ	165	1,363.7	146.0	1,509.7	754.4	107.0
Metal products	L	26	3,447.0	175.1	3,622.1	1,694.9	234.5
except machin-	M	99	758.7	41.3	800.0	489.1	28.1
ery and equip-	Σ	125	4,205.7	216.4	4,422.1	2,184.0	262.6
ment not else-							
where qualified							
Agriculture	L	2	137.0	2.3	139.3	52.6	2.7
machinery,	M	4	3.2	0.5	3.7	0.1	
equipment	Σ	6	140.2	2.8	143.0	52.7	
Other machines	L	15	756.7	49.3	806.0	241.6	33.9
	M	87	138.3	45.8	184.1	85.1	4.6
	Σ	102	895.0	95.1	990.1	326.7	38.5
Radio, TV, com-	L	4	413.4	18.8	432.2	337.1	
munication	M	8	66.6	0.6	67.2	37.1	0.5
equipment and	Σ	12	480.0	19.4	499.4	374.2	0.5
apparatus							
Electrical	L	11	547.9	26.0	573.9	201.2	32.5
apparatus,	M	33	73.2		73.2		
appliances	Σ	44	621.1	26.0	647.1		
Shipbuilding,	L	9	246.5	248.7	495.2	224.7	127.9
repairing	M	9	26.8		26.8		
	Σ	18	273.3		522.0		
Assembling of	L	19	1,388.0	216.9	1,604.9	1,335.6	32.4
motor cars	M	264	40.5	575.0	615.5	31.3	21.5
	Σ	283	1,428;5	791.9	2,220.4	1,366.9	53.9
Assembling of	L						
bicycles	M	10	6.6	n.a.	6.6	n.a.	n.a.
	Σ						
Other transport	L						
equipment	M	2	1.5	n.a.	1.5	n.a.	n.a.
	Σ						
Other manufac-	L	29	445.5	14.3	459.8	95.0	6.3
turing	M	165	654.0		654.0		
industries	Σ	193	1,099.5		1,113.8		

Source: Compiled from Biro Pusat Statistik, Statistik Industri 1970 (Jakarta, the Bureau, 1972).

Fuels, Gas, Electricity (9)	Depreciation (10)	Change of Stocks of Goods in Process (11)	Maintenance and Repairs (12)	Administration and Distribution (13)	Taxes (14)	Miscellaneous (15)	Subtotal (7) – (15) (16)	Value Added (6) – (16) (17)
135.4	98.1	33.3	27.6	6.8	9.3	111.4	693.1	2.2
0.7								
136.1								
885.2	656.7	(-) 109.5	266.4	116.1	182.4	366.2	3,021.7	1,379.4
47.8	24.0	(-) 0.6	12.8	10.6	8.4	5.7	174.9	-9.1
4.4								
52.2								
32.0	32.2	23.2	20.9	9.6	26.6	32.2	599.0	362.9
26.1	10.5		6.7	5.6	18.3	17.4	221.4	521.4
58.1	42.7	23.2	27.6	15.2	44.9	49.6	820.4	884.3
23.9	1.2	(-) 9.4	0.9	12.0	7.0	63.6	178.4	21.0
6.9			0.1	0.8	2.0	0.5	16.0	10.8
30.8	1.2	(-) 9.4	1.0	12.8	9.0	64.1	194.4	31.8
31.0	24.3	16.4	23.4	31.5	24.9	129.5	985.2	210.1
21.0	5.8		14.3	1.2	6.0	20.6	226.1	88.3
52.0	30.1	16.4	37.7	32.7	30.9	150.1	1,211.3	298.4
51.0	73.3	(-) 9.1	39.1	80.8	60.3	132.4	2,357.2	1,264.9
35.2	2.0		7.8	5.9	7.7	20.8	596.6	203.4
86.2	75.3	(-) 9.4	46.9	86.7	68.0	153.2	2,953.8	1,468.3
3.6	0.4	(-) 2.1	1.0	74.8	3.8	29.5	166.3	-27.0
0.2								
3.8								
88.3	53.5	(-) 163.9	13.1	42.6	18.0	98.0	425.6	380.4
9.5	6.2		0.6	2.4	5.8	8.2	122.4	61.7
98.3	59.7	(-) 163.9	13.7	45.0	23.8	106.2	548.0	442.1
2.1	10.7	(-) 13.0	3.3	22.8	50.3	5.6	418.9	13.3
0.3	2.8		0.8	1.5	1.3	3.1	47.4	19.8
2.4	13.5	(-) 13.0	4.1	24.3	51.6	8.7	466.3	33.1
16.3	16.7	9.9	17.3	30.4	183.1	28.1	535.5	38.4
1.7								
18.0								
62.7	74.6	(-) 124.0	31.7	41.3	8.9	123.3	571.1	-75.9
0.4								
63.1								
25.0	13.8	(-) 11.3	1.0	20.6	19.2	122.9	1,559.2	45.7
33.6	7.5		4.1	20.2	15.5	18.0	151.7	463.8
58.6	21.3	(-) 11.3	5.1	40.8	34.7	140.9	1,710.9	509.5
1.0	n.a.	n.a.	n.a.	n.a.	n.a.	n.a.	n.a.	n.a.
0.2	n.a.	n.a.	n.a.	n.a.	n.a.	n.a.	n.a.	n.a.
4.7	6.2	(-) 3.6	2.4	4.4	1.6	13.0	130.0	329.8
3.3								
8.0								

12

ELEMENTS OF A FOOD AND NUTRITION POLICY IN INDONESIA

Saleh Afiff, Walter P. Falcon, and C. Peter Timmer

Indonesia ended the 1970s facing the paradox of difficult problems created by the success of its development effort. The rehabilitation and growth strategy that served the country well in the early years of the New Order will no longer automatically help the rural and urban poor, and the basic strategic paths for both industry and agriculture are at an important juncture. The questions for the food and agricultural sector, the subject of this essay, center on four issues:

1. The most efficient sources of productivity growth in agriculture and the efficiency of the linkages connecting that productivity growth to the rest of the rural sector and to the urban sector

2. The domestic balance between the composition of commodity production and the composition of commodity consumption, and the resulting implications for interregional trade

3. The foreign-trade implications of the domestic commodity balance, including the potential price impact of Indonesia as a buyer or seller in individual commodity markets, concerns for food security, and the foreign-exchange ramifications

4. The employment, nutritional, and rural and urban welfare dimensions of the food and agricultural strategy.

———————————

This essay evolved from a continuing collaboration among the three authors over a decade. The specifics draw from a series of food policy discussion group sessions chaired by Dr. Afiff starting in the summer of 1977.

Each of the four issues has strong linkages with the others and with the rest of the Indonesian economy. These interactions are extremely complex, and in quantitative terms are poorly understood. The interaction mechanisms now operating in the Indonesian rural economy and between the rural and urban economies (which are almost a continuum on Java) make it impossible to treat any of the four issues without reference to the other three. All elements are also related to the macroeconomic policy context—that is, to the economic environment determined by foreign-exchange rates, interest rates, the levels of urban wages, and government fiscal policies. Such integration of sectors and sectoral components is characteristic of maturing market economies. This is one especially important way in which difficult planning problems for the 1980s have been caused by the very successes of the 1970s.

THE RICE SECTOR

The second major source of the paradox relates directly to the success of the rice production program. Indonesia's rice yield gains were quite dramatic from 1967 to 1978, relative both to historical experience and to other countries of monsoon Asia. Yields increased by nearly 50 percent in those years, which is a remarkable performance even discounting the trough-to-peak nature of the calculation. Rice production grew by 70 percent during the same period; and per capita consumption rose, on average, from 91 kilos per year in 1967, the low point of the 1960s, to perhaps 126 kilos in 1978, which may be the high point for the 1970s. The increase of 35 kilos per capita per year is more than one-third the 1967 base consumption level.

The average rice yields in the late 1970s in India, Thailand, Bangladesh, Burma, the Philippines, and Sri Lanka have not reached the levels that Indonesia achieved in the mid-1960s. The spectacular yield gains in Indonesia since then have left these ecologically similar rice producers well behind. At the same time, the gains achieved have narrowed the unrealized yield potential, at least through 1985 or 1990. It is certainly true that countries such as Japan, Taiwan, and the United States have considerably higher yields than Indonesia, but this is partly because of their temperate locations and their levels of environmental control. Consequently, for the immediate future Indonesia's past production successes have bred a set of difficult issues that will take some time to solve.

Plans for Repelita III (the Third Five-Year Plan) reflect these impressions that future gains in rice production will be institutionally difficult as well as expensive to achieve in 1980-85. Production grew 5.0 percent per year from 1967 to 1978, and 3.5 percent from

1968 to 1977, to take the extreme end-point calculations, with the trend averaging an increase of about 4.3 percent per year. There is also a noticeable tendency for the trend line to have a downward curvature. Recognizing this, Repelita III targeted the 1983 crop at 20.6 million tons, an increase of 3.0 percent per year from 1978. Figure 12.1 shows that this is below the linear trend projections of the experience of the years 1965-79, but consistent with a trend of declining growth rates.

Rice production increases of 3 percent per year will have ramifications for rice self-sufficiency and the likely volume of rice imports needed if rice prices are to be held at constant real levels. With the exception of 1976 and 1977, rice imports grew substantially in the 1970s, despite the production gains of 4.3 percent per year, to use the trend figure. If production now grows at only 3 percent per year and total consumption continues to grow at the 1967-79 trend rate of 4.9 percent per year, then the gap between domestic production and consumption will widen even faster. Figure 12.2 shows different plausible trends in rice consumption. When extrapolated to 1983 and compared with the Repelita III target of 20.6 million tons (less approximately 8 percent for seed, livestock feed, and losses), these consumption trends bracket an import gap of between 2 and 3 million tons of rice. Naturally, such figures assume that both production and consumption stay on trend. They make no allowance for the occasional year of drought or pest infestation, which can add 1-2 million tons to the gap between domestic production and consumption.

Gaps exist only in theory. In practice they are closed by one or a combination of three mechanisms. Imports can close the gap between domestic production and consumption; relative prices can rise to reduce domestic consumption to the level of domestic production (which might also rise in response to the higher price); and enforced rationing can limit consumption to the level of domestic production, without using price to allocate supplies. The latter is not likely to be successful in Indonesia, given the potential openness and market orientation of the rice economy. With a given production potential, a gap between rising demand and supply trends of 2-3 percent per year can be closed only by import or price adjustments.

In the past several years Indonesia has been importing approximately 1.5-2.5 million tons of rice from a world rice export market of 8-9 million tons annually. In years of bad weather for domestic production, as in 1977, Indonesia can require up to one-third of the world's exportable supplies in order to maintain price stability. Within the context of present institutional arrangements for rice importing and exporting, Indonesia is already taking a very large share of the total. Even in normal years Indonesia cannot behave as a price

FIGURE 12.1

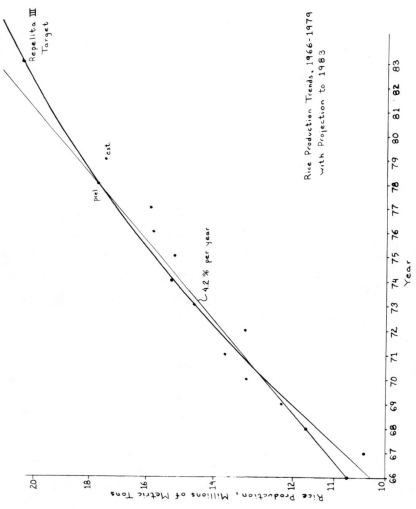

Rice Production Trends, 1966-1979
with Projection to 1983

FIGURE 12.2

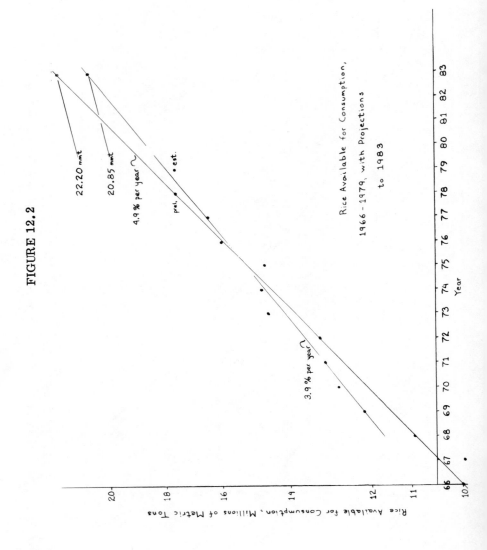

Rice Available for Consumption,
1966-1979, with Projections
to 1983

taker, and in abnormal years it is painfully clear that Indonesian demand largely determines the world price for rice.

The other vehicle for closing the ex ante consumption-production gap is increasing the price of rice relative to prices of other major foodstuffs. This price adjustment has a double-edged effect. Higher relative prices for rice encourage greater rice production, other things being equal. Although the empirical evidence on production response is shockingly scarce, what there is, suggests a supply elasticity of 0.1.* Similarly, high relative rice prices discourage rice consumption as demand shifts to relatively cheaper alternatives.

FOOD CONSUMPTION ANALYSIS

A major research effort has put a new perspective on rice consumption patterns. Although it was possible to argue for substantial flexibility in the composition of the food consumption bundle because of the diverse staples available and consumed, as is seen in the food balance-sheet data in Table 12.1, no reliable estimates of actual price elasticities of demand for rice and other important foods was available until the analysis of cross-section data reported by C. P. Timmer and H. Alderman (1979).

The use of cross-section data to derive price elasticities has been limited for fairly obvious reasons. Households are sampled only once in a particular period when the prices they face are given. If the whole sample is taken during a brief period—for instance, one week—then the only price variation observed will be due to spatial differences.

These price differences will of necessity be faced by different households that may have different tastes. In such a situation it is difficult to infer causality to regionally different consumption patterns

---

*Three dissimilar data sources produce similar estimates for the elasticity of supply of rice in the short run, discounting any area responses. The implicit yield elasticity from Mubyarto and L. Fletcher (1966) is 0.1. Two macro production functions (Timmer 1975; Timmer and Falcon 1975) with area and fertilizer as inputs both produce fertilizer coefficients of 0.1 for a Cobb-Douglas specification, again implying a yield elasticity of 0.1. Given the difficulty of expanding irrigated rice acreage in the short run, these coefficients are probably reasonable estimates of likely rice production response to higher real rice prices.

even when prices are different. However, the Indonesian Socio-Economic Survey V (1976)—SUSENAS—drew a large sample over enough geographical and temporal diversity to capture significant variance in the relevant variables. With three separate samples of 18,000 households drawn in each trimester of 1976, the sample is large enough so that cell means can be used as observations for analysis. This averages out most individual taste differences but leaves adequate variations in incomes and prices for statistical analysis.

TABLE 12.1

Food Consumption Patterns, 1976

Food	Calories per Day	Percent of Total
Rice	1,165	52.22
Corn	175	7.84
Cassava	204	9.14
Other starchy staples	169	7.58
Sugar	105	4.71
Pulses, nuts, seeds	203	9.10
Fruits, vegetables	49	2.20
Meat, eggs, milk, fish	43	1.93
Oil, fats	118	5.29
Total	2,231	100.00

Source: Central Bureau of Statistics, Jakarta, "Indonesia Food Balance Sheet," Pocketbook 1977/78.

So far the analysis deals only with rice, fresh cassava, and total calorie intake from rice, fresh cassava, and corn. Attempts to unravel the factors influencing shelled corn consumption alone have not been successful, and data for gaplek, a form of dried cassava important to the poor, are not yet available for analysis. Since rice, corn, and fresh cassava are the three most important foodstuffs for most Indonesian consumers, accounting for about two-thirds of average calorie intake, whatever functional specification and approach are ultimately chosen must permit accurate estimation of the factors determining their use.

A summary of the important consumption elasticities for rice and fresh cassava is shown in Table 12.2, which indicates that the

TABLE 12.2

Income and Price Elasticities of Demand for Food in Indonesia, 1976

| | Income Class | | | | |
	1 Pcor	2 Low	3 Middle	4 High	Average
Per capita total expenditure (Rp./month)					
Value (TX)	1,548	2,513	3,876	9,085	5,412
Range	<2,000	2,000-3,000	3,000-5,000	5,000	6,151
Proportion of Indonesian population					
SUSENAS sample	0.106	0.185	0.321	0.388	
Population weight	0.154	0.237	0.324	0.285	
Expenditure elasticities					
Rice					
Urban	0.997	0.759	0.533	0.070	0.265
Rural	1.168	0.924	0.704	0.364	0.581
Fresh Cassava					
Urban	0.839	0.522	0.230	-0.369	-0.047
Rural	0.994	0.679	0.394	-0.046	0.410
Calories					
Urban	0.740	0.584	0.435	0.130	0.261
Rural	0.776	0.615	0.470	0.246	0.471
Price elasticities					
Rice	-1.921	-1.475	-1.156	-0.743	-1.105
Fresh cassava	-1.284	-0.818	-0.943	-0.780	-0.804
Calories					
Urban	-0.561	-1.081	-0.943	-0.811	-0.514
Rural	-0.329	-0.849	-0.711	-0.579	
Cross-price elasticities					
Rice with fresh cassava	n.s.	n.s.	n.s.	n.s.	
Fresh cassava with rice	0.996	0.709	0.787	0.685	0.765

n.s. = not significant.

Note: Calories from rice, shelled corn, and fresh cassava only.

Source: Timmer and Alderman 1979.

413

the coefficients are large in absolute size and vary significantly by income class. Such income-class-specific price and income elasticities are critical for any food policy analysis that attempts to trace the nutritional impact of food price changes on the poor. The Indonesian statistical results are the first to allow this to be done with any confidence.

Rice income elasticities are extremely high for the first two income classes, indicating that rice is effectively a luxury good for the bottom 30-40 percent of the Indonesian population. Even high-income populations increase their rice intake with higher incomes, especially in the rural areas. Substitution away from rice because of higher incomes is occurring for less than 5 percent of the Indonesian population.

Income elasticities for fresh cassava also are surprisingly high. They are near 1 for the bottom 10-15 percent of the rural population and remain positive for 50-60 percent of the population. Although the effective income elasticity of demand for cassava in the 1970s no doubt was negative because of the concentration of income growth among upper-income urban groups, higher incomes among the bottom half of the rural population would be likely to generate significant increases in demand for fresh cassava. Graphical analysis of more aggregate data than were used for the statistical analysis shows that virtually all gaplek is consumed by the bottom two income classes, and the income elasticity is probably negative even for these groups.

Price elasticities estimated from cross-section data tend to capture the full adjustment of households to long-run regional differences in prices and to expected seasonal price movements, and hence are not likely to be accurate predictors of short-run response. However, the addition of geographical and seasonal dummy variables in analysis of covariance specifications helps to reduce this effect. For example, analysis of data for rural Java using separate intercepts for each province and each of the three survey rounds reported in the 1976 SUSENAS data results in a rice price elasticity just half the size of the coefficient obtained without separate intercepts. This relationship of short-run responses tending to be about half the long-run response is broadly characteristic of distributed lag models in agriculture, although such models are applied more frequently in supply analysis than in consumption analysis. Consequently the short-run response to rice price changes is likely to be about half the average coefficient in Table 12.2 of -1.105, or perhaps -0.5 to -0.6.

The supply and demand responses together cause a scissors-effect change in the potential import gap. When rice prices rise by 1 percent, supply rises by 0.1 percent and demand drops by 0.5 to

0. 6 percent, in the short run, or a total effect of 0. 6 to 0. 7 percent.
If the trend of production increases is 3 percent per year and the
trend of consumption increases is 5 percent (both in the context of
constant real rice prices), then the trend in the gap to be filled by
imports is 2 percent per year, relative to the consumption or production base (assuming they are of similar magnitudes). In order
to hold the import gap constant—that is, to reduce the trend in the
gap to zero—real rice prices would have to rise by $2 \div 0.6$ or 0.7,
or 2. 9-3. 3 percent per year.

FOOD POLICY ISSUES

Despite the ease with which the above discussion treats the
issues of higher rice prices or increasing imports, neither alternative is easy. Higher rice prices sill significantly reduce the calorie
intake of the poor; and continuously rising imports of rice may not
be feasible from existing world rice markets, especially in bad years
when Indonesia needs the imported rice the most. In these situations
other Asian countries have used substitutes in the literal sense:
barley in Korea, wheat in Japan, corn in the Philippines. After a
decade of significant progress in domestic rice consumption, a feat
exceeded only by increased demand for rice generated by economic
progress and Food Logistics Board (BULOG) policies, Indonesia too
may find that a broader policy perspective emphasizing other commodities as well as rice will make a major contribution to the welfare of the poor and to nutritional well-being. Continued emphasis
on rice along seems likely to involve either a growing import gap
that the international rice market may not be able to fill without substantial price disruptions, or a rapid rise in the relative price of
rice that will have a heavy impact on the poor. Continued concern
with rice production is essential to the well-being of Indonesia, and
some adjustments in rice prices and imports are likely to be needed.
But the rice sector alone should not bear the full brunt of the adjustments required. A broader-based food and nutrition policy that
draws on both the supply and the demand potential of substitutes offers a promising alternative for the 1980s.

If this broader perspective is accepted, the important issues
for a food and nutrition policy turn out to be quite different from
those for a rice policy. In particular the question of efficient mechanisms and programs for improving rural well-being, especially of
the botton one-third to one-half of the income distribution, becomes
uppermost. Not all nutritional problems will take care of themselves as incomes of the rural poor rise, but certainly much of the
existing protein-calorie malnutrition, iron deficiencies, and some

vitamin A problems are linked directly to acute poverty. A successful rural development program that draws on the untapped productivity potential of a handful of important agricultural commodities, including rice, will do much to alleviate simultaneously Indonesia's
poverty and malnutrition problems.

Determining the appropriate composition of the multi-commodity development package on both the production and the consumption sides (with imports and exports doing the balancing) is a task
for further research and, indeed, for market forces over the 1980s
as Indonesians express their preferences through their food purchases. But some of the general issues and principles are already
clear.

Table 12.3 shows comparative yield data for the six basic food
crops for Indonesia and seven other Asian countries with similar
ecological and economic problems. The 1975 data show very clearly the high relative standing of Indonesian rice yields—they are 36
percent above the simple average of the other Asian rice producers.
None of the other five basic food crops even approaches this comparative standard of excellence. Soybeans and peanuts are not significantly different from the average; and corn and cassava, the two
most important calorie sources after rice in Indonesia, are only
three-quarters as productive per hectare as the simple Asian average. Clearly there are major and significant differences between
cropping patterns and ecological resources in Indonesia and these
other countries, yet the stark differences in productivity argue for
significant potential yield gains for the nonrice commodities if technological and institutional resources are put behind the effort.

The Indonesian historical record supports this judgment. Relative to 1961-65 average yields for the six basic food crops in Indonesia, the 1975 yields are virtually unchanged except for rice. This
statistical record, as well as the opinions of many plant scientists
both inside and outside Indonesia, conveys a large, unrealized potential for technical improvement in the nonrice crops.

The important policy questions relate to the appropriate role
for these commodities in three areas: the production set; the consumption bundle; and the composition and magnitude of foreign trade.
Intersecting these three questions are the economic and institutional
packages needed to bring about the changes. And encompassing all
of these issues is the contribution of the changes to rural employment
and improved income distribution. It is not possible at this stage to
present a numerical scenario, but the basic issues and questions are
clear enough.

On the production side the issues revolve around the likely
area substitution effects if the profitability of the nonrice crops improves substantially relative to rice; the marketing, processing,

TABLE 12.3

International Yield Comparisons for Six Basic Food Crops, 1975
(kilos per hectare)

Country	Paddy Rice	Corn	Cassava*	Sweet Potatoes*	Soybeans	Peanuts in Shell
Bangladesh	1,853	—	—	8.3	—	1,400
Burma	1,757	—	10.0	5.3	667	750
India	1,869	1,173	17.3	7.8	750	948
Pakistan	2,298	1,294	—	9.2	—	1,415
Philippines	1,737	863	5.4	4.8	464	611
Sri Lanka	1,933	—	5.0	3.5	—	1,867
Thailand	1,825	2,562	9.0	8.9	1,036	1,167
Simple Asian average	1,896	1,473	9.34	6.83	729	1,308
Indonesia						
1975	2,575	1,079	7.0	6.2	742	1,276
1961–65 average	1,761	977	7.5	6.2	678	1,150
Indonesian yields in 1975 as a percent of						
Simple Asian average	136	73	75	91	102	98
Indonesian 1961–65 average	146	110	93	95	109	111

*1974 data in tons per hectare.
Source: FAO.

and infrastructural improvements that will be needed to provide a stable market at profitable prices, so as to encourage farmers to try the new technology (the parallels to the early rice intensification program are obvious); and the direct and indirect employment effects of these changes. On the production side the emphasis must be on farming systems and rural income. If farmers are provided access to improved technology and adequate incentives, they will determine the best output bundle themselves. With a multi-commodity focus, such decisions are too complex for government bureaucracies to make. Profitable relative prices for the nonrice crops are likely to be a necessary but not sufficient condition for rapid gains in production for these crops. Between 1965-67 and 1974-76, the prices, relative to rice, of corn, cassava, sweet potatoes, and soybeans increased 48, 31, 31, and 89 percent, respectively. But three factors prevented significant increases in yields, especially relative to rice performance: little new technology was available for these crops; the market prices, especially for corn and cassava, show wide variation due to very "thin" markets; and, despite lower relative prices for rice, the new technology and easy access to inputs made rice production more profitable. The combination of new technology, guaranteed markets, and profitable prices for the nonrice crops will be needed to change this pattern.

The consumption issues are in many ways as difficult as the production issues, because of strongly held taste preferences and the political importance of rice. Media campaigns to encourage the consumption of other foodstuffs have not been successful in the past, and there is no reason why they should suddenly be credible or even feasible now. Table 12.4 shows a significant drop in nonrice starchy staple consumption as a proportion of rice consumption, as well as in total consumption of nonrice domestically produced food commodities. Such trends merely strengthen the view that Indonesian consumers strongly prefer rice. While this may be true, it is equally true that Indonesian consumers do not eat only rice. Table 12.1 showed that in 1976 nearly half the average Indonesian's calories came from nonrice sources. More important, this proportion varies directly with income. Analysis of the 1976 SUSENAS data indicates that the poor, especially in rural Indonesia, rely heavily on corn and cassava as primary calorie sources. Table 12.2 reveals positive income elasticities for two-thirds of the income distribution for fresh cassava, although gaplek income elasticities are probably negative except for the very poor. The corn elasticity may be positive over a significant range for rural corn consumers, but the analysis has not been satisfactory thus far. For those groups dependent on cassava and corn for a significant share of their total calories, the 48 percent higher corn price and the 31 percent higher cassava price, relative to rice from 1965-67 to 1974-76, have probably had a negative welfare, and perhaps also nutritional, impact because the price elasticities are also substantial. Although the lower rice prices have more than offset the higher corn and cassava prices for most consumers, those most dependent on the nonrice starchy staples may have suffered in absolute terms. More important, if rice prices now begin to rise, what happens to the caloric intake of the poor will depend critically on corn and cassava prices.

Not all of the changes that occur in domestic output need to be matched by substitution in the domestic consumption bundle, although if incomes of the rural poor rise relative to higher income groups, then demand for corn and especially for fresh cassava is likely to increase significantly. However, international trade can play an important balancing role for both the surplus and the deficit commodities, provided Indonesian producers are competitive with international markets and Indonesian consumers do not demand more rice than the world market can supply. Both issues are a direct function of domestic relative prices, the rate and especially the distribution of income growth, and, very important, of the foreign-exchange rate. Indonesian agricultural and rural labor-intensive enterprises need the encouragement of an exchange rate that is not totally dominated by current world prices for petroleum. The November 1978 devaluation should aid in developing significant export markets for Indonesian agricultural products.

It also is extremely important to recognize the rural employment and welfare dimensions of these macro policy issues. No crop with large area is as labor-intensive, and hence as employment-intensive, as paddy rice. But it is not intended or desirable that paddy rice area be substantially reduced. However, the argument was made earlier that further increases in rice production will be more difficult to achieve, and much of the productive employment growth in rural Java must come from the untapped potential of the nonrice crops. These tend to be crops grown by and for the poorest groups of rural Java, and a technology/incentive package for these crops could have a major impact on subsistence incomes and employment opportunities.

One potentially important dimension of both the import and the domestic pricing issues would be the conscious widening of price differentials between low-quality and high-quality rice, domestic and foreign. For example, if low-quality rice prices remained constant in relative terms while high-quality rice prices were increasing, the impact on consumers in lower income strata would be much less severe than if all rice prices increased equally. Implementing such a policy would involve a conscious recognition of the importance of cheap food (especially in urban areas) for the poor, and the

TABLE 12.4

Staple Food Availabilities for Human Consumption,
in Rice Equivalents, 1968-78
(thousand tons)

	1968	1969	1970	1971	1972
Production[a]					
Rice	11,670	12,250	13,160	13,724	13,183
Corn	3,131	2,268	2,794	2,577	2,229
Cassava	3,441	3,308	3,175	3,239	3,147
Sweet potatoes	636	608	505	595	556
Net trade					
Rice	628	604	956	490	735
Corn	−66	−156	−286	−219	−80
Cassava[b]	−150	−306	−340	−460	−345
Net availabilities for consumption					
Rice	12,298	12,854	14,116	14,214	13,918
Corn	3,065	2,112	2,308	2,358	2,149
Cassava	3,291	3,002	2,835	2,779	2,802
Sweet potatoes	636	608	585	595	556
Total	19,290	18,576	20,044	18,946	19,426
Population (millions)	112.3	114.9	117.5	120.1	123.1
Availabilities per capita (kg.)					
Total	171.8	161.7	170.6	166.1	157.8
Rice	109.5	111.9	120.1	118.4	113.1
Nonrice	62.3	49.8	50.5	47.7	44.7
Nonrice as a proportion of rice	0.57	0.45	0.42	0.40	0.40

[a]Converted to rice equivalents by the following factors: corn, 0.989; cassava, 0.303; sweet potatoes, 0.269.
[b]Cassava exports as gaplek.
Source: Dick 1979.

1973	1974	1975	1976	1977 (prel.)	1978 (est.)
14,607	15,276	15,285	15,844	15,941	17,700
3,649	2,978	2,871	2,574	2,997	2,500
3,389	3,948	3,801	3,694	3,687	3,500
642	664	654	640	660	650
1,600	1,074	672	1,281	1,950	1,850
−39	−197	−51	+65	+4	+15
−73	−396	−281	−89	−174	−235
16,267	16,350	15,857	17,125	17,891	19,550
3,610	2,781	2,820	2,639	3,001	2,515
3,314	3,552	3,520	3,605	3,513	3,265
642	664	654	640	660	650
23,833	23,347	22,851	24,009	25,065	25,330
126.1	129.0	132.1	135.1	138.1	141.1
189.0	180.8	173.0	177.6	181.5	179.5
129.0	126.6	120.0	126.7	129.6	138.6
60.0	54.2	53.0	50.9	51.9	40.9
0.47	0.43	0.44	0.40	0.40	0.30

421

importance of having some rice accessible to most urban consumers. Implementation would require that BULOG import substantial amounts of low-quality rice (presumably at significant discount) for urban distribution, and also stand willing to buy low-quality domestic rice, such as several of the IR (improved rice) varieties. Some of the losses incurred in maintaining low retail prices for such rice should be covered by profit on high-quality imported and domestic rice, which would sell for a substantial premium in urban retail markets.

In addition, the strategy for one nonproduced food commodity, wheat flour, should be an integral part of the overall food strategy. Other things being equal, it is better for Indonesia to import wheat than rice for two reasons. First, on international markets wheat is a cheaper source of calories than rice, and hence it is a better nutritional buy. Consumption patterns can alter this point, but the potential for reaching the urban poor with wheat-flour products is quite substantial, given the apparent price and income elasticities (Timmer 1971). Second, the world wheat market is enormously larger than the world rice market. At present import levels Indonesia takes about 20 percent of total world rice exports, and the projected proportion is rising. If all of Indonesia's food-grain imports were in the form of wheat, it would require less than 2 percent of normal world exports. In this sense wheat imports are not as bad as the lack of potential domestic wheat production might suggest. A further contribution of the domestic wheat-flour economy is its potential for providing an internal market for sorghum, a crop for which Indonesia apparently has great but untapped potential. Excellent white bread and noodles can be made with wheat-flour mixtures containing up to 25 percent sorghum flour, and the nutritional content is marginally better. An integrated wheat flour-surghum program deserves attention, as does the possible development of a wheat flour-cassava flour program.

NUTRITION ISSUES

Nutritional well-being derives from individual decisions in the face of resource availability and the ecological setting of the household and village. It is important that nutrition receive high priority in government policy, but it is equally important that the context of nutritional problems be correctly understood. No commodity market nor operational government agency is organized by nutritional principles. Accordingly, the three major nutritional issues that grow out of the food policy discussions above are the nutritional content of the commodity consumption bundle; the macro and agricultural policy linkages to the distribution of nutrition status; and the scope for and design of direct nutrition interventions.

In present circumstances the nutritional content of the commodity consumption bundle depends much more critically on quantities available to the poor than on the quality (such as protein content) of the bundle. Nutritionists used to downgrade cassava as a human foodstuff, but it is an exceptionally cheap source of calories, especially in dried form. When consumed with the traditional leafy green vegetables and legume products, the cassava-based diet of the poor in Gunung Kidul may be superior to the rice-based diets of similarly poor people at the bottom of the income distribution in rice-rich Krawang because of its higher iron and vitamin A content. Yellow corn is higher in protein than rice and contains significant vitamin A. In short, there is nothing inherently wrong nutritionally with a new dietary emphasis on nonrice foodstuffs. The critical issue will be the quantities available to the poor.

The macro linkages are much more difficult to cope with both conceptually and in terms of policy trade-offs. Table 12.2 shows that the price of basic calories is extraordinarily important in determining the caloric intake of the poor, as are their money incomes. Both prices and incomes are functionally determined by many variables in the macro policy set—foreign-exchange rate, interest rates, choice of technique (in terms of industry choices and techniques within industries), tax policies, and so on. Thinking through the nutritional implications of changes in this macro policy set is equivalent to thinking through the income distribution/welfare effects of those changes. It ought to be done under any circumstance, and a concern for nutritional well-being provides a convenient handle.

The design of direct nutrition interventions is also one appropriate micro response to the broad-scale nutritional problems facing Indonesia. A substantial proportion of Indonesia's nutritional problems will not respond quickly to income and food price changes. The "vulnerable groups"—pregnant and lactating mothers, infants, and toddlers being weaned—must be approached with nutrition intervention programs targeted more precisely to their needs. Calorie supplements for pregnant women can significantly reduce the prevalence of low birth weights. Extended breast feeding substantially lowers infant morbidity and mortality, and also carries an added bonus of temporarily reduced fertility rates. Calorie- and protein-dense weaning foods can eliminate the poor growth of toddlers who are unable to eat enough of traditional, bulky staples to meet growth and energy requirements. Many vitamin and mineral deficiencies could be overcome through nutrition education with increased intake of locally available fruits, vegetables, and leafy greens, some of which are virtually free.

National programs and pilot programs designed to tackle these problems are under way or in the design stage. As a matter of national policy, they should be encouraged, and sophisticated media campaigns probably can be quite effective in speeding changes in dietary habits and patterns. But the policy should go one step further, so that the macro policy changes are consistent with and reinforce the micro nutrition interventions. For example, any use of "fair price" shops and urban rationing in poor districts should coordinate closely with rice price policies that might contain new, wider quality differentials and with presumed wider availability of nonrice commodities, particularly via a BULOG-type market stabilization program. In addition, food diversification promotions can be greatly assisted by changes in relative prices that discourage the eating of rice and encourage the eating of other staples. Efforts to improve intake of vegetables and leafy greens can be coordinated with extension service efforts to diversify the production of foodstuffs and to reach small farmers, even home gardeners, with new technology and improved production techniques. If properly designed and coordinated, such direct interventions might have the potential for significantly improving the welfare of Indonesia's poorest consumers.

It is critical, however, not to lose sight of the most important vehicle for nutritional improvement in Indonesia. Doubling the per capita income of the bottom 25 percent of the population would eliminate much of the overt hunger and protein-calorie malnutrition that now exists. That 25 percent of the population currently receives less than 7 percent of national income. Doubling their incomes by the end of the 1980s would involve less than 1 percent increases in national income per year, provided that the bottom 25 percent of the income distribution could receive it. But designing strategies that reach that lower range of the income spectrum will not be easy, based on current understanding of the Indonesian macro food system.

RESEARCH QUESTIONS

The last joint effort of Saleh Afiff and C. P. Timmer (1972) ended with a list of important research topics in the rice policy area, and it seems appropriate to end this essay with a similar list in the broader food policy area.

First, an ongoing capacity to analyze and project international food-grain prices and trade. BULOG does much of this analysis now, and would welcome an opportunity to upgrade its capacity. As the world's largest rice importer, Indonesia needs more than just good day-to-day trading instincts. A longer-run capacity to analyze basic trends in world grain markets is likely to pay for itself many times over.

Second, a macro food policy model that predicts the nutritional impact on various income groups of changes in basic macro policy variables. In some sense all the other micro studies can be seen as inputs into this study. The assumptions necessary to make a formal macro food policy model computable are unrealistic. The value of such a formal model for Indonesia is dubious, at least for the time being. Nonetheless, the various pieces needed for an understanding of the impact of macro policy on food intake, by income class, should be assembled and major efforts should be devoted to ensuring that the individual pieces are consistent in format, definitions, and analytical methodology.

Third, a functional understanding of micro food consumption patterns by income group. Since price policy and differential income growth are likely to be the two major policy instruments available to the government, it is absolutely critical that an understanding be reached for food consumption patterns and protein-calorie intake, by income group, geographical location, and season; the impact on those patterns of changes in income, for each income group; and the impact of changed relative prices on the consumption of each important food commodity, by income group. Such research involves both straightforward descriptive analysis of household expenditure data, such as the 1969-70 and 1976 surveys, and more complicated and sophisticated econometric procedures using the same types of data.

Fourth, micro food production patterns, by crop, region, and season. The purpose of this research should be to construct a variety of "typical" farms in terms of crops grown, planting and harvesting times of each crop, and area committed during the year. Analysis of cross-section data (some available from the Central Statistical Bureau) should examine the impact of relative farm-gate prices on land allocated to each crop, and on private profitability of various cropping systems; the availability and impact of new technology on crop choice and acreage allocation; the impact of irrigation quality; and the productivity of fertilizer and other inputs.

Fifth, rural income generation and employment. This issue has been neglected so far in Indonesia. The question is how differential price policies are linked to crop selection and output, and the resulting impact on farmer incomes. These incomes should then be traced through their consumption patterns for the second-round effects on employment and income generation. Landless laborers also are affected directly and indirectly by price changes, and these mechanisms need to be understood. They are not simple. For example, a frequently heard criticism is that the BIMAS program has increased landlessness because the larger farmers make more money and buy out the small farmers who have not benefited as much. But an alternative hypothesis would ask what would have happened without BIMAS. Without the more than 50 percent increase in rice production in the 1970s, rice would be a much scarcer commodity than now, large farmers might be doubly well off, and landlessness might well have increased even faster. The research on this topic must get beyond surface phenomena.

Sixth, domestic food marketing, distribution, and price formation. Several connected issues are important here. One is the size of the margin between the farm gate and the urban consumer. Farmers react to prices they receive; consumers, to prices they pay. For a number of important food commodities (especially corn and cassava), relatively little is known about the mechanics or efficiency of the marketing channels. Second, the seasonal movement of food prices, especially in rural areas, is a critical determinant in farmers' production decisions. For instance, the price of corn can be Rp. 50 per kilo for 11 months of the year, but if it falls to Rp. 30 per kilo during the month of harvest and the wet corn cannot be stored on the farm, then the farmer makes his production decisions assuming a corn price of Rp. 30 per kilo even though the annual average is Rp. 48.3 per kilo.

Drying, storage, and processing techniques for the important food crops also need to be studied, partly because they are important in determining how much of the harvest is actually available for human consumption, partly because processing technology may offer significantly more palatable and nutritious foods from crops now known to have little favor with many Indonesian consumers. For example, a village-produced soy- or peanut-fortified cassava product that consumers really liked could totally transform Indonesia's food situation.

Seventh, agricultural input marketing and pricing. Indonesia's agriculture is now heavily dependent on marketed inputs to maintain high levels of output. Research is needed to understand the most efficient way to get fertilizer and pesticides to farmers and to get them appropriate information about use and productivity.

CONCLUSIONS

Indonesia is facing a difficult dilemma as higher rice prices needed for both production stimulus and consumption restraint conflict with marginal calorie intake among the poor, who are very sensitive to rice prices. The perspective offered here suggests that substitutes for rice can play an important role in alleviating the nutritional consequences of higher rice prices if conscious policy attention is focused on the production, marketing, and pricing of nonrice staples, especially cassava and corn in rural areas and wheat flour in urban areas.

As real rice prices rise, price policy for cassava and corn could tilt the income-calorie relationship in favor of the poor, perhaps by subsidizing consumption of these commodities. Widening the differential between low-quality and high-quality rice would also reduce the implicit subsidy that presently exists for well-to-do rice consumers, while helping to keep some rice accessible to the poor, at least in urban areas where BULOG's consumer food price interventions are most successful. Such pricing policies aimed at protecting the food intake of the poor require an understanding of the full food economy of Indonesia, not just its rice economy, which itself is complicated and poorly understood.

The analytical costs of a broader food policy are quite substantial, and Indonesia's food problems are so large and complex that pessimism comes easily. It is easy to be discouraged by the lack of data and research results, by the lack of manpower to analyze the problems and to plot solutions, and by the sheer complexity of trying to think about Indonesia's food economy as an interconnected and dynamic system. While honest appreciation of the difficulties is necessary to avoid naive promises and hopes, despair is inappropriate. The ultimate goal of the research and the food development plan must be to discover in which directions to nudge the market forces.

Above all, Indonesia's food resources remain rich and productive. The country produces more agricultural commodities than it consumes. The commodity composition of that production and of consumption is likely to change because of progressively limited opportunities in the future to exchange rubber, palm oil, or cassava for rice in the international market. But the basic productive capacity of the Indonesian society remains very promising.

REFERENCES

Afiff, S., and C. P. Timmer. 1972. "Rice Policy in Indonesia." Food Research Institute Studies 11, no. 1.

Dick, H. 1979. "Survey of Recent Developments." Bulletin of Indonesian Economic Studies 15, no. 1.

Mubyarto, and L. Fletcher. 1966. The Marketed Surplus of Rice in Indonesia: A Study in Java-Madura. Ames: Iowa State University, International Studies in Economics, Monograph 4.

Timmer, C. P. 1971. "Wheat Flour Consumption in Indonesia." Bulletin of Indonesian Economic Studies 7, no. 2.

_____. 1975. "The Political Economy of Rice in Asia: Indonesia." Food Research Institute Studies 14, no. 3.

Timmer, C. P., and H. Alderman. 1979. "Estimating Consumption Parameters for Food Policy Analysis." American Journal of Agricultural Economics (December).

Timmer, C. P., and W. P. Falcon. 1975. "The Political Economy of Rice Production and Trade in Asia." In Agriculture in Development Theory, edited by L. Reynolds. New Haven: Yale University Press.

INDEX

ABOUT THE EDITOR
AND CONTRIBUTORS

GUSTAV F. PAPANEK is Professor of Economics, Chair of the Department of Economics, and Interim Director of the Center for Asian Development Studies at Boston University. He is currently working on the relationship of development strategy to growth, equity and the political process in Indonesia, India, Bangladesh, and Pakistan. He was Director of the Harvard Advisory Group in Indonesia, an Advisor to the Planning Commission of Pakistan, and Director of the Development Advisory Service at Harvard University. The author of 26 articles and the author or editor of six books, Dr. Papanek holds a B.A. in agricultural economics from Cornell and a Ph.D. in economics from Harvard.

SALEH AFIFF is Deputy Chairman for Economic Affairs at the National Development Planning Agency of Indonesia and Senior Lecturer at the University of Indonesia. Until 1973 he was Head of the Bureau of Agriculture of the Planning Agency. Dr. Afiff has published several articles in the area of agricultural development and food policy in Indonesia. He holds an M.A. from the University of Indonesia, an M.B.A. from the University of California (Berkeley), and a Ph.D. from Oregon State University.

BISRAT AKLILU is Assistant Professor of Economics at Boston University, presently on a leave of absence with the International Fund for Agricultural Development in Rome, Italy. He has been a Research Associate at M.I.T.'s Center for International Studies. He has published principally in the area of agricultural development. Dr. Aklilu holds a B.A. from Carleton College, an M.S. from the University of Massachusetts, and a Ph.D. from Boston University.

DAVID O. DAPICE teaches economics at Tufts University where he is an Associate Professor. He has worked in Indonesia with the Development Advisory Service of Harvard University from 1971 to 1973 and for shorter periods since that time. He has also worked for the World Bank and the Rockefeller Foundation. He holds a B.A. from Williams College and an M.A. and Ph.D. from Harvard University.

BELINDA DAPICE has worked in Malaysia as a Peace Corps Volunteer and anthropologist. Her work in Indonesia during 1971-73 centered on agricultural economics and rural development.

JUERGEN B. DONGES is the Director of the Development Economics Department of the Kiel Institute of World Economics and Professor of International Economics at the Kiel University (F.R.G.). He is a member of the Scientific Board of the German Federal Ministry of Economic Cooperation and has served as a consultant to the World Bank, the OECD, UNIDO, and planning agencies in several developing countries. He is the author of numerous articles and books on development and trade policy issues. Dr. Donges holds a degree in economics and Dr. rer. pol. from the University of the Saar (F.R.G.).

WALTER P. FALCON is Farnsworth Professor of International Agricultural Policy at Stanford University. He is also Professor of Economics and Director of the Food Research Institute. He was on the Harvard faculty between 1963 and 1972, has written extensively on rural development, and in 1979-80 served on the Presidential Commission on World Hunger. Dr. Falcon holds a B.S. from Iowa State University and a Ph.D. from Harvard University.

JOHN R. HARRIS is a Professor of Economics and Director of the African Studies Center at Boston University. Until 1975 he was Associate Professor of Economics at Massachusetts Institute of Technology. He has published extensively in the areas of urban/regional economics, economic theory, and economic development. Dr. Harris's current research includes internal migration in developing countries, the delivery of health services, the internal transmission of inflation, and the financing of basic needs approach to development. He has worked for the World Bank and USAID in Africa, Thailand, and Indonesia. Dr. Harris holds a B.A. from Wheaton College and a Ph.D. from Northwestern University.

RICHARD PATTEN has been advising various agencies of the Government of Indonesia on the labor-intensive works programs and the transmigration programs since 1970. He did his graduate work at the University of Wisconsin.

DANIEL M. SCHYDLOWSKY is Professor of Economics and Senior Research Associate at the Center for Latin American Development Studies at Boston University. He has served as consultant to the major international agencies and has worked in Argentina, Bangladesh, Bolivia, Colombia, Costa Rica, Indonesia, Mexico, Nicaragua, and Peru. Dr. Schydlowsky has published widely in the areas of trade and macroeconomics policies for economic development as well as on benefit-cost analysis. He has recently focused his attention on the problem of how to stabilize the economy of a less developed country with minimum social cost.

FRANCIS SETON is Senior Fellow of Nuffield College, Oxford. He was Resident Associate at Harvard University in 1952-53 and has held Visiting Professorships at Osaka University in Japan, at Columbia and Pennsylvania Universities in the United States, and at the University of Waterloo in Canada. He has held consultancies to the British Department of Economics and Board of Trade, to various United Nations agencies, and to governments of developing countries (Iran, Chile, Indonesia). He has published in the field of theoretical economics, the economics of Communist countries (Soviet Union), and development economics.

G. K. SHAW, presently Reader in Economics at the University of East Anglia, has just been appointed Professor of Economics at the University College at Buckingham. His published work has been primarily in the area of public finance and fiscal policy. He holds the degree of B.Sc. (Econ.) from London University (London School of Economics), and a Ph.D. from Columbia University, New York.

BERND STECHER is a Research Fellow at the Kiel Institute of World Economics. He has written mainly in the area of international economics and lectured in some developing countries. Dr. Stecher received a degree in economics and Dr.sc.pol. from the University of Kiel (F.R.G.).

C. PETER TIMMER is John D. Black Professor of Economics of Food and Agriculture in the Harvard Business School. Dr. Timmer's current research includes a book on food policy analysis for practitioners. He is working with HIID, The Harvard Institute for International Development, on food policy in Sri Lanka. Dr. Timmer holds a B.A. and a Ph.D. from Harvard University.

YOSHI TSURUMI is Professor of Marketing at Baruch College of the City University of New York. Until recently he was Professor of International Management and Director of Pacific Basin Economic Studies Center of the Graduate School of Management, University of California, Los Angeles. Prior to coming to UCLA to found the center, Dr. Tsurumi taught at the Harvard Business School and at the Columbia Business School. Dr. Tsurumi has published extensively in the areas of international business, transfer of technology, and U.S.-Japanese comparative management, as well as in the area of economic development. Dr. Tsurumi holds a B.A. and an M.A. from Keio University, Tokyo, and an M.B.A. and D.B.A. from Harvard University.

FRANK WOLTER is a Research Fellow at the Kiel Institute of World Economics. He has published in the field of industrial and structural policies and has advised the OECD, ILO, UNIDO, and the EEC Commission on these matters. Dr. Wolter graduated in economics from the University of the Saar, Saarbrucken and received a Dr.sc.pol. from the University of Kiel (F.R.G.).